Self and identity
Perspectives across the lifespan

International Library of Psychology

Self and identity

Perspectives across the lifespan

Edited by
Terry Honess
and
Krysia Yardley

Routledge & Kegan Paul
London and New York

First published in 1987 by
Routledge & Kegan Paul Ltd
11 New Fetter Lane, London EC4P 4EE

Published in the USA by
Routledge & Kegan Paul Inc.
in association with Methuen Inc.
29 West 35th Street, New York, NY 10001

Set in 10 on 12pt Baskerville
by Columns of Reading
and printed in Great Britain
by T. J. Press (Padstow) Ltd
Padstow, Cornwall

59794452

Library of Congress Cataloging in Publication Data

Self and identity

(International library of psychology)
Includes bibliographies and index.
1. Self. 2. Identity (Psychology) 3. Developmental
psychology. I. Honess, Terry. II. Yardley, Krysia.
III. Series.
BF697.S45 1987   155.2   87–4499
ISBN 0–7102–0829–4

British Library CIP Data also available
ISBN 0-7102-0829-4

For our parents,
Harry and Iris Honess,
and Marian and Babs Yardley

Contents

Notes on contributors

Frances E. Aboud is an Associate Professor in the Psychology department at McGill University, Montreal. Her research interests focus on social and developmental issues that are relevant to self-concept and peer relations. A second area of interest has been ethnic relations, specifically the development of prejudice and ethnic identity.

John Arnold graduated in Psychology from the University of Nottingham. Subsequently he worked in Health Service Management before moving to the MRC/ESRC Social and Applied Psychology Unit, at the University of Sheffield, where he undertook doctoral research on personal change and stability amongst university graduates during their early career years. He is now Lecturer in Psychology at Plymouth Polytechnic. His research interests include the transition from education to work, career choice and development, and self-concept change and stability during adulthood.

Diane Mitsch Bush is an Associate Professor of Sociology at Colorado State University. She is continuing to examine how adolescents develop beliefs about violence. Related articles published in 1985 examine how theory and ideology influence violence against women. She is currently engaged in research on how paid maternal employment affects girls' and boys' gender-role orientations, occupational aspirations and family expectations. This research is an element of her research programme on how the social organisation of gender, class and race reproduces or changes the content, processes and, therefore, outcomes of socialisation.

Michael Chandler is a Professor of Developmental Psychology at the University of British Columbia and has a history of interest in the developmental study of social cognition. The empirical and conceptual work which underpins this chapter is the result of an ongoing collaborative effort to inquire into the personal and social consequences of progressive cognitive development. Michael Boyes, Lorraine Ball and Suzanne Hala are all graduate students at UBC and are engaged in thesis research focused upon the study of identity formation in populations of normal and disordered adolescents.

William Damon is Dean of the Graduate School, Clark University, in Worcester, Massachusetts. His work is particularly concerned with how social interaction encourages development of social and physical knowledge.

Anne Edwards is Principal Lecturer in Education at West Glamorgan Institute of Higher Education. Her work in the area of identity construction includes a three-year study of the process in nursery school children and two years as research fellow on an ESRC-funded project examining adolescent identity, directed by Dr Terry Honess in the Department of Psychology at University College, Cardiff.

Viktor Gecas is Professor of Sociology and Rural Sociology at Washington State University. He received his Ph.D. in Sociology from the University of Minnesota in 1969. He is currently a council member of the Social Psychology Section of the ASA; and Chair of the Theory and Research Section of the National Council on Family Relations. Most of his research and writing have focused on the topics of socialisation, self-concept development and family relations. Currently, he is working on a book on the social psychology of the self-concept and conducting research on the relevance of self-concept for work-related injury and rehabilitation.

Erica Haimes is a Lecturer in Sociology at Stirling University. She was educated at the University of Durham and has since undertaken research into unemployment, adoption and health care. Her current research is an investigation of the social construction of families through policy making on artificial reproduction. She is co-author with Noel Timms of *Adoption Identity and Social Policy* (Aldershot: Gower, 1985).

Amos Handel is a Senior Lecturer in the Department of Psychology at the University of Haifa, Israel. At present, he is primarily interested in two topics: personal documents, especially autobiographies as a source of information about development and change of self-concept during the life-span; and developmental changes in parental aspirations and concerns.

Daniel Hart is a member of the Psychology Department of Rutgers, The State University, Camden, New Jersey. His research interests focus on the development of the sense of self from infancy through adolescence, and how the sense of self is implicated in day-to-day life.

Irene H. Harwood practises individual, couple and group analytic psycho-therapy in Los Angeles, California, in the USA. She also conducts cross-cultural psychotherapy in Spanish and Russian. Dr Harwood serves as a consultant to various community agencies in addition to teaching at the

University of California, Los Angeles, and at the Postgraduate Center of the Wright Institute, Los Angeles.

Terry Honess is a lecturer in Social Psychology at University College, Cardiff, where his prime interests are in the longitudinal study of adolescent identity and in research methods and theory appropriate for eliciting and interpreting qualitative interview material. His interest in both developmental and social psychology stems partly from his doctoral work at the University of Exeter on children's personal constructions of their social worlds. His journal publications reflect his earlier 'personal constructs' work, but primarily his concern with 'self' and 'identity'. He is currently an Associate Editor of the *British Journal of Psychology*.

Shulamith and Hans Kreitler are a husband-and-wife team, both professors of psychology at Tel Aviv University, Israel. They have developed the cognitive orientation theory that deals with the motivational impact of cognitive contents and the system of meaning for the assessment of meanings and cognitive contents. They have published many articles and six books about cognition (*Cognitive Orientation and Behavior*, Springer, 1976), psychopathology (*The World-view of Schizophrenics*, Reinhardt, 1965), art (*Psychology of the Arts*, Duke University Press, 1972), personality (*The Cognitive Foundations of Personality*) and symbols (*The Psychology of Symbols*).

Brian R. Little is Associate Professor and the Head of the Social Ecology Laboratory in the Department of Psychology, Carleton University, Ottawa, Ontario, Canada.

Julie Maloney began her work on identity when she was a student at Bath University. She continues to be interested in personal identity, but now works for a London publishing firm.

James E. Marcia is a Professor of Psychology at Simon Fraser University, British Columbia, and a clinical psychologist in private practice. His research interests are in the construct validity of ego psychoanalytic theory; his clinical interests are individual psychodynamic psychotherapy.

William J. and Claire V. McGuire have collaborated on numerous articles and chapters that describe their research on the content of the phenomenal sense of self. William McGuire has also published extensively on attitude change research and on other conceptual and methodological topics in social psychology and personality. The programme of research they describe here was conducted while they were at Columbia University in New York, at the University of California, San Diego, and during their current appointments at Yale University in New Haven, Connecticut.

Jeylan T. Mortimer is a Professor of Sociology at the University of Minnesota, where she has taught since 1973. She is currently serving on the editorial boards of *Work and Occupations* and *Contemporary Sociology*. She is also a Council Member of the Social Psychology Section of the ASA, and a member of the Sociology Panel of the National Science Foundation. Her major research interest is the social psychology of work. She has recently completed a book: J. T. Mortimer, J. Lorence and D. Kumka, *Work, Family, and Personality: Transition to Adulthood* (Norwood, N.J.: Ablex, forthcoming). She is currently planning a study of adolescent workers.

Nigel Nicholson is a Senior Research Fellow at the MRC/ESRC Social and Applied Psychology Unit, University of Sheffield. He is the author of books on organisational psychology, absence from work, trade unions, strikes and labour relations. His current research interests are in career development, work-role transitions and innovation at work. He was co-recipient with Gary Johns of the 1983 Academy of Management's New Concept Award for their paper, 'The meanings of absence: New strategies for theory and research'. He received his Ph.D. from the University of Wales, Cardiff.

Barbara Hollands Peevers was awarded the Bachelor of Arts degree, with distinction, by Stanford University in 1953, and received her Ph.D. in Social Psychology from the University of Nevada, Reno, in 1970. She has conducted extensive research on the types of concepts used to understand other persons and the self, and the development of the use of those concepts. The kinds of gender-role models provided by television characters is another of her research interests, and, in addition, she has directed several survey research projects on various topics. She is currently Professor of Sociology at California State University, Chico.

Malcolm Pines is Consultant Psychotherapist in the Adult Department of the Tavistock Clinic in London. He is a member of the British Psycho-Analytical Society and a founder member of the Institute of Group Analysis. His interest in mirroring and child development was stimulated by the use of the concept of mirroring by S. H. Foulkes in group analytic psychotherapy. He has written on this and on the relationship of child development to the psychotherapeutic situation in other publications. He is a past president of the International Association of Group Psychotherapy and previously held consultant posts at Cassel Hospital, St George's Hospital and in the psychotherapeutic department of the Maudsley Hospital.

Gail M. Price has been a clinical psychologist in private practice in Massachusetts for the last ten years. She has done research in parent–infant interaction and has published an interaction measure that assesses sensitivity and empathy in the first months of life. Her current interest is in the treatment of survivors of childhood abuse.

Morris Rosenberg is Professor of Sociology at the University of Maryland.

Most of his research has focused on the self-concepts of school populations. He is author of *Society and the Adolescent Self-Image* (1965) and *Conceiving the Self* (1979), co-author of *Black and White Self-Esteem* (1972), and co-editor of *Social Psychology of the Self-Concept* (1982). He has been the recipient of the American Association for the Advancement of Science Sociopsychological Prize and the Distinguished Contribution to Scholarship Award of the American Sociological Association.

Sheila Rossan is a Lecturer in Psychology in the Department of Human Sciences at Brunel University, Uxbridge, Middlesex. Her interests are in the fields of lifespan developmental psychology, particularly adult develop-ment and identity, and changing family relationships. She is about to undertake a cross-cultural project with Helena Lopata of Loyola University, Chicago, on changes in families as children leave home. She is also a management consultant and managerial trainer in interpersonal skills.

Diane N. Ruble received her Ph.D. in social and developmental psychology from the University of California at Los Angeles and is currently a Professor of Psychology at New York University. Her research interests focus on self-definitional processes in the areas of sex roles, achievement, puberty and motherhood. A second area of interest concerns children's strategies for coping with stress during hospitalisation.

Roberta G. Simmons is Professor of Sociology and Psychiatry at the University of Minnesota. Her research on the self-image focuses on the effects of school structure and puberty on adolescents (*Moving into Adolescence: The Impact of Pubertal Change and Social Context*, to be published by Aldine), as well as the effects of kidney transplantation and donation (*Gift of Life: The Social and Psychological Impact of Organ Transplantation*, Wiley). She has a Ph.D. from Columbia University, has taught at Columbia University, Wellesley College and Barnard College, and conducted research at the National Institute of Mental Health.

Michael West is a Research Fellow at the Social and Applied Psychology Unit, University of Sheffield. He is the author of books and articles on the psychology of meditation, the transition from school to work, work-role transitions, and innovation at work. His current research focuses on the social psychology of innovation at the individual and group level in organisations. He received his Ph.D. from the Department of Applied Psychology, University of Wales Institute of Science and Technology, and has since conducted research at the Social Psychology Research Unit, University of Kent at Canterbury, and at the Bermuda College, Bermuda.

Ruth C. Wylie is Professor Emeritus of Psychology, at Goucher College, in Baltimore, Maryland and Guest Researcher at the Laboratory of Developmental Psychology, National Institute of Mental Health. She is the author of *The Self Concept* (revised edition), vol. 1 (1974), vol. 2 (1978), University of Nebraska Press.

Krysia Yardley is a clinical psychologist working for Mid-Glamorgan Health Authority and an Honorary Research Fellow at University College, Cardiff. She is principally interested in methodological problems in social and clinical psychology, especially those that bear on the development of qualitative research. She has researched and published in the areas of role-play methodology (she is also trained as a psychodramatist) and social skills therapy. Her interest in self arises both from her epistemological interests and from her practice of psychotherapy. She received her doctorate in psychology from the University of Wales.

Preface

'Self', and its counterpart, 'identity', are currently receiving a significant renewal of interest from social scientists and those working in related disciplines. It is not surprising that this is particularly reflected in the human development literature, given the relatively consistent interest in such concepts for an understanding of adolescence. However, this book explores different perspectives across the entire lifespan, from the neonate within the context of an intersubjective relationship with a caretaker to the elderly adult standing alone but expressing his or her identity in response to the interest of a researcher.

The organisation of this book into four parts is not simply a convenient chronological breakdown, nor is it meant to necessarily implicate an argument for several different 'stages' in development. However, it does reflect a clear difference in theoretical foci and choice of research method. Three of the four contributions in the first part draw on new developments in psychoanalytic theory that incorporate 'self' as the key concept. They are heavily dependent upon rich resources of clinical observation and empathic interpretation. A particular strength of such work is its consideration of the infant's psychological vulnerability in the context of the primary 'intersubjective' relationship. Moreover, the propositions that emerge from this work are integrated with the developmental psychology orientations to be found in this volume.

With the advent of the child's language and the typical attainment of an explicit sense of self/other boundaries, the research emphasis, reflected in our second part, switches to using children as research subjects. A concern with the child's developing cognitive competencies (and cross-referencing into the Piagetian tradition) is a feature of much of this work. Moreover, an important bridge is made with the sociological and social psychological literature on accounting through the concepts of 'self-narrative', and 'intention' which reaffirm the significance of the interpersonal context for understanding selfhood.

The changes heralded in childhood point to adolescents' newly emerging capacity to 'construct' rather than simply 'find' meanings. This, in conjunction with considerable biological, social and personal change, underlines the continuing significance of the 'teenage' years for the consolidation of a sense of self. In referring next to the 'post-adolescent' period, we should reiterate that we are not seeking to argue for a particular 'stage' in development, but rather that researchers' emphases have shifted. There are now different forms of institutional socialisation (e.g. work transitions), and an increasing responsibility for others (e.g. in the context of family life). Contributors are particularly concerned with the personal sense making involved in such changes and the necessary reconstructions that these involve.

Psychologists and psychoanalysts predominate in seeking to understand the development of 'self' during the child's earlier years. However, at adolescence, and throughout the adult spectrum, we find a considerable input from sociologists who are particularly concerned to relate 'self' to broader social constraints and enablements. However, sociologist contributors to this book are also concerned to explore individual experience. Moreover, all of the psychology contributions represented here, although largely concerned with intensive interview methods, do in varying degrees seek to articulate the importance of the family and the broader cultural context for understanding 'personal' identity. Hence, the discipline boundaries are, to a large degree, blurred.

This book seeks to further such cross-fertilisation and to acknowledge the high degree of communality between different approaches to the study of 'self' and 'identity'. Such an overriding purpose was also at the heart of the International Interdisciplinary Conference on Self and Identity held in Cardiff in 1984, under the auspices of the Welsh Branch of the British Psychological Society, at which the preliminary work for the chapters in this book first took shape. Indeed, producing an integrated text on development and lifespan issues did not prove to be a contrived task. A consistent theme that can be seen to characterise this book is the consideration of the extent to which research has relied upon inadequate methodologies, and the isolation of limited aspects of 'self' and 'identity' for study. Reference to the concepts of 'distinctness' and 'continuity' are also pervasive, and contributors show a considerable sensitivity to other perspectives for the purpose of properly representing our understandings of the establishment and development of self and identity across the lifespan.

Acknowledgments

Special thanks are due to those who helped shape and plan the 1984 Conference from which the stimulus for this book grew, in particular the steering group, which consisted of Ken Gergen, Rom Harré, Ray Holland, Paul Heelas, William McGuire, Malcolm Pines, Joseph Rychlak, John Shotter and Ralph Turner. The Welsh Branch of the BPS also provided continuous support, and the early encouragement of Tony Chapman and Dave Müller is gratefully acknowledged. Finally, we wish to thank the Department of Psychology, University College, Cardiff, for significant support throughout the planning and execution of the whole enterprise.

1   Perspectives across the lifespan

Terry Honess and Krysia Yardley

Primary relationships – the emergence of self

Many of the contributions to this volume concentrate on the more cognitive aspects of self-awareness, albeit with increasing attention to experiential issues. However, there is little concern with affective aspects and those related phenomena that are not expressed through the verbal medium. In contrast, the first three chapters in this part deal predominantly with such issues and focus upon the experience of both infant and caretaker. These contributions, although based on prior analytic theory, depend heavily upon rich resources of clinical observation and empathic interpretation. Moreover, the findings which emerge via this route can be integrated with more controlled observation and the more traditional psychological orientations to be found in this volume.

The shift in psychodynamic thinking which, not only allows the concept of self for a consideration of psychogenesis, but posits it as essential and central, is a radical one. It liberates psychoanalytic ideas from the profoundly individualistic and biologically deterministic views of conventional psychoanalysis. Of course, such movements do not stand alone, but follow a line of development through ego-psychology and object-relations theory. Of those thinkers who have influenced this shift to self, Winnicott and Kohut have been most influential. In this regard, one of the most significant concepts has been that of 'mirroring'. In Chapter 2 of this book, Malcolm Pines presents a thorough and integrative review of psychodynamic views on mirroring. According to Pines, 'mirroring' in the psychoanalytic literature refers to two types of process. In the first place, it refers to the total social responsiveness of the caretakers to the baby (biological mirroring). In the second place, it refers to the 'specular image' of the French school. In the former, mirroring of the baby by the caretaker has the biologically benign purpose of facilitating and confirming the infant's subjective self (although this process can become malevolent). In the case of the specular image, the experience of being mirrored, via the

1

looking-glass, is one of encountering the objective self. For Lacan, this encounter is intrinsically destructive; he proposes that alienation from the primordial basis of the self commences here.

Pines argues that there is substantial evidence that biological mirroring is a human universal. His review also indicates the extent to which the caretaker is concerned to develop a meaningful reciprocal dialogue with the baby from birth; particularly through an (implicit) assumption of the child's intentionality. This treating of the infant as if it were endowed with particular psychological qualities is intriguingly close to the analysis presented by those social psychologists who take an avowedly social constructionist position (e.g. Shotter, 1984; Harré, 1987). However, a psychoanalyst would also assume that caretakers' response patterns are not simply socially organised or even biologically organised, but convey a great deal about the caretakers' unconscious. This powerfully enters into the child's mode of experiencing self and contributes to 'an *identity* theme which is irreversible but capable of variations throughout the life process'.

Gail Price is also a psychoanalytic psychotherapist. She explicitly draws on the writings of both Kohut and Stern and is, as are many writers in this area, heavily influenced by Winnicottian ideas. Price makes explicit Kohut's and Stern's primary concern with 'intersubjectivity' by positing the need to re-engage or newly engage adult clients in the sort of caretaking relationship that will allow their nascent selves to (re)emerge. Early developmental failures, whether occurring through emotional trauma or physical abuse, are argued to involve the infant's centre of initiative being constituted by a false self (structures which rely on external sources of affirmation and vitality in order to function). In terms more familiar to psychologists, self-esteem may be poorly developed, affect comes under the control of the other, hypervigilance and a preoccupation with others' reactions replace spontaneity and performance may be taken over by the need to placate.

The use of 'true' and 'false' self-structures rests somewhat uneasily with the importance attached to intersubjectivity for the development of self and it merits further consideration. However, the main thrust of Price's chapter is to draw parallels between early child–parent processes and the practice of psychotherapy. The clinician's empathy is seen to be closely related to early intimacy. It is 'an information-gathering process informed by an exquisite sensitivity to communicative signals and enhanced by memories of parallel experiences', a process which Price's evocative clinical descriptions amply illustrate. Essentially, a good 'holding environment' is also regarded as necessary in therapy. This can be sustained by using speech forms which approximate the structure of empathic parent–infant interaction. The precise extent to which good therapeutic practice mirrors the primary relationship is a relatively unexplored research question, yet one which is likely to provide a clearer appreciation of what constitutes a good holding environment for the emergence of a fragile sense of self, whether in infancy or adulthood.

In the next chapter, Irene Harwood draws together the ideas of Kohut and Winnicott. Both of these, Harwood argues, see the infant and caretaker as an indissoluble unit. For Winnicott, the infant self is not pregiven, but rather, through the caretaker's encouraging the experience of 'continuity of being', the infant is able to take the initiative, which is the beginnings of its true self: 'The self comes into being only after the ego nuclei are gathered together through the good mothering of the "holding" and "handling" environments' (Winnicott cited by Harwood). During the second year, the primary unit is seen to break down in that the infant learns to view the other as a whole person, and begins to operate as an independent self that engages with others. When this caretaking process fails, to whatever extent, negative consequences arise for that child's self-development. The child may doubt its own creative gestures and substitute the gestures of the other for its own, leading to the appropriation of a false self.

Harwood argues that Kohut, unlike Winnicott, does not view the self as dependent on prior ego developments. Instead, Kohut sees self as having a rudimentary existence at birth, but one which is intrinsically part of the human intersubjective environment. This intersubjectivity develops through different kinds of mergers until mature reciprocal self/selfobject relations are possible between persons. For Harwood, the most important difference between Kohut and Winnicott is the former's emphasis on the 'good-enough' environment and the latter's emphasis on unnecessary impingements upon the child. In combining these two sets of developmental emphases Harwood enlarges the typology of pathologies of the self and their explanations. An additional feature of Harwood's analysis, which characterises all three psychoanalytic contributions to this part, is the consideration of the anxiety and vulnerability of the infant and the power of the human environment to allay or induce such feelings. This is a particular strength of such work, yet is rarely dealt with in developmental psychologists' accounts.

It has been suggested that the clinicians' focus on more systemic and intersubjective conceptualisations is one which finds accord with developmental and constructivist psychological approaches. However, there are some differences of emphases and conceptualisation, which may be problematic. The emphasis on biological factors may be one such problem, although the 'biological potentiation' involved in Harwood's arguments, for example, is no more or less deterministic than discussion of social constraints or enablements. More problematic is the continued adherence to oedipal dynamics (see Harwood) and to equally androcentric, if more subtle, conceptualisations such as Lacan's law of the name of the father (see Pines). Such views appear strangely insensitive in the context of otherwise sensitive and empathic clinical accounts, and anachronistic in relation to both current child-rearing practices and to current, more feminist, psychoanalytic accounts (see Mendell, 1982).

The final chapter in the first part, that of Wylie, provides a detailed consideration of three mother–child pairs (infants aged 32 to 39 months) interacting in five different contexts. The work reported here is concerned with maternal attributions, i.e. 'any statement made by a mother in the hearing of her child which makes some comment expressing and/or implying some behavioral and/or inner characteristic(s) of the child, whether current or more enduring'. This is an important operationalisation of at least part of the mirroring responses (see the earlier chapters in this section) that the caretaking environment offers. Wylie employs a case-study procedure that Honess and Edwards, in Chapter 16 term 'analytic induction' – categories are inductively derived and Wylie reports 'general propositions' that are true of all three pairs. Methodologically, this is a significant move. Wylie's own authoritative reviews (e.g. 1979) point to the disproportionate attention given to self-regard overall and suggest that, using questionnaire operationalisations, 'many of the theoretically predicted relationships . . . have turned out to be weak or null'.

It appears that attributions addressed to the whole child are relatively rare. Wylie reports an extraordinarily high and varied number of attributions per session – 'a gentle, incessant fall of variously coloured sand grains' from which 'appreciable drifts of various colours' emerge. Given the universal acceptance that the development of self is predicated on the other's reactions to the infant (the mirror metaphor is not, of course, confined to the researchers and theoreticians introduced above, but is a central plank of sociological and social psychological theory) it is curious that Wylie is able to note that there is 'virtually no research literature' on parental attributions. An integration of parental attributions and child responses (the most significant of which might not necessarily be those which are temporally contingent) is likely to be a very important research endeavour. Moreover, her attributional approach could be extended to parents with still younger children by, for example, asking parents to talk through their own videotaped interactions, in order to help articulate the nature of the parents' implicit 'mirror' (Honess, 1986, provides more detail on this kind of research strategy).

Childhood – the conservation and evolution of self

With the advent of the child's language and the typical attainment of at least an implicit sense of self/other boundaries, the research emphasis switches to using children as research subjects. This has the obvious advantage that there can be a more direct focus on their perspective, but the disadvantage that the interpersonal matrix out of which a sense of self develops tends to be lost. However, a concern with the child's developing cognitive competencies is important in its own right, and we shall see that it allows a ready cross-referencing with the Piagetian tradition. The chapter by Aboud and Ruble, the first in this part, clearly relates to this tradition in asking what constitutes the cognitive precursors of the child's perception of self-*constancy*. Aboud and Ruble provide a review of largely experimental literature, which they acknowledge carries a number of special assumptions (in particular, that the experimenter has selected appropriate features for testing) and therefore carries potential pitfalls.

As Flavell (1974, p. 69) asked a decade ago, 'how [are we] to ascertain with any degree of certainty that task X dependably measures social-cognitive ability Y, that child A has "acquired" Y (in exactly what sense? to what level of mastery?) and child B has "not acquired" Y (not even minimally? not even capable of displaying it under ideal testing conditions, or following intensive training?) and so on.' A major problem then is that investigators often devise their own tasks which purport to measure a particular cognitive level, and as Aboud and Ruble note, even minor variations in the way a question is asked can significantly influence the form of a child's response. One possible solution is to seek to maximise the ecological validity of particular tasks, in order to help pre-empt unwarranted experimenter assumptions. A second possibility, followed by Aboud and Ruble, is to retain the particular advantages of experimental control, but to be especially circumspect in moving to imputations of particular cognitive skills. It will be seen that the other chapters in this part cede, in varying degrees, some degree of experimental control, particularly over the form of the subjects' responses, in order to mitigate experimenter pre-emption.

It is noteworthy that even the Aboud and Ruble definition of constancy is not confined to consistency in identification, but involves an achievement of the *understanding* that identification is constant. Of particular interest are the research indications that constancy is achieved at different times for different facets of self (e.g. gender before ethnicity) and that self-constancy is achieved prior to other constancy. This may be related to Wylie's finding that most maternal attributions affirm specific, rather than global, aspects of self.

The argument for the primacy of self-constancy also appears to be consistent with those arguments developed in the previous part (see Harwood's interpretation of Winnicott) that are concerned with the early emergence (given the right environment) of a sense of continuity of being. The psychoanalytic writers necessarily allude more to the experienced internal environment in their discussions of preverbal kinaesthetic responses and to that which Price refers to as the 'cross-modal experience' of identity. In this regard it is appropriate that Aboud and Ruble also warn that current experimental measures may not allow a sufficiently sensitive assessment of the child's sense of sameness.

The three steps proposed by Aboud and Ruble for the achievement of constancy are discussed within the framework of Piagetian stages: (i) expectation of sameness – a preoperational achievement, likened to anticipated conservation; (ii) perceived consistency of essential features – a concrete operational achievement, the ability to identify sameness despite transformation; (iii) perception of stability and consistency – presumably an acquisition related to formal operations, requiring attributions of stability across time and situations. This scheme is especially interesting in that it suggests cognitive developments that are largely complementary to those independently proposed by Chandler and his colleagues in the next chapter.

Chandler, Boyes, Ball and Hala assume that the idea of continuity is established for the children in their sample (the contributions in Part I suggest that this would be the case, although Aboud and Ruble remind us that different aspects of constancy may implicate different levels of cognitive achievement). Children in the Chandler *et al.* study were asked to account for, or warrant, the basis for continuity in the lives of well-known fictional characters. Chandler *et al.* report that (i) preoperational children typically justify continuity on the basis of simple inclusion of specific features, (ii) concrete operational children refer to essential, central features and later to material cause-and-effect relations between past and present and (iii) formal operational children employ foundational warrants, where present identity is seen to be logically related to past self.

Chandler *et al.* characterise the foregoing as 'realistic' attributions in which meanings are 'found'. However, formal operational children can finally achieve constructivist accounts, in which meanings are 'made'. At this stage, the children are said to employ narrative accounts; in Dennet's phrase, 'the self is a narrative centre of gravity'. The work of Chandler *et al.* can be seen to provide an important bridge between the cognitive Piagetian and the social psychological literature on accounting. Moreover, the narrative framework for understanding accounts is one that is increasingly popular (e.g. see Handel; Honess and Edwards; Little; and, especially, Haimes, in this volume). However, a cautionary note might be sounded here concerning the extent to which the 'essentialist' account is seen to be developmentally inferior to the 'narrative' account. Interpretation of the latter might rely too heavily on particular accounting practices, emphasised in some cultures and contexts more than in others. As Harré and Secord (1972, Chapter 11) note, 'preservatory' accounting involves the use of 'back-stop' concepts, such as 'just wanting to'. The complementary responses in the present context are 'I just am', 'It just is' or 'It's still me'. Is this essentialist or constructivist? The important point that Harré and Secord make is that such 'back-stop' responses are *not* properly amenable to further accounting demands.

Hart, Maloney and Damon also focus on the development of self-continuity, but, in addition, explicitly address the related component of distinctness from others. They acknowledge that no sudden emergence of continuity is likely to be charted, but rather note its presence, in some form, at preverbal levels. This is a simple, but important, point: the young infant may experience a strong sense of continuity of being, but not until a decade later be able to publicly warrant that continuity in fully adequate terms. Hart *et al.* note that the response format 'Tell me about yourself' (see discussion below on the McGuires' and Peevers' contributions) should certainly reflect salience of any category, but does not readily allow a between-age comparison of the child's responses to particular tasks. They therefore adopt a similar procedure to Chandler *et al.*, and ask their respondents to defend claims of personal continuity and distinctness.

Hart *et al.* present longitudinal data suggesting that both continuity and distinctness are 'accessible' through employing the above method and, like Chandler *et al.*, show how the basis for justifications markedly shifts as the child gets older. There is a slight difference in emphasis, however. Chandler *et al.* only consider the form of the argument that a child presents, whereas Hart *et al.* also take account of content, particularly the extent to which descriptions implicate an individualised self, with relatively low reference to others.

Wylie's conclusions concerning the disappointing state of the self-esteem literature have already been noted (see discussion of Part I). In this regard, the McGuires, in the next chapter, are not slow to note that self-esteem research is almost exclusively based on pre-emptive questions defined by the experimenter, what they call 'reactive techniques'. Indeed, W. McGuire and his colleagues continue to pursue an extensive programme of examining 'spontaneous' self-concepts in response to the relatively open question 'Tell me about yourself' and more recently 'Tell us what you are not', in order to chart developmental trends in what the McGuires here call 'the subjective experience of self'.

Variations of this approach are becoming increasingly popular with those seeking to examine individual social development, whilst avoiding overly contrived tasks. Thus in the cognitive personality theory of Kreitler and Kreitler (Chapter 21), for example, 'meaning clusters' are derived from the person's descriptions of self from different points of view (which acknowledges in part that descriptions are grounded in particular positions) such as the self in the present, the self in the past, self as described by the respondent to a friend and so on. Similarly, Peevers (in Chapter 10) assumes that aspects of the subjective self 'can be discerned in the verbal accounts which people give when asked to describe themselves'.

The conceptual and methodological roots of the 'Tell me' probe can be traced to the more cognitive interpretations of the sociological interactionist tradition, especially the work of Kuhn. Various forms of the question have been stimulated by the work of Bugental and Zelen (1950) and Kuhn

(1960), which received detailed review in Spitzer *et al.* (1971). It is perhaps ironic that one of the central tenets of symbolic interactionism (especially that encouraged by Blumer, e.g. 1969), that meaning is an emergent quality and one that is highly context bound, was ignored for all practical purposes in this early work. Thus, Tucker (1966) is able to point to the lack of reflexivity on the part of test users.

The modern variants as exemplified in the work of the McGuires are a significant improvement; interviews are now common, the response format is more open and respondents are sometimes asked to take a particular perspective on self. However, it is clear that such researchers do not seek to embrace fully interactionist tenets. Rather, they are examining the wider impact of certain contexts, e.g. ethnicity, gender, family background and particular life experiences, all of which are external to the interview itself. An alternative approach that deserves brief mention here is to go 'inside' the interview, to try to tap the 'accounting process' (see Shotter, 1984, on the distinction between 'accounts' and 'accounting'). This requires that the interview itself must be assessed with respect to its status as a 'context of asking' – a respondent provides an account of self *for* some person *for* some reason (see Yardley, 1987). Within this perspective there can be no 'spontaneous' self-concept, although valuable work is evidently possible through working as if it existed.

A particularly significant feature of the McGuires' work is that they seek to relate spontaneous descriptions to social circumstance. Thus, they are able to extend our understanding of the distinctness component of selfhood; we are more likely to mention a general characteristic to the extent that our position with respect to that characteristic is distinctive. Their 'free-response' data also provide similar findings to those reported by Hart *et al.*, in that self-descriptions of older children become more generalised and there are fewer references to what the McGuires call the 'social aspects of self-space'. The problem of interpretation of such data is addressed by the McGuires in terms of respondents being disposed to provide information that they regard as informative. This does suggest, however, that the most important information may not be spontaneously mentioned, because its importance is taken for granted (a point that is discussed by Peevers in Chapter 10). It may be that frequency of an indicator more usually reflects salience for the given questioning context, rather than importance in a general sense. This would explain why the McGuires' respondents defined themselves more in terms of their pets than of their mothers!

The final chapter in this part, by Peevers, shares a number of the McGuires' methodological assumptions, as discussed above. In particular, Peevers asserts that it is only with a free-response format that one is able to obtain detail on what respondents think is salient. She suggests that if one is interested in self-esteem, for example, it should be maximally effective to look at self-esteem in those areas that respondents believe to be the most salient. The focus on continuity and distinctness as key features of selfhood is sustained in Peevers' contribution, continuity being understood in terms of relations to the past, the future and degree of change. Here, her results are consistent with those of Chandler *et al*. Continuity was spontaneously characterised by lack of change assertions (habitual behaviour) at 6 years, with references to the past generally high. However, references to the future, and warranting of continuity despite changes, occurred later in development.

Self-reflexive statements are reported to increase generally with age, but the first clear agentic statements (as indexed through expressing intentions) do not occur until age 13. This is surprising in that caretakers are argued to act toward their infants 'as if' they had intentions, and, we have seen, that 'initiative' can be regarded as the key element for the development of selfhood. It is less surprising if we see a *statement* of intent, decision or choice as essentially a *public* commitment (see Harré, 1983, pp. 115–119, on the structure of commitment as essentially interpersonal) for which we are held accountable. Indeed, Hart *et al*. argue that the achievement of distinctness and continuity are necessarily prior to considerations of commitment, and we shall see in Chapter 11 that Marcia sees commitment as a key identity task for late adolescence and early adulthood.

Adolescence – the consolidation of self

The assumption that adolescence necesarily involves 'crisis' in the context of identity development is no longer widely held, yet it is undeniably the case that it is a period when a number of social and physical changes confront the individual, and it is a period when young people appear to be especially sensitive to self-evaluation and other appraisal. Moreover, the cognitive changes discussed in Part II point to a newly emerging capacity to construct rather than simply to discover meanings. This series of factors has led researchers to be especially concerned with adolescence, not least because of the influence of Erikson's work. In this regard, the first chapter in this part, by Marcia, is particularly valuable since he, possibly more than any other psychologist, has been associated with the empirical examination of Erikson's ideas.

Marcia's empirical work focuses on the potential identity status 'achievements' of late adolescence and early adulthood. His key constructs for seeking to classify such statuses (which may be different in different areas of the adolescent's life) are (i) 'exploration', which is necessarily related to the distinction between meanings created and meanings discovered or 'conferred', and (ii) 'commitment', a theme discussed above as significantly related to both individual agency and public accountability. The basis for classification of the possible statuses is especially interesting since it derives not only from Erikson's theory, but also from a considerable data base of interviews with adolescents and young adults. The themes discussed in earlier parts – a sense of self-continuity, of distinctness, and the degree of other-reliance for self-validation – are all present. The last feature, in conjunction with the detail of Marcia's reference to the predisposing patterns of family relations, is particularly striking in its high degree of correspondence with the psychoanalytic propositions introduced in the first part.

Simmons, the next contributor, like others in this part, can be seen to contrast with Marcia's position in that it is the number of different transitions, not a particular psychological *stage per se*, that makes adolescence of particular interest. Simmons provides a review of the self-esteem literature, probably the single most researched variable in the adolescent literature. She first addresses some of the criticisms of this concept (e.g. see Wylie's conclusions, discussed above), principally through advocating the need to relate self-esteem to social, biological and behavioural phenomena, rather than other psychological constructs. This is a powerful move, and Simmons is able to demonstrate that simple questionnaire assessments of overall positive or negative attitudes to self do show significant relations with non-questionnaire indicators that are of significance to adolescents. Thus, she is able to provide good empirical support for the notion that changes such as entry into high school, onset of dating, puberty, and so on can be managed, and accommodations made, provided that such changes are met relatively sequentially rather than simultaneously.

Rosenberg is concerned to chart events that threaten a sense of continuity. He focuses on experience of self-change and violations of self-expectations, working on the assumption that the self-system constitutes a system of self expectations. Transitory 'depersonalisation' is shown to be a relatively common occurrence, and one that can usually be related to failures of expectation, not only where one falls short of one's expectations, but also where one exceeds them.

Between the ages of 12 and 16 years, Rosenberg reports significant sex differences, with girls reporting more depersonalisation experiences. The major contributor to this appears to be girls' negative reactions to physical changes – 'I just can't get used to my new looks'. Simmons also reports significant sex differences, for example, that changes in post-puberty body image generally have a positive impact for boys and a negative impact for girls. Furthermore, Simmons reports that overall girls are disadvantaged more by a high number of life-event changes than are boys. This may be related to the Rosenberg finding that 12- to 16-year-old girls report a more 'volatile' self-concept than do boys. In addition, Simmons finds that a too-early allowance of independence from parents appears to be to girls' disadvantage. It is of interest, therefore, that Gecas and Mortimer (in

Chapter 17) report self-esteem as positively related to independence from parents for their all-male sample, although it must be noted that the populations sampled are not directly comparable (see also Honess and Edwards in Chapter 16 on the meaning of independence).

Gender differences such as these receive particular attention in the contribution of Bush. Quoting Gilligan, she summarises the demands of this period thus: 'male gender identity is threatened by intimacy, while female gender identity is threatened by separation'. Hence, she joins Gilligan (1982) in seeing Erikson's *separation* of the stages of 'identity versus role confusion' and then 'intimacy versus isolation' as inappropriate, particularly for understanding female development.

In discussing the cultural construction of gender, Bush stresses the important point that we must be sensitive to changes in cultural expectations. For example, she presents evidence that the popularity versus instrumental polarity (girls are characterised by a focus on popularity, boys by a relative concern with instrumentality) is considerably less marked in comparing 1960s and 1970s cohorts. More profoundly, she argues that the *meanings* of adolescents' understanding of notions such as 'competence' and 'independence' appear to be changing. A particular concern of her chapter is to examine the impact of such changes on young women's participation in violence. Thus, she is critical of the proposition that being a 'non-traditional' female entails being like the 'traditional' male. Her review and her own research give some support to her argument that young women are able to reinterpret instrumentality, without losing their concern for 'connectedness' with others. However, it is likely (as Bush herself acknowledges) that the questionnaire methods she employs are relatively unsuited to charting complicated shifts in meaning, and that methods of the type discussed by other contributors to this section may be more appropriate.

More intensive, individually focused methods are discussed in the final two chapters in this part. Little's 'personal projects' method involves several assumptions that can be seen to be related to a number of the issues introduced so far: such projects, 'extended sets of personally relevant action', are essentially *intentional* in form and operate within ('into' may be a better preposition) a particular ecological context. Moreover, these projects are seen as constituting a system of intentions, each of which is classified according to its meaning, structure, involvement with others, degree of competency and the stress or challenge it involves. Little's work can therefore be seen to have much in common with that of Marcia on 'commitment' (see also our general comments on this issue) and with Rosenberg on the self as a system of self-expectations.

The need to explore individual meanings as well as provide summary data on groups of respondents is also stressed in the final chapter of this part, by Honess and Edwards. Here, the claim is made that the commonly exploited methods of statistical inference, based on comparisons between groups, deserve to be complemented by the relatively underutilised strategy of analytic inference. The latter approach typically draws on qualitative data, which does not mean imprecise data, but rather data that constitute too complex a set (particularly where one is concerned with the nuances of meaning) to be rendered in quantitative terms.

These authors seek to show, in the context of a longitudinal study of poorly qualified school-leavers, how both strategies can complement each other in order to bridge the divide between the complexity of individual lives and the need to generalise to other populations. Little's concern with 'ecological context' is also a significant theme in the Honess and Edwards paper, e.g. their argument that particular 'coping' or 'accommodation' styles can only be properly understood with reference to the cultural and family context.

Beyond adolescence – institutional demands and personal resolutions

The call for a lifespan developmental psychology is now commonplace, yet, as with work in other areas of concern to developmental psychologists, the overwhelming focus in self and identity research is on the first quarter of the expected lifespan for Westerners, i.e. the years from birth to late adolescence. There are good reasons for such an emphasis. Change is more rapid in these early years, putative cognitive developments are more predictable and early experience is assumed to lay the foundations for later years. However, the period beyond adolescence brings a number of unique circumstances – different forms of institutional socialisation (e.g. the workplace), increasing responsibility for others (e.g. family life) – such changes reflecting the broader social acknowledgement that one has come through the rite of passage that confers 'adult' status. Consistent with the emphasis in this book upon the individual person, we are especially concerned with the personal sense-making involved in such changes, and the necessary reconstructions that these involve.

The final part of the book includes chapters by Gecas and Mortimer, by West, Nicholson and Arnold, and by Rossan, all of which reflect a growing interest in articulating the relationship between self and social structure (see general theoretical papers by Stryker, Turner, Wiley and Alexander, and McCall in Yardley and Honess, 1987). In this respect, the three sets of authors seek to distinguish between the personal and social features of identity. For example, Gecas and Mortimer discuss three aspects: (i) 'role identity', a status location conferred on a person largely through forms of institutional socialisation, (ii) 'character', the qualities attributed to the person which are assumed to be constructed through interpersonal negotiation, and (iii) 'existential' identity, which involves, once again, the themes of continuity and distinctness from others, a 'biographical self' that involves a continuing reconstruction.

The research reported by Gecas and Mortimer exploits a similar methodology to that reviewed by Simmons in Chapter 12, and, like her, they report a high level of consistency of reported self-esteem over the adolescent and early adulthood years. However, their finding that quality of relationships is a more important determinant of self-esteem than instrumental achievements is surprising given the gender differences reviewed by Bush in Chapter 14 and the fact that the Gecas and Mortimer sample were males. This might be seen as a helpful corrective to what some regard as the over-reporting of marginal sex differences (see Thoits, 1984, for a discussion of this issue), but replications are required that sample a wider ability and social class range of males. Of possibly greater interest is their report that an assessment of overall self-esteem stability, taken by itself, masks the shifting sources of self-esteem, i.e. from quality of relationship with parents to the quality of relationship with partners.

Gecas and Mortimer also report that 'character' at adolescence is a powerful predictor of future job choice. For example, an adolescent valuing instrumental attributes might select employment that encourages autonomy, and thereby facilitate the development of his or her instrumentality. This is plausible, given a situation where a high level of choice is available to the individual (e.g. the well-qualified men in the Gecas and Mortimer study), but in the majority of situations it might be more profitable to talk of 'mutual adjustment' or 'accommodation' between person and environment (see Honess and Edwards, Chapter 16). The relationship between identity and occupational demands for relatively highly qualified persons is treated in more detail by West *et al.* in Chapter 18. They demonstrate that there is a reciprocal, and to some extent predictable, relationship between personal change, role innovation and particular work-role transitions. This, in conjunction with the Gecas and Mortimer data (and some aspects of the Rosenberg data), gives excellent support for the assumed dynamic relation between role demands and personal resolutions.

This dynamic is further explored in Rossan's contribution, which, as indicated above, shares many of the theoretical assumptions of the previous two chapters. However, her method, an intensive series of interviews and the construction of descriptive case studies (see Honess and Edwards for a discussion of case-study typology) is different. Moreover, her focus, the birth of a first child, appears to be a uniquely interesting transition since it implicates a great number of social and personal changes which would appear to make the warranting of self-continuity problematic. However, this does not appear to be the case, in that active reconstructions appear to be readily undertaken (cf. the closely related 'biographical self' of Gecas and Mortimer). It is likely that this is so because alternative social scripts are readily available for accounting for such transitions for women (see

Haimes, Chapter 22, on the relation between social and personal narratives).

Handel's contribution also explores perceived change of self following transitions (becoming literate, joining the army and undergoing professional training). Unlike Rossan, he is not seeking to access personal changes as particular events are happening, but to tap a retrospective perspective on events. Hence, his focus is on the individual's current state of consolidation of earlier events, when the reconstructions required by such events have, relatively speaking, already been accommodated within the person's overall self-view. For example, it may be that the social scripts that we have suggested are 'on offer' to mothers may meet an immediate need, but *in retrospect* particular mothers might reflect that the reconstructions required were more (or less) radical than realised at the time.

The 'consolidation' argument is helpful in interpreting Handel's finding that his respondents report a global sense of change rather than change in particular features of self. However, it could also be argued that his 'RCI', a reactive technique (see discussion of the McGuires' perspective), would be less sensitive to individuals' specific life changes. Notwithstanding this point, Handel's general summary of his data – 'assimilate if you can, accommodate if you must' – is particularly pertinent in his discussion of the 'progressive self-narrative' that appears to characterise his respondents' reflections. In particular, it appears that there are age-related factors here (which are, no doubt, related to cultural prescription): Handel reports that self-sameness is psychologically central for his middle-aged respondents, where moves to enhance self-esteem call for a 'self-narrative of pronounced stability'.

Kreitler and Kreitler's work, the next contribution, has already been introduced (see discussion of Part II). They employ a free-response strategy in seeking to identify meaning clusters for several different facets of self, working with a wide age range from 16-year-olds to 90-year-olds. A particular strength of their coding system is that it is derived not only from self-attributions, but also from a broad spectrum of attributions (both verbal and non-verbal) concerning other persons and events. This more readily allows an exploration of relatedness between self and other in a manner that is minimally prescriptive. They show that age-related changes reflect an increasing differentiation (compare our earlier references to the conceptual importance of 'distinctiveness'), for example, through an increasing number of negation statements in the post-adolescent period (20 to 30 years). However, this is paralleled by a progressively wider frame of reference for interpreting oneself, leading the Kreitlers to talk about a 'merging of self with the world', which may implicate a lack of flexibility in self presentation for the oldest grouping (60 to 90 years).

An understanding of self in terms of personal narrative (introduced in discussion of Part II) and social accountability (introduced in discussion of

Part III) is the explicit result of the research reported in the final chapter of this book. Haimes cites Barham (1984): 'Problems of personal identity are thus properly understood as problems in the narrative ordering of human lives, as difficulties that arise for the agent' in making one's life intelligible to self or others. Her research, like others in this section, can be seen to focus on a particular transition, in this case, the reasons given by adoptees for seeking information on their biological parents and the restructuring required (for some an assimilation, for others a radical transformation) on receipt of this information. Haimes argues that such information (as well as the 'social narrative', i.e. changing social interpretations of adoption) provides practical tools to account for oneself. In her words, identity then becomes an 'ability', 'the ability to give an account of one's life and to ask others for an account of their part in one's life'.

References

Blumer, H. (1969), *Symbolic Interactionism: Perspective and Method*, Prentice-Hall: Englewood Cliffs, N.J.

Bugental, J. and Zelen, S. (1950), 'Investigations into the self-concept: The W-A-Y technique', *Journal of Personality*, 18, pp. 483–98.

Flavell, J, H. (1974), 'The development of inferences about others', in T. Mischel (ed.), *Understanding Other Persons*, Blackwell: Oxford.

Gilligan, C. (1982), *In a Different Voice: Psychological Theory and Women's Development*, Harvard University Press: Cambridge, Mass.

Harré, R. (1983), *Personal Being*, Blackwell: Oxford.

Harré, R. (1987), 'The social construction of selves', in K. Yardley and T. Honess (eds), *Self and Identity: Psychosocial Perspectives*, Wiley: Chichester.

Harré, R. and Secord, P. (1972), *The Explanation of Social Behaviour*, Blackwell: Oxford.

Honess, T. (1986), 'Mirroring and social metacognition', in C. Antaki and A. Lewis (eds), *Mental Mirrors*, Sage: London.

Kuhn, M. (1960), 'Self: Attitudes by sex and professional training', *Sociological Quarterly*, 1, pp. 39–55.

Mendell, D. (ed.) (1982), *Early Female Development*, MTP Press: Lancaster.

Shotter, J. (1984), *Social Accountability and Selfhood*, Blackwell: Oxford.

Spitzer, S., Couch, C. and Stratton, J. (1971), *The Assessment of Self*, Bawden Bros: Davenport, Iowa.

Thoits, P. (1984), 'Multiple identities: Explaining gender and marital status differences in distress', Paper given at BPS International Interdisciplinary Conference on Self and Identity, Cardiff.

Tucker, C. (1966), 'Some methodological problems of Kuhn's self theory', *Sociological Quarterly*, 7, pp. 345–58.

Wylie, R. C. (1979), *The Self-Concept: Theory and Research on Selected Topics*, University of Nebraska Press: Lincoln.

Yardley, K. (1987), 'What do *you* mean "Who am I?"': Exploring the implications of a self-concept measurement with subjects', in K. Yardley and T. Honess (eds), *Self and Identity: Psychosocial Perspectives*, Wiley: Chichester.

Yardley, K. and Honess, T. (eds) (1987), *Self and Identity: Psychosocial Perspectives*, Wiley: Chichester.

Part I

Primary relationships – the emergence of self

2 Mirroring and child development: Psychodynamic and psychological interpretations

Malcolm Pines

The experimental and observational study of mirroring in children contributes to understanding the developmental lines of:

1. Self as subject
2. Self as object
3. Self with object

To this widely recognised scheme can be added the unusual tangential contribution of Lacan and the French school of:

4. Self as other

Categorisation artificially separates the growth of the whole person into part components, the 'person' in relation to 'others'. For some authors, e.g. Lewis and Brooks-Gunn (1979), following Cooley and Mead, self and object arise together and are different terms in the same equation. However, for clarity and convenience these categorisations will be preserved in reviewing the evidence on the role of mirroring in child development.

At the outset it is of fundamental importance to recognise that authors use the term 'mirroring' in very different senses. For some, mirroring is used as a metaphor; it represents the social responses of others to the infant and therefore includes the study of all the components of relationships. For other authors, the study is of infants' actual responses to their own reflection, the mirror image, the 'specular image' of the French school. In this chapter, the use of the metaphorical mirror will be addressed first, and the observations of both clinicians and psychological researchers will then be drawn upon.

Mirroring as a biological and social phenomenon

The very earliest social responses of caretakers to infants and some of the infants' earliest responses to caretakers have been viewed as 'mirroring' responses at a biological level. The underlying mechanisms have been viewed as imprinting (Lichtenstein), social fittedness (Emde), intuitive parental behaviour (the Papouseks), imitation (Pawlby) and state-sharing (Stern). These observations and concepts are presented in more detail below.

Biological mirroring

Following the suggestions of Emde and other authors, I propose that mirroring is an important function in the developmental line (Freud, 1980) of the process of *organisation* and *coherence* that will lead to self-awareness and to the awareness of the relations between self and objects.

Emde (1983) states that it is generally agreed, partly on the basis of the infant's behaviour towards the literal mirror image, that self-recognition emerges at some time in the infant's second year. Emde asks, does this mean that a new psychic organisation, the 'self', emerges for the first time in the second year? Or, can we conceive of the self as an ongoing developmental process that gains *psychological* representation in the second year and hence becomes observable both subjectively and objectively? He proposes that we regard self as a *process*, a vital set of synthetic functions which increase in depth and complexity as development proceeds through the lifespan, and that prior to the emergence and recognition of self as a *psychological* process we can conceptualise and observe its development as a *biological* process. Part of this biological process we can term 'biological mirroring'.

Three biological processes that apply to the organisation and development of systems are necessary for the coherence of the developing and emerging system that we can later recognise as self. These principles are self-regulation (the physiological homeostasis and maintenance of individual integrity); affective monitoring of pleasurable and unpleasurable experiences and, most important for present purposes, '*social fittedness*'. For this process, the infant is assumed to be pre-adapted to participate in human interaction. Social fittedness involves the actions of both the infant and the caretakers/parents who intuitively adopt appropriate behaviour towards the infant such as baby talk or rhythmic soothing and engage in behavioural synchrony. The aspect that I shall enlarge upon as an example of biological mirroring is the eye-to-eye contact parents adopt with the newborn infant, which has been beautifully investigated and demonstrated by the Papouseks.

The terms 'biological echo' and 'biological mirror' are used by the Papouseks (1979) in their discussion of primary, intuitive parental behaviours, which can be observed cross-culturally, exemplifying Emde's principle of social fittedness. Amongst these primary parental behaviours are facial and vocal behaviours, such as baby talk and exaggerated facial expressions. By speaking to infants in baby talk with its higher pitch, repetitive phrases and free use of nonsense utterances and by the use of exaggerated facial expressions which offer clear indications of emotional states and offerings of joy, greeting, approval, encouragement or even of amused disapproval, the parent acts as a benign reflection to the baby of its presence within the context of a social relationship. This interaction is described by Winnicott (1971) in his discussion of the mother's face as a mirror to the baby (see below).

The Papouseks have demonstrated, cross-culturally, how visual contact between caretakers and infants is established and that it satisfies a basic need for both parties to get to know and to be known by the other. They state that the most important educational principle is 'to deliver knowledge in appropriate amounts at appropriate times through multiple sensory modalities repeatedly and with respect for the recipient's capacity to process them', and that '*intuitive parenting*' seems to guarantee this primary education.

Imitation

Imitative behaviour, also a form of biological mirroring, is another principle of primary intuitive parenting. The capacity for imitation of the adult by the newborn can be seen in the first few weeks of life. Caretakers imitate infants and encourage infants to imitate them. Vocally, they make baby noises and encourage babies to make utterances and then imitate the sounds that come from the infant; they initiate smiling responses and reward the child's smile by demonstrating pleasure when the smile appears; they repeat the infant's gestures; they encourage hitting, grasping, kicking and repeat the movements of the infant; they enter into repetitive sequences, interacting playfully with the infant.

Pawlby (1977) shows that the process begins with the mother being ready to imitate her child. 'Almost from the time of birth there seems to be a marked readiness for mothers to *reflect back* [my italics] to their infants certain gestures which occur spontaneously within the baby's natural repertoire of activities.' By reflecting back imitatively, mother is acting as a psycho-biological mirror, an active partner in the infant's developing capacity for social relations and the beginning awareness of self-representation and object-representation. But that is not all mother does; she does more than that. Whenever baby is likely to repeat an action two or three times, when sequences are observed, 'a mother may skilfully insert her own copy of that action between two of the repetitions and hence create a simulation of a deliberate act of imitation on the infant's part'. The mother's intention seems to be to develop and to sustain a meaningful *dialogue* with her baby and, furthermore, to facilitate the development of a more deliberate imitation by the baby. The mother's answering gesture provides the infant with an interest-holding event which is temporally contingent upon its own performance of a similar event. Thus *intentionality* and *reciprocity* are inserted by the caretakers into their beginning dialogues with their infants. They *assume* that the baby *intends* to perform a motor action; they reward and praise the infant for random actions and encourage him or her to repeat them – 'Who's a clever baby? Go on, do it again'. They reward the child for actions which are contingent on the child's behaviour and also reassure themselves of their child's capacities for such behaviour and for the establishment of communication between them. Pawlby notes that parental imitation of their children's behaviour seems largely unconscious unless it is actually drawn to the caretaker's attention. Thus imitation seems to be a further example of intuitive primary parenting, of parents as the good mirrors assuring the infant that 'you are the fairest one of all' during that blissful early-world state where there is no other to challenge the state of joyful narcissistic self-experience. Mother is the talking, smiling mirror for her child's earliest self-reflection, creating that sense of primary identity to which Lichtenstein has drawn our attention.

Lichtenstein (1977) invokes the concept of '*imprinting*' to describe vital aspects of early infant–mother interaction, defining it as 'the name given to the process by which the releaser of an innate reaction to a fellow member of the species is acquired'. Here he is using concepts derived from ethology as described by Lorenz and Tinbergen. According to Lichtenstein, a mother sends 'messages' to her infant that convey a great deal about her unconscious wishes concerning the child. The way she touches, holds, warms the child, the way in which some senses are stimulated while others are not, forms a kind of 'stimulus cast' of the mother's unconscious. He refers to other analysts like Mahler (1967) who use the term 'mirroring' for these very early selective responses of the parents to the infant and agrees that such mirroring experiences are intimately linked with the emergence of both body image and sense of identity. However, he argues that the term overemphasises the visual element of the experience, that the 'image' of oneself that the mirror conveys is at this early stage outlined in terms of sensory responsiveness, not as visual perception: 'These responses as well as the primitive stimuli that elicit them form a continuous interchange of need creation and need satisfaction between the two partners of the symbiotic world. While the mother satisfies the infant's needs, in fact she creates certain specific needs, which she delights in satisfying, the infant is transformed into an organ or an instrument for the satisfaction of the mother's unconscious needs' (p. 77). Mother imprints upon the infant an *identity* theme which is irreversible but capable of variations throughout the life process. Here Lichtenstein, like Emde, is describing the process that gives continuity and coherence to the individual throughout all the momentous dangers from internal and external environments that characterise the human experience from birth to old age.

Where else do we find the concept of mirroring being applied to infant development in the first year of life? In his masterly summing up and integration of research on very early infantile development and relationships, Daniel Stern (1983) writes of ways of 'Being With' another that can be applied to infantile affective experiences, the experience of 'Self with Other'. Some features of that which he agrees can be called 'mirroring' are amongst the most important of these 'being with' experiences.

Stern proposes that the affective experiences of the baby with the other be integrated with the cognitive viewpoint that self and other are indeed differentiated perceptually and cognitively from birth onwards. He argues that Mahler's 'symbiotic' state as the earliest state of post-natal life is not confirmed by research evidence, which demonstrates that the child is 'an avid learner from birth', competent, predesigned to perceive the world in a highly structured fashion and mentally active in organising prestructured conceptions, of which visual schemata and the recognition of the mother's face are the most important.

In the affective schemata of the mother–infant pair there are three ways of 'being with the other': 'self-other complementarity', 'mental state-sharing', and 'state transforming'. The 'invaluable concept of mirroring' is in fact predicated on the more basic concept '*state-sharing*'. In mental state-sharing and state-tuning, the infant and the mother *share* similar experiences. State-sharing covers events such as vocalising together, games such as pat-a-cake, interactional synchrony, mutual gazing and interactions between mother and infant like smiling, where the smile of the one evokes the smile of the other, which in turn increases the pleasure and the intensity of the smiling response, in a positive feedback loop. State-sharing and those aspects of it which can be termed mirroring are, he argues, clearly moments of great importance for they are the first glimpse of having something like a similar experience with another, that is, a glimpse of intersubjectivity: the sharing of mental states creates the possibility of subjective intimacy. During these moments of state-sharing infants are 'engaged' in the slow and momentous discovery that what they already sense is distinctly their own is not unique and unparalleled but is part of shared human experience. They are establishing subjective intimacy. In order to do that the infant must maintain the separate entities of self and other, because the power of state-sharing lies in a sense of what is happening being between two separate persons. However, not all in this process is joyful. State-sharing can also be negative. Mutual gazing and mimicry can be frightening, provocative and at times intolerably invasive in the sense of negative intimacy. This is the first appearance of the concept of negative mirroring, which will be addressed later on.

Stern writes that 'being with experiences are the stuff that human connectedness, as well as normal intimacy and basic trust, are made of at all points of development. The ability to engage in them is amongst the most needed and healthy of capacities'. This again emphasises the great significance of early biological and psychological positive mirroring experiences in the establishment of the basic building blocks of human personality and of human connectedness.

In his contribution to the same symposium, Louis Sander (1983) does not actually refer to mirroring. His emphasis is on coherency and unity, on how they are enhanced and maintained in infantile development. I suggest that mirroring is one of the ways in which this coherency and unity is advanced and maintained. If we adopt Stern's concept of 'state-sharing', in which the infant becomes aware that what he/she is already experiencing as his/her experience is then mirrored, that is, shared, by another and this other is experienced as already possessing characteristics of coherency and unity, then the state-sharing reinforces the child's own experience of coherency and unity. State-sharing does not lead to fusion, to loss of boundaries, to a regressive de-differentiation; it is a joyful reinforcement of the sense of individuality, of one who is now 'being with the other', the 'fitting together' which Hartmann (1958) emphasised, as does Emde when he refers to 'social fittedness'.

The thrust of current research in infant development is on the infant–mother *system* and not on the isolated individual infant. Previously seen as totally helpless and dependent, the infant seems very different when viewed as an active participant in the 'well functioning' of an organisation that is adapted to its survival, maintenance and development. This systemic viewpoint, which considers both the whole and the parts, sees the parts affecting the structure and function as a whole and the whole concurrently affecting the structure and function of the parts. Development is seen as a creative process in which mirroring has an important part to play through social connectedness, learning and playfulness being inherent in this process.

Within psychoanalytic developmental theory, both Winnicott's dictum 'There is no such thing as a baby' (meaning that the infant is never seen in isolation, only in the context of a caretaker) and Kohut's description of caretakers as the *baby's* 'selfobjects' well exemplify this systemic viewpoint.

D. W. Winnicott

Winnicott's famous contribution to the concept of mirroring is presented in his short paper 'Mirror-role of mother and family in child development' (1971). As Davis and Wallbridge (1981) show, we can set this important contribution in the context of Winnicott's emphasis on ego-relatedness and communication, a relationship between mother and baby that arises specifically from the holding enironment (see Harwood, Chapter 4). Winnicott states that the function of the environment can be summarised as:

1. Holding
2. Handling
3. Object presenting

If the infant is held and handled satisfactorily, and with this taken for granted, at some time the baby begins to look around and looks much more at the face than at the breast. (Indeed, it is striking how much less attention has been placed upon the face in the development of object relationships theory than upon the breast.) Winnicott asks the question, 'What does the baby see when he or she looks at the mother's face?'. I am suggesting that, ordinarily, what the baby sees is himself or herself. In other words, a mother is looking at the baby and what she looks like is related to what she sees there. If she looks with love and with tenderness, the baby experiences him or herself as joyfully alive. If, however, she is depressed and unsmiling, even more so if she does not look back and cannot maintain the reciprocity of looking, the baby experiences him or herself as joyless, unlively, even absent. The mother's face is then all that is seen:

> mother's face is not then a mirror. So perception takes the place of apperception, perception takes the place of that which might have been the beginning of a significant exchange with the world, a two-way process in which self-enrichment alternates with the discovery of meaning in the world of seeing things. . . . A baby so treated will grow up puzzled about mirrors and what the mirror has to offer. If the mother's face is unresponsive then a mirror is a thing to be looked at but not to be looked into (Winnicott, 1971, p. 113).

David Scharff (1982) has utilised Winnicott's observations in his suggestion that there is a developmental line of gaze interaction, and that the exchange of gazes contributes significantly to sexual and emotional life in the adult:

> Gaze interaction is one physical function for which we can draw a developmental line from infancy to adulthood that illuminates the

concepts of growth in object relations and sexuality. Although in practice it is part of the larger context of holding, handling and vocalising, it can be separated out for purposes of study and illustration. . . .

The adult needs for kissing, smiling, and physical caring or lovemaking have their origins in the shared gaze, touch, holding and vocal 'conversations' of infant and mother. The response of each partner to the other is required for a sense of well being. Failures of mirroring in infancy leading to false self problems make it difficult to re-create the mirroring experience in adult sexual life. Without a capacity for mutual mirroring, exchange is severely hampered (p. 24).

To return once more to Winnicott's short but evocative paper, we find here one of his most important statements about psychotherapy, one that my own clinical experience with narcissistically disturbed and damaged patients repeatedly confirms: 'Psychotherapy is not making clever and apt interpretations; by and large it is a long-term process of giving the patient back what the patient brings.' This has profound significance for psychoanalytic technique and has strong parallels with Kohutian technique (see below; Chapters 3 and 4 of this volume; and Wolf, 1987).

Kohut, self psychology and mirroring

On the basis of his clinical experience of the transference manifestations of patients with narcissistic personality disorders, Kohut (1971) postulated that there is a 'normal phase of development of the grandiose self in which the gleam in the mother's eye, which mirrors the child's exhibitionistic display, . . . confirm[s] the child's self-esteem and, by gradually increasing selectivity of these responses, begin[s] to channel it into realistic directions'.

In Kohut's description of object relations there is the developmental line in which the object, before it is experienced and regarded as a separate object, is experienced as a part of the self. Another person invested with narcissistic cathexis is *experienced* narcissistically as a selfobject: 'The expected control over such (selfobject) others is then closer to the concept of the control which a grown-up expects to have over his own body and mind . . .'. The object is important only insofar as it is invited to participate in the child's narcissistic pleasure and thus to confirm it.

Before psychological separatedness has been established, the baby experiences the mother's pleasure in his whole body self as part of his own psychological equipment. After psychological separation has taken place, the child needs the gleam in the mother's eye in order to maintain the narcissistic libidinal suffusion that now concerns, in their sequence, the leading functions and activities of the various maturational phases (Kohut, 1978, p. 439).

The concept of mirroring represents one pole of what Kohut came to call the bipolar self, the other pole representing the idealised parental imago.

It is rather striking that despite the popularity of the terms 'mirroring' and 'mirror transferences' as introduced by Kohut, there has been little systematic correlation of clinical and experimental observation of children and their responses within the mirroring relationship (and their responses to the specular image) with the theoretical corpus of what has now become Kohut's self psychology. Until this is done, the contributions of Kohut to mirroring and child development rest on a somewhat narrow basis. There is no doubt, however, that Kohut's emphasis on the child as the 'gleam in the mother's eye' has led to a great renewal of interest in the concept of mirroring and its application to child development and the clinical situation of psychoanalysis.

The specular image: The French connection

The developmental psychology and psychodynamics of the infant's own mirror image, that is, the child's response to his or her physical reflection in the mirror, the 'specular image', is peculiarly a particular area of interest to and rich speculation by the French psychologists Wallon, Lacan, Merleau-Ponty and Zazzo.

Lacan

In his 1936 work (published in 1949), Lacan put forward the idea of a 'mirror stage', connecting the development of the ego with the mirror stage and the specular image. The following outline of this mirror stage or phase (a preferable term as it denotes an evolving process) is drawn from Lacan (1977), Lemaire (1977) and Laplanche and Pontalis (1973).

Lacan acknowledges the contributions of the American developmental psychologist Baldwin to the study of the child's response to its mirror image. Lacan points out, long before Gallup's more detailed examination of the chimpanzee's response to its mirror image (Desmond, 1980), that the primate, apparently well ahead of the child at an early age in instrumental intelligence, quickly loses interest in the mirror image. The chimpanzee 'once the image has been mastered and found empty exhausts itself in its response'. For its part, the child, far from finding the image empty, responds to it 'in a series of gestures in which he expresses in play the relation between the movements assumed in the image and the reflected environment, and between the virtual complex and the reality it re-duplicates – the child's own body, and the persons and things around him' (Lacan, 1977, p. 1). Lacan places this stage (phase) between 6 and 18 months and states that it represents an *identification*, 'the transformation that takes place in the subject when he assumes an image', his *imago*. The child 'jubilantly' assumes his or her mirror image at the *infans* stage (*infans* means 'without words'), when he or she is still 'sunk in his motor incapacity and nursling dependence'. For Lacan this is the fateful moment when, by identifying with a *fiction*, the idealised image of himself that he perceives in the mirror, the agency of the ego is cast, the primordial basis of the I that is alienated from the subject; man projects himself into a statue, his 'ideal-I'.

The mirror stage is a 'drama', the beginning of the imaginary world,
of the succession of fantasies that will eventually lead to the
assumption of the armour of an alienating identity which will mark
with its rigid structure the subject's entire mental development (p. 4).

Lemaire (1977, p. 177) fills out Lacan's sketch of the mirror phase, describing three successive stages of self-recognition in the mirror:

Phase 1. Child with adult before a mirror confuses reflection and reality. He or she tries to seize hold of the image or to look behind the mirror, but at the same time the reflection is confused with that of the adult.
Phase 2. The child acquires the notion of the image and understands that the reflection is not a real being.
Phase 3. The child realises that this reflected image is his or her own and different from the reflection of the other. Now the intense joy and the classic game of one's own movements seen reflected in the mirror appear.

Parallel to the mirror self-recognition, the child behaves in a typical way towards other children of its own age, who are homologues, more or less, of its own appearance. He or she observes these others with curiosity, imitates, tries to seduce or impose upon them by play-acting, is aggressive towards them and cries when the other falls. This can be understood as the child situating itself socially by comparing itself with another (cf. Atkins, 1983, discussed below). The phase of what is called 'transitivism' (Buhler, 1935) appears. The child who hits will say that it has been hit, a child who sees another fall will cry. This is another instance of the child living in the Imaginary order, of a dual relationship with the merging of self and other. 'It is in the other that the subject first lives and registers himself' (Lemaire, 1977, p. 177).

Thus the mirror stage is based upon observations of (1) the child's response to the specular image and (2) the child's response to the image of its homologues. In both instances the phase observed can be interpreted as the acquisition of, and the response to, a self-image as a fictional totality, to the action of the imagination and to the merger of this new subjective self, the subject, with whatever closely resembles it. This total representation of the self is at the same time the first stage in human alienation through the identification of the self with an image.

> The self merges with his own image and the same imaginary trapping
> by the double is seen in relationships with his fellows . . . the subject
> is ignorant of his own alienation and that is how the chronic mis-
> recognition of self and the causal change determining human
> existence takes shape (Lemaire, 1977, p. 178).

How then does the human being escape from the trap of narcissism to become involved in what Lemaire calls the 'proper dimension to his humanity', symbolic organisation? According to Lacan, this is what is accomplished in the oedipal phase when the third term, that of language (the law of the Name-of-the-Father), leads to a transcendence of the dual relationship of alienation based upon the imaginary relationship of the child and the mother. 'The resolution of the oedipus constitutes the sense of reality in that it is a liberation from the fascination of the image' (Lemaire, 1981, p. 179).

With this reality of persons in relationship, truth can enter. The child can now cease to be Narcissus, who drowned trying to reunite himself with his own image. No longer captivated by his or her own image the child can turn away from his or her reflection to the world of Self with Others, to be a member of a family and to enter into the social order. The child internalises the Law of the Father, accepts that he or she is a small child who has to wait for biological maturity in order to be able to fulfil his/her wishes and desires, as opposed to his/her previous ambition to seduce the mother and to be for her the unique object of her desire, the phallus. Aggression towards father, who intrudes into this world of desire, leads to the recognition of him, eventually to acceptance of the relationship with him and to internalisation of him. To accept reality is to accept *differences*, differences of age, time and generation, differences of bodies.

There is indeed a remarkable strength and even majesty in Lacan's thesis. However, it is based on an intoxicating mixture of sensitive observation and speculation, and I am not aware of any systematic attempt to integrate his theories with the observations and theories of other, more recent, psychoanalytic observers of infants' behaviours towards the mirror image, though Abelin (see below) takes Lacan's mirror stage into account in his reconstruction of early triangulation. Lacan's thesis that mirroring is essentially *alienation* from self, contrasting with Winnicott's thesis that the child first *finds* itself in the mirror of the mother's face, points to the contrast between the integrating aspects of socially responsive mirroring and the alienating experience of aloneness with the self that arises with the specular image. This will be further considered as an aspect of negative mirroring (see below).

Maurice Merleau-Ponty

In 'The Primacy of Perception' (1964) Merleau-Ponty devotes a chapter to 'The Child's Relations with Others', in which he presents a fascinating and comprehensive integration of the world of French and German child psychologists, of Guillaume, Wallon, Charlotte Buhler and others, with the psychoanalytical observations of Lacan on the mirror stage. He outlines the development of the child from birth to 3 years, but the section that concerns us here is the stage after 6 months, 'consciousness of one's own body and the specular image' (pp. 125–151).

Merleau-Ponty outlines Wallon's ideas and observations. Firstly, at the age of 6 months a child situated in front of a mirror, together with a parent, seems to recognise the parent in the mirror reflection prior to recognition of the self-image. If father and child are together before the mirror, the child smiles at the image of father; if the father speaks, the child turns towards him in surprise. Thus the child recognises father through his mirror image at a stage before he/she has shown that he/she grasps the reality of the mirror image as such: 'The image has an existence inferior to that of father's real body – but it does have a sort of marginal existence' (p. 128). It is later, at 8 months, that the child clearly shows surprise at its own mirror image. Wallon concludes that the specular image of one's own body develops later than that of the Other, and the explanation is that the problem to be solved is much greater in the case of one's own body than that of the Other. The child is dealing with two visual experiences of the father: the experience that he or she has of looking at him and that which comes from the mirror. On the other hand, the mirror image is the child's only complete visual evidence of its own body. A child can easily look at feet and hands but not at the body as a whole. Thus, it is first a problem of understanding that the visual image of the body, seen over there in the mirror, is not himself or herself since the child is not in the mirror but here, where the child feels him/herself; and second, the child must understand that, not being located there in the mirror, but rather where he/she feels the self interoceptively, he/she can nonetheless be seen by an external witness of the very place *at which he/she feels the self to be* and with the same visual appearance as in the mirror. In short, the mirror image must be displaced, bringing it from the apparent or virtual place that it occupies in the depth of the mirror, back to the self, whom he/she identifies at a distance with the interoceptive body.

Merleau-Ponty points out that Wallon does not offer a full explanation of why the child is so amused and fascinated by its mirror image. Here he turns to Lacan and to his thesis that the child identifies itself with the specular image. It is through the acquisition of the specular image that the child notices that he/she is visible for himself/herself and for others, that a viewpoint can be taken on him/her, for hitherto the child has never seen himself/herself as a whole. By means of the image in the mirror the child becomes capable of becoming a spectator of itself.

Ernest Abelin and early triangulation

As mentioned above, Abelin (1971, 1980) provides the most notable example of the integration of Lacanian concepts with those of other developmental psychologists. Abelin, trained in the Piagetian tradition and working with Mahler, is aware of the importance of Lacan's theory of the mirroring phase and links this with the momentous development that can be observed at 18 months during the rapprochement phase of separation–individuation. In Lacan's work it is through the development of the specular image that at 18 months the child becomes aware of the self as an entity which exists in space and can now be observed by others. This is a contribution to the developmental line of the image of the corporeal self, the Self as Object. Abelin attempts to create a theoretical bridge between the developmental line of the Self as Object with the developmental line of the Self with Object and Self with Others.

Abelin examines the role of object relations and libidinal wishes and attachments in 'the momentous Copernican revolution of mind' that Piaget demonstrates at 18 months, at the time of the rapprochement phase of separation–individuation. Now the child is able to situate the self within space, to construct the mental image of a space which is bodily inhabited, where the child can imagine the self as being seen from the outside (see Merleau-Ponty, discussed above), where the child is but one cause and effect amongst many others. It is now that the imitation of objects, a *biological* capacity, is superseded by the capacity for mental representations, of the images of objects, a *psychological* capacity. Imitation, which is action in *time*, develops into the capacity for relating to images in *space*. Abelin (1971) invokes the concept of mirroring for his explanation of the mechanism involved.

From birth he sees the infant as involved in one-to-one narcissistic *mirroring* with the mother, a relationship which he considers continues as far as the rapprochement phase. In this narcissistic mirroring phase, the infant operates on sensory-motor schemata. During the rapprochement phase the child becomes capable of symbolic functions and of representing relations. It is this capacity that is necessary for the reduction of the earlier narcissistic mirroring quality of all relationships. How does this change come about?

Abelin (1971) agrees with Lacan that the role of the father is primary here. Whereas Lacan attributes this development to the symbolic father, to language, to the Law of the Name-of-the-Father, Abelin attributes it to the child's burgeoning awareness of father and mother as a loving pair from which he/she is excluded and which he/she is able to observe only from the outside. The child now has a position in space as a separate entity from which it observes the parental couple in their relationship and occupying the same dimension. Now the infant *knows* that he/she is excluded from the relationship of Father loving Mother. Now it knows that it is a self with longings and desires as the affective core, longings which are blocked and frustrated by the rival father. Having a rival means *being* a rival, a birth into a new experience of self. Knowledge of differences is a different kind of knowledge from the knowledge of sameness. Differences are indicated and demarcated by boundaries, which are obstacles that have to be recognised, negotiated with and, if possible, overcome; if not, there is the experience of failure, of separation and of loss. For Abelin this is the foundation of early triangulation experiences, for the mental representation of relations between self and others, of the capacity for symbolic representations. (He does not discuss Kleinian theory, in which very much earlier oedipal triangulation images and concepts are hypothesised.)

This capacity for early triangulation is the psychological matrix for the representation of sets of images, of reciprocal relations, of the 'reversible group' of Piaget, indeed for the representation of the self as a social being.

As we have already seen when discussing biological mirroring, other observers describe the child as entering into social relationships from the earliest neonatal period, because infants are treated as social beings by parents and caretakers who introduce them to the notions of reciprocity and intention by the way in which they interact with them. Abelin does not discuss these findings or look for evidence of the child's own capacity to initiate such relationships and to give them representation. His observations and his theoretical framework are from a different universe of discourse from that of these other observers of early social relationships and have yet to be integrated with them.

Mirroring and early peer-relations

Atkins (1983) argues that psychoanalysis has not yet paid proper attention to the place of 'non-caretakers' in the development of object relationships. However, the close observation of how babies react and respond to the presence of other babies shows that they do indeed interact significantly and that the concept of mirroring can be usefully applied to the understanding of these processes. In this way we can begin to fill in more details of the developmental line of object relatedness in general and peer relatedness in particular.

Atkins invokes the 'gratifying experience of mirroring' to explain this fascinating lure that infants have for one another. Watching the play of two 8-month-old children, he observes smiles, interest in each other and in the other's actions, and he observes actions directed apparently towards the other. Atkins discusses these interactions in terms of the infants responding to some awareness of their similarities to each other, a form of twinship mirroring, which can be analysed in phase-specific sensory, sensorimotor and sensoriaffective integration components.

The infants seem attracted by perceptual similarities, sensing that the other is like oneself. 'Clearly little ones like other little ones – even strangers – even more than they like adults' (p. 237). They manifest socially directed behaviour, responding to each other's play and gestures as a 'primitive sign context of motor recognition which, in turn, precipitates, stimulates and furthers' the child's own actions (p. 238). The other is distinct, yet like oneself, and I suggest that we can infer that the child becomes more aware of being himself or herself through this similarity and differentiation from the other similar person.

Connecting the 'who' and the 'what'

In a notable series of papers Sheldon Bach (1980, 1984) addresses himself to the relation of the experienced self that is proximal, proprioceptively experienced, the self that is experienced *subjectively* 'in here', with the self that exists 'out there' in the mirror, in the reflected appraisals of others, which is *objectified* by others. The synthesis of the subjective and objective self is one of the momentous tasks of the rapprochement phase of individuation–separation.

The subjective self is partly built up upon the internalisation of the mother-of-dual-unity; the objective self on the appraisals of the mother-of-separation. The empathic object (Kohut's selfobject that is narcissistically invested) bridges the gap between the subjective self and the objective self, between the subject and object.

In the context of mirroring, Bach refers to Zazzo's observations that between 18 months and 2 years there is a period when the child can identify the mirror image by the proper name, e.g. answer 'Johnnie' to the question 'Who is that you see in the mirror?', but is unable to use his own name in reference to himself and replies 'me' when asked who he is. This indicates that the child has not yet synthesised the subjective and objective modes of self-awareness.

He has recognised that for others 'Johnnie' and 'me' have the same reference, but he has not yet succeeded in creating that psychic space we call the 'self', within which our multiple subjective and objective perspectives are paradoxically conceived of as transformations of the same invariant ongoing person (Bach, 1984).

When the child does achieve this integration, he or she has then created the psychic space of the self.

Bach addresses himself in particular to the boundary area of subjective and objective self-awareness, delicately applying Winnicott's concepts of paradox, transitional space and play to understand the experiences of patients with predominantly narcissistic pathology who are primarily concerned with *who* the self *is*, in contrast to the more developmentally advanced patients who are trying to find out *what* their ego *wants*; 'In the transference neurotic, thought is trial action, in the narcissistic neurotic, thought is trial identity' (1984, p. 162).

Negative mirroring

Under this heading I include such observations and theoretical constructions as Lacan's, who states that infants' response to their specular images is essentially one of alienation from self, and also the universally recognised developmental stage of the toddler's growing wariness of its mirror image.

From about 14 months onwards, the response of the child who has previously shown delight and enthusiasm at the presence of its mirror image begins to change. It now begins to become wary and to withdraw when placed in front of the mirror. Self-recognition seems soon to lead on to self-consciousness, that is, to a form of painful self-awareness and embarrassment. How is this development to be understood? One approach is that of Amsterdam and Levitt (1980), who argue that at the beginning of the second year of life three key events occur which appear to be critical to the onset of painful self-conscious behaviour.

1.   The beginnings of representational thinking, which allows the body self to be taken as object
2.   The infant's struggle to obtain upright posture and locomotion
3.   Intentional reaching for and self-stimulation of the genitalia

The argument is that the child, through recognising itself in front of the mirror, is also aware that it can be seen by others. Further, that this occurs at a time when he or she is becoming aware that pleasurable sensations which arise from within, in response to his or her own genital stimulation, are now unacceptable to the adult world. Though they think that shame and painful self-consciousness may arise in connection with excretory functions, they argue that the mother is more likely to encourage and to approve of excretory functions, whereas few mothers can observe their children's masturbatory behaviour with unself-conscious approval, at least in Western societies. Thus, the child must begin to learn to inhibit genital sensation and exploration in the presence of others at precisely the same time as he or she also experiences affective self-consciousness before the mirror. Painful self-consciousness seems to occur when the body is experienced as a shameful object and this is a major narcissistic injury in the mother–infant relationship. Because of mother's disapproval and prohibition of genital play the child's bodily display is no longer responded to by the approving gleam and reflection in mother's eyes.

An alternative interpretation of the above observations has been put forward by Paulina Kernberg (1984). She invokes the child's increasing awareness of differentiation from mother. Up until now if the attachment between mother and child has been firm and the mother's attunement to her child's behaviour sensitive and appropriate, then she has on the whole acted as a mirror to her child, enhancing the child's sense of self and bringing meaning to the object world. During this period the child's behaviours in front of the mirror can be seen as 'echoing' the attachment behaviours between child and mother. Because of this, the child's reaction to the mirror includes his or her reaction to the mother whether or not she is actually present with the child in front of the mirror. At this later stage of rapprochement, from 14 to 24 months, the child is increasingly aware of mother and itself as separate entities and therefore is increasingly aware that the reflecting mirror is *not* mother. Children therefore show a type of stranger reaction to their own images, reflecting their unstable sense of self. The toddler is aware of separateness, is perplexed by it, occasionally fascinated but very often withdrawing from this confusing situation. Later, between 24 and 36 months, the child seems to have gained a more secure sense of self-awareness and can again look at itself in the mirror, though now in a more sophisticated manner, sometimes with admiration, sometimes with embarrassment. Now the child is more in possession of a sense of self-constancy and object-constancy, and with this capacity for self-constancy it contains the mirroring function that previously was mother's.

Conclusion

I have attempted to show that the concept of the 'mirror', understood both literally and metaphorically, provides an invaluable contribution to our understanding of the developmental lines of 'self as subject', 'self as object', 'self with object' and 'self as other'. The mirroring concept is used in many different ways by both psychologists and clinicians and we must remain cautious in transferring knowledge between different contexts. However, it has been suggested that there are grounds where such cross-fertilisation would be of significant value.

References

Abelin, E. L. (1971), 'The role of father in the separation–individuation process', in J. B. McDevitt and C. F. Settlage (eds), *Separation–Individuation*, International Universities Press: New York.

Abelin, E. L. (1980), 'Triangulation, the role of the father and the origins of core gender identity during the rapprochement subphase', in R. F. Lax, S. Bach and J. A. Burland (eds), *Rapprochement*, Jason Aronson: New York.

Amsterdam, B. K. and Levitt, M. (1980), 'Consciousness of self and painful self-consciousness', *Psychoanalytic Study of the Child*, 35, pp. 67–83.

Atkins, R. N. (1983), 'Peer relatedness in the first year of life: The birth of a new world', *Annual of Psychoanalysis*, 11, pp. 227–44.

Bach, S. (1980), 'Self-love and object-love: Some problems of self and object constancy, differentiation and integration', in R. F. Lax, S. Bach and J. A. Burland (eds), *Rapprochement*, Jason Aronson: New York.

Bach, S. (1984), 'Perspectives on self and object', *Psychoanalytic Review*, 71, pp. 145–68.

Buhler, C. (1935), *From Birth to Maturity*, Kegan, Paul, Trench, Trubner: London.

Davis, M. and Wallbridge, D. (1981), *Boundary and Space. An Introduction to the Work of D. W. Winnicott*, H. Karnac: London.

Desmond, A. (1980), *The Ape's Reflexion*, Quartet Books: London.

Emde, R. N. (1983), 'The prerepresentational self and its affective core', *Psychoanalytic Study of the Child*, 38, pp. 165–91.

Freud, A. (1980), *Normality and Pathology in Childhood. The Writings of Anna Freud*, vol. 6, Hogarth Press: London.

Hartmann, H. (1958), *Ego Psychology and the Problem of Adaptation*, International Universities Press: New York.

Kernberg, P. (1984), 'Reflections in the mirror: mother–child interaction, self-awareness and self-recognition', in R. Tyson (ed.), *Proceedings of the Second Congress of Infant Psychiatry*, International Universities Press: New York.

Kohut, H. (1978), 'Remarks about the formation of the self', in P. Ornstein (ed.), *The Search for the Self*, International Universities Press: New York.

Lacan, J. (1977), *Ecrits*, (transl. A. Sheridan), Tavistock Publications: London.

Laplanche, J. and Pontalis, J.-B. (1973), *The Language of Psychoanalysis*, Hogarth Press and Institute of Psycho-Analysis: London.

Lemaire, A. (1977), *Jacques Lacan*, Routledge & Kegan Paul: London.

Lewis, M. and Brooks-Gunn, J. (1979), *Social Cognition and the Acquisition of Self*, Plenum Press: New York.

Lichtenstein, H. (1977), *The Dilemma of Human Identity*, Jason Aronson: New York.

Mahler, M. (1967), 'On human symbiosis and the vicissitudes of individuation', *Journal of the American Psychoanalytic Association*, 15, pp. 740–63.

Merleau-Ponty, M. (1964), *The Primacy of Perception*, Northwestern University Press: Chicago.

Papousek, H. and Papousek, M. (1979), 'Early ontogeny of human social interaction', in M. von Cranach, K. Foppa, W. Leperies and D. Ploog (eds), *Human Ethology*, Cambridge University Press: Cambridge.

Pawlby, S. J. (1977), 'Imitative interaction', in H. R. Schaffer (ed.), *Studies in Mother–Infant Interaction*, Academic Press: London.

Sander, L. S. (1983), 'To begin with – reflections on ontogeny', in J. D. Lichtenberg and S. Kaplan (eds), *Reflections on Self Psychology*, Analytic Press: Hillsdale, N.J.

Scharff, D. E. (1982), *The Sexual Relationship*, Routledge & Kegan Paul: London.

Stern, D. (1983), 'The early development of schemas of self, other and "self" with other', in J. D. Lichtenberg and S. Kaplan (eds), *Reflections on Self Psychology*, Analytic Press: Hillsdale, N.J.

Winnicott, D. W. (1971), 'Mirror-role of mother and family in child development', in *Playing and Reality*, Tavistock Publications: London.

Wolf, E. (1987), 'Some comments on the selfobject concept', in K. Yardley and T. Honess (eds), *Self and Identity: Psychosocial Processes*, Wiley: Chichester.

3 Empathic relating and the structure of the self: Parallels in mother–infant and patient–therapist interaction

Gail M. Price

The self is composed of innate structural units having functional potential which develop into response patterns within the context of a dialectic of intimacy and autonomy. Intimacy may be defined as sharing the subjective experience of oneself with another and experiencing in oneself the subjective experience of the other. Autonomy consists in having the right of self-expression and in perceiving oneself as a self-governing centre of initiative.

Maturity has been defined as an ability to form a sense of connectedness with the inner self and with the other in a way that is caring of each (Gilligan, 1982). The highest level of morality has been related to a concern for the individual's right of self-expression (Pingleton, 1983). In psychological health, an integration of the two takes place as the self creates itself through self-expression within the context of interpersonal relationships. In the formation of the self, the innate or subjective self, experienced within, reaches out by means of a creative gesture and receives an evaluation in the response of the other. When this evaluation is caring, the self is affirmed and objectified. When the evaluation is unempathic or uncaring, the self loses some of its right of self-expression in the process of connecting. If enough of the right of self-expression is lost, a subordinate form of connectedness takes precedence. When the right of self-expression is given up in the presence of traumatic assaults on the self, whether physical or emotional, remaining connected requires introjection of the other's centre of initiative and the formation of a false self that contains within it the unmetabolised other. This introjected other erodes the innate centre of initiative of the self, from which it gains its sense of creativity and vitality. (See Harwood, Chapter 4, for an integration of Kohut's and Winnicott's views of the innate self.)

When the parental introject caps the true self and prevents its emergence, its centre of initiative is replaced with false self-structures which require external sources of vitality to function. A primary function of therapy is to restore the patient's centre of initiative through creating a setting where the self may emerge from beneath the introjected prohibitions, experience restoration of the right of self-expression and form caring connections with self and other. A great deal of true self-formation takes place in infancy, being created within patterns of empathic parent–infant interaction. In his work with adult patients, Leston Havens (1977, 1978, 1979, 1980) has developed forms of speech that restore the developing self by fostering the removal of false self-structures and exposing the innate self for further growth. The uniqueness of his method lies in the fact that the speech forms approximate the structure of the empathic parent–infant interactions which enter into the initial formation of the self.

William James (quoted in Damon and Hart, 1982) developed a theory of the self in which four innate structural units combine in health to form the 'I' or the experiencing self. The 'I' is the 'self as knower'. The four innate structural units are the body/motoric unit, the cognitive/intellectual unit, the affective/relational unit and the spiritual/motivational unit. These macro-structures correspond closely to three micro-structures of the self defined by Beebe[1] and also by Stern,[2] albeit in somewhat different terms. Beebe defines the interactive structures of the self as composed of three components: affect, cognition and perception. Stern speaks in terms of a 'lived episode' of the interacting self composed of affect, perception and cognition, stored together in memory. That is, the self does not normally function in discrete parts, but in patterned structural units. When these structural units are composed of the innate patterns of perception, affect, thought and motivation, they form true self-structures. When the patterns are composed of the perceptions, affect, thought and motivation of another, the structures become false self-structures.

In James's model, the 'I' knows the innate 'Me', or the innate self-structures, through interpersonal experience. That is, the self comes to know itself by being known to another. Stern (1983a) has stated that 'self-experience involves an affective, sensorimotor and cognitive part of the self that cannot be experienced without a concomitant complementary experience of the other; it cannot be experienced alone' (p. 73). Mack (1983) proposes the existence of an 'experiencing self', paralleling the 'I' in James's theory, as the agent through which we become concerned with or know other selves. Sander (1983) argues that coherence of the experiencing self requires connectedness with another. This connectedness creates 'inherent polarities' resulting in a synthesis of 'creative integrative mechanisms as solutions to the inherent polarities', thus creating self-coherence and self–other connectedness. In his model, as with Stern's (1983a), self-awareness, the self as knower of the self, develops from the experience of feedback within the interpersonal interaction. Kohut and Wolf (1978) describe a somewhat different innate structure of the self, organised teleologically, but place its development within an interpersonal context. In their theory, the self has three constituents. The first constituent develops from interactions with a mirroring selfobject that confirm the innate vigour and greatness of the child, and evolves into autonomous strivings for power and success. The second constituent evolves from connectedness with significant others that permits the self to achieve a sense of calmness and infallibility, and contains basic idealised goals. Intermediate between these are the innate talents and skills which develop out of 'the tension that establishes itself between ambitions and ideals' (p. 414).

According to Kohut and Wolf (1978), 'it is the interplay between the newborn's innate equipment and the selective responses of the selfobjects through which certain potentialities are encouraged in their development while others remain unencouraged or are even actively discouraged' (pp. 416–17). They further propose that attributes which are mirrored and affirmed are structured into the self, and those which are inhibited or altered are left underdeveloped or discarded. In this way, enduring patterns develop that then organise experience and are organised by it. Stern (1983b) proposes a similar model of structure formation in that the internal relational world of the infant is 'determined by which self-experiences are communed with and thus supported, and which are under parental pressure to be altered' (p. 22). An early example of this phenomenon is seen in the work of Sander (1983) on sleep–wake cycles. Within empathic encounters in the early interactions between mother and infant, the infant begins to develop feeding and sleeping cycles that approximate circadian rhythms, with shorter sleep periods and more feedings during the day, and the reverse at night. In the absence of sensitive empathic caregivers, the sleep–wake periods tend not to vary over the twenty-four-hour period.

Infant development research has demonstrated the presence of innate interactive structures available to the newborn and very young infant which facilitate autonomy and connectedness between mother and infant (see Beebe, 1983; Lozoff *et al.*, 1977; Samuels, 1984; Stern, 1983a,b for comprehensive reviews). Among the innate cognitive/intellectual structures are recall and recognition memory, the capacity to recognise boundaries, such as the phoneme boundaries of speech, hue or colour boundaries and geometric shape boundaries. Innate affective/relational structures include the preference for the adult human face and voice, the ability to express emotion through subtle changes in facial expressions and the ability to communicate internal need states with distinctive vocalisation patterns. Body/motoric innate structures include the capacity for imitation and the ability to engage in interactional synchrony in moments of high arousal. Spiritual/motivational innate structures include the tendency to seek stimulation and intimate contact manifest in long episodes of mutual gaze. With regard to the 'I' as the knower of 'Me', the newborn infant manifests some capacity to recognise its own self in that it will cease crying when it hears a tape of its own cry, but not when it hears another infant's cry (Martin and Clark, 1982).

There are two basic patterns of intimacy in which the infant is able to participate from the earliest weeks of life (Stern, quoted in Beebe, 1983). Stern describes these as coactive and alternating. In the coactive pattern, each partner emits the same response simultaneously. This pattern tends to produce intense positive affect and high arousal bonding. The second is alternating or turn-taking, which provides the basic structure of conversation. Stern (1983b) found that the most frequently expressed goal of mothering is for the coactive mode, manifesting a wish to be with or commune with the infant. The other major goals of the mother are cognitive, in the wish to communicate information to the infant, and motoric, to 'tune the baby up or down', or to restructure the interaction.

Stern (1983b) has noted that the 'language' used by the parent to connect with the infant enables her to recruit and hold attention, to engage the infant in communal being together and in communication designed to receive and send information. The primary channels are vocal and kinetic ones in which stimulation is repeated in structural units with or without elaboration. The structural units increase in complexity from a single behaviour (e.g. a vocalisation or smile), termed a 'phrase', to a repeating sequence of vocal or kinetic phrases, or a 'run', permitting 'connectedness in the form of maintained engagement'. The various structural units of the interaction play over a temporal rhythm of matched cycles which parallels matching of phrase–pause cycles of adult conversation (Beebe, 1983).

In parent–infant attunement the parent matches the infant's behaviour by bringing her own into alignment with the intensity, timing, rhythm, duration and/or shape of the infant's behaviour. The infant's innate ability to perceive the abstract characteristics of behaviour, i.e. the rhythm, intensity, timing, and so forth, enables him to realise that the parent is attuning or responding to the unique behaviour he is emitting. For example, a mother watches her 9-month-old boy shake a rattle and nods her head in matching rhythm and intensity contour, in shared motoric engagement (Stern, 1983a).

The infant is born with an innate integrative ability, termed cross-model equivalency (Stern, 1983b), to relate information gained in one stimulus modality or self unit to another and to relate components of the infant self to those of other selves. Cross-modal equivalencies occur within the infant self and between self and other. In within-self cross-modal equivalencies, information received in one modality such as touch is transferred without prior learning to another modality, such as vision. For example, Meltzoff and Barton (1979, quoted in Stern, 1983b) permitted 2- to 3-week-old infants to mouth a cube while blindfolded. When the blindfold was removed, the infant could recognise the cube when it was placed next to a sphere in a visual field, indicating integration of cognitive and motoric self-experiences.

In the between-self interpersonal cross-modal equivalency, the channel or modality of expression used by the other to match the infant's behaviour may be different from the channel or modality used by the infant. Stern (1983b) gives the example of a 9-month-old girl who expressed delight as she grabbed a desired toy. Her mother tuned into her delight with a joyful shimmy of her body that matched her daughter's vocalisation in intensity and affect. In this example, the mother's motoric self-component matched the daughter's affective self-component.

In securely attached parent–infant pairs, self-development is co-determined and permitted to achieve a receptive and expressive balance between self and other. The parent perceives the infant as an individual having his/her own goals which it is the parent's function to facilitate. Manifestations of autonomy which result in disengagements and mis-matches do not disrupt the overall state of connectedness and intimacy. Very early in the relationship, secure parent–infant pairs tend to achieve a state of mutual attentiveness in which mirroring and affirmation can take place (Price *et al.*, 1982). The overall impression in these relationships is of two unique individuals in a state of mutual adaptation. The parent provides the infant with experiences and information needed for growth, development and socialisation. The infant responds sensitively to the parent by providing feedback which mirrors the parents' responsive care. Securely connected infants demonstrate age-appropriate expression of all the component self-structures. They exhibit a predominately happy mood, the ability to self-soothe and to be soothed and comforted. Their actions are oriented toward maintaining social encounters, exploration and affective sharing (see Ainsworth *et al.*, 1978).

When the engagement between parent and infant is sensitively tuned by the parent to repeat and elaborate infant behaviour, the infant experiences aspects of the self as being affirmed. For example, infants are most likely to smile when the content of their behaviour is reproduced within the structural units of 'phrases' or 'runs' (Stern *et al.*, 1977). Beebe (1983) and Beebe and Stern (1977) propose that aspects of the interaction between infant and caregiver are internalised as a central rule of 'who acts when'. When the infant self-representation is internalised as acted upon rather than acting in mutuality, the autonomous self-structures will be poorly developed and less available for later expression. Research done in the home during the first 3 months of life (Ainsworth and Bell, 1969) has demonstrated manifestations of impaired autonomy and connectedness in the earliest feeding interactions. In certain of these mother–infant dyads, there is a near-total absence of positive social interactions. Intrusive non-empathic interactions require pathological adaptations that result in a turning away from the parent in autisticlike withdrawal (see Beebe and Sloate, 1982; Mahler *et al.*, 1975). The intrusiveness of the parent appropriates the infant's centre of initiative and results in infant failure to achieve independent self-expression. There is therefore a need to rely on parental directives, which become internalised as unmetabolised parental structures capping the innate self. Gradually, the infant must relinquish portions of the self-structures to the governing of the parent, resulting in an internalisation of the parent at the point where infant self-expression has been suppressed, creating a merger between parent and infant so that infant self-structures are replaced by parental ones. The infant then becomes dependent upon the parent for functioning, since the centre of autonomy of the self-structures involved in the merger resides within the parent, and not the infant. To cite an example, a toddler is brought for psychological evaluation. During the course of the testing, the child is offered a crayon and asked to make marks on a paper. He looks briefly at the crayon, then turns away, eyes filled with terror, and begins to cry. The examiner is told that he has been forbidden to use crayons, an instruction reinforced by repeated slaps to his hands, because of a fear that he would write on the wall. The child had not written on the wall at the time of the initial injunction. The examiner asks the mother if she could give the child permission to use the crayon. She half-heartedly attempts to do so, to no avail. In this example, the parental prohibition of this form of creative self-expression replaced the normal toddler's pleasurable interest in beginning to write and draw. The tool for this task that is normally received with interest and delight is now perceived as dangerous. As a result, the cognitive, affective, motoric and motivational self-structure of the child was severely inhibited and replaced by a punitive parental introject. At the point where the environment presents the forbidden task to the child, the child of necessity becomes very dependent, mired in conflict between inclination and prohibition. This toddler looked helplessly at the examiner, then turned frozen in anxiety and clung to his mother, unable to separate from her prohibitions, needing her protection from the internal wish and environmental offering and surrendering his centre of initiative in order to remain connected to her.

The concept of selfobject has relevance here. In self psychology theory, the selfobject consists of a parent (or surrogate) who performs those functions which serve to complete the immature self. In a study of acting-out patients, Berkowitz (1982), following Kohut, describes the selfobject in the following way:

> The notion of the selfobject refers to the manner in which the infant
> and small child, whose self is not yet fully cohesive and self regulating,
> utilizes parental figures . . . to externally provide certain functions
> which he cannot yet perform endopsychically. Provision of these
> functions which include soothing, anxiety reduction and self-esteem
> regulation will enable him through the gradual internalization of
> psychic structure to progressively provide them for himself from
> internal sources (p. 17).

Infancy researchers, notably Stern, believe that selfobjects represent pathological manifestations inasmuch as infancy research has demonstrated that the infant is capable of providing these and other functions through its own innate mechanisms of self-soothing, attention-focusing and contact-seeking if the self is not overwhelmed by stimulation. Stern (1983a) states that concepts like symbiotic objects, selfobjects and part-objects, which imply an undifferentiated self, derive from 'emotional experience occurring in states of psychopathology' (p. 71). (See Beebe and Sloate, 1982.) For the purposes of this presentation, the selfobject relationship aptly described by Berkowitz will be termed a self-other relationship, and pathological mergers will be termed selfobject relationships, following Stern. In the example presented above, the toddler was unable to participate in the proffered self-other relationship around the use of the crayon because the sternly prohibitive parental introject created unbearable anxiety for the integrity of the self should he do so. Instead, he relinquished once again his centre of initiative to the introjected and real parent. He turned to her for direction, for soothing and regulation of anxiety and tension created by the parental prohibition which conflicted with innate self-structures. In this way, he used his mother as a selfobject to complete an environmentally created deficit structure. If the child had experienced a conflict around a wish to use the crayon and a developmental inability to do so, and had sought soothing and tension regulation, the mother's empathic response would have been experienced within a self-other relationship in which the centre of initiative of each would have remained intact.

Recent research indicates a significant proportion of psychopathology to be correlated with physical and emotional abuse (Carmen *et al.*, 1984), much of it perpetrated on young children. In abusive or neglectful experiences, self-development is altered in significant ways, in that self-structures containing innate patterns of talents and ambitions are abandoned, suppressed or distorted. In their place, patterns develop that are designed to ensure survival. Failing to gain the recognition and affirmation needed for an integrated self, the self becomes empty, enfeebled or fragmented by the powerful other now internalised (see Harwood, Chapter 4). In the words of a severely abused woman who later became alcoholic, 'Whenever I would attempt to play my trumpet my mother wanted to know why I didn't do it her way. But if I did, she criticised that. I couldn't think. She was always asking who, what, why. And I wasn't sure I knew how to answer her so she wouldn't yell or hit. Finally, I gave the trumpet up.' (See Wylie, Chapter 5, for a discussion of maternal attributions and their influence on the child's self-concept.) As Berkowitz (1979) has pointed out, low self-esteem results either from experiences of failure to achieve a sense of power and competence through expressing innate talents and abilities or from a sense of not having this innate self, valued and idealised. In the presence of threats of abuse, cognition is disrupted by attention deficits as the child concerns herself with pleasing the parent in order to avoid abuse. Boundaries between cognition and affect are disturbed by intrusions of anxiety and fear. Self-esteem is poorly regulated because the child experiences the abused self as bad, deserving the abuse and therefore the cause of it, which it relabels punishment. Affect is experienced as under the control of parental behaviour and mood. Hypervigilance replaces spontaneity generated by the expression of one's own inner patterning of goals and preferences. Performance is taken over by a need to placate and please the parent, so that motivation and intent are perceived as residing within parental wishes rather than in the self. For example, Ainsworth and Bell (1969) in a home-observation study of early parent–infant interaction, describe parents who control infant experience of hunger by feeding the infant when the parent is hungry. These infants learned to eat rapidly and greedily when fed and were highly task-oriented. Their crying lacked signal quality and seemed to express despair. The absence of affirmation for the infant's attempt to create a self from within its own centre of initiative results in a self that is experienced as being lost, hidden or eroded (Havens, 1982–83).

The dialectic between autonomy and connectedness is essential to the organisation of the self in that it provides patterns of expectancies around which the self can form structures. Cohn and Tronick (1982) have demonstrated that within the first weeks of life the infant develops expectancies of certain responses from the mother. When she violates these expectancies, disorganisation of infant self results. For example, if the mother presents a still or immobile face to an infant instead of the anticipated social smile for even three minutes, the infant becomes significantly distressed, ceases playing and develops a wary, watchful attitude. Beebe and Stern (1977) analysed the interaction of a 4-month-old infant and its mother in a relationship characterised by a relatively massive failure in the area of autonomy and connectedness. The mother repeatedly interrupted sustained mutual gaze by looming into the infant's face, which was followed by the infant moving away, pulling away and finally becoming limp and unresponsive. In this 'chase and dodge experience', the infant could escape the controlling aversive experience at the cost of cognitive, emotional, motoric and motivational self-components, resulting in the loss of even a semblance of connectedness. Beebe (1983) reports, 'No matter how vigorously the mother bounced, poked, or pulled, the infant remained motionless, giving the impression of a profound refusal to engage' (p. 24). Beebe and Stern suggest that this form of interaction may be a model for the origins of the persecutory object. The infant will make strong bids to restore the interactive expectancies to avoid intrusive interaction (Beebe and Stern, 1977) or to re-engage a withdrawn mother (Cohn and Tronick, 1982). In such aversive encounters, however, it may learn only that its own behaviours appear to produce either the intrusiveness or parental unresponsiveness. The infant's centre of initiative is invalidated. Withdrawal and passivity may then become an enduring pattern to avoid the aversive connectedness. When a parent is unable to modify aggressive impulses toward an infant, the infant becomes a helpless victim of the parent's need to control its self-expression and responds ultimately with extreme dependency (see Beebe and Sloate, 1982).

Berkowitz (1979) proposes that in this form of interaction, the parent is using the infant as a selfobject to complete his own incomplete self-structures. The result is an inability to connect intimately because of fear of losing what self is available. There is also an inability to individuate and become self-governing as a result of inadequate structures. Further, autonomous bids have often resulted in rejection and punishment. The repair and restoration of damaged self-esteem involves removal of those unmetabolised parental introjects that have capped the innate structures and inhibited development and mutual regulation. Empathic interventions that connect with the innate self-structures and with the introjects enable the therapist to reach the hidden self and release it for further development.

Empathy is defined differently by different disciplines, in part because the varying forms focus on different self-structures. In the clinical literature, empathy is spoken of with a cognitive emphasis, primarily as an information-gathering process informed by an exquisite sensitivity to communicative signals and enhanced by memories of parallel experiences (see Grostein, 1983). Developmental studies of mother–infant interaction (see Ainsworth *et al.*, 1978) and social psychological studies of children (Hoffman, 1977) emphasise motoric/behavioural aspects that combine the information-gathering component with a behavioural element. Maternal empathy, for example, is defined in terms of sensitive, responsive maternal behaviour. Interpersonal theorists (Sullivan, quoted in Havens, 1980) cast empathy in an affective/relational historical context in which the past is carefully and empathically reconstructed so that it has the clarity of the present for the patient and therapist. Existential theorists define empathy with a spiritual emphasis as having the goal of achieving communion for the sole purpose of being with the other, much like the motivations of love (see McAdams, 1982; Havens, 1982–83). Fogel *et al.* (1982) suggest that empathy promotes an internal and interpersonal connectedness between mother and infant that finds its closest analogy in adult lovemaking. In a comprehensive discussion of the role of empathy in psychoanalysis, Basch (1983) sees empathy as a natural process of understanding, informed by affective communication that may create a wish to move closer to the object of empathy as in love or to move away as in empathic resonance with the hatred of a demagogue. The Greek word *eleos*, translated as 'mercy', may best express the clinical definition of empathy as it is used in this chapter, in that it encompasses all the structural units of the self. Its meaning is to enter into the world of the other, seeing through his eyes, thinking through his thoughts, feeling his feelings, experiencing the existential moment of the other in its full intensity. It assumes compassion, recognising need on the part of the recipient and resources adequate to meet the need on the part of the other. It is a close correlate of intimacy.

In his work with adult patients, Leston Havens (1977, 1978, 1979, 1980) has developed empathic 'speech forms' that are designed to modify hostile introjects, expose innate interactive structures and restore vitality through affirmation that restores the centre of initiative to the self, motivating further growth. These speech forms encourage the patient to turn into his own perceptions and establish the therapist–patient relationship as a self–other relationship rather than the selfobject merger in the original pathological parent–child interaction patterns. Although developed independently of theories of parent–infant interaction, certain of these speech forms are closely allied with parent–infant behaviours that promote the birth of the self initially.

The removal of the hostile introject involves recovering memories of the original trauma that is suppressing innate structures and avoiding transferences that would re-create the original trauma. To recover memories, Havens has developed 'projective speech', in which the therapist makes remarks that elicit the details and emotions surrounding past experience, tapping into cognitive and affective interactive structures in the present and seeking recovery of all four interactive self-structures involved in the memories of the experience. The result is an increasingly accurate picture of experience. To cite a clinical example, an artist came for therapy as a result of being unable to work for some years. The therapist commented, 'You drew a lot as a child,' to which the patient replied, 'I was always drawing. I filled the kitchen floor with paper and drew until it was all used up. When I got older, my mother complained that I was different from my sisters, that I could not make any money if I studied to be an artist, which I did anyway.' The therapist responded, 'Your parents were concerned about money,' to which the patient replied, 'Yes, and so is my husband. It was just after we were married that I stopped drawing and painting and went to work.' The session continued with a discussion of the patient's sadness that she never felt her considerable talent was valued. She realised she was unable to begin to draw again until she began a pottery business which gained her husband's respect. In this way, the patient reveals the nature of the original injury to the emerging self as it has been re-created in the marriage to her scientist husband. In projective speech, the therapist suggests details to which the patient may respond, elaborate on, or disagree with and correct, adding detail that will bring with it the suppressed affect. Havens believes this speech form to be less intrusive and therefore less painful than direct questioning. Through projective speech, the therapist and patient are able to achieve episodes of maintained engagement that enable traumatic memories to emerge.

When patients have been treated aversively as children, they are inclined to project their mistrust onto the therapist. As the past comes increasingly into view, it is important for the therapeutic alliance to remove the projections from the interpersonal field of patient and therapist. This may be done through the use of counterprojective statements. Counterprojective statements move the introjects outside the self onto an imaginary screen that both patient and therapist can speak about, sharing feelings about and experiences of those figures. For example, a patient projects his confusion onto the therapist, complaining that things are not being clarified by the therapist. The therapist relates this to similar feelings the patient has expressed toward his employer and toward his girlfriend and then to his experience of confusion from his parents. The therapist empathises with the patient's experience of confusion in significant relationships, and in doing so helps the patient to acknowledge and accept the validity of his experience. As the parental introject is more clearly observed and experienced as now outside the patient, it is possible to distinguish between the introject and self. This is accompanied by an experience of barrenness and manifestations of depressive affect resulting from the emerging sense of the empty, eroded self and lost opportunities for growth. Havens finds that the hostile introject may be reincorporated because the individual has so little self available for connectedness and intimacy or autonomous strivings that she or he cannot tolerate the barrenness inherent in giving up the introject. In clinical experience with abused patients, this barrenness represents the underdeveloped true self in the absence of intimate connectedness. To reach it requires a complex combination of the break-up of denial and a resultant despair as the patient re-experiences the memories of the trauma and loss of the self that 'could have been'. At such times both adults and children experience all at once rage toward the now externalised abusive introject, accompanied by strong denial expressed as 'This didn't happen to me', followed by feelings of not wanting to live because the pain of the traumatic memories seems unendurable. It is important to empathise with the emotional pain and with the true self that is beneath it.

At this point in the therapy, speech forms that call forth and affirm aspects of the true self enable the patient to separate slowly from the traumatic experience. These empathic speech forms are similar in structure to patterns of relating between parent and infant. They are called exclamatory joining, imitative statements, translations and extensions. The empathic speech form of exclamatory joining is created when the therapist responds to the patient with a short exclamation, adjective or utterance which joins self and other by placing the therapist within the feelings of the patient. These have a parallel in the 'phrases' described by Stern (1983a), as when an infant stretches and reaches for a toy and his accelerating behaviour is matched by his mother in rhythm and effort with a slow crescendo groan. In the example of the abused patient in despair, the therapist joins the patient in a non-verbal utterance of the fear, rage and grief, providing for the patient a sense of being 'held' in the experience of the therapist. At this point, the patient will often put forth some aspect of the true self for affirmation. It may be rudimentary and barely noticeable, the way a tiny infant will raise its arm in a searching gesture for some as-yet-unnamed and unknown response. If this gesture is met by the mother with a matching gesture, such as enfolding the infant's fingers within her own, meaning will be given to the experience and an affective/cognitive/ motoric/motivational bond will connect self to other. In the case of the patient, the therapist affirms the patient's expression of the innate self, however rudimentary.

The speech form termed imitation involves an interaction in which the therapist mirrors or imitates the patient's verbalisations and gestures. In imitation, statements are made which articulate the thoughts, feelings, motivation and/or behaviour of the other in the way maternal imitation faithfully reproduces an observable infant behaviour. Imitative statements permit closeness without intrusiveness by echoing and mirroring the self-experiences. These speech forms parallel the vocal or kinesic phrase or run of mother–infant interaction in which a mother might make a cry-face and say to her infant, 'Ooh, you're gonna cry'. Imitation between mother and infant has a quieting effect and fosters attentiveness (Field, 1977). In Haven's model, the therapist might imitate a patient's experience of feeling paralysed with fear by saying, for example, 'How does one find the courage to act in the face of all this?' Or, one might respond to the other's sense of hopelessness with the softly stated comment, 'What hope is there?'

A third empathic speech form involves primarily cognitive self-structures, which are termed 'translations' and 'bridging statements'. These enable the patient to integrate the conflict that the present experience with the therapist is different from the past. Havens (1979) gives an example of a bridging statement in the comment 'No one understands', made to a patient whose experience is one of being misunderstood and abandoned. This bridge expresses the past reality and the paradoxical present reality of having been misunderstood and now being understood. Bridging state-ments can bring together behaviour and affect, motivation and perception, in the way the responsive mother may match the infant's affect with her own motoric response or define the motivation behind an affective response.

The fourth speech form, termed 'extension', is primarily motivational and involves moving with the other through tracks of space and time, bringing together past and present and/or future. In classical analytic terminology, the therapist aligns herself with the transference and moves the issue back to the original relationship. For example, a patient's fear of appearing inadequate is related to his mother's wish that at thirteen he function like an adult. There is in addition an existential component to this speech form in that the patient may also be brought to the consideration of another form of relationship. Havens (1983) gives an example of a man wishing to connect in a caring, supportive way with his girlfriend who is having legal difficulties. However, the man was under attack from a hostile introject to abandon her. The therapist affirmed the caring in a comment that spoke to both past experience and future possibility, 'Can I stay with what I love?' A similar phenomenon occurs in the mother–infant interaction in which the mother 'extends' by interacting with her regressed infant, offering comfort appropriate both to an earlier time and to her 'potential infant', the infant she expects him to become. Stern describes this as especially evident in maternal speech, which may regress to meet the infant's regression, but which is often ahead of the infant's productive competence.

Malin[3] has stated that optimal positive experience is important in the building of self-structure. He contends that vital structure occurs as a consequence of positive experience, and that the experience of empathic resonance leads to transformations which result in growth of new structure. As the innate self of the patient begins to emerge in therapy, a new empathic speech form is required, termed by Havens 'counterintrojective' or 'performative' speech, which he defines as 'structure building admiring appraisals'. They serve to acknowledge and affirm the behaviour, wishes or motives, feelings and thoughts of the true self 'against the testimony of the introjects' and thereby replace or modify the hostile introjects.

To cite a clinical example, a mother projects her own neediness and internalised hostile parental introject onto her son, labelling him 'selfish' and depriving him of much-needed shoes. He is so ridiculed when he wears his tattered shoes that he refuses to go to school. His mother responds with a brief moment of concern for his plight and purchases shoes for him. This empathic concern is an expression of her true self, and it needs affirmation to become structuralised. Her son fails to admire and affirm her for what he rightly feels is his due. She becomes enraged and in her rage severely beats him, keeping him home from school. She has returned the self to the control of the introject (her own abusive parent). The following day, discussing the incident with her therapist, she was given detailed praise for her efforts. This affirmation quieted the patient and strengthened the therapist–patient bond sufficiently for the therapist to offer an interpretation. She suggested that the mother was treating her son like an adult in wanting praise for something children take for granted. That evening, the mother again wanted praise from her son, remembered her therapist's words as she was raising her arm to hit him for refusing to offer the desired praise and stopped as she registered the meaning and truth in the therapist's interpretation. The following day, she telephoned the therapist to tell her of the event, giving evidence of a beginning structure formation in covert praise to the therapist and of trust in her expectation that the therapist would continue to affirm her.

Performative statements also enhance autonomy. For example, a diabetic child whose parents were in the midst of divorce was found to have stored several pounds of sweets in her room around the time her mother was scheduled for an elective surgical procedure. Careful questioning indicated that she was eating 'only a handful' each day. This was understood as a bid to be in control of what happened to her rather than as an attempt to destroy herself. The therapist affirmed her wish for autonomy, leading to her willingness to assume a greater role in her own care. In the building of self-structures, performative statements parallel the way a mother admires first the crayon mark on a piece of paper in preparing the child for realisation of her full potential to turn that mark into a representation of three-dimensional form.

Once the hostile introject has been released, and the patient has experienced sufficient affirmation of the exposed self-structures, clinical experience indicates that the individual now experiences a profound sense of freedom to exist in past and present. Often, the patient will spontaneously return to the site of past traumas and make strong efforts to heal past relationships based on the new understanding gained from the perspective of the newly discovered true self. This self, with its own centre of initiative, is able to integrate the structures of the self into response units in which thought, affect, motivation and behaviour originate from within. The self has now reached a state of maturity in which the inner true self may connect with the other in a self–other relationship in which each respects the right of the other to exist.

Notes

1 Beatrice Beebe, 'Mutual influence in mother–infant interaction', paper presented at the Eighth Annual Conference on The Psychology of the Self, New York City, October 4–6, 1985.
2 Daniel Stern, discussion of paper by Beatrice Beebe, Eighth Annual Conference on The Psychology of the Self, New York City, October 4–6, 1985.
3 Arthur Malin, introductory comments by the Chair, Plenary Session no. 1, Eighth Annual Conference on the Psychology of the Self, New York City, October 4–6, 1985.

References

Ainsworth, M. D. S. and Bell, S. M. (1969), 'Some contemporary patterns of mother–infant interaction in the feeding situation', in J. A. Ambrose (ed.), *Stimulation in Early Infancy*, Academic Press: London, pp. 133–70.

Ainsworth, M. D. S., Blehar, M. C., Waters, E. and Wall, S. (1978), *Patterns of Attachments*, Erlbaum: Hillsdale, N.J.

Basch, M. F. (1983), 'Empathic understanding: A review of the concept and some theoretical considerations', *Journal of the American Psychoanalytic Association*, 31, pp. 101–26.

Beebe, B. (1983), 'Mother–infant mutual influence and precursors of self and object representations', in J. Masling (ed.), *Empirical Studies of Psychoanalytic Theories*, vol. II, Erlbaum: Hillsdale, N.J.

Beebe, B. and Sloate, P. (1982), 'Assessment and treatment of difficulties in mother–infant attunement in the first three years of life: A case history', *Psychoanalytic Inquiry*, 1, pp. 601–23.

Beebe, B. and Stern, D. N. (1977), 'Engagement–disengagement and early object experiences', in N. Freedman and S. Grand (eds), *Communicative Structures and Psychic Structures*, Plenum Press: New York.

Berkowitz, D. A. (1979), 'The disturbed adolescent and his family: Problems in individuation', *Journal of Adolescence*, 2, pp. 27–39.

Berkowitz, D. A. (1982), 'Implications of the selfobject concept for the therapeutic alliance', *Hillsdale Journal of Clinical Psychiatry*, 4, pp. 15–24.

Carmen, E., Ricker, P. and Mills, T. (1984), 'Victims of violence and psychiatric illness', *American Journal of Psychiatry*, 141, pp. 378–83.

Cohn, J. F. and Tronick, E. Z. (1982), 'Communicative roles and the sequential structure of infant behavior during normal and depressed interaction', in E. Z. Tronick (ed.), *Social Interchange in Infancy: Affect, Cognition, and Communication*, University Park Press: Baltimore, pp. 59–77.

Damon, W. and Hart, D. (1982), 'The development of self-understanding from infancy through adolescence', *Child Development*, 53, pp. 841–64.

Field, T. M. (1977), 'Effects of early separation, interaction deficits and experimental manipulations on infant–mother face to face interaction', *Child Development*, 48, pp. 763–71.

Fogel, A., Diamond, G. R., Langhorst, B. H. and Demos, V. (1982), 'Affective and cognitive aspects of the 2-month-old's participation in face-to-face interaction with the mother', in E. Z. Tronick (ed.), *Social Interchange in Infancy. Affect, Cognition, and Communication*, University Park Press: Baltimore, pp. 37–57.

Gilligan, C. (1982), *In a Different Voice*, Harvard University Press: Cambridge, Mass.

Grostein, J. S. (1983), 'Some perspectives on self psychology', in A. Goldberg (ed.), *The Future of Psychoanalysis*, International Universities Press: New York, pp. 165–202.

Havens, L. (1977), 'The choice of therapeutic method', *Journal of the American Academy of Psychoanalysis*, 4, pp. 463–78.

Havens, L. (1978), 'Explorations in the uses of language in psychotherapy: Simple empathic statements', *Psychiatry*, 41, pp. 336–45.

Havens, L. (1979), 'Explorations in the uses of language in psychotherapy:

Complex empathic statements', *Psychiatry*, 42, pp. 40–48.

Havens, L. (1980), 'Explorations in the uses of language in psychotherapy: Counterprojective statements', *Contemporary Psychoanalysis*, 16, pp. 53–67.

Havens, L. (1982–3), 'Models of the mind', Lectures given at Cambridge Hospital, Cambridge, Mass., September 1982 to May 1983.

Havens, L. (1983), Chapter 10, unpublished manuscript.

Hoffman, M. L. (1977), *Empathy: Its Development and Prosocial Implications*, *Nebraska Symposium on Motivation, 1977*, 25, pp. 169–217.

Kohut, H. and Wolf, E. S. (1978), 'The disorders of the self and their treatment: An outline', *International Journal of Psychoanalysis*, 59, pp. 413–25.

Lozoff, B., Brittenham, G. M., Trause, M. A., Kennell, J. H. and Klaus, M. H. (1977), 'The mother–newborn relationship: Limits of adaptability', *Journal of Pediatrics*, 91, pp. 1–12.

Mack, J. E. (1983), 'Self-esteem and its development: An overview', in J. E. Mack and S. L. Ablon (eds), *The Development and Sustenance of Self-esteem in Childhood*, International Universities Press: New York, pp. 1–42.

Mahler, M. S., Pine, F. and Bergman, A. (1975) *The Psychological Birth of the Human Infant*, Basic Books: New York.

Martin, G. B. and Clark, R. D. (1982), 'Distress crying in neonates: Species and peer specificity', *Developmental Psychology*, 19, pp. 3–9.

McAdams, D. P. (1982), 'Experiences of intimacy and power: Relationships between social motives and autobiographical memory', *Journal of Personality and Social Psychology*, 42, pp. 292–302.

Ornstein, A. (1981), 'Self-pathology in childhood: Developmental and clinical considerations', *Psychiatric Clinics of North America*, 4, pp. 435–53.

Pingleton, J. P. (1983), 'An integrated model of relational maturity', *Journal of Psychology and Christianity*, 3, pp. 57–67.

Price, G. M., Walker, L. and Penticuff, J. (1982), 'Maternal sensitivity at four weeks and attachment status at one year as manifestations of maternal empathy', Paper presented at the Tenth International Congress of the International Association for Child and Adolescent Psychiatry and Allied Professions, in Dublin, July 1982.

Samuels, C. A. (1984), 'I am born: Now do I exist?', Paper presented at the International Conference on Infant Studies, New York City, April 1984.

Sander, L. S. (1983), 'To begin with – reflections on ontogeny', in J. D. Lichtenberg and S. Kaplan (eds), *Reflections on Self Psychology*, Erlbaum: Hillsdale, N.J., pp. 85–104.

Stern, D. N. (1983a), 'The early development of schemas of self, other and "self with other" ', in J. D. Lichtenberg and S. Kaplan (eds), *Reflections of Self Psychology*, Erlbaum: Hillsdale, N.J., pp. 49–84.

Stern, D. N. (1983b), 'Affect attunement', Paper presented at the World Association for Infant Psychiatry, Cannes, France.

Stern, D. N., Beebe, B., Jaffe, J. and Bennet, S. L. (1977), 'The infant's stimulus world during social interaction: A study of caretaker behaviors with particular reference to repetition and timing', in H. R. Schaffer (ed.), *Studies in Mother–infant Interaction*, Academic Press: New York.

4 The evolution of the self: An integration of Winnicott's and Kohut's concepts

Irene H. Harwood

By integrating Winnicott's and Kohut's theories this chapter will help us understand the identity of the self, which is based on both identification (Winnicott, 1960b) and merger (Kohut, 1977). These two men expound complementary views on the emerging self and the caretaking environment. They both agree on the need for an optimally available and responsive human environment in order for an authentic self to evolve. Whereas Winnicott stresses impingements, however, Kohut points to deficiencies in the environment as interfering with the emergence of a true or nuclear self. When the two theories are integrated, the theoretical framework that emerges appears to be more complete and thus more useful than either theory used alone.

Winnicott's true and false self

For Winnicott, as illustrated in Figure 4.1, the starting point for the true self occurs when mental organisation begins in the individual. At this point it is little more than the summation of sensorimotor aliveness (Winnicott, 1960b). The ego, then, is a definite precursor to the self. Only with the beginnings of self-awareness or self-consciousness, after the child has begun to differentiate 'me' from 'not-me' and her/his own feelings and perceptions from those of others, does Winnicott (1962) believe that the self has any meaning.

Infant–maternal care unit

Winnicott views the ego as developing within a unit consisting of the infant and its maternal care, which allows the inherited potential to experience a continuity of being. When that continuity is not interfered with, the infant has an opportunity to come forth with her or his own productions, or what

55

Winnicott (1960a, 1960b, 1971) calls 'creative gestures' or impulses. He states (1960a) that the infant could not exist without maternal care and therefore that where one finds an infant, one finds maternal care. The only reason that the infant's ego is usually able to master and include the id is that the maternal ego is able to implement the infant's ego and thus make it powerful and stable. To Winnicott (1962) the relative strength or weakness of the ego largely depends on the mother's ability to respond appropriately to the absolute dependence of the infant at the very beginning, before the infant separates the mother from the self. When good-enough mothering is lacking, the maturation of the ego either fails or is distorted in important aspects. With good-enough mothering, the infant's ego can eventually let go of mother's ego support as mental detachment from the mother is established and differentiation into a separate personal self is achieved (Winnicott, 1960a, 1960b). The self comes into being only after the ego nuclei are gathered together through the good mothering of the 'holding' and 'handling' environments (Winnicott, 1962).

Integration from holding

From the start, when the infant is in a state of absolute dependence, it is not only through physical holding, but also through 'total environmental provision', that the mother helps to assemble the ego nuclei for the infant into a feeling of integration. The holding environment for Winnicott performs an important function by providing the setting for the fusion of aggression and love, which in turn allows the individual to experience both ambivalence and concern, as well as to feel and accept responsibility (Winnicott, 1963a). Another function of the holding environment is to protect the infant at the beginning from experiencing unthinkable or archaic (early primitive) anxiety as she or he proceeds from a state of unintegration to a state of integration (Winnicott, 1962). Little by little, while experiencing a 'continuity of being' without having to attend or react to outside stimuli, the infant initiates spontaneous creative gestures that become the bedrock of the true self. Winnicott also saw the beginnings of ego-relatedness as born out of the paradoxical experiences of being alone in someone else's presence (1958). Eventually, with a good-enough holding environment, the child becomes able to forgo the mother's presence and establish an internal environment that becomes the essence of the self.

Personalisation from handling

Personalisation for Winnicott occurs when a close relationship is achieved between the body and the psyche. Such an achievement can be aided by experiencing a harmonious gestalt, which comes as a consequence of 'active and adaptive handling'. Personalisation can occur through adaptive handling by a caretaker who enfolds the baby in such a manner that it is neither overwhelmed nor feels that it consists merely of a collection of organs and limbs surmounted by a wobbling head. Appropriate active handling also adapts to the mood of the child as well as encouraging the evolution of vital (as opposed to passive) being.

Object-relating from object-presenting

Good-enough holding and handling environments allow the infant's rudimentary ego to initiate object-relating by discovering presented objects. For Winnicott, the object must not thrust itself on the infant, but must present itself casually so that the infant can discover it and delight in it as if it were its own spontaneous creation. If the caretaking environment consistently stimulates the infant to react and respond to external stimuli outside the context of ego-support, a pattern of 'reactive doing' is built up that may lead to the emergence of a false self, unlike 'active being', which allows for the emergence of a true self.

With the beginning of personalisation and with non-impinging object-presenting, there occurs a clearer differentiation between me and not-me (or between the subjective and objective object), and a self starts to emerge that is able to relate creatively and spontaneously to other objects and to the world around it. A self that is an integrated collection of experiences, details of aliveness and of feelings of realness is a 'true self'. The true self has a thirst for life. It can emerge only when impingements are held to a minimum and the infant's creative gestures are allowed to emerge. If impingements from the environment predominate, a false self emerges instead.

False self

For Winnicott (1960b), the false self develops because in the beginning of life the caretaker (owing to inability, lack of desire or the caretaker's own early deprivation) failed to be good enough at understanding, allowing or implementing the infant's sense of omnipotence when responding to the infant's gestures. In these cases, the caretaker substituted her or his own gestures instead, to which the infant compliantly started relating. Such continuous compliance gives birth to the false self, whose essential feature is lack of creative originality. At one extreme, when there is a drastic split between the false and true self, people are to be found who experience great restlessness and who virtually seek out impingements in external reality in order to have something to react to and thus to experience some sense of being or realness.

Winnicott (1960b) has described the process of a false self-organisation moving through several steps in the direction of health and of the true self. These can be summarised as follows. At one end of the progression, the false self sets itself up as real and appears so to others. But when called upon to respond as a whole person, particularly in intimate relationships, it cannot do so. The spontaneity of the true self emerges only when some instrumental figure such as a therapist, through communication with the false self, is able to convince the nascent true self that its creative gestures will be allowed and safeguarded.

As the false self-organisation sets out on its progress towards health, it tries to perpetuate its original function – to hide or protect the true self. Such organisation is characteristic of people who have developed enough of a sense of self to be aware of its potential, but whose true self can only be expressed through clinical illness which, through symptom formation, preserves the early pain experienced by the emerging true self when its creative gestures were met mostly with disapproval or impingements. In its further progression towards health, the false self searches for conditions that will allow the true self to emerge. If conditions are extreme and there is no possibility of putting an end to exploitation of the true self from the outside, the false self has been known to reorganise and take recourse to the extreme defence of suicide. Of course it destroys itself in the process, but it protects the true self from any further exploitation.

Sometimes what looks like a true self is a self built on identifications with objects in its early environments, but this type of self still lacks that which is uniquely her own or his own. In Chapter 3, Price describes a similar type of selves who are 'self-absorbed in a caricature of autonomy' and who 'disappear into another self and achieve a caricature of connectedness'.

In contrast to either a true or a false self, Winnicott (1963b, 1963c) also described a self that has suffered deprivation at the stage of relative dependence but has not been particularly discouraged in expressing its emerging true self. He contrasted 'deprivation' with 'privation', the latter being a failure experienced at the early stage when the infant has no real awareness of maternal care. In contrast, at the stage of relative dependence, an infant is aware of dependence on an object and the environment. With a loss of the experienced good-enough environment, the child at this stage of development is able to perceive the environmental maladjustment. If the deprivation is so prolonged that the child cannot cope with it or keep the experience of the good-enough environment alive, even though there has been a certain degree of integration of the self, the child will develop an antisocial tendency upon experiencing failure or withdrawal of ego support (Winnicott, 1956).

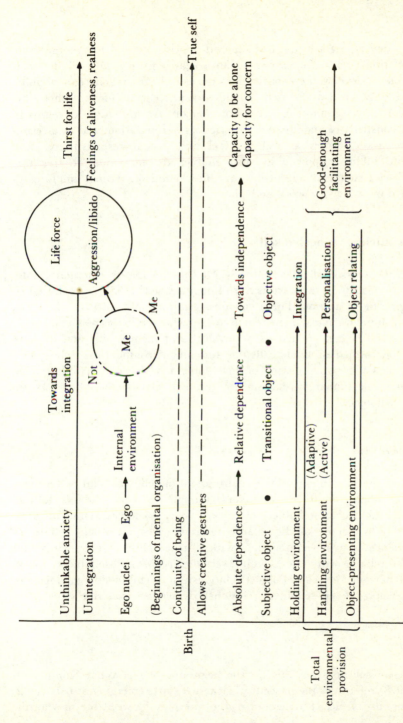

FIGURE 4.1   *Winnicott's emerging self*

The true self

Unlike a developing self that has suffered deprivation and has reorganised at an inferior level to encompass an antisocial tendency, an evolving true self is able to develop the capacity for concern. That capacity can be fully achieved only toward the end of the second year of life or when the individual can view another as a whole person. An individual develops it through constructive and creative experiences of reparation, and as a result can care about others as well as feel and accept responsibility. For Winnicott, taking responsibility also enables the individual to free the constructive elements of aggression (or what Winnicott termed 'life force'), which are necessary for work and play.

Kohut's nuclear, cohesive self

Kohut's theoretical self does not rely on the ego for its emergence into being, but exists from the start as a 'rudimentary self' (1977) – a self that is just beginning to appear. There can be a rudimentary self from the start because a human environment reacts to a newborn baby as a 'virtual self' (1977), a self that is treated as a physical and mental unit and as if it already had formed a self. He calls that human environment the 'selfobject'. During the self's earliest period of development, which can be followed in Figure 4.2, the human caretaking environment can be thought of as an 'archaic selfobject'.

Self–selfobject unit

For Kohut the human caretaking environment or selfobject can be mother, father or other committed caretakers, though he usually refers to the mother as the archaic selfobject of early infancy. Whereas Winnicott sees the child growing out of the infant–maternal care unit when a state of independence is achieved together with a true self that can engage in concerned relating with others, Kohut sees the archaic self–selfobject unit of early infancy and the self–selfobject relationships of childhood evolving into mature reciprocal self–selfobject relationships between cohesive selves.

Nuclear self

The nuclear self does not exist at the beginning of life. What Kohut and Wolf (1978) refer to as the nascent nuclear self starts emerging at between 2 and 5 months of life. It arises out of the interplay between the newborn's biological givens, the rudimentary self and the selective empathic responses of the human environment. Kohut and Wolf (1978) state that the nuclear self emerges probably during the second year of life. Kohut (1971, 1977) conceptualises the nuclear self as a bipolar structure. The nuclear ambitions cluster at the pole of the 'grandiose self' and the nuclear ideals at the pole of the 'idealised parent imago'. Rudimentary talents and skills, the child's natural attributes, are enhanced through satisfactory or optimum mirroring or validation by the selfobject. (In Chapter 2, Pines describes various types of mirroring, while Wylie's chapter on mothers' attributions to their young children discusses an aspect of mirroring.) Later, the natural talents and developed skills are modified by whatever ideals (or lack thereof) have emerged under the complementary pole of the idealised parent imago. For example, someone with highly developed manual dexterity, who has evolved in his/her ambitions within a context of ideals, can become a locksmith, or a lockpicker. Kohut (1977) refers to interplay between nuclear ambitions and nuclear ideals as the 'tension arc' that keeps the bipolar structure in balance. In his last book, Kohut (1984) added a third developmental line, twinship, where the emergent self experiences merger with the strength of another similar to itself. In twinship, as in the other developmental lines, archaic forms evolve into mature expressions. For development to proceed and psychic structure to build, the availability of caretakers has to be optimum, neither too gratifying nor too frustrating. For Kohut (1971, 1977, 1984), it is through transmuting internalisation that optimum or non-traumatic, phase-appropriate, selfobject 'failures' build psychic structure. As a result of the transmuting internalisation, there is new psychological structure. The growing child can now, on its own, perform the function for which the selfobject was previously needed.

Empathic introspection

Through the use of empathy, an archaic selfobject (the newborn's caretaker) can temporarily immerse itself into the state of the infant (while maintaining its own cohesion) in order to understand that state and to respond to it appropriately. Kohut termed such immersion 'empathic introspection'. For example, when through empathic immersion the selfobject has determined that the infant's own tension release has gone beyond the usual sensory-muscular discharge, it can step in to provide a regulatory function through soft, reassuring verbalisation or singing, through gentle holding or stroking and through containing the infant's emotional and physical discharge by its own calm presence. The archaic merger involves the infant's absorption of the selfobject's state of the self, through which the infant is able to take in the regulatory function of the archaic selfobject. That reciprocity between the infant and the selfobject

Kohut (1977) calls the 'matrix of mutual empathy'. The regulatory function that the archaic selfobject provides the infant is within the developmental pole which Kohut calls the 'idealised parent imago'.

Disorders of the self

Within the self–selfobject unit, when the selfobject fails for whatever reasons to respond empathically to the evolving self within the realm of optimum frustration, the self experiences a narcissistic injury. Depending on the degree, frequency and impact of the lack of responsive empathy (as subjectively experienced by the child), the effect can be momentarily disruptive (mild enfeeblement); temporarily breaking up, enfeebling and distorting the self (narcissistic and behaviour disorders); protractively breaking up a self with more or less effective defensive or compensatory structures (borderline disorders); or permanently or protractively breaking up the self (psychotic disorders) (Kohut, 1977).

Evolving self

The evolving self requires a different responsiveness from the selfobject(s) as it progresses through archaic, twinship and mirroring mergers and as it internalises (not identifies) – and integrates into already existing configurations – the state or values of selfobjects. The child takes in what the parents or selfobjects are and do, not what they profess to be or say that the child should be or do.

Archaic merger

Under the developmental pole of the grandiose self, through the first year and somewhere up to the first 18 months of life, the beginning nuclear self interplays with the admiring, confirming responses of the archaic selfobjects (Palombo, 1981). It is important for the selfobjects to confirm the total self of the child as well as emerging skills or talents. Confirming responses or the lack of them make the difference in whether the evolving self can own, without much question, a characteristic or a specific sense about itself.

When self psychologists speak of the archaic selfobject as part of the self, they are not referring to the perception or recognition of an object as being physically separate. Self psychology stresses the archaic self's experience of the *functions* of the archaic selfobject as part of the self, since the selfobject functions are the very psychological oxygen that Kohut (1977) says an infant needs in order to survive.

Under the developmental pole of the idealised parent imago, during the same developmental period, the archaic selfobjects are utilised primarily as tension regulators. The merger of the rudimentary self with the archaic selfobject(s) is believed to be total (Palombo, 1981). Through the archaic merger the infant can absorb the selfobject's state of the self – calmness or agitation, as well as the quality of the selfobject's responsiveness.

Twinship or alter-ego merger

At the next level of development, the selfobject is perceived as more separate from the self. Probably because of the insecurities that differentiation from the selfobject arouses, the evolving self voices demands that the selfobject be more like itself. The child does not give up its demands for the still-needed functions of the selfobject(s). At the pole of the grandiose self, it is not unusual to hear requests for confirmation, such as 'You have brown hair like me, don't you, Mummy?' or 'You like to play ball like I do, right, Daddy?' Self psychologists type this phenomenon as the twinship or alter-ego merger, which Kohut later (1984) recognised as yet another developmental line along which the evolving self travels en route to becoming a cohesive self.

During the same 18- to 36-month period of the beginning of life, although some capacities for tension regulation are evident, the role of the selfobject, under the idealised parent imago pole, is that of soothing. During this period, along with the further development of language, symbolic thought begins. By the end of the period, the nuclear cohesive self is formed, unless the self is traumatised (Kohut, 1977).

Mirroring mergers

Under the pole of the grandiose self, from 36 months to 5 years of age, the evolving self, which by now can experience selfobjects as quite separate from the self, no longer needs to maintain a twinship merger, but has grown into a mirroring merger with selfobjects (Palombo, 1981). The child at this stage does not require the selfobjects to be, feel or act like him/herself, but does need the mirroring function of the selfobjects to further confirm his/her total evolving self, achievements, goals and values.

During the oedipal period (3 to 5 years), the parental imagos are related to differently by the child. Though both parents are needed to accept and confirm the oedipal strivings of the child within an appropriate familial context, both parents need to remain idealised within their sexual roles (Harwood, 1983b; Lang, 1982). Thus, for the oedipal boy, even though the mother gently limits his libidinal aim and redirects it toward other future selfobjects, she confirms that his amorous ambitions are a positive indication of his growth and capacities and will surely be welcomed by a peer of the opposite sex when he becomes older. Under the pole of the grandiose self, she reassures him that she remains a loving mother while admiring, confirming and accepting the masculinity of the evolving self. With this type of affirmation, the mother can remain an idealised parent imago if she holds herself as a person worthy of esteem and is content with her role (traditional or non-traditional), and if the father does not undermine the worth of her role. For his part, the father of the oedipal boy gently curbs his son's rivalrous aggression, while admiring his developing capacities and strength. The father remains an idealised imago, a source of power and wisdom whom the son can choose to emulate (Kohut, 1984).

For the oedipal girl, the mother can accept the daughter's turning her libidinal aim to the father, while curbing appropriately, though firmly, her daughter's aggressiveness. A mother who is secure in her relationship with her husband and in other roles she has chosen need not be threatened by her daughter's turning away from her (Harwood, 1983b). Instead, the enjoyment of the mother's own role, whatever it may be, can become a source of idealisation for the daughter, who can also look forward to becoming a capable woman who enjoys her work (Harwood, 1983b; Lang, 1983).

The father of the oedipal girl needs to accept her developing femininity while not forgetting to confirm her other growing talents, skills and ambitions, whether they conform to his own ideals of a woman's role or not. With such affirmation of her total self, the girl can emerge from her oedipal phase while still seeing her father as an object worthy of respect and admiration. Based on this positive interplay between her affirmed evolving grandiose self by both parental imagos, who did not become traumatically de-idealised, the adolescent, and the postadolescent woman as well, can continue exploring her ambitions and working towards her goals, confident that she will meet a peer of the opposite sex who, like her father with her mother, will be a reciprocally confirming, accepting, mature selfobject (Harwood, 1983b).

The consolidation of cohesion

Between 5 and 7 years old, for both sexes, the evolving self continues through progressive transmuting internalisations. Self-confidence and self-assurance continue to consolidate under the pole of the grandiose self. There is continued but lesser dependence on the idealised parental objects as other idealised objects gain importance (Palombo, 1981). Between 7 and 11 years of age there is a continued consolidation of a cohesive self. While ambitions emerge more clearly, grandiosity is more realistically modified.

	Beginning of life	2 months	5 months	1 year	18 months	2 years	3 years	4 years	5 years	7 years	11 years	18 years
Self	Tension state → Nascent or beginning nuclear self Archaic self					Nuclear cohesive self			Cohesive self			
Idealised parent imago pole	Archaic mergers Tension-regulating function ie soothing – containing	Beginning internalisation of regulatory function		Regulatory functions are being internalised		Tension – regulation function acquired	Idealised parent imagos needed for idealisation and to provide values or ethics				Ideals Enthusiasm
Twinship pole		Archaic forms				Mature forms						Joy Pride
Grandiose self pole		Responding; smiling, playing with infant Archaic mergers		Twinship mergers Selfobjects needed to be like self		Mirroring mergers Selfobjects needed to confirm self					Ambitions Self-esteem
Selfobject		Archaic selfobject									Mature selfobjects
		Selfobject not functionally differentiated		Beginning of functional differentiation of selfobject			Functions of selfobjects are seen as separate from self		Emergence of mutuality and reciprocity with selfobject			Reciprocity Mutuality

FIGURE 4.2   *Evolution of the self in Kohut's self psychology*

There is a further redirection of idealisation from parental imagos to heroic figures. With continued untraumatic affirmation from parental imagos, the evolving self can enter adolescence with a stabilised sense of self-esteem (Palombo, 1981).

If the parental imagos continue their affirmation of the evolving self during the adolescent period while gently and firmly guiding in the direction of ideals, an adult self will emerge somewhere around the eighteenth year with a balanced sense of self-esteem, pursuing one's own ambitions within a framework of ideals, and feeling enthusiasm, joy and pride in one's own pursuits as well as in oneself (Palombo, 1981). At this point, the evolving self will have consolidated into a mature cohesive self. The adult self does not devoid itself of all selfobjects, but no longer relates to others in an archaic fashion. Selfobjects are related to as separate persons with their own goals, ambitions and ideals. At the same time, the cohesive self has come into its own as a selfobject, and interactions are now based on mutuality and reciprocity with appreciation and acceptance of the other's strengths as well as weaknesses. This type of mature understanding of other mature selfobjects readies the cohesive self to enter into a possibly even more evolved state – that of becoming, in turn, an archaic confirming and soothing selfobject to a brand-new virtual self.

Integration of a true and cohesive self

We now compare and integrate Kohut's theoretical view of the self with that of Winnicott. Figures 4.1 and 4.2 describe how each of them viewed the evolution of self on a continuum. Figure 4.3 (Harwood, 1983b), as discussed in this section, speaks to an integrated continuum, but also points out fixations on that continuum at different developmental stages. The particular points of fixation will be labelled in Winnicott's and Kohut's terminology.

The centre line of Figure 4.3 combines Winnicott's and Kohut's concepts of the self and describes the optimal evolution of the creative, true, cohesive self within the context of an indestructible, non-retaliating, soothing and accurately mirroring human environment that allows an integrated self to emerge. The upper line describes the development of a self that has suffered from a deficiency in tension regulation or has been unprotected from internal and external impingements. This developmental line represents, on a continuum, the disorders that Kohut calls both the psychotic, as well as borderline and narcissistic *behaviour* disorders, and Winnicott describes as unfused aggression and antisocial behaviours with lack of concern for others (acting-out personalities). The lower line describes the development of a self that may have received adequate tension regulation but subsequently has been overwhelmed by external impingements or experienced a deficiency in mirroring. This developmental line represents a continuum of Winnicott's false self and what Kohut calls both the psychotic, as well as borderline and narcissistic *personality* disorders (acting-in personalities).

Potential for a creative, true, cohesive self

Both Kohut and Winnicott believe that the potential for vital creativity is inborn in the biologically healthy infant. Whether it develops fully or only partially depends largely on the interactions with the human environment, and, for Kohut, how the child subjectively experiences that environment. Winnicott (1971) believes that when a child is allowed a basis for being, a basis for a sense of self follows. Thus, a natural evolution of the self occurs when the environment does not unnecessarily impinge on the infant by substituting its own impulses while curtailing or redirecting the infant's creative gestures (centre line of the figure). Winnicott finds that a separate personal self (which acquires integration, personalisation and object-relating within the holding, handling and object-presenting environment) is formed from the building blocks of creative gestures. Each separate, personal self is structured uniquely using its own pattern, while acquiring its own shape and texture, instead of being squeezed into a mould.

When Kohut (1977) speaks of the newborn being reacted to as a 'virtual self', he assumes that the interaction from the caretaker carries within it the respect one naturally gives a formed and adult fellow human being. In the natural evolution of the self, Winnicott emphasises the importance of the infant's being allowed to *be* (without having to react); Kohut, though not disagreeing, emphasises responsiveness to the rudimentary self. He spells out the need for particular selfobject responsiveness along the two parallel developmental poles of the grandiose self and the idealised parent imago (centre line of Figure 4.3).

Need for an indestructible, non-retaliating, containing, soothing and accurately mirroring human environment

Before an infant can offer the types of gestures that become the building blocks for its uniqueness and future creativity, it needs to experience what Winnicott calls continuity of being. An infant who is distressed and crying is not experiencing continuity of being, but is offering a creative gesture of sorts. To return to the state where the infant can experience a resumption of continuity of being, homeostasis must be restored. An infant often can do this on its own; but when its distress reaches what Winnicott calls unthinkable anxiety, or what Kohut calls a panic state, the human environment is needed to act as a protective shield, to contain that anxiety and to restore the infant's equilibrium. The human environment thereby performs as Kohut's tension regulator or as Winnicott's holding environment without impinging with its own anxieties. But if it fails in that role, the beginning self can experience the caretaker's anxieties as the result of its own self destroying the environment through its own lack of equilibrium. The human environment therefore needs to maintain or restore its own sense of well-being before it can act as a soothing tension-regulator.

Continuity of being allows creative gestures

Within the context of the good-enough, consistent, reliable and non-intrusively available environment, psychic integration proceeds as continuity of being persists. With continuing psychic integration, there can be a beginning discovery of the self, or parts of the self, including one's own creative gestures. Winnicott considers the act of discovering and sucking one's own thumb and the self-satisfied smile that occurs after a good feeding to be creative gestures, because they are within the infant's control.

When such creative gestures are interfered with, an impingement occurs that interrupts the infant's continuity of being, suggesting to the infant that its spontaneous impulse is wrong and that the environment knows better. If the infant or child resists by repeating the creative gesture, and the environment consistently interferes and substitutes its own gesture, any of several outcomes are possible. The self may become overwhelmed; it may react with anxiety to further impingements; it could experience the substance of its own self only in opposition to impingements and in opposition to others; or eventually it could acquiesce and cease or hide its own gestures, curtailing its ability to create new gestures. In the last case, the self may find no other recourse but to mimic and identify with its caretaking environment. In Kohut's terminology, lack of validation of the productions of the beginning self can be viewed as an inappropriate interference. It is no exaggeration to say that when the evolving nuclear self is impinged upon or interfered with, it is distortedly mirrored.

In contrast, the calm, loving appreciation of the infant that emanates through a selfobject's smile mirrors the goodness and loveliness of the self. If the selfobject offers the smile as a creative gesture of its own without impinging on the nascent self (in the spirit of Winnicott's idea of object-presenting), the nascent self has the opportunity to find within its own biological vitality a creative and lovely smile of its very own. Thus, the give and take of pleasurable human relations is set into motion.

Having been allowed continuity of being and its own creative gestures, a unique self can emerge that can begin to appreciate the uniqueness and individuality of others as well as develop its own ambitions. In another paper (Harwood, 1983a), I described how the group therapist can try to

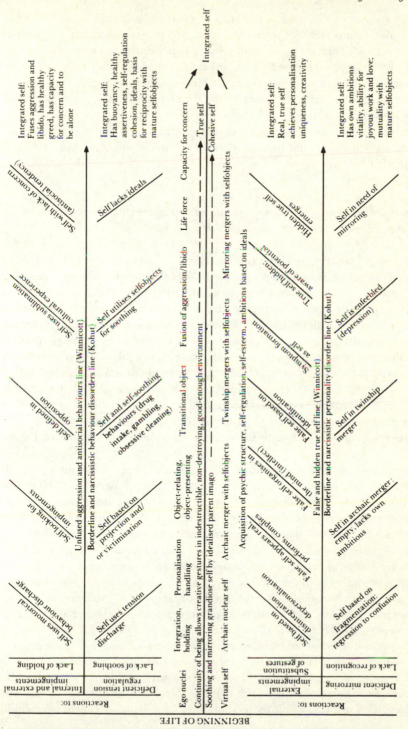

FIGURE 4.3 *Winnicott's and Kohut's concepts of self: An integration*

ensure the emerging nuclear strivings of each nuclear self and protect the vulnerable group member from ensuing group pressures, much as a parent intervenes to shield a young child who is experiencing impingements or a sense of being overwhelmed by its environment. Becoming aware of one's uniqueness – within an environment that neither neglects nor intrudes unnecessarily, but instead celebrates the developmental achievements of the self – allows the emerging self to proceed in its evolution toward maturity in a context of respect, joy and mutual appreciation. This type of self can eventually experience its unique identity within its own culture and as a member of humanity.

An emerging self copes with internal and external impingements and deficient tension regulation: Attempts at self-regulation and self-definition

Therefore, depending on how the emerging self has been responded to or not responded to, it organises or disorganises differently. The evolving self that has not received enough soothing, holding or containing of internal impingements or has not been protected from external impingements seems to cope primarily along the developmental continuum through motor or behavioural discharge to soothe itself and to restore some sense of internal equilibrium. From this developmental continuum evolves a self that tends to act out, rather than act in – a self that lacks ideals and coincides closely with what Kohut (1977) described as the borderline and narcissistic behaviour disorders. Winnicott (1956, 1963b) described this type of self as having unfused aggression, exhibiting antisocial behaviours or a character disorder without the capacity for concern for others (upper line of Figure 4.3).

Depending on where the self is on the evolutionary continuum, it will discharge its tension or attempt to soothe it differently. These selves are identified in the upper line of the figure. *The self that uses tension discharge, either motorically or behaviourally*, is one with little or no self-regulatory capacity. Because it has experienced external impingements while not receiving adequate soothing, it will not be able to regulate, modify or keep some kind of firm boundary against a build-up of impingements, internal and/or external. Examples of this may be conversions, as in some forms of epilepticlike seizures or different kinds of aggressive behaviours. These behaviours fall into the reactive-to-injury categories, which Kohut called 'fragmentation by-products of disintegrating rage' (1971, 1977).

The self that seeks out impingements either through projection or self-victimisation is one which, not having been soothed sufficiently, gives way to a predominant state of anxiety that interferes with continuity of being. To modify such an unpleasant and painful state, the empty self seeks out contact with others who, by responding, penetrate the semipermeable membrane of this vulnerable and empty self and are thereupon experienced as violating and impinging upon the barely formed boundaries. While the impingements are experienced as an affront, at the same time they bring this type of self out of its emptiness and make it feel alive. Examples of this are children who bang their heads against walls and furniture.

A self that has sufficiently differentiated self from non-self, but is restless and feels too overwhelmed by internal impingements that it cannot bring under its control, can use the early defence mechanism of projection to experience the impingement as if it were outside itself, to attempt to bring it under its control, or in order to find an explanation for not having it under its control.

The self that uses self-soothing behaviours such as overeating, gambling or drugs may have had caretakers who, instead of making themselves available for comforting the child, propped it up with a bottle or left it with some article to keep it amused. *The self that defines itself in opposition* has differentiated itself enough to know that it exists, but cannot trust or implement its own creative gestures. It obtains a sense of aliveness or power from opposing others; otherwise, it feels empty and restless, while always dissatisfied. This emerging self identified with its restless and aggressive environment, which was never satisfied with itself, with the evolving self or with others. Abused children who grow up to be abusive parents fall into this category. *The self that utilises selfobjects for soothing and uses sublimation* is a self further along the evolutionary pathway which has experienced optimal soothing and responsiveness and has been able to channel the discharge of its tension through socially approved channels, such as sports or music. *The self that lacks ideals and concern for others* appears paradoxically placed this far on the developmental continuum; but this type of self has experienced enough soothing and holding to consolidate its boundaries and experience a sense of cohesiveness. However, because it has suffered a traumatic disappointment or loss from its early good-enough human environment and has not, with time, received equivalent functions from other sources, it organises itself alloplastically without empathy or concern for others. *A vital, integrated self that maintains its boundaries and does not fragment from impingements* can emerge around 3 years if no significant fixation has occurred. Although appropriately and empathically considerate and reciprocating with others, the self that has a capacity to be alone will be able to hold onto its own point of view, as well as integrate a novel one, without fear that its separateness will result in damage to self or others.

An emerging self copes with external impingements and deficient mirroring: A true self attempts to emerge with self-esteem and its own ambitions

The other type of evolving self, which did *not* suffer from an inordinate amount of tension build-up due to internal impingements or *did* initially receive a good-enough holding and soothing environment, may later on be externally impinged upon by the very environment that originally served it so well. If that occurs, the evolving self tends to resign itself to the deficiency or to the demands of the caretaking environment by complying and by setting aside its own creative gestures or by losing touch with the fact that they even existed. A phenomenon not too dissimilar to this may happen to an empty older self that encounters and is drawn to a cult.

From this developmental continuum a self evolves that tends to be empty, to fragment, to be out of touch with parts of itself, to be depressed, or to hide its true self and potential. Again, these are what Kohut (1971, 1977) dubbed the borderline and narcissistic personality disorders, while Winnicott (1960b) saw them as exemplifying a false self or a partially hidden true self (lower line of Figure 4.3).

Depending on where the self is on the evolutionary continuum, it may or may not have awareness to what degree its self is authentic. These different types of selves are identified on the lower line of Figure 4.3.

The *self that disintegrates, fragments and depersonalises* is at the extreme end of the developmental line. It is a type of self that was so overwhelmed by the environment, or so lacking in a good-enough adaptive and active handling environment, that it could not emerge personally at all. Some nascent selves, on the other hand, may be biologically predetermined in such a way that even a better than average good-enough environment may not suffice. Autistic, catatoniclike states, as well as childhood schizophrenia, may fall into this category.

The *false selves that appear real, organise in the mind and are based on identification* are selves that mostly feel empty, lack their own ambitions and are enfeebled. The basis of how they came into being is very similar to that of the preceding type; they differ primarily in the degree to which their particular or spontaneous, authentic gestures were interfered with by their environment. A self that *has had* a containing, indestructible, good-enough human environment and has been able to internalise its tension-regulating functions is not necessarily well equipped to deal with external impingements. The initial holding, soothing environment can subsequently substitute its own gestures for those of the emerging self and/or impinge by being deficiently responsive to the evolving self's discovery of its own uniqueness.

If the psychobiological predisposition of the newborn is a calm, passive, receptive or compliant one and especially if the impingements or substitute gestures are presented in a manner that is pleasant and loving to the state of the self, but still overwhelming, the unformed self tends to merge archaically not only with the structure but with the identity of the powerful or idealised object. This concept is an extension of Lichtenstein's (1977) and Pines's (1982) views that the mother (or caretaker) mirrors selectively those parts of the self that eventually consolidate into a particular identity.

What may look like a real self is not. It is what Winnicott (1960b) calls a false self. Its own sense of self was never integrated into its own unique configuration, nor did it develop its own unique ambitions. Instead, it has been overwhelmed and seduced into complying, through gross introjections, to take on the identity of its caretaking environment. In Chapter 3, Price substantiates this view.

This self tends to follow rules, regulations and authority without question. A self whose own creative gestures were not allowed, not recognised and not mirrored is an empty self and will remain in an archaic merger with early or later selfobjects, or will look for powerful others to merge with in order to fill itself up with borrowed strength, ideals or goals. This phenomenon may help explain the tragedy of Jonestown, Guyana, where so many people were attracted to the Reverend Jim Jones, who 'lovingly' assured them he had the answers to the complex existential questions of living.

At the least-developed level of this stage is a *false self that appears real, but functions mostly by complying and performing*. It is a self that can function by following directions mechanically, but falls short when asked to be real and to relate spontaneously in creative tasks or social and intimate relationships.

Farther along the continuum is the self whose whole identity is vested in its intellectual functioning, either because the caretaking environment did not interfere with a gifted biological predisposition or because it primarily singled out this area of the young self to affirm. A *false self that organises in the mind* chooses professions where, through perseverance and hard work, it attains status and recognition, but it cannot fully own or enjoy its success, since it does not resonate with the rest of its empty life, which is totally split off from its high intellectual functioning. The more success this self attains, the more unreal it feels.

The *false self based on identification* is somewhat farther along the continuum. It is a self that appears more balanced in the different aspects of living, but its balance is based on identifying almost in total with its early objects. In contrast to transmuting internalisations that occur in small doses, Wolf (1983) states that gross identifications, which can become a compensatory part of the self, occur for defensive reasons because of disavowal of aspects of the self that seem discordant with an idealised selfobject. Disavowal and gross identification leave the self to relate and function primarily by copying or mimicking its archaic or later idealised parent imagos and call into question the proud notion of 'like father, like son'.

This type of self, when removed from its familiar cultural milieu or exposed to severe conditions of stress and struggle for survival, tends to rely on old cultural rules and has difficulty integrating new ones. Instead of taking recourse in its own armamentarium of creative solutions, it tends to look towards a leader, a family, a religious group, a political organisation or a cultural or national identity.

In Kohut's (1971; 1977; 1978) framework, the uncohesive self needs to maintain an archaic merger with an apparent, powerful, idealised parent imago, from whose putative or real strength it attains a sense of well-being and illusory power. While in this blissful merger, the relatively empty, enfeebled self does not have to face its own powerlessness and vulnerability. The caretaker of this type of self, while not minding admiration and merger with its own ideals (insisting on them, more likely), did not validate separate, unique goals in the emerging self (and probably discouraged them strongly). Though Kohut talked of the developmental importance for the nuclear self to merge with the power and ideals of the idealised parent imago (1971; 1977; 1984), he did not speak of how equally important it is for that idealised caretaker not only to mirror the unique qualities of the emerging self, but also to give the message that it can become *as powerful as*, or possibly *even more powerful or wise* than, its idealised caretaker.

Failing that, the compliant, overwhelmed self, because of its fixation in development (which hinders the capacity to come up with several creative solutions, sort them out, integrate them and differentiate among various shades of reality and meaning), tends to settle for the prepackaged 'right solution' against other 'wrong ones'. When it encounters inconsistencies, this type of self tends to deal with them by splitting and compartmentalising rather than by integrating, sorting out or finding similarities.

This typology makes it easier, though no less alarming, to comprehend why types of upbringing that strongly emphasise early and unquestioning obedience to authority would produce people who unreflectingly and blindly join ranks behind tyrannical leaders, charismatic political groups or messianic religious sects.

The *enfeebled self or the self that organises into symptom formation* is very close on the developmental continuum. Defining oneself through physical or emotional symptoms can include an identification with a significant person who was also ill. When the symptom formation is an expression of a true self, it is the manner in which the emerging self found that it could exist without being overwhelmed by its environment or without having its creative gestures replaced, denied or ignored. It may have also been the only manner in which the evolving and yet vulnerable self received positive attention.

A *true self that is aware of its potential* may stay *hidden* until its need for mirroring is satisfied and it feels safe to emerge as a separate and *cohesive true self*. A self that is not in an archaic merger and is aware of its existence, its capacities, ambitions, skills and values often stays *hidden* until it finds someone − often *like* itself at first − to whom it feels safe to reveal its potential, goodness or uniqueness.

Only after the evolving self has experienced empathy and appreciation from those whom it perceives as *different* from self can it experience that its own feelings, qualities, ambitions, skills and ethics are truly valued. It is at this point that the self can begin to feel and understand what empathy is and begin experiencing it freely with others. It can then become a truly personal, unique, true self. It embodies cohesion, vitality and self-esteem. It is capable of joy, empathy and concern for others while being aware of its own healthy appetites. It can give and take within the matrix of comfortable mutuality and reciprocity with peers. Thus, at this point we could say that Winnicott's true self, with its capacity for concern, would be able to act as a mature reciprocal selfobject to Kohut's cohesive self.

This chapter has described several states of the self along the developmental continuum, which became more three-dimensional when Kohut's and Winnicott's conceptualisations of the self were integrated. Thus, Winnicott's 'true self' was able to acquire a more specific validation of its real qualities from its human caretaking environment as well as further understanding of how it copes with tensions when experiencing impingements. Kohut's 'cohesive self' acquired more intuitively sensitive, as well as poetic-selfobjects, who object-present and appropriately share their own uniqueness with another self who is also recognised as unique and creative from the very start.

References

Harwood, I. H. (1983a), 'The application of self psychology concepts to group psychotherapy', *International Journal of Group Psychotherapy*, 33, pp. 469–87.

Harwood, I. H. (1983b), 'The evolution of the self in group psychotherapy' (unpublished manuscript), abridged version presented at the American Group Psychotherapy Association in Toronto, Canada.

Kohut, H. (1971), *The Analysis of the Self*, International Universities Press: New York.

Kohut, H. (1977), *The Restoration of the Self*, International Universities Press: New York.

Kohut, H. (1978), 'Creativeness, charisma, group psychology', in *The Search for the Self*, vol. 2, ed. P. Ornstein, International Universities Press: New York.

Kohut, H. (1984), *How Does Analysis Cure?*, University of Chicago Press: Chicago.

Kohut, H. and Wolf, E. S. (1978), 'The disorders of the self and their treatment', *International Journal of Psychoanalysis*, 59, pp. 413–25.

Lang, J. (1982), 'Notes towards a psychology of the feminine self', Presented at the Fifth Annual Conference of Self Psychology, Atlanta, Georgia.

Lichtenstein, H. (1977), 'Narcissism and primary identity', in *The Dilemma of Human Identity*, Jason Aronson: New York.

Palombo, J. (1981), 'Parent loss and childhood bereavement: Some theoretical considerations', *Clinical Social Work Journal*, 9, pp. 3–33.

Pines, M. (1982), 'Reflections on mirroring', *Group Analysis*, 15, supplement.

Winnicott, D. W. (1956), 'The antisocial tendency', in *Collected Papers: Through Paediatrics to Psychoanalysis*, Basic Books: New York, 1958.

Winnicott, D. W. (1958), 'The capacity to be alone', in *The Maturational Processes and the Facilitating Environment*, International Universities Press: New York, 1965.

Winnicott, D. W. (1960a), 'The theory of the parent–infant relationship', in *The Maturational Processes and the Facilitating Environment*, International Universities Press: New York, 1965.

Winnicott, D. W. (1960b), 'Ego distortion in terms of the true and false self', in *The Maturational Processes and the Facilitating Environment*, International Universities Press: New York, 1965.

Winnicott, D. W. (1962), 'Ego integration in child development', in *The Maturational Processes and the Facilitating Environment*, International Universities Press: New York, 1965.

Winnicott, D. W. (1963a), 'Communicating and not communicating leading to a study of certain opposites', in *The Maturational Processes and the Facilitating Environment*, International Universities Press: New York, 1965.

Winnicott, D. W. (1963b), 'Psychotherapy of character disorders', in *The Maturational Processes and the Facilitating Environment*, International Universities Press: New York, 1965.

Winnicott, D. W. (1963c), 'Morals and education' in *The Maturational Processes and the Facilitating Environment*, International Universities Press: New York, 1965.

Winnicott, D. W. (1971), 'Playing: Creative activity and the search for the self', in *Playing and Reality*, Basic Books: New York.

Wolf, E. S. (1983), 'Discussion of papers by Drs. Lichtenberg and Ornstein', in J. D. Lichtenberg and S. Kaplan (eds), *Reflections on Self Psychology*, Analytic Press: Hillsdale, N.J.

5 Mothers' attributions to their young children

Ruth C. Wylie

The research reported here involves looking at three mothers' verbal attributions to their young children during two 2½-hour sessions in a semi-naturalistic setting, an apartment within the laboratory.

As used in this research, the term 'attribution' means 'any statement made by a mother in the hearing of her child which makes some comment expressing and/or implying some behavioral and/or inner characteristic(s) of the child, whether current or more enduring' (Wylie, 1984, p. 1).

The goal of the research is to explore in an ethological way one of the many possible kinds of opportunities afforded to children to learn about themselves, i.e. to acquire self-conceptions. The protocol calls for observing mother and child behaviours when a stranger is present, when the mother is preparing to leave the child with the stranger and when she returns, when a 'doctor' is examining the child, and when the mother and child are eating, resting, doing a block task, reading a prescribed book, looking at pictures of babies expressing different emotions and interacting freely.

This chapter begins by outlining the broad background of theory and research underlying this study. Then theoretical reasons are given (1) for defining attribution in the way the term is used here, (2) for selecting certain aspects of each attribution to be coded and (3) for expecting certain descriptive outcomes.

An overview of theory and research on the self-concept shows that almost all the attention has been given to global or overall self-evaluation, sometimes called self-esteem or self-acceptance (Wylie, 1979). This is true despite the fact that all the theoretical definitions of self-concept state that it includes many descriptive dimensions.

In view of the disproportionate attention to overall self-regard, it is quite provocative that many of the theoretically predicted relationships between self-regard and other variables have turned out to be weak or null, whereas some stronger associations have been found in the much smaller number of studies of more specific aspects of self-conception, e.g. self-conceptions of schoolwork abilities (Wylie, 1979). These considerations suggested the idea of directing the present research primarily to the study of separate aspects of self-conception, while taking into account their respective evaluative connotations.

All personality theories, in attempting to account for behaviours, assign explanatory importance not only to self-conceptions and self-evaluations, but also to parental behaviours, including those which might influence the development of self-conceptions and self-evaluations during the child's first 5 years. (Some of these theories are considered in other chapters of this part of the book, e.g. in Pines's review of theories involving social mirroring, in Price's comments about the self's being formed by empathic encounters through a process of affirmation and suppression of innate components and in Harwood's allusions to Kohut's and Winnicott's views that human interaction is crucial in accurate mirroring and validation of the child's emerging talents, achievements and ambitions.) Additionally, Piagetian theorists such as Kohlberg (1969) have incorporated some comments on the development of self-conceptions into their general views about cognitive development. Actually, however, there is virtually no research literature explicitly directed to these issues.

Unexpected results of certain self-concept research using subjects older than 5 years suggest indirectly that influences during the first 5 years may be especially important. For example, race and socioeconomic status are *not* associated with self-regard (Wylie, 1979, Chapters 3 and 4), which led some researchers (e.g. Rosenberg and Simmons, 1972) to suggest that the level of self-regard developed in the early home life might be relatively immune to later influences.

Other examples of results suggesting the importance of early influences are (1) the frequent occurrence of self-favorability biases (Wylie, 1979, Chapter 12) and (2) the skew toward poor self-regard scores on several reliable instruments (e.g. Piers, 1969; Rosenberg, 1969). To account for such findings with older children and adults, it has been suggested that, during most children's earliest years, the relatively high frequency of parental praise and the relative lack of invidious comparisons might build up immunities to more modest or derogatory information about self encountered later in life.

In addition to *a priori* arguments for the special importance of parental behaviours for development of self-conceptions, one can cite Rosenberg and Simmon's finding that children aged 8 to 11 years have 'even greater faith in their parents' knowledge of their moral, intellectual, and aesthetic characteristics than in their own' (Rosenberg, 1979, p. 243). Most of these children reported that their mothers knew what they really felt and thought 'deep down inside', and that their parents would be 'mostly right' in what they would say about them.

Of the many ways by which parents could plausibly influence a child's self-conceptions (some of which are considered in Chapters 2, 3 and 4), the mother's use of language seems worthy of consideration. More particularly, the characteristics of what we call *maternal attributions* should reveal much concerning the opportunities the child has to learn self-descriptive and self-evaluative language. As said above, our brief, non-operational definition of maternal atribution is 'any statement made by a mother in the hearing of her child which makes some comment expressing and/or implying some behavioral and/or inner characteristic(s) of the child, whether current or more enduring'. (No assumption is made that the mother is consciously aware of what attribution she may be making, or even that she is intending to make any attribution at all. Nor does this phase of the study attempt to deal with whether the child recognises the mother's attributions in the same terms as the researchers see them.)

Some ideas about possibly relevant aspects of maternal language usage come from the arguments and research of Livesley and Bromley (Livesley and Bromley, 1973; Bromley, 1977a, 1977b). They contend that lay persons' 'personality theories' (which are presumably the partial bases for personal and interpersonal actions) are framed in terms of 'ordinary language'. Relevant to this, their analysis of children's free descriptions of self and others shows that 6-year-old children's descriptions tend to refer to peripheral behaviour categories, e.g. specific aspects of appearance, routine actions, actual incidents, life events, possessions, rather than referring to central categories such as traits, abilities, values, beliefs or attitudes (Bromley, 1977a, pp. 15–17). A trend toward the use of central categories occurs with age. Moreover, to the extent that the younger children employ a trait vocabulary, they tend to use vague, general terms at first, e.g. 'nice', 'kind' or 'naughty', with the trait vocabulary increasing in number and precision with age. Finally, the transition to young adulthood (Bromley, 1977a, p. 18) brings with it the use of more syntactical qualifying/organising terms (e.g. 'He is very patient with his children except when he has headaches').

Rosenberg (1979) also remarks that his younger subjects were 'more likely than the older to describe themselves in behavioral, moral, and specific terms' (p. 200).

These trends fit well with theory and research findings about children's general conceptual development and their use of language.

Students of child language have shown that adults spontaneously adapt their speech addressed to very young children in such ways as using short, uncomplicated sentences spoken clearly and slowly. Moreover, it has been demonstrated that a great deal of adult speech to babies and young children is in terms of the 'here and now' (Gleason, 1977, p. 204). Presumably, these features of adult language facilitate very young children's acquisition of language and conceptual behaviour at the level their developmental stage permits.

It follows from the above considerations that maternal attributions will be found to have certain characteristics. First, many of them will provide the child with an opportunity to acquire self-descriptive language mostly of a very specific sort, e.g. when the mother says, 'Yes, you do have one like this at home', or when she says 'Yes' in reply to the child's assertion 'I can hit him very hard'. Occasionally an attributional statement might summarise a number of instances of a particular kind of behaviour, thus providing the child with an opportunity to learn somewhat more abstract self-descriptive language. For example, the mother might say, 'She often plays with trucks' or 'I know you like hot dogs'. Only rarely would one expect to hear the mother making an attribution which summarises a wide range of instances in a much more abstract way, e.g. 'You have a good memory' or 'Aren't you generous?' In short, since the mother is expected to adapt her speech to the conceptual level of the child listener, few opportunities for directly learning more abstract self-relevant language are expected to occur when she is speaking to the child.

Also of interest is the lexicon of self-applicable words used by the mother to label the child's inner states and cognitive processes and his or her abilities, traits, identities and evaluative status. For example, such words as 'baby', 'big', 'careful', 'can', 'girl', 'honey', 'hungry', 'like' and 'remember' are included in the lexicon frequency counts.

It is contended above that research should focus more on the various dimensions or aspects of the self-concept than on overall self-regard. Accordingly, it is necessary to use a set of substantive categories of mothers' attributions by which one could classify these allusions to the children's behaviours, states and characteristics.

As described below, the mother's verbalisations are seen as attributing such behaviours/states/characteristics as needs, emotions, physical characteristics, competencies and cognitions. Of particular relevance to self-concept theory is the possibility that the mother will attribute not only cognitions regarding not-self, e.g. 'Yes, that is yellow', but also cognitions about self, e.g. 'You know what you like'. We wanted to see to what extent, even at this very early age, the child is given an opportunity to learn that she or he supposedly knows things about self.

When we first thought of the idea of maternal attributions, we had in mind what we now call explicit attributions. These are utterances which seem to be telling the child in so many words (i.e. literally) that one or more of the traits/states/characteristics in the substantive-category list describe(s) him or her. Two obvious examples are 'You're a tall boy' and 'I know you love your sister'.

However, close attention to the videotapes and transcripts soon made it obvious that many utterances which do not take an explicit form could nevertheless be offering important, self-relevant information to the child. For example, if the mother says 'Please set the table', this seems to imply that she considers the child competent to carry out this task. Or, if the child offers the mother a candy, and the mother says 'Thank you', she is implicitly attributing generosity. At the level of commonsense theorising, it seems obvious that we all convey and receive much self-relevant information in these implicit ways, possibly more than by explicit attribution.

Of course, classifying maternal statements as explicit or implicit attributions is a tricky business, involving a discomfiting amount of subjectivity. One way to cope with this would be to deal only with the most clear-cut explicit attributions. But, intuitively, all of us who have wrestled with this problem have felt that implicit messages are being sent, and they are plausibly very influential on self-concept development.

Although one purpose of this research was to avoid the usual practice of focusing solely on global self-regard, we were theoretically interested in (1) the extent to which maternal statements relevant to particular aspects of the child (e.g. cognitions, body characteristics) could be said to carry evaluative messages; (2) the distribution of evaluative levels of these messages; (3) the frequency with which maternal statements seem to direct evaluations to the 'whole child' as opposed to more limited aspects of the child; and (4) the distribution of evaluative levels of these 'whole child' attributions.

Our interest in this information stems partly from the common assumption of educators and clinicians that it is more educational and more emotionally salutary to direct attributions, especially negative ones, toward an aspect of the child rather than to the whole child.

In addition, we expected that 'aspect attributions' would greatly predominate, suggesting that, in the long run, 'overall self-regard' is plausibly determined more by many thousands of minute, specific, evaluatively tinged inputs than from global evaluative statements.

Moreover, in line with the findings concerning self-favourability (mentioned above), we expected to find a predominance of positive maternal attributions.

For a number of theoretical reasons, we considered it important to keep track of what occasioned the mother's attributional verbalisations. Were they intimately related to the child's behaviours/questions/comments; to another's behaviours/questions/comments; to situational characteristics; or to nothing discernible? With respect to this question, we expected to find that the mother was almost always relevantly monitoring the situation and the interaction.

We also expected to find that opportunities to learn specificity/abstractness of maternal attributional language would vary as a function of whether the language was occasioned by the child's behaviour/question/comment (where more specificity is to be expected) or by another's behaviour/question/comment (where more abstractness is to be expected). The latter should provide the child with an opportunity to learn more abstract self-relevant language. Moreover, we wanted to see whether evaluative levels of maternal attributions are related to type of occasion, e.g. whether positive evaluations are associated more often with child language than with child behaviour, or whether positive evaluations were associated more often with child behaviour/question/comment or with another's behaviour/question/comment.

It seems most meaningful to look at such cross-tabulations within each mother–child pair, which implies the need to analyse a large number of attributions per pair. This is one of our reasons for looking at the maximum available time sample for each of three pairs, as opposed to going immediately to shorter time samples on a larger number of pairs.

(Research is currently in progress to attempt to cross-validate some of the findings on a smaller time sample [35 minutes] taken from each of 35 additional mother–child pairs. In both the present study and the more extended one, the focus is on descriptive results applicable to all subjects, as opposed to an examination of individual differences and their correlates, or group differences, e.g. sex differences.)

Method

Subjects were three middle-class mothers and their children (two females, aged 32 and 33 months, and one male, aged 39 months) who participated in a larger study of depressed and non-depressed mothers at the Laboratory of Developmental Psychology, National Institute of Mental Health, Bethesda, Maryland. Each child had at least one sibling about 5 years older than she or he, and the mother was the child's primary caretaker. The three pairs were chosen from the files, and their videotaped records were transcribed and coded without knowledge of whether the mother had experienced periods of depression. Each pair interacted in an apartment within the laboratory, following a protocol calling for various kinds of activities, as listed at the beginning of this chapter.

Transcriptions were made of two 2½-hour sessions for each pair, and data analyses were made within each of the six sessions. The transcriptions included (1) mother's, other's and child's speech; (2) 'paralinguistics', e.g. facial expressions, laughing, crying, voice tones and gestures which could throw light on how to interpret verbalisations, especially on how to infer their evaluative levels; (3) information about the situation (e.g. phone rings, lunch time); (4) listing of general behaviours (e.g. mother fixing lunch, mother handing to child, child climbing into booster seat). The transcripts show all the above in correct time relationships to each other, i.e. whether they were concomitant and/or sequential.

Consistent with the purposes of the research described earlier in this chapter, a coding system was developed, which is fully described in a coding manual (Wylie, 1984). When applying the code, the coder frequently reviewed the videotape, especially if any questions rose as to alternative interpretations of the transcript.

Once a maternal attribution had been identified, it was coded with respect to what occasioned it; what opportunity it gave the child to learn self-descriptive language of varying degrees of specificity/abstractness; its temporal referent (a current occurrence or an enduring characteristic); the lexicon words it contained; its explicit/implicit nature; its evaluative level, and whether the evaluative coding was determined at least in part by paralinguistics; its direction toward the total person or just an aspect of the person; its substantive content. (Detailed intercoder reliability information is given in Wylie, 1984.)

Although not inspired by the theories discussed by Pines, Price and Harwood in other chapters of this book, our decisions to take account of occasions, paralinguistic behaviours and substantive referents of maternal verbal attribution seem consonant with the theories they consider.

Results and discussion

Space limitations necessitate selecting only certain results for presentation here. Information about separate dimensions is given first, cross-tabulations between dimensional scores later.

As already mentioned, the study was conceived, the coding system developed and the data analyses planned with the aim of ascertaining what descriptive statements about maternal attributions may be applicable to any mother, as opposed to examining possible individual differences and their correlates, or possible group differences.

Frequency distributions for separate dimensions

Number of attributions per session. These numbers range from 821 to 1093 (median, 912). Of course we have no way of knowing whether or how the child is processing and interpreting all this input. Nevertheless, it seems clear that, even if many allusions are lost on the child, considerable self-referent learning *may* be going on during each session. Considering the various substantive referents of attributions, one sees a picture emerging of the child's being subjected to a gentle, incessant fall of variously coloured sand grains (the colours representing the various substantive categories of the attributions). Most of the grains are very small, i.e. specific or instantial; but they gradually pile up into appreciable drifts of various colours. An analogous point may be suggested regarding the possible formation of 'overall' self-regard from the incessant input of evaluations attached to a wide variety of particular, substantively limited attributions.

Occasion. For each attribution, the coder is allowed to check either 'no discernible occasion', one type of occasion (out of eight listed on the code sheet) or a combination of two types of occasion. This yields thirty-seven possible types of occasion coding for any one attribution. In all six sessions, attributions associated with no discernible occasion are infrequent (the range across sessions is 0.5 to 4.7 per cent of all attributions; median, 1.2 per cent). This clearly supports the hypothesis that the mothers monitor interpersonal interactions and/or the general situation, and they do not speak 'out of the blue', as it were. Among the thirty-seven possibilities, the five most common types are: child comment only (40.1–56.5 per cent; median, 46.6 per cent); child behaviour only (7.6–17.9 per cent; median, 11.2 per cent); child comment and child behaviour combined (7.8–17.1 per cent; median, 11.2 per cent); situation only (6.9–13.6 per cent; median, 10.6 per cent); child question only (0.7–14.3 per cent; median, 2.0 per cent). Obviously there is considerable similarity across subjects with respect to what occasions maternal attributions.

Opportunities to learn self-descriptive language. The commonest occurrence is a maternal verbalisation which provides an opportunity to acquire very specific self-descriptive language (39.9–60.2 per cent; median, 48.0 per cent of all coded maternal verbalisations). Much less frequent are maternal verbalisations providing the opportunity to learn somewhat abstract or quite abstract self-descriptive language (0.2–9.8 per cent; median, 4.8 per cent and 1.7–5.3 per cent; median, 1.8 per cent, respectively). These trends are strongly in the hypothesised direction and are in agreement with previous studies of general maternal language used in mother–child conversations.

Of considerable theoretical interest is the fact that many maternal utterances which we identify as attributions contain no opportunity for the child to learn self-relevant language (37.7–48.3 per cent; median, 45.8 per cent). For example, the mother may simply say 'No' when the child picks up a forbidden object, giving the child a clear conception that she or he is violating prohibitions. Or she may say, 'Yes, that one is bigger than the other one', confirming the accuracy of the child's size judgment, but involving no child-relevant language.

Lexicon words. For the three pairs of subjects, the numbers of lexicon words used by the mother in the two sessions combined are 457, 665 and 663; and the total numbers of different words are 60, 79 and 109 respectively. Obviously, each child was afforded many opportunities to learn vocabulary words concerning his/her inner states and/or processes and/or characteristics; traits, physical or psychological; evaluative status; name, gender and developmental status. Lexicon words were grouped into twelve categories: (1) abilities/competencies; (2) cognitions; (3) desires/wants/

needs/emotions; (4) developmental level; (5) evaluations; (6) gender; (7) permission/requirements (including ability and permission); (8) physical characteristics; (9) state of health; (10) willingness combined with ability; (11) name; (12) miscellaneous. Within each of the six sessions, lexicon words classified in Category 3 (desires/wants/needs/emotions) are most frequent, i.e. they rank first in each session. The median ranks across six sessions for the next most common categories of lexicon words are: cognitions (median rank 2.5); name address (median rank 3.2); abilities/competencies (median rank 3.8). Obviously, there is considerable similarity across subjects regarding the sorts of lexicon items to which each is exposed.

Explicit/implicit characteristics of attributions. According to our view of attributional information contained in maternal verbalisations, such information is implicit in the verbalisation more often than it is explicit. For six sessions, the ratios of number of implicit to explicit attributions range from 1.8 through 6.9 (median, 3.4). If our rationale and procedure for inferring implicit attributions are defensible, it is obvious that much of importance would be missed by excluding implicit attributions.

Evaluative levels of the attributions. Each attribution was rated as being highly positive, positive, neutral, mixed message (+/−), negative, highly negative or not able to be classified evaluatively. Detailed guides for assigning evaluative ratings were developed, taking into account (1) the mother's evaluation words, e.g. 'right', 'good'; (2) her paralinguistic behaviours, e.g. facial expression or voice tone; and (3) what we agreed to be the desirability or undesirability of the attributed behaviour, state or characteristic.

Regarding our agreed-upon assumptions about evaluative connotations, we take for granted, for example, that mothers prefer knowledge to ignorance, competence to clumsiness, carefulness to carelessness, generosity to stinginess, cleanliness to messiness, etc.; but that a mother's attributions of drives, emotions or preferences carry no positive or negative evaluations unless the context or her paralinguistic behaviours suggest otherwise.

For reasons explained in the introduction, we expected positively evaluated attributions to be most frequent. When attributions coded high positive and positive are combined into one positive category, the range of percentage values across six sessions is 50.2 to 65.3 per cent (median, 59.2 per cent). When attributions coded negative or high negative are combined, the range is 16.6 to 28.2 per cent (median, 25.4 per cent). Percentages of mixed-message attributions range from 5.0 to 13.7 per cent (median, 6.4 per cent). Percentages of attributions coded evaluatively neutral range from 4.5 to 19.7 per cent (median, 6.7 per cent).

Direction of attributions. Considerable importance has been assigned to the issue of whether a maternal attribution *is directed to the total person or to some aspect of the person* (see Wylie, 1984). Generally, it is regarded as more educational and more emotionally salutary to direct attributions, especially negative ones, to an aspect of the person. Thus, it is interesting to note that relatively few attributions are judged to be directed toward the total child (6.7–14.8 per cent; median, 9.8 per cent). These include name address, developmental level, gender, family-relationship status and terms of endearment or the opposite, as well as occasional statements such as 'You're terrible' or 'I love you'.

Substantive categories. The fifty substantive categories (some with separately coded subheadings) were mostly derived inductively from attempts to code the first subject's transcript. When a subsequent transcript alluded to something not codable by the original list, an appropriate new category was introduced, and the earlier transcript(s) were inspected for possible oversights of that substantive category.

The category list of main substantive headings includes: aesthetic appreciation; age/developmental level; aggressive/hostile/violent/rough behaviour; appearance; attention; carefulness/cautiousness; cleanliness (non-personal); power/ability to make acceptable choices; cognitions; competencies; compliance; consistency across behaviour situations; dawdling; decisiveness; desires/wants/needs; eating behaviours; emotions/feelings; family/friendship status; forbidden behaviour; gender; generosity/helpfulness/altruism; good/bad behaviour (general); health; honesty; imitation; lovability; manners/politeness; ownership status (possessions); name identity; patience; physical characteristics; play (general ability to); preferences/likes/interests; pretending (behaviour/ability); quietness; racial status; religious status; routines; sense of humour; sex-typed behaviour; silliness; socioeconomic status; socialising behaviour; speech and language characteristics; tantrum behaviour; teasing; trying/not trying.

The numbers of different main substantive categories for two sessions combined are 38, 42 and 39 for the three mothers. For each mother, the number for two sessions combined exceeds the number for either of the two separate sessions. Thus, the use of an extended time period (5 hours versus 2½ hours) allowed more different substantive-category allusions to emerge, affording a more accurate estimate of the number of topics which might occur in such mother–child interactions. Obviously, even when interacting with such young children, the mothers cover many different substantive areas.

For each subject, the three most frequent substantive categories of attribution are: cognition (as in perceiving, knowing, understanding, remembering) (18.0–38.6 per cent of all attributions; median, 31.4 per cent); power/ability to make acceptable, appropriate choices (inferred from offering a choice or agreeing/disagreeing with one) (12.5–23.9 per cent; median, 18.4 per cent); and competencies (as in building, table setting, climbing, etc.) (7.1–22.1 per cent; median, 9.7 per cent).

Of particular interest to self-concept theories are the large percentages of attributions of cognition which impute to the child *knowledge about self* (17.9–39.6 per cent of all attributions of cognition; median, 23.6 per cent). The mothers seem to imply that their children have quite a few rudiments of self-knowledge, even at this young age.

Cross-tabulations between variables

Of the many possible cross-tabulations between coded aspects of attributions, perhaps the most interesting are those involving the evaluative tone of the attributions.

Consider first the relationship between evaluation levels and the following two types of occasion: (1) child behaviour/comment/question involved or (2) child behaviour/comment/question not involved in occasioning the maternal attribution. In all six sessions, larger percentages of *negatively* evaluated attributions occur when the occasion involves child behaviour/comment/question (differences in percentages between the two classes of occasion range from 7.3 to 26.4 per cent; median, 19.7 per cent). Also, larger percentages of mixed-message attributions occur when the occasion involves child behaviour/comment/question (differences in percentages between the two classes of occasion range from 1.7 to 13.4 per cent; median, 5.0 per cent). It appears that the child's chances of avoiding negative and mixed attributions are greater if the mother's child-relevant remarks are occasioned by the situation and/or by a person other than the child. (There is no tendency for percentages of positively evaluated attributions to differ between these two types of occasion.)

Next, one can separate the above occasions involving the child into (1) those involving child's comment/question (but *not* behaviour); (2) those involving *behaviour* (and, for some of these occasions, comment or question as well). For each of six sessions, percentages of *positive* attributions are larger when occasioned *only* by child language (differences in percentage values range from 2.3 to 26.2 per cent; median, 19.8 per cent). Conversely, for each of six sessions, percentages of *negative* attributions are larger when occasioned by child *behaviour*, even if language is also involved in the occasion. Differences in percentage values between the two classes of occasion range from 6.5 to 37.6 per cent; median, 15.8 per cent. This suggests that the mother's attention may be drawn more by child language deserving favourable comment, i.e. the mothers may be missing opportunities to reinforce behaviours positively. Perhaps many acceptable child behaviours are taken for granted since they are expected and do not 'demand' maternal verbalisation to the same degree that the child's comments or questions do.

For each session, of the few attributions directed toward the total person, the majority were coded as evaluatively positive (59.5–74.2 per cent; median, 62.6 per cent), the minority as negative (8.1–24.5 per cent; median, 13.1 per cent). The negative ones comprised almost entirely the use of name address (coded 'total person') in the context of a negative attribution concerning an aspect of the child. Thus, contrary to the assumptions of some professionals, it is rare in this study for the total child to be evaluated, in the sense of being called a wonderful, good, bad or terrible boy, girl or person.

Only seldom did the occurrence of paralinguistics in the transcript play any part in assigning an evaluative code level to an attribution (6.4–13.0 per cent of all attributions; median, 9.0 per cent). In five out of six sessions, negative attribution codings are more frequently determined by paralinguistics than is the case with positive ones. Differences in percentage values for the five sessions range from 4.6 to 12.1 (median, 10.7). Thus, when making attributional remarks, mothers display negatively toned non-verbal behaviours in connection with negative remarks more often than they display positively toned non-verbal behaviours in connection with positive remarks.

In the case of either positive or negative attributions, any determining paralinguistics are at least in agreement with the general direction of the evaluation suggested by the mother's words, precluding confusion on the child's part. By contrast, when paralinguistics enter into determining a mixed-message coding, an ambiguous evaluation is necessarily created. This sort of ambiguity occurs with some frequency for mixed-message attributions (17.8–37.5 per cent; median, 28.5 per cent). The question remains as to the psychological import this sort of information has for the child.

Evaluative level is also associated with the substantive content of the attributions. Table 5.1 shows this for the most common substantive categories. Here, conceptually related categories are combined as indicated and are listed from those most frequently positive to those most frequently negative. The median percentage values across session are based on the evaluative category which was most common for each session. For example, the median of 78.4 per cent positive for cognition and related categories is based on all six sessions because, for attributions of cognition, positive evaluations are the commonest kind of evaluation in every session. In a contrasting example, the median of 45.2 per cent positive for name identity is based on the three sessions in which the commonest evaluative level associated with name address was positive, and the median of 38.9 per cent negative for name identity is based on the three other sessions in which the commonest evaluative level for name was negative.

TABLE 5.1   *Median percentage values of evaluative levels of attributions in the most frequent substantive categories in six sessions*

Substantive category	Evaluation levels			
	Positive	Neutral	Mixed	Negative
Family/friend status	100.0(6)			
Lovability	100.0(5)		52.6(1)	
Ownership status	100.0(5)	50.0(1)		
Choice ability/power[a]	97.0(6)			
Competencies	83.2(6)			
Cognitions[b]	78.4(6)			
Socialising behaviour[c]	63.4(6)			
Body characteristics[d]	56.5(1)	50.2(4)		45.0(1)
Name identity	45.2(3)			38.9(3)
Choice ability/power[e]	42.1(2)			48.5(4)
Motivation/emotion[f]		68.0(6)		
Carefulness				86.2(6)
Forbidden behaviours				91.8(6)

The numbers in parentheses indicate the number of sessions on which the median value is based. See text for explanation.
[a] Inferred from mother's offer of choice
[b] Cognition and related categories including aesthetic appreciation; language imitation, usage and communicativeness; pretending ability
[c] Socialising behaviours and related categories of compliance; generosity/helpfulness/ nurturance; social play
[d] Includes characteristics of body and body parts, personal appearance, health, gender
[e] Inferred from mother's acceptance/rejection of child's choice
[f] Includes attention; desires/wants/needs/emotions/feelings; preferences/likes/interests; trying/ not trying; tantrums; aggressive/hostile/violent/rough behaviour

In part, the evaluative ordering of the substantive categories in Table 5.1 depends artificially on constraints imposed by the coding system. For example, one can easily find instances of the mother's offering the child a choice (considered to imply a positive attribution concerning the child's power/ability to choose acceptably). However, there is no way of discerning systematically when the mother might reasonably have offered a choice, but has failed to do so (implying attribution of inability or powerlessness to choose acceptably). Therefore, 'choice offered' attributions are overwhelmingly positive (a very few being coded 'mixed message' because, for example, they offer a choice, then immediately retract the offer). As another example, an *a priori* decision was made to assign a neutral evaluative coding to substantive references to motivational/emotional states unless context and/or paralinguistics warranted a positive, negative or mixed code. Hence, for all six sessions, the commonest evaluative coding of attributions of motivational/emotional states is neutral.

However, the evaluative level of most substantive attributions is free to vary. Among these, it is interesting to observe that mothers' comments on choices already made by children are not very favourable (in contrast to the overwhelmingly favourable codings for 'choice offered'). In the same vein, mothers' comments on carefulness and forbidden behaviours are over-whelmingly negative, even though there were opportunities to comment on carefulness and self-restraint regarding forbidden behaviours. In other words, mothers were probably missing opportunities for positive reinforce-ment of carefulness, self-restraint and child-initiated choices of behaviour.

In Chapter 3, Price (citing Berkowitz) contends that 'low self-esteem results either from experiences of failure to achieve a sense of power and competence through expressing innate talents and abilities or from a sense of not having this innate self, valued and idealised'. Possibly relevant to these theoretical ideas are the present findings that, for each mother, the three most frequent substantive topics of attributions – cognitions, competencies and ability/power to choose acceptably (as inferred from offered choice – are predominantly coded in the positive evaluative direction, as seen in Table 5.1.

Finally, I include one interesting set of cross-tabulations not involving evaluative levels. As predicted, the child's opportunity to learn self-relevant language of varying degrees of specificity tended to vary as a function of whether the maternal attribution was occasioned only by something the child said and/or did, or only by what another (adult) person said and/or did. In five out of six sessions, greater percentages of the child-occasioned attributions involved a maternal verbalisation affording the child an opportunity to learn highly specific language. Differences in percentage values for six sessions range from 0.9 to 45.4 (median, 24.2). In five out of six sessions, greater percentages of other-occasioned attributions involve a maternal verbalisation affording the child an opportunity to learn somewhat abstract language (a generalisation across specific instances, e.g. 'She likes to play with trains'). Differences in percentage values across six sessions range from −0.3 to 46.7 (median, 27.2).

However, in only four out of six sessions did greater percentages of other-occasioned attributions afford an opportunity to learn very abstract language. Differences in percentages across six sessions range from −2.5 to 10.8 (median, 1.2). On the other hand, this comparison is somewhat misleading, since terms of endearment comprise most of the abstract attributive statements occasioned by the child and these would not tend to occur in an attribution occasioned by another person.

All in all, the results of this preliminary intensive study of three mother–child pairs provide an encouraging basis for believing that the newly developed code is appropriate for studying those aspects of maternal attributions which theory suggests are relevant to the development of the self-concept. Thus far it appears plausible that a larger-scale study will continue to support certain general statements concerning such characteristics of maternal attributions as their language characteristics, their explicit/implicit nature, their evaluative level, their substantive contents, what occasions them and the interrelationships among attributive dimensions.

Acknowledgment

This work was supported by the National Institute of Mental Health, Bethesda, Maryland, and by the John D. and Catherine T. MacArthur Foundation Award on the Transition from Infancy to Early Childhood, Chicago. The following persons made insightful and thought-provoking contributions to the development of the coding system used in this and related studies: Ona Brown, Rochelle Levin, Peggy Jo Miller, Gail Owen, Olive Quinn, Morris Rosenberg, Susan Staib, Sally Wall and Marian Yarrow.

References

Bromley, D. B. (1977a), *Personality Description in Ordinary Language*, Wiley: London.

Bromley, D. B. (1977b), 'Natural language and the development of self', in H. E. Howe, Jr. (ed.), *Nebraska Symposium on Motivation*, vol. 25, pp. 117–67.

Gleason, J. B. (1977), 'Talking to children: Some notes on feedback', in C. E. Snow and C. A. Ferguson (eds), *Talking to Children: Language Input and Acquisition*, Cambridge University Press: London, pp. 199–205.

Kohlberg, L. (1969), 'Stage and sequence: The cognitive-developmental approach to socialization', in D. A. Goslin (ed.), *Handbook of Socialization Theory and Research*, Rand McNally: Chicago, pp. 347–480.

Livesley, M. J.. and Bromley, D. B. (1973), *Person Perception in Childhood and Adolescence*, Wiley: London.

Piers, E. C. (1969), *Manual for the Piers-Harris Children's Self-Concept Scale (The Way I Feel about Myself)*, Counselor Recordings and Tests: Nashville, Tenn.

Rosenberg, M. (1965), *Society and the Adolescent Self-image*, Princeton University Press: Princeton, N.J.

Rosenberg, M. (1979), *Conceiving the Self*, Basic Books: New York.

Rosenberg, M. and Simmons, R. B. (1972), *Black and White Self-esteem: The Urban School Child*, American Sociological Association: Washington, D.C.

Wylie, R. C. (1979), *The Self-concept: Theory and Research on Selected Topics* (rev. ed.), vol. 2, University of Nebraska Press: Lincoln, Neb.

Wylie, R. C. (1984), *Characteristics of Mothers' Verbal Attributions to Their Children in a Semi-naturalistic Research Setting: Guide to Identifying and Coding Maternal Attributions*, Unpublished manuscript, Laboratory of Developmental Psychology, National Institute of Mental Health, Bethesda, Maryland.

Part II

Childhood – the conservation and evolution of self

6 Identity constancy in children: Developmental processes and implications

Frances E. Aboud and Diane N. Ruble

The question of how we know that we remain ourselves despite the transformations we undergo in appearance, thoughts, values and behaviours has intrigued philosophers and psychologists for many years. It is the question of personal identity constancy. Perceptions of continuity and consistency of different aspects of self are believed to be crucial to emotional and interpersonal stability. Mental health problems associated with a fragmented personality and identity loss are widely recognised (Erikson, 1968). Even experimental procedures have been used to demonstrate that when their identifiable features are masked by covering the head and body with nondescript material, people tend to act in unusual ways, often asocial and irresponsible (Dipboye, 1977). One interpretation is that loss of identity is an unpleasant experience, and that the bizarre behaviour is an attempt to restore some individuality. It was therefore with considerable surprise that developmental psychologists discovered how fragile was the young child's identity constancy.

Our goal in this chapter is to examine the developmental sequence of perceptions of constancy and possible cognitive precursors. A clear understanding of these issues has remained elusive, in part because of the large variation in the ages at which different types of constancy (e.g. gender vs. ethnic constancies) are attained. By integrating the findings across different forms of constancy and thereby examining the relationship between the demand of the task and the age of acquisition, we hope to shed some light on questions originally raised by philosophers, i.e. what cognitions underlie a sense of continuity (Rorty, 1976; Waterbor, 1972).

The phenomenon of constancy

The term 'constancy' refers to a consistent identification of oneself or another, as well as to the understanding that identification is consistent. In a typical study of constancy, children are told about or see the transformation of a person's appearance or behaviour and then are asked about the person's identity. Constancy is indexed by the use of the same label that was applied before the transformation, a label not based on the changeable attribute of appearance or behaviour. One procedure for assessing the global identity constancy of other people, for example, involves a standard picture of a person along with a number of test pictures showing transformations of that person (e.g., shirt colour, eyeglasses) and distractor pictures of another person. The question asked about each test picture is 'Is he the same or different?' or less ambiguously 'Is it he or is it someone else?' Regardless of the question, children younger than 9 years of age mistakenly identified the standard man dressed differently as someone else on 25 per cent of the trials (Aboud, 1984; Novack and Richman, 1980). Thus, for example, a father may unwittingly produce this reaction in his young child if he shaves off his beard.

Other procedures involve in-depth interviews. Peevers (in Chapter 10 of this volume), for example, asked children of different ages to 'tell what you are like'. Responses were coded in terms of four indicators of continuity, meaning the sense of self existing over time. The results showed that only six out of sixteen 6-year-olds referred in any way to consistency, primarily by referring to activities in which they habitually engaged. A few spoke of past and future events. It is clear from this research that continuity is not a salient feature of the young child's self-concept.

Another more elaborate procedure, developed by Chandler *et al.* (see Chapter 7), involves presenting children with stories in which the main character changes in some dramatic way. For example, Scrooge in Dickens's *A Christmas Carol* changes overnight from a stingy, mean man to a warm philanthropist. Children are asked if Scrooge is still the same person he was before Christmas, and why or what is the connection between the old and the new Scrooge. Of major interest here is how children justified the constancy, given that Scrooge had already been identified. No information was provided about age differences in how many children accepted the idea of constancy in the first place. Interestingly, the implication is that even the youngest (preoperational) children accepted this presupposition, although the procedure may not have allowed an alternative. Preoperational children made the connection in terms of observable and physical qualities, whereas most concrete operational children referred to the continuity of certain essential internal qualities or to the material causal connection between selves. Many children in the formal operational stage also perceived a causal connection, but more imaginatively reinterpreted the past identity in light of its effect.

Much of the research focuses on the constancy of a specific aspect of identity, such as gender, ethnicity, ability and trait, as opposed to personal identity as a whole. The typical procedure is the one developed by Slaby and Frey (1975) to study gender constancy. Along with questions of identity ('Which is the boy? girl?') and continuity ('When you grow up will you be a mommy or a daddy?'), there are two questions related to consistency of gender despite transformations of appearance and behaviour. These are: 'If you wore [opposite-sex] clothing, would you be a boy or a girl?' and 'If you played [opposite-sex] games, would you be a boy or a girl?' Similarly, Semaj (1980) asked, 'If a Black child wore a blond wig, would she be a Black or a White?' These studies indicate that perceptions of constancy of various sorts develop after early childhood. There are variations in the age at which constancy develops, however, depending on the target (self or other), the attribute (gender, ethnicity, ability, trait) and the mode of transformation (verbal or visual).

First, with respect to target, the research suggests that self-constancy is expressed before awareness of another's constancy. For example, children say that they will remain the same gender even though they wear opposite-sex clothing at a younger age than they say that someone else would (e.g. Gouze and Nadelman, 1980; Marcus and Overton, 1978).

Second, with respect to attribute, gender constancy seems to develop earlier than ethnic constancy and personality constancy. Gender constancy is present in 4- and 5-year-olds in many samples (Gouze and Nadelman, 1980; Ruble *et al.*, 1981; Slaby and Frey, 1975), whereas ethnic and personality constancy do not appear until 8 or 9 years of age (Aboud, 1984; Aboud and Skerry, 1983; Semaj, 1980; Rotenberg, 1982; Ruble and Flett, in preparation).

Third, when the mode of transformation is visual, constancy is expressed later than when the transformation is described verbally as a hypothetical event. For example, gender constancy appears at 8 years when children see a photograph of themselves with a picture of opposite-sex clothing superimposed on it, and at 4 to 6 years when they are asked the question, 'If you wore boys' clothes, would you be a girl or a boy?' (Gouze and Nadelman, 1980; Marcus and Overton, 1978).

Steps involved in the development of constancy

Taken together, the different findings suggest that there may be several steps or levels involved in the development of constancy. In this section, we postulate three such steps based on the discrepancies observed across studies varying target, attribute and mode of transformation. We also suggest possible cognitive precursors associated with these steps.

Expectations of sameness

The mode-of-transformation results suggest that an early form of constancy appears when the procedure involves a verbal, hypothetical event as opposed to a visual transformation. Results from the former procedure fit Piaget's (1968) view that identity constancy was a preoperational structure because it required the understanding that a particular quality was conserved, but did not require an understanding of quantity conservation. He considered it akin to the identity form of the water beaker test, i.e. that the water poured from one beaker into a differently shaped beaker was the same water even though its outline looked different (Hooper, 1969). Interestingly, it seems that identity conservation is not necessarily acquired before equivalence, or quantity, conservation. Studies comparing responses of children aged 5 to 9 years on the identity and the equivalence forms of the conservation test found no significant differences (Aboud, 1984; Marcus and Overton, 1978). Both were acquired around the age of 8 years. Thus, there is no strong evidence that person constancy should be a preoperational acquisition on account of its similarity to identity conservation.

Anticipated conservation may represent a closer analogue of preoperational identity constancy. The anticipated conservation procedure requires the child to predict whether a quantity such as volume would be the same *if* the operations were to be performed. The transformation is hypothetical, as it is in the Slaby and Frey (1975) gender constancy test. According to Acredolo and Acredolo (1980), anticipated conservation precedes the perceived form of conservation. Two factors may account for this. One is that one's understanding of conservation is not challenged by misleading perceptual information and so perhaps need not be as strong. The second is that some children (18 per cent in Acredolo and Acredolo, 1980) do not even anticipate a change in the water level. Thus, their conservation answer was based on the assumption that no perceptual transformation took place. Similarly, the 'anticipation' form of the constancy test may demonstrate preoperational constancy in the form of an expectation that people remain constant, though the expectation is too weak to withstand disconfirming perceptual data.

Another interpretation of this early form of constancy is that a child may give a constancy answer based on the belief that some identity marker, such as shoes or name, still exists. Support for this kind of 'categorical' basis of constancy is provided by Emmerich *et al.* (1977), who found that when 6- and 7-year-olds gave a constancy response to the transformation test, their reasons most often referred to an external identity marker such as a name that remained the same despite a clothing change. Similar findings are reported by Chandler *et al.* (in Chapter 7). The increase in this type of justification between 4 and 7 years of age suggests that children are viewing the constancy task as a categorisation one. Assigning people to categories based on their physical features has been shown to develop during this period (Gelman *et al.*, 1985; Vaughan, 1963). Furthermore, once a person is placed into a social category, he or she is ascribed an array of features and is thought to be rigidly tied to that category (Kuhn *et al.*, 1978). This tendency has often been noted in children under the age of 7 years. Thus, constancy in this case may be viewed as a product of the rigidity of the category rather than as truly an understanding of identity. In fact, one might predict that some children who manifest constancy at 4 or 5 years might lose it at 6 or 7 if there is a breakdown in the rigid application of categories without a concomitant increase in understanding identity.

The recent findings that gender constancy is associated with understanding the distinction between reality and the hypothetical may also be viewed as supporting a possible categorisation basis for early constancy (Martin and Halverson, 1983; Trautner, 1985). For example, adding a modifier to the basic question – 'If you wore boys' clothes would you for real be a girl or for real be a boy?' – appears to emphasise a focus on the gender category rather than the transformation and results in a higher percentage of constancy responses (Martin and Halverson, 1983). Thus, the emphasis on the category may minimise the chance of being misled by the transformation.

Although findings that gender constancy occurs before 'person' constancy support the notion of a categorical basis, findings of the relatively late development of ethnic constancy, another kind of category, suggest that other factors are involved. Such factors are considered next with respect to a second step in the development of constancy.

Perceived consistency of essential features

The second step appears to be associated with a deeper understanding of personal identity, including the ability to identify someone as the same despite perceived transformations. The relatively later development of gender constancy given visual/perceptual transformations supports this description and is consistent with Kohlberg's (1966) view that constancy requires concrete operational thought. The description of this second step is also consistent with the relatively later development of personal identity constancy, in that generally this task can only be accomplished by going beyond an external, category marker.

Three skills seem to appear around the ages of 7 to 9 years, which may be viewed as cognitive precursors of this second step. One is the ability to infer features beyond what are merely observable. A second skill is to focus on essential features, those that are central to the person, gender, ethnicity or trait. The third is the understanding that such features are stable and consistent. By examining each of these skills in greater detail, we hope to clarify which factors are associated with particular constancy tasks and whether these skills have a development order.

Inferring non-observable features. The first skill is the ability to infer features of the person rather than relying on the category or the observable qualities associated with that category. Constancy seems to mature as one moves from focusing on only one perceptual feature to several perceptual features, and from perceptual to inferred psychological features. Presumably several features are less likely to change in their entirety than is one feature, and internal features are more enduring and less dependent on situational variability than are external features. Two types of indirect evidence support the importance of these two advances in the development of step 2 constancy. First, conservation is thought to entail both factors, and it appears to precede this more advanced form of constancy in children (e.g. Aboud, 1984; Marcus and Overton, 1978; Semaj, 1980). Second, early studies on what formed the basis of self-identity (Guardo and Bohan, 1971; Mohr, 1978) found age differences in children's reports of what features would have to change for them to become another person. There was a shift in focus from one external attribute at 7 years, to several external behaviours constituting a unit at 9 years, and finally to an internal attribute at 12 years (Mohr, 1978). This skill in particular may account for the emergence of self-constancy before other constancy since it appears that internal states are acknowledged in self prior to others (Keasey, 1977). Similarly, ethnic constancy may develop late because the internal attributes of ethnic members remain unnoted longer than they do for other person concepts (Aboud and Skerry, 1983).

One might well ask whether step 2 constancy is simply the social form of conservation or is something different. The data suggest that the two are not highly enough correlated to be considered equivalent. Conservation in fact precedes constancy in that children who evidence constancy have already acquired conservation (Aboud, 1984; Marcus and Overton, 1978; Semaj, 1980). Thus, constancy seems to require certain skills involved in conservation, such as going beyond observables to infer internal qualities, but also requires some additional skill.

Focus on essential features. The second skill is the selection of features importantly associated with a person or category. Regardless of the number or location of the focused attributes, certain ones will be better identifiers. Aboud and Skerry (1983) found that 5- to 8-year-olds, unlike adults, did not describe themselves in terms of essential attributes, and those they mentioned were external rather than internal. Children who spontaneously mentioned essential and internal attributes were more likely to express constancy. Similarly, Chandler *et al.* (see Chapter 7) found that around 8 years of age children began to abandon their arguments that constancy was due to the persistence of observable and physical parts and to focus instead only on central and essential parts. These authors suggested that essentialist arguments were more sophisticated because they required the hierarchical organisation of a person's attributes along a continuum of centrality, with stability only in the most essential ones being necessary for constancy.

This skill, more than the previous one, may account for the variation in age of acquisition of gender, ethnic and personality constancy. Once the child understands the notion of centrality, the application of the skill seems to depend largely on the acquisition of social knowledge about people and categories. We know that knowledge about gender in particular is acquired early. Lewis and Brooks-Gunn (1979) reported that the identification of oneself on the basis of age and sex cues begins at 15 months of age. Gender labels are applied correctly by most 3-year-olds (Ruble and Ruble, 1982), and associated attributes are learned in the following year or two. Social knowledge about ethnic groups and about their associated and essential attributes develops later (Aboud and Skerry, 1983). Personality traits and abilities also enter late into the child's base of knowledge (e.g. Peevers and Secord, 1973; Rholes and Ruble, 1984). If social knowledge is necessary for the child to determine which attributes are essential, then the essential attributes of gender might be understood before the essential attributes of ethnicity or personality.

Perception of stability and consistency. The third skill involves understanding that certain features are stable over time and consistent across situations, enabling the child to predict that a person's ability, for example, will be exhibited at other times (stability) if it has appeared once and that it will be exhibited in other situations (consistency). This skill requires a perception of the equivalence of behaviours and attributes over time and situation.

Adults appear to assume high stability and consistency for their internal attributes (Eisen, 1979). Young children, however, do not. Several studies suggest that although 5-year-olds can make internal attributions of traits, and can predict their temporal stability, they do not assume cross-situational consistency until after 7 to 8 years of age (Barenboim, 1981; MacLennan and Jackson, 1985; Rholes and Ruble, 1984; Rotenberg, 1982; Ruble and Flett, in preparation). This developmental progression parallels the acquisition of first expectations of sameness (step 1) and then constancy despite a transformation (step 2).

The ability to recognise consistency would seem to involve at least two processes. First, the equivalence of behaviours must be noted even though they appear at different times and embedded in various contexts. One way to test for perceived equivalence is to measure recall of the behaviours. Waters and Waters (1979) argued that the memory trace for behaviours perceived in different contexts would increase in strength as a function of frequency of exposure only if the behaviours were perceived as equivalent. If they were perceived as different because of their different contexts, then the memory trace would not be strengthened with exposure. The results of this research indicated that 7-year-old children were poorer than 10-year-olds at recalling behaviours presented in various contexts (comparable to the consistency problem) but were no different at recalling behaviours presented in the same context at different times (the stability problem) (Aboud, 1982; Waters and Waters, 1979). Thus, younger children do not note the equivalence of stimuli embedded in different contexts.

Second, recognising consistency would seem to involve making cross-situational comparisons. Barenboim (1981) claims that comparisons across time, situations and persons allow one to integrate behaviours. He found that this step peaked around 8 and 9 years. Similarly, recent research has indicated that young children (5 to 6 years) tend not to integrate trait-related behaviours observed in the past with recently observed behaviour, when the behaviours are separated in time, even to form a simple impression (Rholes and Ruble, 1986). Furthermore, even though pre-schoolers can observe and compare themselves with their peers, they tend not to integrate this information into their self-knowledge until much later, at approximately 7 to 9 years (Aboud, 1985; Ruble *et al.*, 1980). Thus, it appears that the integration of comparative information occurs after early childhood and, by facilitating an understanding of the consistency of certain attributes, is likely to contribute to step 2 identity constancy.

Summary. Step 1 constancy – expecting one's identity to remain constant – is an important step in understanding constancy. However, to demonstrate a clear, unassailable understanding of constancy, the child should indicate the ability to attend to, but not be misled by, a featural transformation. Those who correctly answer the anticipation form of the constancy test demonstrate a constancy expectation, but it is not clear whether they are overcoming the change in appearance or simply minimising its salience. Those who correctly answer the perception form of the constancy test (step 2) demonstrate that they can overcome the misleading change in appearance. To explain the discrepancy in the age at which these two steps are passed, we would have to say that the expectation is acquired at 4 or 5 years, but that it succumbs to perceptual challenges before 8 or 9 years. A similar resolution of the discrepancies found in the role-taking research (Higgins, 1981) has been more useful than simply claiming that the construct is not unitary. Many role-taking tests did not present the child with a contrary view and require that his or her own view be salient, but controlled, when inferring the other's perspective (Higgins, 1981). When only one of those two components was salient in the test, the child appeared to role-take during the preoperational stage. Similarly, when only the identity is salient, but the transformation is not, constancy may appear during the preoperational stage.

Inferred qualities viewed as foundations for later, different qualities

A possible third step in constancy involves the recognition that certain inferred qualities determine later and different qualities. This has been described by Chandler *et al.* (see Chapter 7), who extended the study of constancy to preadolescents and adolescents. This cognition is viewed as more sophisticated than the essential cognition because it is not tied to attributes that maintain a similarity between the original person and that person's transformed self. The connection can be maintained even though many internal and essential features have changed, because the connection is a causal one. So far this work has been applied only to personality transformations; but it has interesting implications for gender and ethnic constancy.

Implications of constancy for development

In what way does the acquisition of constancy affect other social developments? How does the lack of constancy affect young children? These questions are important if we are to understand the role of constancy in the child's overall self and social development.

There are a number of possible motivational and behavioural consequences of acquiring identity constancy (Kohlberg, 1966). Once an attribute of oneself or others is perceived as relatively stable and consistent, the personal significance of that attribute and of any single instance of the attribute changes. For example, attributes perceived as constant are likely to lead to expectations about future behaviours. Furthermore, constancy provides a reason to seek information about another's trait-related behaviours that is not available to preconstancy children – to predict and thereby control, in part, future interaction.

Although there has been little research examining links between the developmental changes in constancy and associated motivations and behaviours, the available evidence is generally consistent with these predictions. The most direct evidence concerns gender constancy. Slaby and Frey (1975) found that preschool boys (but not girls) at advanced stages of gender constancy spent more time selectively attending to a same-sex model in a movie than boys at lower stages. They also subsequently played with the same-sex model's toy significantly longer than children who had seen opposite-sex children play with the toy (Ruble *et al.*, 1981). In contrast, children at low levels of gender constancy showed no effect of the sex of the models (see Ruble and Stangor, 1986, for a review of other related studies).

One noteworthy implication of the relationships that have been observed is that the attainment of gender constancy may represent a point where change in sex-stereotypic behaviour would be possible if children viewed same-sex models exhibiting non-stereotypic behaviour. Indeed, greater flexibility of stereotypes has been shown in children at advanced levels of gender constancy (Urberg, 1982). Similarly, ethnic constancy appears to be related not to own-group preference but to a less biased evaluation of one's own and other groups, i.e. to less ethnocentrism (Clark *et al.*, 1980; Semaj, 1980).

In the area of achievement, several studies are consistent with the conclusion that the development of constancy-related cognitions has important motivational implications. For example, only children perceiving ability as a stable characteristic seem to show indications of learned helplessness after receiving consistent failure at a task (Rholes *et al.*, 1980; Rholes and Jones, 1985). Children also tend not to use social comparison information in self-evaluation of ability until this age (Aboud, 1985; Nicholls, 1978; Ruble *et al.*, 1980). Until the relative constancy of ability is recognised, more unstable elements of self-evaluation, such as absolute performance, may be more salient or preferable. Finally, children's increasing appreciation of the comparative basis and long-range significance of performance has implications for self-esteem. Indeed, several studies indicate a drop in ability-related self-esteem or self-confidence between the early and middle-elementary school years (Frey and Ruble, 1985; Parsons and Ruble, 1977; Stipek, 1984). Moreover, in one observational study in classrooms, perceiving ability as a general dispositional characteristic was associated with a drop in overt statements about performance, suggesting that such topics of conversation had become sensitive or anxiety-provoking (Frey and Ruble, 1985).

Finally, future research might consider the implications of the lack of identity constancy in young children. Possibly young children are not as severely handicapped as adults by a lack of constancy because their self-concept is not as central to behaviour and emotions. On the other hand, there seems to be some need for constancy which children may obtain through social rather than cognitive means. That is, they may rely on the perception of significant others' recognition of their constancy (Erikson, 1968). It is also conceivable that children possess more constancy than the studies indicate, basing it on features not tested such as their name, their heart or their parents. The phenomenon of constancy raises interesting questions about how children cope with something adults take for granted.

References

Aboud, F. E. (1982), 'The effect of context variability on recall and the inference of traits', unpublished manuscript, McGill University.

Aboud, F. E. (1984), 'Social and cognitive bases of ethnic identity constancy', *Journal of Genetic Psychology*, 145, pp. 217–29.

Aboud, F. E. (1985), 'Children's application of attribution principles to social comparisons', *Child Development*, 56, pp. 682–8.

Aboud, F. E. and Skerry, S. A. (1983), 'Self and ethnic concepts in relation to ethnic constancy', *Canadian Journal of Behavioural Science*, 15, pp. 14–26.

Acredolo, C. and Acredolo, L. P. (1980), 'The anticipation of conservation phenomenon: Conservation or pseudoconservation', *Child Development*, 51, pp. 667–75.

Barenboim, C. (1981), 'The development of person perception in childhood and adolescence: From behavioral comparisons to psychological constructs to psychological comparisons', *Child Development*, 52, pp. 129–44.

Clark, A., Hocevar, D. and Dembo, M. H. (1980), 'The role of cognitive development in children's explanations and preferences for skin color', *Developmental Psychology*, 16, pp. 332–9.

Dipboye, R. L. (1977), 'Alternative approaches to deindividuation', *Psychological Bulletin*, 6, pp. 1057–75.

Eisen, S. V. (1979), 'Actor–observer differences in information inference and causal attribution', *Journal of Personality and Social Psychology*, 37, pp. 261–72.

Emmerich, W., Goldman, K. S., Kirsh, B. and Sharabany, R. (1977), 'Evidence for a transitional phase in the development of gender constancy', *Child Development*, 48, pp. 930–6.

Erikson, E. H. (1968), *Identity, Youth and Crisis*, Norton: New York.

Frey, K. S. and Ruble, D. N. (1985), 'What children say when the teacher is not around: Conflicting goals in social comparison and performance assessment in the classroom', *Child Development*, 56, pp. 550–562.

Gelman, S., Collman, P. and Maccoby, E. E. (1986), 'Inferring properties from categories vs. inferring categories from properties: The case of gender', *Child Development*, 57, pp. 394–404.

Gouze, K. R. and Nadelman, L. (1980), 'Constancy of gender identity for self and others in children between the ages of three and seven', *Child Development*, 51, pp. 275–8.

Guardo, C. J. and Bohan, J. B. (1971), 'Development of a sense of self identity in children', *Child Development*, 42, pp. 1909–21.

Higgins, E. T. (1981), 'Role-taking and social judgment: Alternative developmental perspectives and processes', in J. H. Flavell and L. Ross (eds), *Social-cognitive Development: Frontiers and Possible Futures*, Cambridge University Press: Cambridge.

Hooper, F. H. (1969), 'Piaget's conservation tasks: The logical and developmental priority of identity conservation', *Journal of Experimental Child Psychology*, 8, pp. 234–49.

Keasey, C. B. (1977), 'Young children's attributions of intentionality to themselves and others', *Child Development*, 48, pp. 261–4.

Kohlberg, L. A. (1966), 'A cognitive-developmental analysis of children's sex-role concepts and attitudes', in E. E. Maccoby (ed.), *The Development of Sex Differences*, Stanford University Press: Stanford, Calif.

Kuhn, D., Nash, S. C. and Brucken, L. (1978), 'Sex-role concepts of two- and three-year-olds', *Child Development*, 49, pp. 445–51.

Lewis, M. and Brooks-Gunn, J. (1979), *Social Cognition and the Acquisition of Self*, Plenum: New York.

MacLennan, R. N. and Jackson, D. N. (1985), 'Accuracy and consistency in the development of social perception', *Developmental Psychology*, 21, pp. 30–6.

Marcus, D. E. and Overton, W. F. (1978), 'The development of cognitive gender constancy and sex role preferences', *Child Development*, 49, pp. 434–44.

Martin, C. L. and Halverson, C. F. (1983), 'Gender constancy: A methodological and theoretical analysis', *Sex Roles*, 9, pp. 775–90.

Mohr, D. M. (1978), 'Development of attributes of personal identity', *Developmental Psychology*, 14, pp. 427–8.

Nicholls, J. G. (1978), 'The development of the concepts of effort and ability, perception of academic attainment and the understanding that difficult tasks require more ability', *Child Development*, 49, pp. 800–14.

Novack, T. A. and Richman, C. L. (1980), 'The effects of stimulus variability on overgeneralization and overdiscrimination errors in children and adults', *Child Development*, 51, pp. 55–60.

Parsons, J. E. and Ruble, D. N. (1977), 'The development of achievement-related expectancies', *Child Development*, 48, pp. 1075–9.

Peevers, B. H. and Secord, P. F. (1973), 'Developmental changes in attribution of descriptive concepts to persons', *Journal of Personality and Social Psychology*, 27, pp. 120–8.

Piaget, J. (1968), *On the Development of Memory and Identity*, Clark University Press: Barre, Mass.

Rholes, W. S., Blackwell, J., Jordan, C. and Walter, C. (1980), 'A developmental study of learned helplessness', *Developmental Psychology*, 16, pp. 616–24.

Rholes, W. S. and Jones, M. L. (1985), 'Developmental trends in vulnerability to learned helplessness as related to the acquisition of stable dispositions concept', Manuscript submitted for publication.

Rholes, W. S. and Ruble, D. N. (1984), 'Children's understanding of dispositional characteristics of others', *Child Development*, 55, pp. 550–60.

Rholes, W. S. and Ruble, D. N. (1986), 'Children's impressions of other persons: The effects of temporal separation of behavioural information', *Child Development*, 57, pp. 872–878.

Rorty, A. O. (1976), *The Identities of Persons: Introduction*, University of California Press: Berkeley, pp. 1–15.

Rotenberg, K. J. (1982), 'Development of character constancy of self and other', *Child Development*, 53, pp. 505–15.

Ruble, D. N., Balaban, T. and Cooper, J. (1981), 'Gender constancy and the effects of sex-typed televised toy commercials', *Child Development*, 52, pp. 667–73.

Ruble, D. N., Boggiano, A. K., Feldman, N. S. and Leobl, J. H. (1980), 'A developmental analysis of the role of social comparison in self evaluation', *Developmental Psychology*, 16, pp. 105–15.

Ruble, D. N. and Flett, G. (in prep.), 'Developmental changes in seeking information for self-evaluation'.

Ruble, D. N. and Ruble, T. (1982), 'Sex stereotypes', in A. G. Miller (ed.), *In the Eye of the Beholder*, Praeger: New York.

Ruble, D. N. and Stangor, C. (1986), 'Stalking the elusive schema: Insights from developmental and social psychological analyses of gender schemas', *Social Cognition*, 4, pp. 227–261.

Semaj, L. (1980), 'The development of racial evaluation and preference: A cognitive approach', *Journal of Black Psychology*, 6, pp. 59–79.

Slaby, R. G. and Frey, K. S. (1975), 'Development of gender constancy and selective attention to same-sex models', *Child Development*, 46, pp. 849–56.

Stipek, D. J. (1984), 'Young children's performance expectations: Logical analysis or wishful thinking?' in J. Nicholls (ed.), *The Development of Achievement Motivation*, JAI Press: Greenwich, Conn.

Trautner, H. M. (1985), 'The significance of the appearance–reality distinction for the development of gender constancy', Paper presented at the Biennial meeting of the Society for Research in Child Development, Toronto.

Urberg, K. A. (1982), 'The development of the concepts of masculinity and femininity in young children', *Sex Roles*, 8, pp. 659–68.

Vaughan, G. M. (1963), 'Concept formation and the development of ethnic awareness', *Journal of Genetic Psychology*, 103, pp. 93–103.

Waterbor, R. (1972), 'Experiential bases of the sense of self', *Journal of Personality*, 40, pp. 162–79.

Waters, H. W. and Waters, E. (1979), 'Semantic processing in children's free recall: The effects of context and meaningfulness on encoding variability', *Child Development*, 50, pp. 735–46.

7 The conservation of selfhood: A developmental analysis of children's changing conceptions of self-continuity

Michael Chandler, Michael Boyes, Lorraine Ball and Suzanne Hala

The *object* of this chapter relates to the general process of identity formation, and our particular *aim* is to explicate the usual developmental course by which young persons come to achieve a stable sense of selfhood. The *orientation* which we have followed in pursuit of this purpose has been cognitive-developmental in its focus, and the specific *target* of our remarks will be the changing ways in which young persons, characterised by different levels of intellectual maturity, differently undertake to warrant their own sense of numerical identity. The thrust of our argument is that the maintenance of a satisfactory sense of numerical identity first demands access to some successful means of warranting personal continuity in the face of inevitable change and, second, that the level of one's current cognitive-developmental maturity sets limits upon the particular form of warranting practice that can be called into play in an effort to interpretively rationalise the differences which set apart one's past and present selves. Our work has consisted of attempts to outline a formal typology of such alternative continuity warrants, to specify the nature of their dependence upon supportive cognitive competencies and, through a series of empirical studies, to evaluate the match between this proposed developmental model and the actual struggles toward identity achievement which we have observed in our subjects.

To elaborate upon this skeletal outline, we will begin by clarifying what we intend by the somewhat cryptic notion of numerical identity and by justifying the importance which we have attached to it as a linchpin in the developmental train toward the achievement of a stable sense of identity. These definitional matters are followed by a line of argument in which we differentiate five alternative strategies for potentially warranting one's numerical identity. Further, we conceptually link these contrasting warranting practices to their necessary cognitive prerequisites. The chapter ends with a summary of our empirical efforts to test the descriptive adequacy of both this proposed typology and the developmental model which, we propose, ties these separate warranting practices to particular stages in the course of cognitive development.

Numerical identity

Since this chapter is primarily about matters of numerical identity, and since such notions are little spoken of in the contemporary literature on self-concept formation, it is important to begin by being clear about how we intend the term. By 'numerical identity' we mean to refer to the self in its diachronic aspect and to address the potentially problematic question of whether or not, across time, persons can be said to be identical with themselves (Perry, 1975). That which makes the matter of numerical identity appear at first to be something of a misnomer is that we typically reserve the term 'identity' for discussions about the potential similarities which obtain between two different things – the extreme case being something like the degree of synchronic similarity to be found between two identical twins or two peas in a pod. Numerical identity, in contrast, refers to single things in their historical aspect and involves a judgment as to whether, as one looks backward or forward along the tunnel of time, individuals can be said to be in any sense identical with themselves.

Although there is nothing in the available research literature to signal its importance, the assumption that numerical identity is foundational to the concept of selfhood is fundamental to Western thought and can be traced back at least as far as Locke (Wiggins, 1971). Within more recent history, William James (1910) has argued, for example, that 'consciousness of personal sameness' is an essential characteristic of the self; as did Erikson, who equated a sense of identity with an 'inner continuity and sameness' and 'a subjective sense of continuous existence' (also see Rosenberg, Chapter 13). These arguments pertain not to simple sameness, but to the idea that knowledge of one's history as one's own is a necessary condition for selfhood (Harré, 1979). Any single notion of self at any given moment is fundamentally nonsensical unless it can be linked in some fashion to one's own past (Gergen and Gergen, 1983). Numerical identity, consequently, represents a necessary condition over which the terms 'self' and 'person' are reasonably allowed to operate (Shotter, 1984; see also Luckman, 1979). The importance of continuity in grounding the notion of selfhood is nicely captured in B. Reed Whittmore's poem 'The Mother's Breast and the Father's House':

> Your seemingly small mind is in truth an enormous
> warehouse devoted to documenting and buttressing the persistence of
> you
> Stuff with the dust of decades is in it
> books, faces, tears, fears,
> loves, hates, games, names
> all in relation to
> you

colors, odors, textures, travel incredible distance with us
even the weakest among us is a sort of god of preserving of that which
would be wholly trivial if it were not ours
which is why we lecturers are sometimes uneasy as we travel the circuit
patting sweet selves on the head
the selves on closer inspection turn out to be gobble-ups. . . .
yet at least there remains the inexhaustible fact of the self
it does not leave
it persists
its essence is that it persists

(*New Republic*, 4 Dec., 1971)

If, as the previous remarks are intended to suggest, having a functionally adequate self-concept is predicated upon the achievement of some conceptual means of warranting the continuity of successive forms of the self, then a number of central but unanswered questions follow: How and when are the abilities to formulate such a continuous personal history acquired? Do such autobiographical accounts come in more than one variety? Are differences in such warranting practices age-graded or dependent upon certain cognitive-developmental prerequisites? What are the consequences of failure to maintain such a coherent account and to successfully redeem one's numerical identity in the face of inevitable personal change? Shortly, attention will be turned to the presentation of empirical findings which provide answers to some of these important questions by suggesting that the different ways in which persons undertake to justify matters of numerical identity do in fact vary as a function of their cognitive-developmental status. Before presenting these results, however, it will be necessary to consider in some detail the range of possible ways in which persons might, in principle, reasonably undertake to justify their own or others' numerical identity and to organise these alternative warranting practices into some coherent typology.

A proposed typology of possible continuity warrants

In the broadest possible sense, all serious claims for numerical identity reduce to the specification of some means of assigning continuous meaning to one's self or to others. The variable ways in which this task may be accomplished hinge upon the sorts of answers that are supplied to a nested series of questions concerning the *what*, *where* and *how* of such meanings. Once settled, the alternative answers to these orienting questions yield the three general classes and the half-dozen separate varieties of possible continuity warrants which together form the typology of alternative warranting practices to be discussed. The first juncture in this hierarchicalised network of possibilities concerns the basic question of precisely *what* meaning is taken to be (see Figure 7.1). Here the available options centre upon the question of whether meanings are understood to be in need of *discovery* or *invention*, that is, whether they are to be *found* or *made*. By adopting the first of these alternatives one commits one's self to a 'realistic' or 'copy theoretic' epistemology (Chandler and Boyes, 1983), according to which continuous personal meaning must be ferreted out of the constantly shifting details of one's life. By contrast, commitment to a more constructivistic epistemology, according to which meanings are understood to be the product of human invention, results in a radical re-reading of the issue of numerical identity. When meaning is taken to be made rather than found, the task of establishing one's numerical identity becomes a matter of personal inventiveness, reflected in the ability to reconstruct one's past interpretively in light of one's present. This first choice point in the decision tree depicted in Figure 7.1 is meant, then, to distinguish between what are described as *constructivistic* or best-explanation warrants for numerical identity and a residual class of four additional *realistic* warranting practices to be discussed in the paragraphs which follow.

Subordinate to the choice between such broad epistemological commitments concerning the reality status of meaning, there arises, for those individuals who favour the realist assumption that personal meanings are matters of literal discovery, the subsidiary question of precisely *where*, in the details of one's life, such meanings are likely to be found. Here the possible alternatives break along the lines of the usual form/content dichotomy, with some individuals committed to a search for the continuous meaning in their lives among imagined, change-resistant *features or attributes* of themselves, while others search for such invariants among the *relations or forms* which are thought to hold between such attributes at different points in time. This bifurcation point yields the two remaining general classes of continuity warrants referred to in the present typology as *simple similarity* and *relational* arguments. Finally, the option remains of searching at a high or low degree of abstractness. How *concrete* or *abstract* a set of features or relations one searches for in one's bid to warrant one's numerical identity represents, then, the third and final distinction in that *what*, *where* and *how* sequence.

Projected as a linear sequence, this hierarchical arrangement of alternative answers to questions of continuous personal meaning results in a series of five distinct approaches to the task of warranting claims to numerical identity. Individuals who make use of what we have termed *simple similarity arguments* glean evidence of their numerical identity by searching for more or less concrete personal descriptors which they imagine to have somehow stood outside the ravages of time to persist unchanged from past to present. Depending upon the level of abstraction of the shared parts which such individuals have in mind, the warranting strategies which they adopt are described here as: (1) *simple inclusion* or (2) *essentialist*

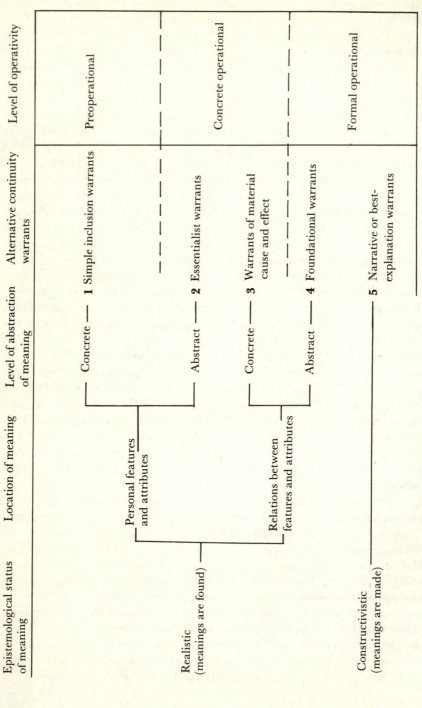

FIGURE 7.1 *Typology of alternative continuity warrants*

warrants. By contrast, individuals who share these same realistic assumptions about the objective status of meaning, but who search for evidence of persistent personal sameness in what we have referred to as enduring relational forms, tend to rest their case for numerical identity upon what we will term: (3) *concrete warrants of material cause and effect* or (4) *foundational warrants of relatedness*. Finally, by exclusion, individuals who see meaning-making as a subjective or constructivistic affair employ what we have referred to as (5) *narrative or best-explanation warrants*.

Presenting a more detailed version of this five-part typology of possible continuity warrants, and linking their use to the kinds of underlying cognitive competencies which support them, will be the agenda of the sections which follow.

Realistic, content-centred, simple similarity arguments

1. Simple inclusion warrants

Simple inclusion warrants are predicated upon a synchronic conception of the self in which one's various concrete or physicalistic parts are treated as integers that add up to a sum; understood as a static assemblage or simple composite collection. Changes, when they do occur, can only be understood within this interpretive context as the simple addition or deletion of parts. Within such a framework of understanding, numerical identity is guaranteed if and only if a 'sufficient' number of the features descriptive of one's self at time A are assumed to stand outside the process of change and to make up a wholly retrievable or non-reducible part of the list of features descriptive of one's self at time B. While the precise number of such features which would need to be held in common at points A and B in order to guarantee such a sense of continuity is indeterminate, it would seem to follow that with the passage of increasingly long intervals of time, A would come to play a diminishing role in B, and the felt persistence of the self would be placed in increasing jeopardy (Campbell and Richie, 1983).

2. Essentialist warrants

Essentialist warrants, like continuity claims based on connections of simple inclusion, also support a belief in the continuity of selfhood by pointing to the persistence of one's parts. The critical difference between these two forms of claimed connectedness lies in the fact that essentialist arguments, unlike simpler inclusion claims, presuppose that the component parts of one's self are stratified along some dimension of increasing centrality, and that the most abstract, deep-lying or definitional of these attributes are the most critical in guaranteeing continuity. The strategic advantage afforded by such essentialist arguments is that assumed similarities need no longer depend upon some major transmigration of one's parts from one point in development to another. Disruptive changes in surface attributes can be discounted easily, and only the possibility of changes within the essential core of the self need pose any real threat to one's sense of continuity.

Maturational warrants, or what Flavell (1982) refers to as modification arguments, represent a minor variation on the theme of essentialist arguments generally. Within arguments of this type, continuity of selfhood is secured through vague allusions to some maturational or epigenetic growth model, according to which the present and the as-yet-unrealised future are understood to have been wholly preformed, lying in wait within one's past like a tightly wound spring. Although identity warrants of this calibre might be easily mistaken for other more complex and adequate foundational accounts which employ abstract relational claims, they fall short of this standard through their effective 'spatialisation' of time. In such accounts, the future is understood to have only that sort of unknowability characteristic of distant and as-yet-unexplored regions of space (Shotter, 1984). All that will be revealed in the fullness of time is already present, though for the moment simply hidden from human knowledge. It is this feature of maturational accounts which reduces them to a subspecies of the realistic, content-centred, simple similarity arguments discussed in this section.

Realistic relational arguments

In contrast to the simple similarity arguments just outlined, the general class of relational warrants to be detailed below are not grounded in any assumption regarding shared parts. Instead, numerical identity is vouch-safed by referencing some pattern of material relations seen to link present and previous ways of being. That is, for those who employ such relational arguments, personal continuity in the face of change is made possible on the grounds that one's past is understood to be somehow foundational to, and lawfully productive of, one's present. In short, such continuity arguments amount to the claim that one is numerically identical with one's self for the reason that one's past is taken to be the progenitor of one's present. Such relational arguments are more sophisticated than simple similarity claims, in that they tolerate the possibility of wholesale personal change. Nevertheless, they retain a common commitment to the assumption that the shared meanings which constitute the grounds for numerical identity actually reside, and require literal discovery, within the material course of ontogenetic events.

The dimension of difference which divides the categories of (3) *material cause and effect* and (4) *foundational arguments*, which make up this general class of relational warrants, concerns their contrasting readings of the possible alternative means by which earlier ways of being can be understood to stand in some parenting relation to later ways of being. Of the two, arguments of mechanical cause and effect, to be discussed in the section which follows, are seen to be the more concrete, on the grounds that the effects of such mechanical causes are commonly understood to be entirely contained within their prior causes (Bunge, 1979).

3. Arguments of mechanical cause and effect

By the notion of mechanical cause, which embeds the more familiar ideas of efficient and material cause (Overton and Reese, 1973), and which is referred to by Campbell and Richie (1983) as a relation of non-implicative mediation, we mean to reference those external forces or material mediators which operate as non-logical prerequisites, bridges, scaffolds or other enabling support structures to serve as means for the accomplishment of effects which are not their own. When turned to the purpose of warranting claims of personal continuity, such relations of mechanical determination take the form of arguments to the effect that one is what he or she is today precisely because of some externally induced and passively suffered cause-and-effect sequence which led one mechanically, albeit continuously, from past to present. Such mechanical causal accounts, then, undertake to justify personal continuity in the face of change by demonstrating that outcomes, of the sort represented by the person one has become, satisfy some general, trans-individual, covering law to the effect that, under conditions of the type specified, outcomes of the sort that have obtained typically occur. In short, by such accounts the person that one has become is understood to be the effect of that which the person once was.

4. Foundational relations

As suggested above, relations of mechanical causation, with their distinct mark of externality and 'leading-to' type of determination (Freeman, 1984), constitute only one of a range of possible determinant relations. As Smedslund (1969) points out, certain forms of mental processes are best understood to be related, not by mechanical causation, but by logical forms of determination (Shotter, 1984). Such continuity warrants, which Flavell (1982) refers to as 'relations of implicative mediation', effectively argue that the person that one has become is somehow continuous with the person one once was because it is logically impossible to be the latter without having previously been the former. One's prior self, in effect, is held to be a logical prerequisite for one's present self, which is in turn understood to hierarchically integrate one's past. Cognitive developmental theorists, such as Piaget and Kohlberg, employ such foundational forms of determination in explaining the relations between the various stages which they postulate, as do individuals who persuasively argue their own numerical identity on the grounds that the person they once were logically requires that they be as they now are. The crucial difference, then, between arguments of mechanical cause and effect and other foundational arguments generally is that the former involve the specification of hypothesised relations between logically *independent* phenomena, which must be shown empirically to succeed one another, whereas the latter involve what are argued to be logically *dependent* phenomena (Shotter, 1984).

Constructivistic arguments

5.   *Narrative or best-explanation warrants*

Each of the four alternative warranting strategies outlined in the preceding sections, while differing in other details, nevertheless share the common realistic assumption that the persistent meanings which serve to guarantee numerical identity are in some literal sense discoverable features of actual experience. By contrast, persons who adopt, instead, what we have labelled narrative or best-explanation warrants hold to the contrasting and more constructivistic view that meaning is *made* rather than *discovered*. Such individuals consequently understand the task of justifying their own numerical identity as one of imaginatively constructing an interpretive framework in which both their past and present can be brought within a common horizon or context of meaning (Shotter, 1984). One's self-concept, in these terms, becomes something like the narrative centre of gravity of one's own unfolding autobiography (Dennett, 1978), and the warranting of numerical identity is understood as equivalent to the writing of a presentist historiography (Buss, 1979), in which the past is creatively reconstructed in ways that make the present comprehensible. By recasting the past in terms of the present, such accounts, then, enable their authors to embed their earlier self-concepts within an enlarged narrative which makes them retrospectively intelligible. In this sense, such narratives satisfy the same criterion to which all successful theories are held, that is, they not only replace, but subsume, their predecessors (MacIntyre, 1977).

Cognitive competence and the use of alternative warranting strategies

Although the typology outlined above lists strategies for warranting numerical identity as though they were simple alternatives, there is, in the way in which they are framed, the clear suggestion that some of these alternatives are more mature or adequate than others and that access to their use is dependent upon different cognitive prerequisites. Continuity arguments of the narrative or best-explanation variety, with their tacit commitment to a constructive epistemology, obviously rest upon the sorts of reflective abstractions which Piaget (1970) took as definitional for his stage of formal operational thought. Similarly, what we have labelled as foundational warrants, while suffering a quality of lingering realism, require for their use the ability to consider relations of relations or similarities of form, which again are thought to be defining features of formal operations. By contrast, continuity warrants of the essentialist and cause-and-effect variety seem to involve only first-order abstractions and the navigation of only shallow hierarchies, of a calibre well within the competence range of concrete operational thinkers. Finally, children whom Piaget would classify as preoperational, because of the concrete, transductive and non-relational form of their thought, should be reduced to the use of concrete, realistic arguments of simple inclusion. The study to be reported in the following pages represents an attempt (a) to apply this proposed typology of alternative continuity warrants and (b) to evaluate the expectation that the kinds of warranting practices which people invoke in justifying assumptions of numerical identity vary as a function of their level of cognitive-developmental maturity.

Method

Using a standard battery of Piagetian procedures, we selected fifty young persons representative of preoperational, concrete operational and formal operational levels of cognitive development. These subjects were then asked to consider the continuity or lack of continuity in the lives of various well-known fictional characters, portrayed as having come through periods of radical personal change. John Locke's story of the prince and the cobbler who exchanged memories; Scrooge on Christmas Eve and Christmas Day; and Jean Valjean as galley-slave and factory owner were among the characters whose stories were presented and whose continuity of selfhood was inquired into. The responses of our subjects were transcribed and segmented into discrete explanatory accounts. These explanatory statements were then coded as to which of the five alternative continuity warrants they expressed.

Results

The coarsest cut which can be made through these data concerns the contrast in performance between those subjects who did and those who did not demonstrate formal operational competence. As can be seen from an inspection of Table 7.1, better than half of the formal operational subjects based their best claims for persistent personal identity on what we have termed foundational and narrative continuity warrants. Specifically, they most frequently argued that the story characters continued to be themselves, not because certain of their earlier concrete parts or relations stood outside the ravages of time, but because personal pasts were seen to be capable of being narratively reconstructed in light of the present. By contrast, all of the preoperational and concrete operational subjects based their claims for continuity on one or another of the four alternative forms of realistic argument detailed above. In particular, all of the preoperational subjects employed arguments of simple inclusion and based their claims for continuity upon the literal persistence of manifest and material parts (i.e. 'It's still Scrooge because he is still wearing the same clothes', or 'He still has the same looks'). In the views of these young subjects, persons are the same from one time to another precisely because the mosaic formed by their physicalistic attributes is seen to be sluggish and subject to only piecemeal, quantitative change. So long, then, as the differences noted were neither too sweeping nor qualitative in character, continuity was guaranteed for these preoperational subjects on the grounds that more bits and pieces remained the same than changed.

TABLE 7.1   *Type of continuity warrant by level of cognitive competence*

Level of operativity	Alternative continuity warrants		
	1. Simple inclusion	*2. Essentialistic 3. Cause and effect*	*4. Foundational 5. Narrative*
Pre-operational (n = 12)	12		
Concrete operational (n = 17)	5	12	
Formal operational (n = 18)		8	10

χ^2 (4 *df*) = 45.1; $p < 0.001$

By contrast, the concrete operational subjects most often abandoned such simple inclusion warrants and argued instead that individuals persist in being themselves because of the presence of some deep-lying core of essential sameness or because the person that they have become was seen to be the material effect or causal consequence of their former selves. By these lights, Scrooge was seen either to have had hidden within him some necessary kernel of goodness which simply germinated overnight or as having been frightened into a superficial change in self-serving strategies.

Finally, as already suggested, a majority of our formal operational subjects rejected both simple similarity and relational arguments in favour of more foundational or best-explanation warrants, in which the former lives of these story characters were narratively reconstructed in light of knowledge of the sorts of persons they had later become. Thus, Scrooge's former tight-fisted ways were, for example, reinterpreted in light of his morning-after behaviour as a necessary staging ground for his later bent-over-backwards brand of philanthropy.

In summary, we offer several general conclusions. First, we would hope to have persuaded you that any coherent conception of selfhood must necessarily make provision for judging persons to be somehow numerically identical despite the inevitability of personal change. Second, we would like you to have been convinced that a series of progressively more mature and adequate solution strategies are available with which one might hope to win such continuity arguments. Finally, we hope to have provided some evidence leading you to share with us the view that the use that can be made of these various continuity warrants is related to, and perhaps dependent upon, specific levels of cognitive-developmental maturity.

While these results speak primarily to the normative course by means of which persons successfully manage threats to the numerical identity of others, parallel research efforts have demonstrated that similar solution strategies are employed by persons in settling continuity questions about their own lives. These results also suggest that young persons sometimes find themselves between stages, which leaves them without a successful means of justifying their own continuity across time. We see in such lapses a conceptual means of accounting for certain of the crises of identity characteristic of adolescents and other risk groups. Our ongoing research has turned to an examination of the human consequences of these and other failures to maintain a stable sense of one's own numerical identity.

Acknowledgment

This research was supported by a grant (No. 410-83-1049) from the Canadian Social Sciences and Humanities Research Council and by a grant from the Youth Employment Program of the Ministry of Labour, Province of British Columbia. The authors wish to thank David Soy, Jim Carney, and the students and staff of Osler Elementary and Killarney Secondary Schools for their help and cooperation. Very special thanks are due to Susan Calvert and Sherry Henderson for their thoughtful assistance and diligent efforts in the collection, scoring and analysis of these data.

References

Bunge, M. (1979), *Causality and Modern Science*, Dover Publications: New York.

Buss, A. (1979), *A Dialectical Psychology*, Irvington: New York.

Campbell, R. L. and Richie, D. M. (1983), 'Problems in the theory of developmental sequences: Prerequisites and precursors', *Human Development*, 26(3), pp. 156–72.

Chandler, M. and Boyes, M. (1983), 'A developmental analysis of children's changing conceptions of selfhood', Paper presented at the meeting of the International Society for the Study of Behavioral Development, Munich.

Dennett, D. C. *Brainstorms*, Bradford Books: Montgomery, VT.

Flavell, J. H. (1982), 'Structures, stages and sequences in cognitive development', in A. Collins (ed.), *Minnesota Symposia on Child Psychology*, vol. 15, Erlbaum: Hillsdale, N.J.

Freeman, M. (1984), 'History, narrative, and life-span developmental knowledge', *Human Development*, 27, pp. 1–19.

Gergen, K. and Gergen, M. (1983), 'Narratives of the self', in T. R. Sarbin and K. E. Scheibe (eds), *Studies in Social Identity*, Praeger: New York, pp. 254–73.

Harré, R. (1979), *Social Being: A Theory for Social Psychology*, Blackwell: Oxford.

James, W. (1910), *Psychology: The Briefer Course*, Holt & Co.: New York.

Luckman, T. (1979), 'Personal identity as an evolutionary and historical problem', in M. von Cranach *et al.* (eds), *Human Ethology*, Cambridge University Press: Cambridge.

MacIntyre, A. (1977), 'Epistemological crisis, dramatic narrative, and the philosophy of science', *The Monist*, 60(4), pp. 453–72.

Overton, W. F. and Reese, H. W. (1973), 'Models of development: Methodological implications', in J. R. Nesselroade and H. W. Reese (eds), *Life-span Developmental Psychology: Methodological Issues*, Academic Press: New York.

Perry, J. (1975), *Personal Identity*, University of California Press: Berkeley.

Piaget, J. (1970), 'Piaget's theory', in P. Mussen (ed.), *Carmichael's Manual of Child Psychology*, vol. I, Wiley: New York.

Shotter, J. (1984), *Social Accountability and Selfhood*, Blackwell: Oxford.

Smedslund, J. (1969), 'Meanings, implications, and universals: Towards a psychology of man', *Scandinavian Journal of Psychology*, 10, pp. 1–15.

Wiggins, D. (1971), *Identity and Spatio-temporal Continuity*, Blackwell: Oxford.

8 The meaning and development of identity

Daniel Hart, Julie Maloney and William Damon

Over the past thirty years, the meaning and development of personal identity has increasingly come under the scrutiny of philosophers and psychologists. Philosophers have been particularly interested in identifying what dimensions of the individual provide the sense of sameness into the future (e.g. Williams, 1970). The concept of personal identity is important to philosophers because, as Parfit (1971) has pointed out, questions of morality and self-interest depend upon individuals having a sense of identity. When an individual makes a decision that sacrifices immediate gratification for later benefit, the underlying assumption is that he or she will be the same person in the future, and therefore he or she will be the one to benefit from this decision. An individual does not purchase a pension maturing in twenty years if he or she expects to die in six months, or if he or she believes the beneficiary of the pension in twenty years will be an unknown, unrelated person. This latter case is what would exist if persons had no sense of sameness into the future.

More than anyone, Erikson (1950, 1968) has been responsible for the emergence of the concept of identity in the clinical literature. Through the life histories of both well-known and unknown individuals, Erikson has convincingly communicated the value of the construct of identity for interpreting and understanding the actions and thoughts of adolescents and young adults. Although Erikson's own work has focused on adolescence, he has claimed that the development of identity is a lifelong task that begins in infancy, assumes prominence in adolescence and continues to challenge the individual through adulthood. Even though Erikson's model of development, especially his construct of identity, has gained widespread attention in developmental psychology and has been integrated into clinical practice, the many connotations of identity found in Erikson's works make it difficult to apply the construct in research. As Erikson himself admitted, 'The term identity covers much of what has been called the self by a variety of workers, be it in the form of a self-concept, a self-system, or in that of fluctuating self experiences' (1956, p. 102). Of course, the sense of personal

121

identity is one type of experience associated with a person's sense of self, but little is gained by simply identifying as 'identity' what used to be known as the 'self-concept and self-system'.

If identity is to become a meaningful construct within psychology, then the threads that tie together the many diverse meanings of identity found in the philosophical and clinical work must be identified. By far the most successful current attempts to develop an empirically verifiable dimension of identity have followed Marcia's (1966) pioneering work. Marcia pointed out the importance of commitment in Erikson's writings on identity and formulated an interview procedure that assesses an individual's commitment to a vocation, to an ideological stance and to a sexual orientation. The value of this operational definition of identity is clearly demonstrated by the associations found between Marcia's measure and other theoretically related constructs such as self-esteem, authoritarianism and moral reasoning, to name but a few (see Chapter 11 and Marcia, 1980, for a complete review of these studies). Indeed, Marcia's approach has been so empirically robust that it has become a paradigm for identity research, with most investigations building upon Marcia's original operationalisation of the term identity.

There is much more to the concept of identity, however, than commitments to vocations, ideologies and sexual orientations. First of all, commitments in these areas can be made only by adolescents and adults who are relatively independent of parental influence. If the construction and maintenance of identity is a task faced by infants and children, there must be more to it than simply making commitments. More importantly, we believe that commitment in various areas of life does not adequately encompass all that inheres in the sense of identity as described in the philosophical and clinical literature.

Components of identity

It is our claim that there are two additional, and possibly more basic, components characteristic of the sense of personal identity. These two additional components are knowing both that the self is continuous over time and that the self is unique, or distinct from others.

In perhaps the most interesting account of the philosophical problems inherent in the concept of personal identity over time, Nozick (1981) offered the *closest continuer* schema as a framework within which intuitions about personal identity might be organised. According to this schema, the sense of personal identity over time is based on two judgments: first, to what degree is the future self causally related to the present self, and, second, to what degree is the future self unique. For instance, for an individual to believe that she will be the same person five years from now, she must suppose that the person that will be her in the future has developed out of the person she is now (causally related). She also must believe that she will grow into *only* one person in the future (unique); if there are many people who could be her in the future, then her sense of personal identity would be disrupted.

In the psychological literature, the senses of personal continuity and distinctness from others have also drawn the attention of theorists and clinicians concerned with the construct of identity. William James (1961; 1948) was one of the first to consider these dimensions. For James, the sense of personal identity was most closely associated with the 'I' or the 'self-as-knower'. A stable self-identity derives from a sense of the continuity of the self-as-knower. As James wrote, 'each of us spontaneously considers that by "I" he means something always the same' (1961, p. 63). James believes that 'the worst alterations of the self' (1948, p. 207) are associated with disruptions in the sense of personal continuity. Interestingly, James identified adolescence as the period of the lifespan during which the sense of personal continuity is lowest. Very similar connotations of identity can be found in Erikson's work: 'Identity, then, in its subjective aspect, is the awareness of the fact that there is a self-sameness and continuity to the . . . *style of one's individuality*' (1968, p. 50). Like James, Erikson believed that adolescence is the period of the lifespan during which an awareness of self-continuity is most difficult to achieve. This is because the adolescent must maintain a sense of personal continuity in the face of obvious physical and psychological changes in the self. Leahy and Kogan (in press) have suggested that commitments in adolescence are made in order to provide a sense of continuity to one's adult life; the sense of continuity may be said, then, to underlie the commitment aspect of identity studied by Marcia.

A feeling of individuality, of distinctness from others, also derives from the subjective nature of the self-as-knower. According to James, 'Other men's experiences, no matter how much I may know about them, never bear this vivid, this peculiar brand' (1961, p. 71). The special feeling associated with one's own experience is the basis for the sense of personal uniqueness. Similarly, Erikson has pointed to the sense of distinctness as essential for 'the basis of a sense of "I" ' (1982, p. 45).

Research problems

Of course, James and Erikson are not the only two psychologists who have identified the experience of personal continuity and a sense of uniqueness as central components of the phenomenology of selfhood. Among clinicians, Josselson (1973) has related the experience of little continuity in one's life to the failure to form an identity and Laing (1968) has interpreted psychotic cases in terms of a weak sense of personal distinctness. Reviewers, too, have commented on the importance of these dimensions for interpreting self-understanding (Aboud, 1979; Harter, 1983). It is somewhat surprising, then, to note that there has been relatively little empirical research on the development of these two components of identity (Damon and Hart, 1982). One reason that these components of identity have proven elusive to developmental study is that even toddlers have some sense of personal continuity and distinctness from others (Damon and Hart, 1982). Therefore, the time-honoured developmental approach of describing age-norms for those without a particular quality, those who have part of the quality and those who have the quality completely is not appropriate. A second reason that these components of identity have not received the attention they deserve is that it is difficult to operationalise them. A brief consideration of the most important studies that are relevant to an account of the development of continuity and distinctness can highlight these difficulties, as well as provide an overview of what is currently known about the development of these two identity components.

In a very interesting study, McGuire and Padawer-Singer (1976) asked children to describe themselves, using whatever adjectives they wished. Then the children were asked to provide specific information about their own physical characteristics (e.g. height) and family histories. McGuire and Padawer-Singer were able to demonstrate that children were more likely to use adjectives that differentiated between them and their classmates. For instance, children who were not within 6 months of the class modal age were more likely to mention their age spontaneously when describing themselves, and similarly children who were not born in the United States more frequently offered their birthplace as a descriptor of self than U.S.–born children (see also Chapter 9). These results clearly demonstrate that the self-concept includes within it those features that serve to distinguish between the self and others. The central problem with this methodological approach, however, is that it cannot be easily applied to the great majority of traits that an individual might use to describe the self, since it would be very difficult to obtain objective information about how unique a child's psychological qualities are in respect to his classmates.

Peevers (Chapter 10; Secord and Peevers, 1974) has also used free-response descriptions of the self for data. Instead of trying to obtain objective information regarding the degree to which an adjective differen-tiates between self and other, Peevers looked for descriptors that in *themselves* suggest distinctness from others (e.g. 'I am a better baseball player than my brother') or continuity over time (e.g. 'I always wear a ring'). The central advantage of Peevers's approach is that it allowed her to chart age-related changes in the *salience* of these dimensions. For instance, Peevers showed that there are many more references to the presence or lack of a sense of personal continuity in the self-descriptions of 17-year-olds than in the self-descriptions of 13-year-olds, which suggests that this dimension is more prominent in the experience of self in the older teenagers. The major problem with this method is that many children and adolescents do not include in their spontaneous description of self information relevant to these dimensions, even though virtually all children and adolescents believe that they are coninuous over time and distinct from others. In other words, the method does not efficiently or fully elicit information about each child's sense of continuity or distinctness.

The third approach, the one utilised in the research to be described in the next section, is to ask children and adolescents to defend their claims to personal continuity and distinctness from others. In an early study, Guardo and Bohan (1971) asked children whether or not they could assume the identity of a same-sex peer (testing for the sense of distinctness) and whether they were the same individuals as they were in the past (testing for a sense of continuity). Guardo and Bohan then asked the children why they believed that they were distinct from others and continuous over time (since virtually all the subjects expressed these beliefs). Their analysis of these responses revealed the oft-noted physical to psychological, or 'surface to depth', shift in social cognition, with older children using more psychological traits to defend their beliefs in their own continuity and uniqueness. One of our research goals (and that of Chandler in Chapter 7), was to describe with more clarity the developmental transformations that occur in the sense of personal identity, by asking children and adolescents to explain their claims of personal continuity and distinctness from others.

This is a very different sort of task from the free-response descriptions of self used by McGuire and by Peevers. Free-response descriptions of self require only that a person list the different characteristics of self that seem relevant. Asking individuals to defend their claims to personal continuity and distinctness requires reflection of a second-order nature: not only are subjects asked to describe themselves, but they are requested to explain *why* they believe those characteristics truly describe them. One advantage of this approach is that data relevant to the sense of continuity and distinctness from others can be collected for each subject, since subjects are asked to explain why they believe they are continuous over time and distinct from others. Implicit in efforts of this type is the postulation that the extent of the individual's awareness and resolution of the twin dilemmas of change and continuity of self and the similarities and dissimilarities between self and others is implicated in a real way in psychological functioning; however, to date there is only anecdotal evidence to suggest that this sort of second-order reasoning about self has this effect (Broughton, 1980).

A second aim of the research to be described was to examine the relationship between the development of the sense of personal continuity and distinctness from others and the development of the sense of the *objective self*. Referring once again to James's theory, the sense of personal continuity and distinctness from others is an aspect of the 'self as subject' or the 'I'

(Damon and Hart, 1982). The other major component of the experience of self is the 'self as object' or the 'me', which consists of those characteristics that the individual uses to define the self and which include the physical (e.g. 'I have brown eyes'), active (e.g. 'I play kickball'), social (e.g. 'I am friendly') and psychological (e.g. 'I am smart') self-features. It is the objective self that most subjects describe when asked about themselves, rather than the more elusive dimensions of self like continuity and distinctness from others. It is also the features of the objective self that individuals use to describe others (Hart and Damon, 1985a). In other words, when a person is asked to describe her friend, she describes the other's physical, active, social and psychological characteristics, rather than attempting to describe the other in terms of the degree of continuity over past and future time or the degree to which the friend is distinct from others.

TABLE 8.1   *Four developmental levels of self-understanding*

Level 1	The self is considered in terms of its surface features, direct actions, group memberships or simple thoughts and feelings. The various characteristics of self are not related to each other, and therefore there is no integrated, coherent self-conception.
Level 2	The different aspects of self are considered in light of information garnered through comparison with others or with social standards. Comparisons between the self and others often focus on relative capabilities. Characteristics of self that influence the self's performance are related to the self's capabilities.
Level 3	The influence of the social context on the individual's consideration of the self's characteristics is extended further. The understanding of self focuses on the effect of various self-characteristics on both the self's interactions with and its attractiveness to others. The social characteristics of self are now integrated by the individual into a consistent personality.
Level 4	The importance of the immediate social context for a consideration of the self's characteristics wanes. All the different characteristics of self are united by, and draw their meaning from, their contribution to the self's personal, moral or philosophical belief systems.

Using cross-sectional, longitudinal and cross-cultural research (Damon and Hart, 1982; Damon and Hart, in preparation; Hart and Damon, 1985b; Hart *et al.*, 1985), we have described development in the sense of the objective self during childhood and adolescence in terms of the four developmental levels that are presented in Table 8.1. The levels represent qualitative changes along two dimensions. The first is the extent of organisation in self-understanding. With development, the individual becomes more capable of both formulating integrations of information and making the comparisons between the bits of information necessary to reject those that are inconsistent with the integration. Each level represents a discrete increase in the integration of self-understanding characteristics. The second dimension represented by the developmental levels is the degree to which self-understanding is directly related to the immediate social context. Although all self-knowledge is social, there are important differences in the degree to which individuals relate specific self-characteristics to specific individuals and social standards in the immediate social context. At Levels 1 and 4, the individual makes few explicit references to specific persons, groups or standards in explicating the meaning of particular self-characteristics. These references are very prominent in the self-understanding of individuals at Levels 2 and 3. Our hope was that developmental transformations in the sense of continuity and distinctness from others, corresponding in some way to the developmental levels of the objective self, could be identified.

An empirical investigation into the development of the sense of personal continuity and distinctness from others

Method

Subjects. At the first round of testing, there were 82 children and adolescents distributed fairly evenly across Grades 1 to 10 and equally divided by sex. In the second round of testing, eighteen months later, 52 of the children and adolescents were again interviewed.

Procedure. Each child was given a comprehensive self interview. The questions that are relevant to the sense of personal identity study include 'If you change from year to year, how do you know you are always you?', tapping the sense of personal continuity, and 'What makes you different from everyone else in the world?', eliciting the sense of distinctness from others. The sense of the objective self was elicited through questions such as 'What kind of person are you?' and 'How would you describe yourself?' Initial responses to these questions were followed with probe questions. Eighteen months later, the children and adolescents who agreed to participate again answered the same questions. The questions relevant to the sense of distinctness were asked only at the second testing time, and not all subjects answered all the questions.

Coding. One-half of the transcribed interviews were used to construct two developmental scoring manuals, one for the sense of continuity and one for the sense of distinctness. Each scoring manual has four developmental levels. For continuity, these levels are:

Level 1: The self's continuity over time is defended by reference to

externally observable physical or behavioural characteristics of self (e.g. 'If you change from year to year, how do you know that you are still you?'
'*My eyes stay the same colour.*').

Level 2: The sense of personal continuity is based on immutable, permanent psychological characteristics of self in addition to physical and behavioural characteristics of self (e.g. 'If you change from year to year, how do you know that you are still you?' '*Because I have always been smart.*').

Level 3: Self-continuity is related to the social context that extends beyond the self. One's sense of self-continuity is in part dependent upon others recognising the sameness of the self over time (e.g. 'If you change from year to year, how do you know that you are still you?' '*I will have the same friends and they will be able to tell that I am the same old person.*').

Level 4: The self's characteristics and properties are believed to be constantly, if slowly, changing over the lifespan. At any one moment, however, the properties and characteristics of the self are believed to be directly related to, although not identical with, the self's characteristics of earlier periods in life. This relationship between characteristics of the self past and present is the basis of the sense of personal continuity (e.g. 'If you change from year to year, how do you know that you are still you?' '*Well, nothing about me always stays the same, but I am always kind of like I was a while ago, and there is always some connection.*').

The four developmental levels for the sense of distinctness from others are as follows:

Level 1: Distinctness from others is asserted on the basis of observable physical features (e.g. 'What makes you different from everybody you know?' '*Nobody else has my hair colour.*').

Level 2: Distinctness from others is believed to stem from differences between self and others along one character or personality dimension (e.g. 'What makes you different from everybody you know?' '*Nobody else in my class is as smart as me.*').

Level 3: The sense that the self is distinct from all others derives from one's belief that the self is a unique combination of psychological and physical qualities (e.g. 'What makes you different from everybody you know?' '*Nobody else has the same things like me, like smart, friendly, short, and blue eyes.*').

Level 4: The individual's sense of distinctness from others arises out of the self's own unique subjective experiences and subjective interpretations of the world (e.g. 'What makes you different from everybody else you know?' '*Nobody else sees things or feels the same way about things as I do.*').

The developmental levels for the two aspects of identity show similar trends along two dimensions. First, there is an expanding awareness that the experience of continuity and distinctness of self cannot be easily explained by reference to monistic physical or psychological characteristics. Second, in common with the developmental levels of the objective self, responses at levels 2 and 3 make explicit comparisons or references to individuals, groups or standards in the immediate social context.

Responses relevant to the sense of the objective self were coded using a third scoring manual that is described elsewhere (Hart and Damon, 1985b; Damon and Hart, in prep.). Responses were coded for a developmental level only if the rater judged that the interviewer had fully elicited the subject's reasoning.

Interrater reliability was calculated for 25 per cent of the interviews. The reliability cases were evenly distributed across the age-range of the study, and were coded by two scorers who were familiar with both scoring manuals. The two raters agreed on whether a response was sufficiently probed by the interviewer to allow it to be coded in 85 per cent of the instances. Of those codable responses, the scorers agreed on the developmental level for 87 per cent of the continuity responses and 86 per cent of the distinctness responses.

Results

The results support the developmental nature of the levels for continuity and distinctness as described above. The correlations between age and developmental level of continuity for the first and second testing times were, respectively, $r=.59$, $p<.001$ $(df=64)$, and $r=.56$, $p<.001$ $(df=40)$. The longitudinal trends for levels of continuity further confirmed the developmental nature of the sequence, with eighteen movements from lower levels to higher levels over the 18-month interval between testing times, and only two movements down the sequence (with fourteen subjects having the same score for both testing occasions). The correlation between age and levels of distinctness for the second testing time was $r=.80$, $p<.001$ $(df=43)$. A significant association was also found for developmental levels of continuity and distinctness at the second testing time, $r=.59$, $p<.001$ $(df=37)$.

Development in the sense of personal continuity and distinctness from others was also related to development in the sense of the objective self. At the first testing time, there was a correlation of $r=.41$, $p<.001$ $(df=64)$, for the relationship between developmental level of continuity and developmental level of the objective self. At the second testing time, the correlation between developmental level of continuity and developmental level of the objective self was $r=.58$, $p<.001$ $(df=38)$, and the correlation between developmental level of distinctness and developmental level of the objective self was $r=.49$, $p<.001$ $(df=40)$. Since the levels of continuity and distinctness require, as discussed earlier, more reflection than the levels of the objective self, it is not surprising that development in the sense of personal continuity and distinctness appears to lag behind development of the sense of the objective self. At the first testing time, 48 per cent of the subjects were at the same developmental level in the sense of continuity and in the sense of the objective self, 35 per cent were at a lower development level for the sense of continuity than for the objective self and only 17 per cent had a higher developmental level for the sense of continuity than for the objective self (the corresponding percentages for the second testing time were 45 per cent at the same level, 31 per cent at a higher objective self level and 21 per cent at a higher continuity level). For the sense of distinctness from others, 63 per cent of the subjects were at the same developmental level in this domain as they were in the sense of the objective self, 27 per cent were at a lower level in the sense of distinctness than in the sense of the objective self and 10 per cent were at a higher level in the sense of distinctness than in the sense of the objective self.

Conclusions

Psychology has paid little attention to the construct of personal identity. Consequently, there are few established research perspectives on its meaning or its development. In this chapter we have attempted to synthesise aspects of the philosophical and psychological discussions of identity, in order to present one starting point for future research. Our synthesis places special emphasis on the sense of personal continuity over time and distinctness from others, two dimensions of identity that are at least latent in the work of a number of psychologists besides ourselves.

We have also tried to outline the difficulties faced by ourselves and others in empirical investigation of development in the sense of continuity over time and distinctness from others. It is probably safe to conclude that any single methodology, including our own, is insufficient for a thorough investigation of identity development as construed in this paper. None the less, based upon our previous review of literature (Damon and Hart, 1982), the results presented in this chapter, the findings of Chandler and Peevers presented in Chapters 7 and 10 and the study by McGuire and Padawer-Singer (1976), a few conclusions can be offered.

First, by the end of their second year, toddlers are aware that they are distinct from others and remain the same at least in some ways over time (Damon and Hart, 1982). Not only are children aware of their continuity and distinctness, but their self-concepts are constructed in such a way as to incorporate those features of self that distinguish themselves from others (McGuire and Padawer-Singer, 1976). Developmentally, the sense of continuity over time is much more salient in the self-descriptions of 17- and

21-year-olds than in the descriptions of younger adolescents, but by age 21 the sense of distinctness from others appears to be so well-established that explicit reference to one's distinctness becomes infrequent (as Peevers suggests in Chapter 10). Not only does the salience of continuity and distinctness in self-awareness change with time, but also the underlying system of beliefs that secure for the individual the sense of continuity and distinctness. Children are most likely to base their continuity and uniqueness on particular static physical or psychological characteristics. In early adolescence, given the rapid physical, cognitive and status changes that accompany this period, the teenager can no longer believe in immutable self-characteristics and instead constitutes his or her identity as based upon the self's position in a social network. Finally, in late adolescence, continuity and distinctness from others are related to the unique nature of one's experience and to the connected succession of states of self (this chapter; Chandler, Chapter 7).

As discussed earlier, both Erikson and James speculated that the sense of identity is most elusive during adolescence. Our own findings and those of others provide some evidence for these speculations. In addition, this body of research suggests some explanations for the identity difficulties of adolescence. During childhood, the sense of continuity and distinctness is attributed to immutable self-characteristics, an attribution that adequately protects the sense of identity. It is adequate, however, only because of the child's relative lack of cognitive sophistication and life experience. The child finds it difficult to remember the important changes that occurred between infancy and childhood, and the slow evolution since that transition may be obscured by the constancy of the same school, same family and the same social world. Given this life experience, and cognitive difficulties in imagining transformations, it is not surprising that the sense of continuity is easily attained by children. The child's restricted social world may make the sense of distinctness from others self-evident, again by reference to immutable self-characteristics. It is quite possible that a child could be the only person among his parents, siblings, friends and classmates to have red hair, or to play basketball well.

But adolescence kicks these props out from under the individual's sense of identity. Physical and cognitive changes are occurring rapidly and apparently; new schools, friends and responsibilities reflect a new social status; and social awareness expands to include people and social groups that are not within the circle of family or classmates. All these changes, in combination with the cognitive skills necessary to appreciate them, make adolescence an especially difficult time to maintain a sense of personal identity. Since static physical or psychological traits no longer suffice as a base, the adolescent instead builds the sense of personal identity upon his or her location in a social network of family and friends. Disruptions in these relationships can be threatening to the adolescent, because the sense of identity is invested almost totally in these others. Emergence from this slavish concern for relationships with others occurs when adolescents become aware of other sources of continuity and distinctness such as their own unique point of view, or the special connections that exist between their successive selves. This change may preserve the sense of identity from the difficulties that beset it at the onset of adolescence, and allow the individual to be once again confident in his or her sense of continuity and distinctness.

Of course, these findings present only the barest outlines of identity development. The degree to which developmental transformations in identity are described in this chapter affect psychological functioning has yet to be assessed. But it is a start, and it is only by beginning the investigation that the insights into personal identity offered by the theories of Erikson, James and others can be explored.

Acknowledgment

The research described in this paper was supported, in part, by a grant from the Spencer Foundation to William Damon.

References

Aboud, F. (1979), 'Self: An identity, a concept, or a sense?' in L. Strickland (ed.), *Soviet and Western Perspectives in Social Psychology*, Pergamon Press: New York.

Broughton, J. M. (1980), 'The divided self in adolescence', *Human Development*, 24, pp. 13–32.

Damon, W. and Hart, D. (1982), 'The development of self-understanding from infancy through adolescence', *Child Development*, 53, pp. 841–64.

Damon, W. and Hart, D. (in press), 'Stability in self-understanding', *Social Cognition*, details to come.

Damon, W. and Hart, D. (in preparation), *The Development of Self-understanding in Childhood and Adolescence*, Cambridge University Press: Cambridge.

Erikson, E. (1950), *Childhood and Society*, Norton: New York.

Erikson, E. (1956), 'The problem of ego identity', *Journal of the American Psychiatric Association*, 4, pp. 56–121.

Erikson, E. (1968), *Identity: Youth and Crisis*, Norton: New York.

Erikson, E. (1982), *The Life Cycle Completed*, Norton: New York.

Guardo, C. and Bohan, J. (1971), 'Development of a sense of self-identity in children', *Child Development*, 42, pp. 1909–21.

Hart, D. and Damon, W. (1985a), 'Contrasts between understanding self and others', in R. Leahy (ed.), *The Development of Self*, Academic Press: New York.

Hart, D. and Damon, W. (1985b), *Developmental Trends in Self-understanding*. Manuscript submitted for publication.

Hart, D., Lucca-Irizarry, N. and Damon, W. (1985), 'The development of self-understanding in Puerto Rico and the United States', Paper presented at the meeting of the Society for Research in Child Development, Toronto.

Harter, S. (1983), 'The development of the self and the self-system', in M. Hetherington (ed.), *Carmichael's Manual of Child Psychology*, 4th ed., Wiley: New York.

James, W. (1948), *Psychology*, World Publishing Co.: New York.

James, W. (1961), *Psychology: The Briefer Course*, Harper & Row: New York (originally published 1892).

Josselson, R. (1973), 'Psychodynamic aspects of identity formation in college women', *Journal of Youth and Adolescence*, 2, pp. 3–52.

Laing, R. D. (1968), *The Divided Self*, Penguin Books: New York.

Leahy, R. and Kogan, N. (in press), 'Social cognition and identity achievement', in S. Messerick (ed.), *Development in Young Adulthood: Characteristics and Competencies in Education, Work, and Social Life*, Jossey-Bass: San Francisco.

Marcia, J. (1966), 'Development and validation of ego identity status', *Journal of Personality and Social Psychology*, 35, pp. 551–8.

Marcia, J. (1980), 'Identity in adolescence', in J. Adelson (ed.), *Handbook of Adolescent Psychology*, Wiley: New York.

McGuire, W. and Padawer-Singer, A. (1976), 'Trait salience in the spontaneous self-concept', *Journal of Personality and Social Psychology*, 33, pp. 743–54.

Nozick, R. (1981), *Philosophical Explanations*, Harvard University Press: Cambridge, Mass.

Parfit, D. (1971), 'Personal identity', *Philosophical Review*, 80, pp. 3–27.

Secord, P. and Peevers, B. (1974), 'The development of person concepts', in T. Mischel (ed.), *Understanding Other Persons*, Blackwell: Oxford.

Williams, B. (1970), 'The self and the future', *Philosophical Review*, 79, pp. 161–80.

9 Developmental trends and gender differences in the subjective experience of self

William J. McGuire and Claire V. McGuire

The vast outpouring of self-concept research carefully reviewed by Wylie (1974, 1979) and by Rosenberg (1979) has focused so heavily on the single dimension of evaluation that the whole field could be adequately included under the much narrower rubric of 'self-esteem'. The research programme described in this chapter broadens the scope of enquiry by going beyond evaluation to investigate additional dimensions of self-conceptualisation that are spontaneously salient in the phenomenal sense of self. Our spontaneous self-concept approach gives the participants the choice of dimensions on which to describe themselves in response to a general 'Tell us about yourself' probe, thus providing information on the content and processes in the natural as-is experience of self. In contrast, the usual reactive approach to the self-concept limits participants to describing themselves on some researcher-chosen dimension, typically self-esteem, and so yields only hypothetical as-if information on where the person would place the self on the researcher's dimension if he or she ever thought of it, without providing information on the extent to which the person ever does think of it. We shall first describe briefly the purposes and procedures of our more permissive approach and then summarise four areas of findings that have come out of this research programme.

Purposes of our phenomenal self research programme

The almost exclusive concentration on self-evaluation in the thousands of self-concept studies (Wylie, 1974, 1979) is inappropriate, not because evaluation is unimportant and does not deserve to be studied, but because there has been an excessive focus (over 95 per cent of self-concept studies) on this one self-esteem dimension. Our studies (McGuire and Padawer-Singer, 1976), which allowed children to choose the dimensions upon which to describe themselves, indicate that less than 10 per cent of all self-descriptive thought units are explicitly evaluative. The present programme of research on the spontaneous self-concept allows a more ecologically valid distribution of effort.

The thousands of past self-concept studies have had a somewhat disappointing conceptual yield relative to the effort expended because they typically restrict participants to describing themselves reactively on some researcher-chosen dimension, thus closing off the opportunity of investigating what personal characteristics are spontaneously salient and what determines this salience. To allow study of the neglected salience issues, our spontaneous self-concept approach non-directively asks the participant to describe him/herself and leaves to the participant the choice of self-descriptive dimensions, thus providing information on the dimensions in terms of which the person actually thinks of him/herself. We have long been describing, both in the U.S.A. (McGuire, 1966) and in the U.K. (McGuire, 1970), this more open, availability-revealing approach to the study of the self-concept. In common with our approach, this volume and its companion volume (Yardley and Honess, 1987) include chapters describing a variety of less-reactive approaches that open up salience and process issues for study.

Methods used in the present studies

The participants in our research programme were schoolchildren living in a middle-sized inland industrial city in the northeastern United States. Half were boys and half girls and they ranged from first-graders (7-year-olds) to twelfth-graders (18-year-olds). The data were obtained by asking the children open-ended questions such as 'Tell us about yourself' and 'Tell us what you are not'. Written responses were elicited from 1,000 students and oral responses from 560 others. Their 5-minute uninterrupted responses were transcribed and content-analysed. After these open-ended self-descriptive responses were obtained, yielding dependent variable measures of characteristics' salience, additional background information was collected about each child's actual position on various dimensions to obtain measures of the independent variables such as characteristics' distinctiveness, age, gender, etc.

The child's written or oral responses to the open-ended probes were transcribed verbatim in a standard typewritten format and then, to facilitate computer scoring of the salience or process-dependent variables, the child's continuous uninterrupted response to each probe was content-analysed by a three-step procedure. First, it was divided into individual thought segments; then the contents of each segment were transformed into a standard three-unit subject/verb/qualifier format to allow aggregate computer analysis with only minor distortions of what the child had said or written (e.g. the rare passive constructions had to be converted to active; some adjectives and adverbs had to be eliminated); then the contents of each of the three units of every segment were translated into the terms in a 1000-word basic concept dictionary.

Some results of this programme of spontaneous self-concept studies

We shall illustrate the yield of this programme of research on the spontaneous self-concept by describing four lines of work: (1) the extent to which the distinctiveness of one's characteristic on a dimension affects its salience in the self-concept, i.e. one's likelihood of spontaneously mentioning that characteristic in describing oneself; (2) contrasts between affirmation and negation self-concepts, i.e. what characteristics are salient when one describes what one is as compared with describing what one is not; (3) the extent to which, and ways in which, self-space is social, and how gender and age affect how one describes oneself in terms of other people; and (4) how the modes of thinking about the self change during childhood and adolescence, as manifested by developmental shifts in the verbs one uses to describe oneself.

Characteristics' distinctiveness and their salience in the self-concept

Distinctiveness theory. Distinctiveness theory (McGuire, 1984) postulates that one perceives not so much what is there as what is absent. Applied to person perception it predicts that one perceives self and others, not as they are in themselves, but as they differ from others; hence, one exists to oneself and others in so far as one is different and in terms of these peculiarities. The theory has basic epistemological and even ontological implications, but we shall leave these background speculations for discussion elsewhere (McGuire, 1984). Here we shall report results that bear on the hypothesis that one thinks of oneself in terms of a given characteristic in so far as one's position on it distinguishes one from others in one's usual social milieu (i.e. in so far as it is distinctive, unpredictable, information-rich). We shall describe findings on the extent to which three different types of personal characteristics – one's physical appearance, one's ethnicity and one's gender – become more salient in one's sense of self as one's position on the dimension becomes more distinctive (unpredictable, informative) within one's comparison groups.

Salience of physical characteristics. To test the distinctiveness hypothesis in terms of the spontaneous salience of physical characteristics, we chose (McGuire and McGuire, 1980; 1981) the four physical characteristics most commonly mentioned in people's written self-descriptions (height, weight, hair colour and eye colour) and added four other commonly mentioned quasi-physical characteristics (age, birthplace, wearing eyeglasses and handedness). The children's actual positions on each of these eight dimensions were determined from their written responses to a structured questionnaire completed by the 1,000 fifth- through twelfth-graders (including 100 girls and 100 boys at each of five age levels, i.e. 11-, 13-, 15-, 17- and 18-year-olds) after they had first given 5-minute responses to the 'Tell us about yourself' non-directive probe. From responses on the structured questionnaires each student's actual height, weight, etc., was calculated along with its distinctiveness in terms of distance from the average on the given dimension for schoolmates of his/her own gender at his/her own grade level. The children could then be partitioned on each of these eight independent-variable dimensions into those with average positions that fell in the middle range (of height, weight and age) or in the modal category (as regards hair colour, eye colour, birthplace, eyeglass wearing and handedness) versus those with atypical positions that fell in the extreme range or uncommon category on the given dimension. The distinctiveness prediction could then be tested for each of the eight dimensions by determining whether or not the given dimension was spontaneously mentioned in response to the 'Tell us about yourself' probe with greater frequency by the more distinctive group of respondents.

TABLE 9.1 *Percentages of various subgroups of children who spontaneously mentioned specific physical characteristics as part of their 5-minute written self-description*

Characteristic	All	Gender subgroups		Age subgroups		Distinctiveness subgroups		
		Males	Females	17 and 18 Years	11 and 13 Years	Unusual		Common
Height	19%	21%	17%	18%	18%	27%	*	18%
Weight	11	11	11	13	* 8	12	*	6
Hair colour	14	10	* 18	11	* 17	17	*	13
Eye colour	11	8	* 15	9	13	13		11
Age	31	28	* 33	24	* 38	33		30
Birthplace	6	6	6	7	6	10	*	4
Eyeglasses	1.5	0.5	* 2.5	0	* 3	3	*	0.5
Handedness	>1	>1	>1	>1	>1	1.5	*	0.5

* = difference between the adjacent percentages is significant at .05 level.

It can be seen in the last two columns of Table 9.1 that, for each of the eight characteristics, children in the unusual category were more likely spontaneously to describe themselves in terms of this dimension than were children in the typical category or range, and that for six of the eight characteristics taken separately, the greater salience for those in the distinctive category was significant by chi-square at the .05 level. For example, as regards weight (shown in Table 9.1 to have been mentioned spontaneously by 11 per cent of the participants, equally often by girls and boys, but decreasingly with age), only 6 per cent of the average-weight children (those within six pounds – 2.7 kg. – of the class mean) spontaneously described themselves in terms of their weight, whereas a significantly greater 12 per cent of the heavy and light children (those with weights at least one stone – 6.4 kg. – above or below the class mean) spontaneously mentioned their weight.

Salience of ethnicity as a function of school ethnic composition. Several distinctive-ness predictions regarding ethnicity salience were tested and confirmed (McGuire *et al.*, 1978), indicating that the salience of ethnicity in the child's self-concept increases as the representation of her/his ethnic group in the student body of her/his school declines. Five-minute oral responses to 'Tell us about yourself' were collected individually from 560 schoolchildren including 70 girls and 70 boys at each of four grade levels (7-, 9-, 13- and 17-year-olds) and each child was scored on the salience-of-ethnicity dependent variable by whether or not her/his 5-minute response contained at least one mention of her/his ethnicity. The independent variable of actual ethnicity and the distinctiveness of this ethnicity in the child's classroom were measured by having the interviewer judge each child's ethnicity, on the basis of appearance, accent and name, as being in one of four ethnic categories (English-speaking white, black, hispanic or other/uncertain); the obtained percentages in these four categories were 82, 9, 8 and 1 per cent, respectively.

As predicted, the members of the black and hispanic minority groups were much more likely spontaneously to mention their ethnicity, 17 per cent of the blacks and 14 per cent of the hispanic minority children doing so as compared with only 1 per cent of the whites. Also, the smaller the proportion of the students in a classroom who were members of a given ethnic group, the more probable it was that the members of that group would spontaneously describe themselves in terms of this ethnicity.

Salience of gender as a function of household sex composition. The distinctiveness postulate predicts that people will be more conscious of themselves as male or female to the extent that the other gender predominates in their usual social settings. Since it is school policy to assign approximately equal numbers of boys and girls to any classroom, we used gender asymmetry in the household rather than in school as the independent variable to test this gender-salience prediction. The proportion of males to females in the child's household was measured by asking each child at the end of the session to list those who lived in her/his house or flat and to indicate the age, gender and relationship of each listed person. The dependent variable, spontaneous salience of gender in the self-concept, was measured by scoring each of the 560 children for whether she/he mentioned her/his sex at least once in the 5-minute oral response to 'Tell us about yourself'.

We found (McGuire *et al.*, 1979), as predicted, that boys are increasingly more likely spontaneously to describe themselves in terms of their maleness as the predominance of females in their household increases; and girls mention their femaleness increasingly as the proportion of males in their households increases, the trend being significant at the .05 level for each gender. A second test of the hypothesis involved the effect of father-absence on boys' consciousness of their maleness. Social learning theory predicts that diminished modelling and reinforcement of their male role-playing will make boys from fatherless homes less likely to develop a masculine self-image; distinctiveness theory makes a rather opposite prediction, that boys from fatherless homes are more likely to be conscious of their being male because maleness tends to be a more distinctive characteristic in homes without fathers. The distinctiveness prediction was confirmed in that among the 33 boys in the sample who came from fatherless homes 18 per cent spontaneously mentioned that they were male, while among the 227 boys from homes in which both mother and father were present only 7 per cent spontaneously mentioned that they were males, a difference significant at the .05 level.

These findings have relevance for both theory and public policy. As regards theory, they support the partial view of the person as an information-processing machine, noticing aspects of a stimulus that are most distinctive (that is, which are least predictable and thus contain the most information). This information-processor concept of the person is confirmed even when the method of strong inference is used by pitting it against opposite predictions from social desirability or from the social learning/modelling concept of the person. As regards practical implications, the results on ethnicity and gender salience correct common misperceptions sufficiently accepted to have influenced public policy. For example, the U.S. Government's Moynihan (1965) report popularised the notion that boys growing up in fatherless homes develop an inadequately male self-image which contributes to high unemployment rates; and since father-absence from the household has increased sizeably since World War II, perhaps promoted by aid-to-dependent-children laws, it has been suggested that these laws be changed. The present results show that, on the contrary, boys from fatherless homes are more conscious of their maleness – although it is possible that they are less knowledgeable about what males are expected to do with this distinctive characteristic. These results have relevance also to the recent policy of discouraging cross-racial adoption because of the argument by black social work associations that black children brought up in white adoptive households would tend to lose their black ethnic identity. The findings reported here suggest that, on the contrary, black children adopted into white homes will be more conscious of their distinctive blackness than will black children adopted into black households.

The affirmation versus negation self-concept

The distinctiveness hypothesis implies that one forms one's concept of what one is by negation, by noticing a difference between oneself and another, the absence of the characteristic in oneself making salient its presence in the other. If one's affirmation self-concept of what one is thus derives from what one is not, the interesting question arises of how one forms one's negation self-concept of what one is not, and so we have studied (McGuire, 1984) the negation self-concept elicited by asking, 'Tell us what you are not', as contrasted with the affirmation self-concept so far discussed, which is elicited by asking, 'Tell us about yourself'. Here we shall report some obtained contrasts between the affirmation and negation self-concepts as regards the spontaneous salience of ethnicity and of gender.

As regards the salience of ethnicity in one's sense of self, the distinctiveness hypothesis predicts that the minority group members will think of themselves in ethnic terms more in the affirmational than negational self concept; while the majority group members will think of themselves in ethnic terms more in the negational self concept (as not having a minority ethnicity) than in the affirmational self concept (as being of the majority ethnicity). Underlying this prediction is the assumption that the more distinctive (unpredictable, information-rich) minority ethnicities will be more salient than the majority ethnicity. The results confirm the interaction prediction. For the majority English-speaking white group, five times as many people mentioned other-ethnicity in their negation self-concepts of what they are not as mentioned their own ethnicity in their affirmation self-concepts of what they are. Minority-group black and hispanic children show the reversed contrast: twice as many mentioned their own rare ethnicity in their affirmation of what they are as mentioned not being the common white ethnicity as part of their negation self-concepts of what they are not.

The affirmation-versus-negation self-concept interacted with own gender in affecting the salience of gender in self-descriptions. Gender, like ethnicity, is much more salient in the negation than in the affirmation self-concept, three times as many participants mentioning the other gender as something that they are not when giving their negation self-concept as mention their own gender as something they are when giving their affirmation self-concept. This affirmation-versus-negation salience difference is significantly higher in girls than in boys: in the affirmation self-concept, girls are only slightly more likely than boys to mention their own gender spontaneously as something that they are; but in giving negation self-concepts, girls mention not being boys half again more often than boys mention not being girls.

Social aspects of self-space

Humans are a social species and so it can be expected that other people will loom large in a person's self-concept. Freud (1975) asserted that all our thoughts involve other people, not only when we are in social situations but even in our most autistic thinking. We shall illustrate the roles played by significant others in self-space by reporting here four sets of findings regarding the social self in our affirmation self-concept studies (McGuire and McGuire, 1982).

Prevalence of significant others in self-space. Children's self-concepts are highly social: 23 per cent of the contents of the first (subject) plus third (qualifier) units of all segments of self-descriptions are mentions of significant others. Half of these mentions are of family members, another quarter of friends, and the remainder are divided about equally among school-related people, broad categories of people and animals. Of the family mentions, one-half are of siblings, one-third of parents and the remainder of the family in general or of extended family members. In Chapter 21 the Kreitlers likewise report the prevalence of interpersonal references in self-descriptions.

Girls' self-concepts are even more social than boys' in several respects: girls describe themselves in terms of other people half again more often than do boys, and mention others more favourably and as individuals rather than as depersonalised categories of people more than do boys. Girls tend to be more 'parochial' as regards the significant others in terms of whom they define themselves, concentrating more on family members and on age peers than do boys.

Prevalence of animals in the child's self-concept. Mentions of non-human animals in children's self-descriptions are surprisingly frequent, accounting for 11 per cent of all significant-other mentions; e.g. more children define themselves in relation to their pets than to their mothers, even though all had mothers and only some had pets. Of the animal mentions, 80 per cent were of pets (especially dogs, to a slightly lesser extent cats, and with decreasing frequency fish, birds, small mammals and reptiles) and 20 per cent were of wild animals, the latter mentioned more often relative to pets by boys than by girls. We expected the proportion of animal mentions to decline with age but the obtained age trend was non-monotonic, 9-year-olds mentioning animals in their self-concepts more often than younger or older children. This peaking at age 9 occurs consistently whether we consider dogs, cats, other pets or wild animals. Indeed, 19 per cent of all references to significant others by 9-year-olds were to non-human animals, exceeding their mentions of siblings or parents or friends. With puberty the salience of animals declines, so that by the time the person reaches 17 years of age non-human animals constitute only 3 per cent of all significant-other mentions; but until this late-adolescent age is reached animals loom surprisingly large in self-space.

Desocialisation of self-space with age. The self becomes progressively less social with age. For 7-year-olds 29 per cent of all first- and third-unit contents are mentions of significant others but the percentage drops steadily with maturing through childhood and adolescence until by age 17 only 16 per cent are mentions of significant others. Further evidence of a developmental decline in defining self in terms of others is that mentions of significant others become increasingly depersonalised with age, consisting of categorical references to 'people', 'adults', 'boys', etc., rather than to specific individuals, such categorical references increasing progressively from 6 per cent of all significant-other mentions for 7-year-olds to 27 per cent for 17-year-olds. Thinking in more categorical terms with maturity could also serve the purpose of facilitating the sense of self-continuity discussed by Chandler in Chapter 7 and invites comparison to the developmental trends reported by Wylie in Chapter 5 toward increasing specificity in some aspects and greater abstractness in other aspects. Another kind of desocialisation of the self with maturity is that mentions of disliked others increase progressively from 4 per cent for 7-year-olds to 13 per cent for 17-year-olds. Not surprisingly, there is a cosmopolitan trend with age, family members constituting a decreasing proportion of all significant others as the child grows older.

Self-definitions in terms of siblings and parents. An analysis of the socialisation task of the child (McGuire and McGuire, 1982) suggests that children should describe themselves in relation to the same- rather than the other-gender parent (since children must focus more on own-gender parents as their models to master the socially expected adult role behaviour), but should describe themselves in relation to other-gender rather than same-gender siblings (since the prescribed heterosexual role acquisitions involve relating to age peers of the other sex). Results are in keeping with these predictions. As regards self-definition in relation to parents, boys mentioned their fathers half again more often than their mothers, whereas girls mentioned their mothers twice as often as their fathers. As regards self-definition in relation to siblings, the sex difference was less pronounced but still in the predicted cross-gender direction, with boys mentioning their sisters more often than their brothers and girls mentioning their brothers more often than their sisters.

These four varied sets of findings regarding significant others in self-space illustrate that, by allowing participants more freedom in selecting the referents in terms of which to describe themselves, a broader set of issues can be addressed and more meaningful salience information can be obtained than is revealed by the usual reactive approach, which yields only hypothetical information about where people would see themselves on the researcher's dimension if they ever thought of it.

Self-concept differences as revealed by the ontogeny of verbs

Our content-analysis procedure involves dividing the children's self-descriptions into individual thought segments and transforming each segment into a subject/verb/qualifier format. In the preceding section on the social self we described findings revealed by the segments' first- and third-unit noun contents; in this final section we shall describe some trends revealed by the middle-unit verb contents. We shall first describe the verb classification system used for the content analysis of these middle-unit contents and then report findings regarding how changes in self-conceptualisation during childhood and adolescence are detectable by the changing distribution of verbs used in self-descriptions.

The verb classification system. We used published word-frequency counts, verb classifications and prestudies to develop a dictionary of 108 verb concepts for encoding the contents of the middle units of the subject/verb/qualifier thought segments, these verb concepts being grouped into a hierarchical organisation on the basis of *a priori* theorising about the psychologically meaningful categories of verbs relevant to person perception. Our broadest division follows the traditional grammatical dichotomy into verbs of action versus verbs of state. The state verbs were subdivided into 'being' versus 'becoming' verbs. The action verbs were subdivided into overt actions versus covert reactions. It was hypothesised that as the child matures his or her self-descriptions use an increasing proportion of the more sophisticated member of each verb pair. Specifically, it was predicted that as the child grows older there is an increase of state verbs relative to action verbs, of becoming relative to being verbs of state, and of covert-reaction relative to overt-action verbs of action. A fourth division dichotomised all verbs into affirmations versus negations, to test the prediction that the more difficult negation thinking (of the self in terms of what one is not) would increase with age relative to affirmation thinking of the self in terms of what one is.

Results regarding ontogenetic trends in verb usage. The predicted maturation of the self-concept during the childhood and adolescent years was confirmed as regards the four verb ratios just described (and as regards additional verb ratios that will not be discussed here because of space limitations). The prediction that as the child matures he or she thinks of the self in more abstract terms, in terms of what one is rather than what one does, was confirmed by the proportion of all verbs which are verbs of state increasing steadily from 21 per cent for the first graders to 45 per cent for the twelfth graders, a developmental trend that was replicated in both oral and written response modalities. Other chapters in this volume, including Wylie's and Chandler's, report additional signs of increasing abstraction of self-thought with age. The second prediction, that among state verbs there will be an increasing proportion of becoming verbs relative to being verbs as the child grows older was also confirmed: in the oral-response condition the proportion of state verbs that were verbs of becoming increased from .19 for 7-year-olds to .36 for 17-year-olds; and in the written-response replication, becoming verbs increased from 16 per cent of all state verbs for 11-year-olds to 28 per cent for 18-year-olds ($p < .001$ for the age trend in each modality). The third prediction, that the child becomes more deliberative and reflective with age, exhibited by a shift among verbs of action from those describing the self as overtly reacting to those describing the self as covertly acting, is confirmed in the oral-response condition where the proportion of all action verbs that refer to covert reactions increases progressively from .29 for 7-year-olds to .53 for 17-year-olds ($p < .001$); in the written condition, covert reaction verbs likewise increase from .60 of all state verbs for 11-year-olds to .67 for 18-year-olds, but this age trend in the written condition falls short of the .05 level of significance. A fourth age-trend prediction, that the use of negative verbs in self-descriptions will increase relative to affirmative verbs, was confirmed by a clear age trend ($p < .001$) toward increasing negation in both the oral and written response modes. The research reported in the Kreitler's chapter (Chapter 21) indicates that this developmental trend towards increasing use of negation continues through adulthood into old age.

Summary

This programme of studies utilises a less reactive approach than most self-concept research in that it allows people to select the dimensions on which to describe themselves rather than confining them, as in the usual reactive approaches, to describing themselves on dimensions presented by the investigator. Our open-ended approach is more labour-intensive in that it requires the construction and utilisation of a content-analysis system but in return it allows investigation of neglected process and salience issues that cannot be studied as well by the usual reactive methods.

We have illustrated the programme by describing issues studied and results obtained in four lines of research. One line of work, investigating the distinctiveness theory implication that what is salient in one's phenomenal sense of self is one's peculiar (unpredictable, information-rich) characteristics, demonstrated that a given physical dimension is salient in one's self-concept to the extent one's characteristic on it is unusual; that one's ethnicity is salient to the extent that most of one's schoolmates are of other ethnicities; and that one thinks of oneself in terms of one's gender to the extent that the other gender predominates in one's household. A second line of research contrasts what is salient in the affirmation versus negation self-concepts, what one thinks of when describing what one is versus what one is not. The social self is the focus of a third line of research, showing that the self is defined largely in relation to other people and that children define themselves in terms of the same-gender parent and the other-gender siblings. A fourth line of work, focusing on age shifts in the types of verbs people use in free self-descriptions, shows that the self-concept becomes progressively more abstract, dynamic, introspective and negational as the child matures. The use of a demanding and unusual approach has enabled this programme of research to discover new answers to neglected questions.

Acknowledgment

The research reported here was substantially aided by Grant No. MH 32588 from the National Institute of Mental Health, Interpersonal Processes and Problems Section, of the U.S. Government's Department of Health and Human Services.

References

Freud, S. (1975), *Group Psychology and the Analysis of the Ego*, transl. and edited by J. Strachey, Norton: New York (original edition 1921).

McGuire, W. J. (1966), *Attitude Change and Social Perception*, National Science Foundation proposal, Washington, D.C.

McGuire, W. J. (1970), 'Perceptual selectivity and the self-concept', Invited lecture presented at the British Psychological Society Conference, University College, London.

McGuire, W. J. (1984), 'Search for the self: Going beyond self-esteem and the reactive self', in R. A. Zucker, J. Aronoff and A. I. Rabin (eds), *Personality and the Prediction of Behavior*, Academic Press: New York, pp. 73–120.

McGuire, W. J. and McGuire, C. V. (1980), 'The salience of handedness in the spontaneous self-concept', *Perceptual and Motor Skills*, 50, pp. 3–7.

McGuire, W. J. and McGuire, C. V. (1981), 'The spontaneous self-concept as affected by personal distinctiveness', in M. D. Lynch, A. Norem-Hebeisen and K. Gergen (eds), *The Self-concept*, Ballinger: New York, pp. 147–71.

McGuire, W. J. and McGuire, C. V. (1982), 'Significant others in self-space: Sex differences and developmental trends in the self', in J. Suls (ed.), *Psychological Perspectives on the Self*, Erlbaum: Hillsdale, N.J., pp. 71–96.

McGuire, W. J., McGuire, C. V., Child, P. and Fujioka, T. (1978), 'The salience of ethnicity in the spontaneous self-concept as a function of one's ethnic distinctiveness in the social environment', *Journal of Personality and Social Psychology*, 36, pp. 511–20.

McGuire, W. J., McGuire, C. V. and Winton, W. (1979), 'Effects of household sex composition on the salience of one's gender in the spontaneous self-concept', *Journal of Experimental Social Psychology*, 15, pp. 77–90.

McGuire, W. J. and Padawer-Singer, A. (1976), 'Trait salience in the spontaneous self-concept', *Journal of Personality and Social Psychology*, 33, pp. 743–54.

Moynihan, D. P. (1965), *The Negro Family: The Case for National Action*, U.S. Department of Labor: Washington, D.C.

Rosenberg, M. (1979), *Conceiving the Self*, Basic Books: New York.

Wylie, R. C. (1974), *The Self-concept*, vol. 1, University of Nebraska Press: Lincoln, Neb.

Wylie, R. C. (1979), *The Self-concept*, vol. 2, University of Nebraska Press: Lincoln, Neb.

Yardley, K. M. and Honess, T. M. (eds) (1987), *Self and Identity: Psychosocial Perspectives*, Wiley: Chichester.

10 The self as observer of the self: A developmental analysis of the subjective self

Barbara Hollands Peevers

A good deal of the psychological research on the concept of self has focused on self-esteem and its relationship to individuals' competence in various life spheres. The results of this work, however, have been disappointing, generally characterised by weak or non-significant findings (Wylie, 1979), despite the seemingly obvious practical importance of self-esteem. One of the several problems with the attempt to measure self-esteem, particularly that of children, is that little is known about the conceptual bases upon which individuals of various ages evaluate themselves. Indeed, not a great deal is known about the development of self-understanding. The research to be reported represents an attempt to increase that knowledge.

George Herbert Mead (1934) conceived of the self as socially constructed through interaction with others within the context of a particular culture and a common language. Consistent with this formulation is Harré's (1983) contention that individuals' concepts of self are derived from the theory of selfhood prevalent in the society in which they live, and that this theory is implicit in the grammatical forms of the language of that society. Mead's notion of the self is illustrative: he enlarged upon the ideas of William James (1961) in formulating a conception of the self which included the components of the objective and the subjective selves. As designations for these components he used the equivalent grammatical terms, the 'Me' and the 'I'. The 'Me', the objective component, consists of the collection of perceived facts regarding the self in an individual's repertoire. The 'I', the subjective self, observes, organises and reflects upon the 'Me'. Subjective processes are elusive because they are instantaneous, and as completed, can become a part of the 'Me'.

The content of the objective self, and its development across various age levels, has received a good deal of research attention. Methods employed have included adjective checklists on which participants indicate the extent of their possession of selected traits; the 'Who am I?' technique, which elicits twenty responses to that question from participants (Kuhn, 1960); and, in a few studies, participants have responded in their own words to a general question about what they themselves were like (Livesley and Bromley, 1973; Secord and Peevers, 1974; Keller *et al.*, 1978). Findings have accumulated regarding the kinds of self-facts (e.g. possessions, physical appearance, activities, interests, values, traits) which comprise the objective self of individuals of different ages.

Study of the 'I' component has received considerably less attention, partially because of the logical impossibility of directly observing it, and partially because of the reluctance of psychologists to accept language, or verbal accounts, as observable human behaviour (Farr, 1981). Nevertheless, the subjective self is amenable to study through the accounts which people give, directly or indirectly, of their subjective processes.

Two examples of the direct approach are those of Broughton (1978) and Selman (1980). Broughton interviewed individuals of different ages, asking open-ended questions about the nature of the mind and the self and their relationship to the body. On the basis of these data, he distinguished six levels of the development of self-understanding, extending from childhood through young adulthood. During the first of these, which includes ages 4 to 7, children make no distinction between mind and body, and conceive of themselves in terms of their physical selves only. At about age 8 some differentiation of mind and body occurs, though self-consciousness is not yet articulated reflectively. Ideas about the self begin to include some psychological concepts, as noted also by Secord and Peevers (1974) and by Keller *et al.* (1978). Around age 12 a beginning of recognition of two selves appears: the self in itself (the 'I') and the self for others (the 'Me'). The individual begins to be able to view the self as an object. Later levels of development (from age 18 onward) include, first, a perception of 'truth' as objective; next, as purely subjective; and finally, as a combination of the two. Broughton suggested that there may be further developmental levels of self-understanding, as yet unidentified.

Selman (1980) asked his participants to resolve a dilemma posed to them which involved taking the perspective of another person, and he also formulated a developmental model. In the first of his stages, characteristic of very young children, no distinction is made between inner psychological experience and outer experience. Later, in the late preschool and early elementary school years the 'subjective' level emerges, in which the child is aware of the separation of inner experience and actions, but views them as consistent. The idea that one can 'fool oneself', to the child at this level, means that one can do so only by changing one's own subjective experience, or by discovering that one was wrong about it. The 'self-reflective' level begins in early elementary school and middle childhood, and involves the emergence of an introspective self, which views inner experience as reality and actions as reflections of that reality. The individual becomes aware of the 'I', the self's ability to monitor the self's thoughts and actions. The 'mutual' level is a preadolescent phenomenon in which the individual develops the ability to view the self from the viewpoint of another person. For George Herbert Mead (1934), this ability is a critical component of a mature concept of self. Adolescence and young adulthood mark the acquisition of the 'in-depth' level, in which the existence of unconscious experiences and motivations is understood.

Damon and Hart (1982) reviewed the research on the development of self-understanding and summarised what is currently known about the development of the objective and subjective selves, conceptualising a three-dimensional model of this development from infancy through adolescence. The model emphasises the necessity of considering the interaction of the multiple dimensions of the self during various stages of development, and incorporates as dimensions aspects of the 'Me' and the 'I' derived from William James (1961), as well as four developmental levels. Aspects of the 'Me' are the physical, active, social and psychological selves, and of the 'I', understanding of continuity, distinctness from others, volition and self-reflection. The developmental levels are infancy and childhood, late childhood, early adolescence and late adolescence.

Research design

The research to be reported represents an indirect approach to the study of the development of self-understanding. It is based on the premise that references to subjective self-processes, or aspects, can be discerned in the verbal accounts which people give when asked to describe themselves. Free-response self-descriptions were examined for indicators of aspects of the subjective self, and the development of the appearance of those indicators across ages was traced.

Eighty individuals participated in the research, eight persons of each gender at the ages of 6, 9, 13, 17 and 21. These individuals were classified as upper-middle class by use of Hollingshead's Two-factor Index of Social Position (1965) and lived in a moderately sized city in the western United States. The participants were interviewed individually and were first asked to describe three friends and one disliked peer. When this portion was completed, they were asked to 'tell what you are like' and were free to say what they wished, for as long as they wished. The interviewer remained as non-commital as possible, both verbally and non-verbally, and said only, 'What else can you tell me about yourself?' at appropriate intervals. The interviews were tape-recorded and subsequently transcribed verbatim for analysis.

It should be noted that participants were not asked direct questions about subjective self-aspects; indicators of these processes occurred spontaneously in the course of the self-descriptions. Consequently, the absence of indicators in no way implies the absence of that process in an individual. Indeed, at older ages absence may indicate the internalisation, or 'taken-for-granted', quality of an aspect. The results are interpreted as evidence not only for the presence of a process, but for the salience of that process to the individual at the time of the interview.

The aspects of the subjective self studied were those conceptualised by William James (1961): individuals' conceptions of (1) continuity of the self, (2) distinctness of the self, (3) self as agent (volition) and (4) self-reflection. A content-analysis system was developed to identify indicators of these aspects of self, as follows.

Continuity refers to the sense of self existing over time, or the permanence of the self. Evidence cited by Damon and Hart (1982) indicates that continuity, defined as recognition of a mirror image of the self, occurs early in human development, certainly by the end of the second year. For the content analysis of verbal self-descriptions, continuity was defined as references to (1) things which the self did, which happened to the self or which were true of the self in the past (e.g. 'When I was in the Scouts I learned to tie knots'); (2) the future of the self (e.g. 'Perhaps I will understand when I grow up'); (3) change in the self over time (e.g. 'I have really changed since high school'); and (4) lack of change in the self over time (e.g. 'I really haven't changed that much').

Distinctness refers to the sense of the self as unique and different from all others. Evidence previously cited indicates that in early childhood distinctness is perceived in purely physical terms, and that the conception of self as psychologically unique appears at around age 8. Indicators of distinctness were defined as references to the self's being different from one or more others in either a general way or in terms of a specific physical or psychological attribute, ability or condition (e.g. 'I'm really different from the other kids' and 'I guess I read more than most people').

Agency refers to the concept of self as capable of making decisions and acting purposefully. Earlier work (Peevers and Secord, 1973a; Secord and Peevers, 1974) suggested that the concept of agency in free-response person descriptions begins to occur in early adolescence and develops more completely in late adolescence. Three types of indicators of agency were identified: (1) references to trying to accomplish something (e.g. 'I try to stick to a schedule'); (2) an intention to do, or to have done, something (e.g. 'I'm working on being nicer to my father'); (3) choices or decisions to be made, or which have been made (e.g. 'I haven't decided whether I want to play football or basketball').

Self-reflection refers to the direct consideration of the self as an object, and the work of Broughton (1978) and Selman (1980), as well as that of Secord and Peevers (1974), suggests that the ability to self-reflect develops in early adolescence. Indicators of self-reflection were defined as (1) references to the reflexive self, in the sense of seeing oneself, answering to oneself, liking oneself, etc. (e.g. 'I keep learning about myself'), and (2) explanations of self-attributes and behaviour (e.g. 'They really scare me, so I suppose I act stuck-up').

The coding procedure consisted of reading the self-descriptions and underlining words, phrases or sentences defined by the code as indicators. Two coders independently coded 55 of the 80 self-descriptions, and disagreements on coding were resolved through discussion. One coder coded the remaining descriptions.

The reliability of the coding system was tested by comparing the independent coding by two coders of seven randomly selected self-descriptions by older participants (i.e. 17- and 21-year-olds). These seven descriptions contained 316 indicators, or 37 per cent of the total indicators for all participants.[1] Two tests were made on these independent codings: first, for agreement on the identification of indicators, and second, for agreement on the coding of the mutually identified indicators.

The coders agreed on the identification of 217 indicators, or 69 per cent of the total. The most frequent disagreement in identification was a failure to code past-tense references to the self, which are indicators of continuity. These omissions were readily agreed upon through discussion, and the coding directions were amended to require a first reading of the descriptions for continuity indicators, and a second for other indicators. The percentage agreements on identification for each self-aspect were: continuity, 65 per cent; distinctness, 79 per cent; agency, 68 per cent; and self-reflection, 73 per cent.

Of the 217 indicators which were mutually identified by the two coders, 202 were coded identically, an agreement of 93 per cent. The percentage agreements for self-aspects were: continuity, 96 per cent; distinctness, 85 per cent; agency, 91 per cent; and self-reflection, 93 per cent.

The *results* of the content analysis demonstrated dramatic changes in evidence of aspects of the subjective self with increasing age. They are presented in the form of percentages in order to control for the increasing length of self-descriptions with increasing age. For example, the number of items descriptive of the self in these protocols had previously been determined by use of a different and independent coding system, the Person Concept Code (Peevers and Secord, 1973b). The mean numbers of descriptive items thus calculated reflected the length of the descriptions, and ranged from 4.5 items for 6-year-olds to 46 at age 21.

In the present study the mean numbers of subjective self-indicators for participants who gave self-descriptions at each age were: 6-year-olds, 0.7; 9-year-olds, 2.4; 13-year-olds, 3.9; 17-year-olds, 17.3; and 21-year-olds, 26.7. The findings will be discussed first in terms of specific ages and, second, in terms of each aspect. The percentage distribution of each kind of indicator for each age is shown in Table 10.1

TABLE 10.1   *Percentage distribution of indicators for each age*

Indicators	Age				
	6 Years (N=13)	9 Years (N=15)	13 Years (N=16)	17 Years (N=16)	21 Years (N=15)
Continuity					
Past	33%	37%	31%	31.5%	31%
Future	22	20	1.5	12	14.5
Change	0	0	5	7	6.5
Lack of change	45	11.5	5	3	6
Distinctness	0	17	15	9	3
Agency					
Trying	0	0	33	8	7
Intention	0	11.5	0	16	3
Decision	0	0	0	1.5	4
Self-reflection					
Reflexivity	0	0	1.5	6	15
Explanation	0	3	8	6	11
Total	100%	100%	100%	100%	100%
Total indicators	N=9	N=35	N=61	N=277	N=401

Six-year-olds. Continuity was the only aspect of the subjective self which was evident in self-descriptions at this age, and only 6 of the 16 children used these types of indicators. Indeed, 3 children were unable to give any description of themselves at all, although each had just previously said something descriptive of several peers. The children who did give evidence of continuity spoke most frequently of activities in which they habitually engaged, which were coded as lack of change in the self (e.g. 'I always play with my Hot Wheels'). They spoke also of a specific event in the past ('When I was three years old I spilled some milk'), and to a lesser extent, of their future ('I'm going into Brownie Scouts next year'). There were no references to change in the self. The mean number of indicators of continuity for 6-year-olds who gave self-descriptions was 0.7.

Nine-year-olds. Indicators of aspects of the subjective self were present in the descriptions of 8 of the 15 children who gave self-descriptions, and the mean number was 2.4. Indicators of continuity were the most frequent at this age, as they were for all the ages studied, comprising two-thirds of the indicators used by 9-year-olds. More than one-half of these were references to the past, followed by future references (e.g. 'I hope someday I'll become an artist'), and a few references to lack of change ('I always wear a ring'). As was true of the 6-year-olds, there was no mention of change in the self.

Indicators of distinctness were next in order of frequency, but all emanated from one boy, who compared himself with other members of his family in terms of expertise in athletic activities. There were a very few indicators of agency, and those were statements of intentionality (e.g. 'I'm going to learn to swim better'). There were no references to trying or to decision-making.

One indicator of self-reflection was present: 'I do what my mom wants me to do cause she gets mad', which was coded as an explanation of behaviour.

Thirteen-year-olds. Twelve of the 16 participants in this age group used at least one indicator of an aspect of self, and the mean number of indicators was 3.9. The most frequent aspect was again continuity, comprising nearly one-half of the total indicators. Three-quarters of the continuity indicators were references to the past. There were three references to lack of change in the self (e.g. 'I always have to be busy') and one reference to the future. For the first time, indicators of change in the self were present, contributed by one person (e.g. 'Since I've gone to Central I've changed a lot in my personality').

Indicators of agency were almost as frequent at this age as those of continuity and consisted entirely of references to trying to accomplish something. There were no statements of intentionality, and again no references to decision-making.

Indicators of distinctness were present to a small degree, as were indicators of self-reflection, which were most frequently explanations of attributes or behaviour. There was one reference coded as reflexivity: 'It's hard to get me to sit down and do it (learn the guitar)'.

Seventeen-year-olds. There was a sharp increase, to 17.3, in the mean number of indicators at this age, and, in addition, for the first time all of the participants used indicators. A little more than one-half of the indicators were of continuity. Of these, the majority were references to the past, followed by future references and by references to change and to lack of change.

Next most frequent were indicators of agency, which comprised one-quarter of all indicators. About two-thirds of these were statements of intention, and the second most frequent were references to trying. For the first time, references to decision-making appeared (e.g. 'I've been thinking about if I want to go to college'), but were very infrequent.

Indicators of self-reflection were third most frequent, and they consisted equally of reflexive references and of explanations. Indicators of distinctness were least frequent.

Twenty-one-year-olds. The mean number of indicators increased over the previous age to 26.7, and again all of the participants used indicators. Indicators of continuity once more comprised more than one-half of all indicators, and the types of indicators used closely followed the pattern of the 17-year-olds, with references to the past occurring most frequently.

For the first time, self-reflection indicators occurred second most frequently, comprising one-quarter of the indicators. In addition, also for the first time, these indicators consisted of more reflexive than explanatory references.

Indicators of agency were third most frequent, and they, together with indicators of distinctness, had dropped in frequency of use from the 17-year-old level. Indicators of agency were most frequently references to trying, second most frequently to decision-making (which increased in use from the 17-year-old level) and third, to intentionality.

The percentages of the total indicators for each aspect of the subjective self at each age are shown in Figure 10.1. The results demonstrate the spontaneous emergence, in the language of self-description, of aspects of the subjective self. The high points in the distributions for each aspect can also be interpreted as representing the salience of that aspect at that particular age (i.e. the importance of the aspect, perhaps reflecting its recent

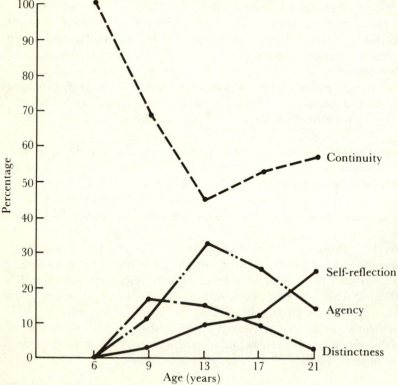

FIGURE 10.1   *Percentage distribution of each aspect for each age*

acquisition). A progression can be seen in the emergence of these aspects: continuity is the most salient, and indeed the only, aspect present in the descriptions of 6-year-olds; distinctness peaks at age 9; agency at age 13; and self-reflection at age 21.

A closer examination of the types of indicators used to express aspects of the subjective self suggests a sequence in verbal expressions of these aspects. Table 10.2 shows the percentage distribution of indicators within the aspects of continuity, agency and self-reflection at the different ages. (Distinctiveness is not included because there was only one indicator for that aspect.)

TABLE 10.2   *Percentage distribution of indicators within aspects for each age*

Indicators	Age				
	6 Years (N=13)	9 Years (N=15)	13 Years (N=16)	17 Years (N=16)	21 Years (N=15)
Continuity					
Past	33%	54%	73%	59%	53.5%
Future	22	29	4	22.5	25
Change	0	0	11.5	13	11.5
Lack of change	45	17	11.5	5.5	10
Total	100%	100%	100%	100%	100%
Agency					
Trying	0%	0%	100%	32%	48%
Intention	0	100	0	62	24
Decision	0	0	0	6	28
Total	0%	100%	100%	100%	100%
Self-reflection					
Reflexivity	0%	0%	17%	50%	58%
Explanation	0	100	83	50	42
Total	0%	100%	100%	100%	100%
Total indicators	N=9	N=35	N=61	N=277	N=401

Continuity, the most frequently occurring aspect at all ages, was expressed most often by 6-year-olds as lack of change in the self. Such reference at this age was invariably a statement about 'always' doing some activity, and appears to be the early representation of continuity of self in verbal descriptions. This reference appeared in the same form for 9-year-olds, but considerably diminished in frequency, and was replaced by an increase in references to the past. At age 13 references to lack of change shifted from activities to mention of stability in psychological attributes, and this trend continued for the two older groups. References to change in the self were the last of the continuity indicators to appear, at age 13, and they remained constant at ages 17 and 21. References to the past were most frequent for all ages except 6, and peaked at age 13. At the same time, of all ages, 13 showed the lowest frequency of references to the future of the self.

Agency indicators appeared for the first time at age 9 in the form of statements of intention, but these constituted only a small percentage of the total indicators at that age. At age 13, however, all agency indicators were references to trying to achieve something, frequently some type of self-improvement of skills or psychological attributes. In addition, these indicators represented one-third of all indicators at that age, suggesting that 'try' statements are the first significant representation of agency in verbal self-descriptions, and that this aspect is highly salient at age 13. It should be noted that this kind of reference implies a future orientation, although it was not coded as such, and may substitute for direct references to the future at this age. References to decisions or choices made the last appearance of any indicator, being first evidenced at age 17 and increasing in frequency at age 21.

Self-reflection manifested itself more slowly than the other aspects of self, but at the same time it was the only aspect which increased in frequency steadily with increasing age. Explanations of behaviour or attributes appeared with some frequency first at age 13, and were considerably more frequent at that age than were reflexive statements. However, with increasing age, explanations decreased proportionately, while the frequency of reflexive statements increased.

The results of this research are congruent with those of previous work (e.g. Broughton, 1978; Selman, 1980; Secord and Peevers, 1974) regarding the order and the approximate age levels of the acquisition of the four aspects of self-understanding. They add further validity to these findings by demonstrating the extent to which indicators of these aspects appear spontaneously in self-descriptions. This kind of analysis can be interpreted to demonstrate the salience of different aspects of the self at different developmental levels. Salience may reflect the recent acquisition of the aspect, and the subsequent lessening in proportionate frequency of that aspect may reflect its internalisation in the self-understanding of the individual.

The results of this study also provide new information on the order of acquisition of concepts, or of the verbal means of expressing them, within aspects of the subjective self. That is, reference to habitual behaviour appears to be an early way of expressing continuity; 'trying' statements emerge first as indicators of agency; and self-reflection manifests itself originally as explanations of self-attributes and behaviour. These findings may be useful both in furthering knowledge of self-understanding and in enabling a linkage between this knowledge and other variables, such as self-esteem. For example, measures of self-esteem addressing aspects of the subjective self which are salient at particular age levels may be found to yield more fruitful results than have present approaches. Study of individual differences in spontaneously expressing aspects of the subjective self might yield information relevant to the differential acquisition of self-esteem.

Much of the research in this area, because it is social class and society specific, leaves unanswered the question of whether the emergence of these indicators is reflective of universal developmental trends, or of a theory of self implicit in a particular society. The late appearance of references to decision-making, in particular, raises questions of this nature. Cross-cultural research is needed to clarify this issue.

Finally, research efforts should be directed at comparing and linking the development of aspects of the subjective and objective selves across ages, as proposed in the Damon and Hart (1982) model, and extending this study to include adults at various life stages. Such efforts are needed to further increase knowledge of the developmental progression and unity of self-understanding.

Acknowledgment

This research was completed while the author was spending a sabbatical leave as a visitor at the Department of Experimental Psychology, Oxford University. The support of Michael Argyle and Rom Harré is gratefully acknowledged. The assistance of Roz Burnett in the development of the coding system and in coding self-descriptions was of critical importance to the completion of the project. Solomon Asch and Peter K. Manning read an early version of the manuscript and made invaluable suggestions.

Note

1 The coding system includes four categories which were not included in the present analysis. The total number of indicators in the seven descriptions used for the reliability tests included those categories, and totalled 316. The total number of indicators in the final sample, including those categories, was 849.

References

Broughton, J. (1978), 'Development of concepts of self, mind, reality, and knowledge', in W. Damon (ed.), *New Directions for Child Development*, vol. 1, Jossey-Bass: San Francisco.

Damon, W. and Hart, D. (1982), 'The development of self-understanding from infancy through adolescence', *Child Development*, 53, pp. 841–64.

Farr, R. (1981), 'The social origins of the human mind: A historical note', in J. P. Forgas (ed.), *Social Cognition: Perspectives of Everyday Understanding*, Academic Press: London.

Harré, R. (1983), *Personal Being*, Blackwell: Oxford.

Hollingshead, A. (1965), *Two-factor Index of Social Position*, Yale University Press: New Haven.

James, W. (1961), *Psychology: The Briefer Course*, Harper & Row: New York (originally published 1892).

Keller, A., Ford, L. H., Jr., and Meacham, J. A. (1978), 'Dimensions of self-concept in pre-school children', *Developmental Psychology*, 14, pp. 483–9.

Kuhn, M. H. (1960), 'Self attitudes by age, sex and professional training', *Sociological Quarterly*, 1, pp. 39–55.

Livesley, W. J. and Bromley, D. B. (1973), *Person Perception in Childhood and Adolescence*, Wiley: New York.

Mead, G. H. (1934), *Mind, Self, and Society*, University of Chicago Press: Chicago.

Peevers, B. H. and Secord, P. F. (1973a), 'Developmental changes in the attribution of descriptive concepts to persons', *Journal of Personality and Social Psychology*, 27, 1, pp. 120–8.

Peevers, B. H. and Secord, P. F. (1973b), 'The Person Concept Code', *Catalog of Selected Documents in Psychology*, American Psychological Association: Washington, D.C.

Secord, P. F. and Peevers, B. H. (1974), 'The development and attribution of person concepts', in T. Mischel (ed.), *Understanding Other Persons*, Blackwell: Oxford.

Selman, R. (1980), *The Growth of Interpersonal Understanding*, Academic Press: New York.

Wylie, R. C. (1979), *The Self Concept: Theory and Research on Selected Topics*, rev. ed., vol. 2, University of Nebraska Press, Lincoln, Neb.

Part III

Adolescence – the consolidation of self

11 The identity status approach to the study of ego identity development

James E. Marcia

As a clinical psychologist and a psychotherapist, I have three criteria for the value of a concept: it should be definable and measurable so that it yields predictions within a scientific hypothesis-testing context; it should be part of a fairly complex and internally consistent theoretical framework so that overall understanding of human nature is increased; and, finally, it should be useful for psychotherapy. Hence, in this paper I shall be discussing some of the empirical, theoretical and psychotherapeutic implications of the identity status approach to the study of identity development.

Psychosocial developmental theory

The identity status approach to the study of ego identity development began as an attempt at establishing construct validity for Erik Erikson's (1959) fifth stage of psychosocial development, which occurs in late adolescence. Erikson, like other ego psychoanalytic theorists such as Rapaport, Hartman, Kris, etc. (Rapaport, 1958), sought to elaborate and extend the description of the ego, i.e. those cumulative personality processes whose essential function is delay of impulse expression. Although the concepts developed by these theorists are far richer and more complex than mere 'delay mechanisms', still it is this notion of progressively more structured and sophisticated processes intervening between impulse and expression that establishes ego psychoanalytic theory as an extension of, rather than as an alternative to, more id-oriented psychoanalytic theory. Erikson's major contribution has been the formulation of a scheme, not quite a theory, of life cycle development which attempts to account for changing individual needs and capabilities on one hand and changing societal demands and rewards on the other. A series of epigenetically based issues in individual psychosocial growth is assumed to be more or less matched by a series of institutionalised social practices. These are culturally furnished milieux within which each specific stage of ego development takes place. For example, in our society, the stage-specific crisis of late childhood, industry-inferiority, occurs generally within the context of the social institution of the primary school. If Erikson's developmental scheme is correct, then social institutions can be evaluated with respect to the degree to which they facilitate or inhibit the ego growth expected within a particular period.

Contrary to the generally conservative bias discernible in Erikson's theory, the responsibility for a lack of this psychosocial meshing or mutuality does not always lie with the individual. Once created, social institutions have their own agendas and seek their own survival, often at the expense of individual growth. We in North America, particularly those in the United States, went through a very evident period of disjunction with respect to our late adolescents during the late 1960s and early 1970s. In this case, I think that it was some social institutions (the military draft and sex role stereotyping) that gave way, to some extent, to pressures from the individual side of the psychosocial partnership. Hence, there is room within this scheme of ego developmental stages for societal as well as individual adaptation, although this is an admittedly underdeveloped aspect of Erikson's theory. Its thoroughgoing study awaits a taxonomy of environments construed in terms of their relevance to each psychosocial stage.

The identity status paradigm was developed to permit measurement of Erikson's central, and only truly structural, concept of identity – identity diffusion. Resolutions of other stage-specific issues lead to what Erikson refers to as 'a sense of' or 'a capacity for', e.g. 'a sense of industry', 'a capacity for intimacy', etc. Only the concept of identity refers to a synthesis of parts into a new structure that is subsequently reorganised, as well as re-experienced, at succeeding life cycle stages. All life cycle stages including identity recur at subsequent stages and take on a different colouring or tone according to the dominant issue of that stage. But the quality of the other stages is more that of experience than of structure.

The identity statuses

The identity statuses are four outcomes of the identity crisis period. They are four differing modes of identity formation and are intended to be exhaustive; hence, any late adolescent (ages 18 to 22) should be categorisable into one of these four statuses.

Placement of an individual into an identity status is done by means of a semi-standardised, semi-structured interview. The interview is semi-standardised in that interview content areas can change with changing social conditions; it is semi-structured in that the interviewer is allowed some latitude in terms of asking probing questions. Currently, the interview content areas are occupational choice, ideological beliefs (comprising religious and political attitudes) and sexual-interpersonal beliefs (composed of attitudes towards sex roles and sexuality). Although the content areas are important in that they must reflect issues salient to, and discriminating among, late adolescents, of most significance to identity status determination are the *process* variables of exploration of alternatives ('crisis') and commitment. Identity status is determined on the basis of the degree of exploration and subsequent commitment.

The four identity statuses are as follows. *Identity Achievement* is the most developmentally advanced status. The individual has gone through a period of exploration of alternatives and has made well-defined commitments. *Moratorium* is the predecessor to Identity Achievement. Here, the person is *in* the exploration period with commitments only vaguely formed. *Foreclosure* refers to the individual who has undergone no, or very little, exploration and remains firmly committed to childhood-based values. Finally, *Identity Diffusion*, the least developmentally advanced of the statuses, is comprised of persons who, whether they have explored alternatives or not, are uncommitted to any definite directions in their lives.

Some empirical characteristics of the identity statuses

The results of approximately twenty years of research and about 150 studies have established construct validity for the identity statuses and, by extension, for Erikson's notion of identity formation as a distinguishing developmental task of late adolescence. (Studies upon which these descriptions are based are reviewed in Bourne, 1978a, 1978b; Marcia, 1980; Waterman, 1982; Marcia *et al.*, work in progress.) This research covers roughly two areas, studies dealing with personality characteristics of individuals in the different identity statuses and studies concerning psychosocial developmental implications of the identity statuses. Some representative findings are that Identity Achievement subjects are the most cognitively and integratively complex and flexible of the statuses and least resistant to self-esteem manipulation and conformity pressure. They are at high levels of general ego development, as conceptualised by Loevinger (1976), and advanced over the other statuses in their capacity for intimate relationships. Moratoriums are the most overtly anxious of the statuses and are morally and interpersonally the most sensitive. They tend to have ambivalent relationships with their families and are sometimes preoccupied with resolving oedipal issues. They show contrasting patterns of rebellion and acquiescence. Foreclosures subscribe to authoritarian values and tend to be cognitively rigid. They are very close to their families, whom they perceive as warm and child-centred, and from whom, of course, it is very difficult for them to differentiate. Interpersonally, they tend to form stereotyped and superficial relationships. Identity Diffusions are easily manipulable by others in terms of their self-esteem and, among the statuses, are at the lowest levels of ego development and of cognitive and moral development. They feel generally rejected by their families, particularly by the parent of the same sex whom they perceive as non-emulatable. More than the other statuses, they tend to be interpersonally isolated.

Theoretical propositions concerning identity

Ideally, theory and research are reciprocally interactive in that theory gives rise to research, which in turn explicates, sometimes truncates, sometimes elaborates theory, which then indicates new research directions. This has been the case with identity theory and identity status research. The following theoretical propositions concerning identity development are based upon an integration of Erikson's theory and the foregoing research on the identity statuses.

1. *Identity formation occurs within a sequence of developmental stages.* The nature of the resolution of each psychosocial stage is dependent upon the nature of the resolution of prior stages and contributes to the style of resolution of succeeding stages (Erikson, 1959). Given an 'average expectable environment', identity formation is a naturally occurring event in human personality development (the epigenetic principle: Hartmann, 1958). The style of identity (the identity status), although not necessarily the content of a particular identity, is predictable from previous psychosocial stage outcomes and can predict subsequent psychosocial stage outcomes.

Theoretically, every stage-specific crisis (e.g. identity) has both precursors (e.g. an Identity issue during the oral, Trust–Mistrust stage) and consequences (e.g. an Identity issue during the Generativity stage). The assumption is that the issue relevant to a particular stage takes on the colouring or tone of the dominant crisis of that stage. For example, Intimacy during the Industry–Inferiority stage might be related to peer relationships in school, whereas Intimacy at the Generativity–Self Absorption stage would likely centre around a chosen individual with whom one shares joint responsibility in caring for the life cycles of others. The implications for research are these: if the theory is correct, then the resolution of identity issues in stages prior to late adolescence should yield finer predictions about identity in adolescence than the resolutions of the prior stage-specific crises. That is, while Autonomy, as the stage-specific issue of toddlerhood, should be related to Identity at adolescence, the Identity aspect of the Autonomy stage should be even more highly related to Identity at adolescence. Similarly, Identity should be related to Intimacy, but identity resolution at late adolescence should be even more highly related to the identity aspect of Intimacy at young adulthood than to Intimacy *per se*.

2. *Identity is a psychological structure – a process with a slow rate of change – similar to Piaget's cognitive developmental structures.* Identity is 'really there' in the same sense that a theory is 'really there'. An identity is a theory one has about oneself (not necessarily wholly conscious) and having it usually makes a positive difference in how one feels about oneself. This self-theory, or identity structure, is usually below the level of awareness (*assimilative* in Piaget's sense), except when it is challenged by potentially disconfirming input (*disequilibrated*), at which time one becomes more aware of one's identity (Erikson's 'crisis' state). Optimally, one then modifies the identity structure somewhat in order to *accommodate* to the new experience.

3. *The cognitive, physiological and social-expectational ingredients necessary for a mature identity are present for the first time at late adolescence.* Although precursors to identity exist in prior developmental stages, adolescence is at least the crucial, and, perhaps the critical, period for the formation of the first full identity configuration (Meilman, 1979). This first identity configuration is not the last. Identity status at late adolescence represents only a first answer to the identity question. It is assumed that a successful solution at this age permits that openness to experience that will initiate subsequent periods of disequilibration, identity crisis and re-resolution. In other words, initial identity achievement at late adolescence should guarantee a Moratorium–Achievement–Moratorium–Achievement cycle throughout adulthood, similar to the process discussed by Daniel Levinson *et al.* (1978), in *The Seasons of a Man's Life.* Unsuccessful identity resolutions at late adolescence do not necessarily mean that an identity will never be constructed. Even if one has not moved out of Foreclosure during late adolescence, there are plenty of disequilibrating events in a life cycle to elicit identity crises. However, the older one gets, the more difficult it is to move from the Foreclosure position. There are not many social supports for identity crises at age 40; by then, one has to contend both with the internal conditions of one's self-esteem ('standards' that one has to live up to) and with the external expectations of others that one will be a certain person and will behave in a certain way. Possibilities for later identity construction for Identity Diffusions exist, especially if they are fortunate enough to find themselves in a relationship that supplies the self-affirming supports that were absent in their relationship with their parents. However, the likelihood is that their identity will take on a conferred (from the partner) form rather than a constructed one. In other words, if one is a Diffusion in late adolescence perhaps his or her best hope is for a kind of belated Foreclosure.

4. *The initial identity formed at late adolescence may be the result of either a sum or a synthesis of childhood identifications, social appraisals, unique abilities and needs, physiological givens, and positive and negative results of social experimentation.* To the extent that a society and one's family permits and encourages decision-making about occupational choice and ideology, an individual's identity

will be based more upon ego *synthetic* processes. To the extent that a society and one's family prescribes occupational choice and ideology, an individual's identity will be more the *sum* of influences from his or her childhood. The presence of an identity does not mean that an identity has necessarily been constructed. Given an average expectable environment, an identity can 'happen' as one becomes progressively more aware of one's most basic characteristics and position in the world. One comes gradually to realise that one is separate from one's mother, the child of certain parents, the possessor of certain skills and needs, a pupil in a particular school, a member of a certain religious and social group, the citizen of a particular country. All of this describes a *conferred* identity of whose elements the individual becomes progressively aware. In contrast, identity begins to be *constructed* when the individual starts to make decisions about who to be, with what group to affiliate, what beliefs to adopt, what interpersonal values to espouse and what occupational direction to pursue. Most, though not all, individuals 'have' an identity; however, only some have a *self-constructed* identity based upon the superimposition of a decision-making process on the given or conferred identity.

5. *The identity status interview content areas (e.g. occupation, religion, sexuality, etc.) may be considered as topographic features indicating the presence or absence of underlying structure.* An identity status may be assigned to each interview content area; i.e. an individual may be Moratorium in occupation, Foreclosure in religion, etc. Usually, one identity status predominates across a majority of areas. But the relationship between identity status in the different content areas and overall identity status may be, and has been, considered in two ways. Identity has been treated as a sum of interview areas, so that the individual is assigned to the most frequently appearing status. The assumption underlying this procedure is that overall identity is a kind of sum of identity in different areas; e.g. the more areas called Identity Achievement, the more 'identity' is present. The alternative being suggested here is that the areas are indicators of the presence or absence of underlying structure; some areas are more important for indicating this structure than others. The importance, then, of a number of areas having the same status rating is not that they are summative to an overall identity but that they increase the accuracy of the probability of the existence of a given underlying structure.

6. *Identity is always changing, but after adolescence it does so at a progressively slower rate.* Identity formation, particularly after the initial adolescent synthesis, is a process of maintaining continuity by changing. Peaks of change occur during focal crisis periods in subsequent psychosocial stages (e.g. a divorce during the Intimacy stage; one's child's adolescence during the Generativity stage; a serious illness during the Integrity stage).

Psychotherapeutic implications of the identity status approach

Perhaps the most demanding context within which to determine the validity of psychosocial developmental theory is psychotherapy – the task of enabling individuals to effect significant changes in their lives. In terms of clinical implications, the presence, in some form, of each psychosocial stage at every other stage offers the possibilities of remediation. The nature of the Eriksonian stages is that they are crucial, but not critical. It is difficult to form a positive sense of Identity if one's resolution of Industry is tilted negatively toward the Inferiority side. But the game is not necessarily over. For an Industry issue can be expected to arise again at Identity. Then, of course, one has two life cycle issues to deal with at adolescence: Identity and the preceding Industry. So the chances of an individual's resolving both crises, unaided, are slim. Most 'average expectable' social institutions at adolescence assume that Industry is in place and do not provide a context for its development. It is here, I think, that one can construe psychotherapy within an Eriksonian framework as the provision of a 'better-than-average expectable environment' for the purpose of remediating previously negatively resolved psychosocial issues.

Since the identity statuses have their basis in psychodynamic theory, involve differing modes of decision-making and yield fairly discernible character types, they have implications for counselling and psychotherapy.

Identity Achievement persons seldom come in for psychotherapy; they are more likely to seek 'growth' or educational experiences, or to be undergoing time-limited crises. A crisis-intervention, short-term counselling approach would probably be indicated in most cases.

Moratoriums are the most likely to appear for treatment because of their transitional, 'in-crisis' position with respect to identity. However, since their discomfort is meaningful in terms of the identity formation process, the therapist must be careful not to label them as 'patients' and not to treat an identity crisis as an affliction. In general, Moratoriums will do quite well if the therapist is not too intrusive. A Rogerian approach is probably the most useful.

Foreclosures seldom come in for therapy except when external events force them to reconsider their previously unexamined beliefs and goals. The problem here is that one is dealing with an unreconstructed ego ideal, which, if confronted too directly, will result in the Foreclosure's fleeing therapy or experiencing an acute depressive episode as the individual is deprived abruptly of his or her inner source of self-esteem. What is called for here is an initial alliance between the psychotherapist and those parts of the individual's ego ideal that he or she finds congenial and benign. From this position of a non-threatening alliance, then, the therapist can enable the Foreclosure to use the precipitating crisis to effect a gradual change in identity – to go through a successful moratorium period. Psychodynamically oriented psychotherapy with an emphasis on the relationship aspects of treatment is likely the intervention of choice here.

Identity Diffusions present the widest range of pathology and the greatest therapeutic challenge. For less-disturbed Diffusions, the task of the therapist is to help the individual to draw together disparate identity elements into a coherent, meaningful identity structure. In more severe disturbances, such as borderline disorders, the therapist him/herself becomes an identity element, a primary object, that the person can incorporate or identify with, and around whom the Diffusion can begin to build some identity. Obviously, this is a lengthy process and requires the provision by the therapist of better-than-average expectable interpersonal conditions in order to remedy severe developmental deficits. Psychoanalytically oriented psychotherapy is recommended for this condition.

Current salient issues in identity research from an Eriksonian perspective

In this brief overview, I have indicated some of the empirical, theoretical and clinical implications of the identity status approach to identity development. Some important questions to be considered by those working in this area are as follows.

Is identity, in fact, an internal structure representing more than the sum of learned behaviours? Answering this question would involve longitudinal studies in which identity elements (occupational directions, social-religious-political beliefs, interpersonal attitudes) could be assessed at a fairly early age (10 to 11 years), and change in their content, especially in the organisation of content, could be observed throughout adolescence. The key issue is whether or not there is an individual organisational, structural contribution to an identity gestalt that supersedes a simple combination of elements. Elements can be learned; organisational principles can be learned more or less; but a unique organisation of elements would indicate the individual's own structure-building contribution. Some evidence for this may be found in the relationship between identity and formal operational thought (Wagner, 1976; Rowe and Marcia, 1980; Leadbeater and Dionne, 1981) and between identity and integrative complexity (Slugoski *et al.*,1984).

What is the relationship between the *content* of one's identity and the *process* of identity formation; do some contents preclude or foster subsequent identity development? The research on identity status formation has been assiduously process-based. Interviewers are specifically instructed not to consider the content of a subject's belief in assigning an identity status. However, there are indications that content may affect process. In a 6-year follow-up study, Marcia (1976) found that three out of seven persons who were Identity Achievement in 1970 were Foreclosures in 1976. One of the explanations proffered for this theoretically anomalous finding was that the *content* of the initial identity was so constricting that it resulted in a Foreclosure-like position. Taking another tack, it appears that the content of women's social-political beliefs is related to their identity status. Stein and Weston (1982) reported that women with non-Traditional attitudes toward women's role were higher in identity than women with Traditional attitudes; and Prince-Embury and Deutchman (1981) found pro–Equal Rights Amendment women to be higher in identity status than anti-ERA women.

How does women's identity formation process, based as it is as much on interpersonal as on occupational and ideological contexts, differ from men's identity formation process? At least, it must be more protracted while the social forms (engagement, marriage, childbearing) are fulfilled. Jane Kroger, currently studying identity development in adult women in New Zealand, states: 'Support is obtained for the psychoanalytic view that identity formation for women is a lengthy and complex process; in fact, it may not be until well past the thirties that vocational, political, and religious issues can be resolved' (1985, p. 6, unpublished manuscript). Findings also support the view that questions of identity for women in the age range studied (17 to 47) centre primarily in interpersonal areas.

The identity statuses are *outcome* categories applicable to late adolescence; how can they be used to investigate the *process* of identity development through adolescence? Some recent methodological innovations look promising in terms of a more refined assessment of the process aspects of identity. Grotevant and Adams (1984) have developed an objective (questionnaire) measure of identity status that yields separate scores on the variables of exploration and commitment in the individual interview content areas. A similar attempt at developing a process-oriented measure relating both to the identity statuses and to Coleman's 'focal' theory of adolescent identity development is underway in the Netherlands (Bosma, 1985). What is especially valuable about both of these efforts is that they provide dimensions for measuring changes in the processes underlying identity, exploration and commitment, so that these can be considered separately rather than lumped together in the rather unwieldy form of identity status categories.

How far back developmentally can one trace the identity formation process that reaches its first complete expression at late adolescence? Recent research by Schiedel and Marcia (1985) on the relationships among gender, sex, role, identity and intimacy suggests that sex-role learning during the oedipal period affects later identity and intimacy development. Studies on the psychosexual level of early memories by Josselson (1982), replicated and extended by Orlofsky and Frank (in press), indicate preoedipal as well as oedipal forerunners. Finally, using Hansberg's separation–individuation index to measure concepts of attachment and individuation (Bowlby, 1969; Mahler *et al.*, 1975), Kroger (in press) found that persons high in identity were less anxiously attached and more secure in dealing with separation issues than were those in low identity statuses. Taken together, these studies indicated that important preconditions for successful identity formation may exist from earliest childhood.

The incompleteness of the answers to the above questions indicates the need for continued research into them. The partial answers presented suggest possible directions. However, identity considered as a psychosocial developmental stage reaching its initial, but not final, resolution at late adolescence has proven to be empirically and theoretically fruitful.

References

Bosma, H. (1985), 'Identity development in adolescence: Coping with commitments', Unpublished doctoral dissertation, University of Groningen, Groningen, The Netherlands.

Bourne, E. (1978a), 'The state of research on ego identity: A review and appraisal (Part I)', *Journal of Youth and Adolescence*, 7, pp. 223–51.

Bourne, E. (1978b), 'The state of research on ego identity: A review and appraisal (Part II)', *Journal of Youth and Adolescence*, 7, pp. 371–92.

Bowlby, J. (1969), *Attachment and Loss: I. Attachment*, Hogarth Press: London.

Erikson, E. H. (1959), 'Identity and the life cycle', *Psychological Issues*, 1 (monograph no. 1).

Grotevant, H. P. and Adams, G. R. (1984), 'Development of an objective measure to assess ego identity in adolescence: Validation and application', *Journal of Youth and Adolescence*, 13(5), pp. 419–38.

Hartmann, H. (1958), 'Ego psychology and the problem of adaptation', *Journal of the American Psychoanalytic Association*, Monograph 1, International Universities Press: New York.

Josselson, R. L. (1982), 'Personality structure and identity status in women as viewed through early memories', *Journal of Youth and Adolescence*, 11, pp. 219–99.

Kroger, J. (in press), 'Ego identity status and separation–individuation', *Journal of Youth and Adolescence*.

Kroger, J. (1985), 'A developmental study of identity formation among late adolescent and adult women', Unpublished manuscript, Department of Education, Victoria University of Wellington, Wellington, New Zealand.

Leadbeater, B. J. and Dionne, J. P. (1981), 'The adolescent's use of formal operational thinking in solving problems related to identity solution', *Adolescence*, 16(61), pp. 111–21.

Levinson, D., Barrow, C. N., Klein, E. B., Levinson, M. H. and McKee, B.

(1978), *The Seasons of a Man's Life*, Ballantine: New York.

Loevinger (1976), *Ego Development*, Jossey Bass: San Francisco.

Mahler, M. S., Pine, F. and Bergman, A. (1975), *The Psychological Birth of the Human Infant*, Basic Books: New York.

Marcia, J. E. (1980), 'Identity in adolescence', in J. Adelson (ed.), *Handbook of Adolescent Psychology*, Wiley: New York, pp. 159–87.

Marcia, J. E. (1976), 'Identity six years after: A follow-up study', *Journal of Youth and Adolescence*, 5, pp. 145–60.

Marcia, J. E., Waterman, A. S. and Matteson, D. (in preparation), *Ego Identity: A Handbook for Psychosocial Research*, Erlbaum: Hillsdale, N.J. (Simon Fraser University, Burnaby, B.C., Canada.)

Meilman, P. W. (1979), 'Cross sectional age changes in ego identity status during adolescence', *Developmental Psychology*, 15(2), pp. 230–1.

Orlofsky, J. and Frank, M. (in press), 'Personality structure as viewed through early memories and identity status in college men and women', *Journal of Personality and Social Psychology*.

Prince-Embury, S. and Deutchman, I. E. (1981), *Journal of Mind and Behaviour*, 3, pp. 309–21.

Rapaport, D. (1958), 'A historical survey of psychoanalytic ego psychology', *Bulletin of the Philadelphia Association for Psychoanalysis*, 8, pp. 105–20.

Rowe, I. and Marcia, J. E. (1980), 'Ego identity status, formal operations, and moral development', *Journal of Youth and Adolescence*, 9, pp. 87–99.

Schiedel, D. G. and Marcia, J. E. (1985), 'Ego identity, intimacy, sex role orientation, and gender', *Developmental Psychology*, 21(1), pp. 149–60.

Slugoski, B. R., Marcia, J. E. and Koopman, R. F. (1984), 'Cognitive and social interactional characteristics of ego identity statuses in college males', *Journal of Personality and Social Psychology*, 47(3), pp. 646–61.

Stein, S. L. and Weston, L. (1982), 'College women's attitudes toward women and identity achievement', *Adolescence*, 17(68), pp. 895–9.

Wagner, J. (1976), 'A study of the relationship between formal operations and ego identity in adolescence', Unpublished doctoral dissertation, State University of New York at Buffalo.

Waterman, A. S. (1982), 'Identity development from adolescence to adulthood: An extension of theory and a review of research', *Developmental Psychology*, 18(3), pp. 341–58.

12   Self-esteem in adolescence

Roberta G. Simmons

Of all dimensions of the self-image, self-esteem has been the most studied (see Wylie, 1961, 1974; Damon and Hart, 1982). In fact, the great emphasis on self-esteem has led many of the major theorists in the area to plead for studies of other dimensions of the self-picture to redress the balance (e.g. Rosenberg, 1979). Nevertheless, probably as a reflection of the importance of self-esteem maintenance to overall well-being (Allport, 1961; Murphy, 1947; Rosenberg, 1979), self-esteem studies continue to be plentiful.

In this chapter we shall concentrate on the impact of adolescence on global self-esteem. As a time of complex social, physical, emotional and cognitive changes, adolescence is an important period in the life course in which to examine all aspects of self-image and identity, including global self-esteem. This chapter will first review some basic issues related to the conceptualisation (and therefore measurement) of global self-esteem, will then briefly present theories of adolescence that predict effects upon self-esteem, as well as empirical findings concerning these effects, and finally discuss some of our work in this area. Much of the theoretical and empirical work on global self-esteem has involved its relationships to other psychological constructs and to cognitive changes rather than its relationship to the social, biological and behavioural phenomena that are changing during adolescence (Harter, 1983). Our own work has focused on some of the latter social, biological and behavioural issues: e.g. would one expect the way society structures the entry to adolescence to affect the child's reaction to it? Do the biological changes of puberty have consequences for global self-esteem?

Global self-esteem

If the self-image is classified as an attitude toward the self, then self-esteem involves the evaluative dimension. Global self-esteem has been described by Rosenberg (1965; 1979) as the overall negative or positive attitude toward the self, and it is this definition which we have utilised in our own work (Simmons *et al.*, 1979). In this conceptualisation, high self-esteem does not signify arrogance or conceit but simply acceptance of oneself as a person of worth; low self-esteem means a view of oneself as unworthy.

Wells and Marwell (1976), Harter (1983) and Wylie (1974; 1979) review alternative definitions. To Epstein (1973), an individual's level of self-esteem is a higher-order postulate in the collection of abstractions that constitute the self-theory. As Wells and Marwell (1976) note, another alternative definition stems from James's view that self-esteem is the result of the discrepancy between aspirations and the extent to which persons believe they have attained these aspirations. This definition, in fact, suffers from the complexity of conceptualising aspirations (fantasy level, realistic level, floor of satisfaction), as well as the methodological problems of discrepancy scores. If one instead utilises the simpler definition of an overall positive versus negative attitude toward the self, one can investigate empirically the extent to which this attitude varies as a function of one's aspirations and of one's attainments (Rosenberg and Simmons, 1972).

Wells and Marwell (1976) note that some definitions place greater emphasis on the emotional or affective dimension of self-esteem (also see Epstein, 1973). However, the Rosenberg definition assumes that a favourable self-esteem carries with it positive emotions and that a very negative self-esteem implies some pain. Nevertheless, global happiness/depression can be distinguished from global self-esteem both conceptually and in terms of measurement; and it can be shown that the two variables correlate but are not identical (Rosenberg, 1965; Rosenberg and Simmons, 1972, Chapter 2).

Despite the great number of studies of self-esteem and the major emphasis placed by many theorists on the human motive to maintain high self-esteem, there has been controversy about the utility of such a concept. First of all the question has been raised as to whether there is such an entity as global self-esteem, or whether instead the individual evaluates himself or herself segmentally. That is, do individuals rate themselves differently depending on the task at hand, the situation at issue or the role-relationship or identity involved (Savin-Williams and Demo, 1983; Harter, 1983; Gecas, 1972; Rosenberg, 1979)?

On the logical level, there is nothing to preclude both segmental/situational self-evaluations on the one hand and global self-evaluations on the other (Rosenberg, 1979). A consensus to this effect seems to be emerging. Epstein (1973) and Harter (1983)[1] emphasise global self-esteem on one hand (perhaps as the superordinate construct in a hierarchy) and more specific dimensions of self-evaluation on the other – particularly, ratings of self-competence (or self-efficacy), of worthiness in the moral dimension, of power or control and of social acceptance (or love-worthiness). Clearly, these subdimensions can be broken down into more precise subratings.

The important issue is not whether global self-esteem is a useful theoretical construct, but rather that measurements should clearly distinguish between global indicators and indicators suitable for more specific evaluations. As Harter (1983) notes, many prior measures of self-esteem have included a pot-pourri of items that tap different subdimensions and varying levels of abstraction.

The Rosenberg self-esteem scale and our translation of that scale for younger children focus only on the global dimension. With the use of these scales, there has been much fruitful research related to the construct of global self-esteem; there has also been considerable work on validating instruments. (See Wells and Marwell, 1976; Wylie, 1974, 1979; Rosenberg and Simmons, 1972, Chapter 2; Rosenberg, 1965; Hoge and McCarthy, 1983, 1984; Robinson and Shaver, 1969). It should be noted that large longitudinal studies show that whatever momentary changes occur in overall self-regard owing to situational differences, stability over the long term is substantial. In our own work on adolescents, the average one-year correlation was .54 ($p < .001$) with reliability uncorrected and .68 ($p < .001$) with reliability corrected (Simmons and Blyth, 1987).[2] McCarthy and Hoge (1984) show similar one-year correlations of .50 ($p \leq .05$) on the Rosenberg self-esteem scale. The size of these coefficients gives evidence both of the existence of the construct global self-esteem and of some fluctuation in self-evaluation due perhaps, in part, to situational changes.

An additional issue related to the existence of global self-esteem is a developmental one. Harter (1983) reports, based on pilot data, that children aged 4 to 7 years do not appear to possess a concept of general self-worth but rather seem able to evaluate specific behaviours only. Adolescents, on the other hand, appear to be comfortable with the idea of a general self-evaluation.

If Harter is correct, then the question of interest involves the age range at which such a concept usually emerges. We have measured global self-esteem at age 8 in Grade 3 and validated these measurements (Rosenberg and Simmons, 1972). However, Damon and Hart (1982) and Harter (1983) both note that because younger children's cognitive views of self differ from those of adolescents, the same measure may not be appropriate at both age periods. In our current studies, to be reported below, we compare the global self-esteem of children in Grades 6 through 10. We utilised a confirmatory factor analysis in LISREL VI to develop a measurement model for self-esteem, and found that the same measurement model (the same factor structure) was appropriate for children from Grades 6 to 10 (Simmons *et al.*, 1987). Further work on the development of global self-esteem and its relationship to specific self-evaluations would be advised, however.

In general, the linkage between specific and global self-esteem is of great interest. With the principle of psychological centrality, Rosenberg (1979) hypothesises that specific self-evaluations have a greater impact upon global self-esteem if these evaluations are in areas about which the individual cares a great deal. Utilising Stryker's theoretical framework, a similar hypothesis can be derived: role-performances related to salient identities (identities to which one is more committed) will have greater effect on global self-esteem than role-performances related to less salient identities (Wells and Stryker, in press; Stryker, 1982).

Given the view that global self-evaluation is a theoretical construct of importance to study, another question involves the combination of positive and negative attitudes along the same dimension. This question has been raised because of factor analyses of the Rosenberg self-esteem scale. Despite high Guttman scale coefficients and reasonably high Cronbach's Alphas (Hoge and McCarthy, 1983, 1984; Wells and Marwell, 1976; Fleming and Courtney, 1984), in factor analysis the positively worded items ('I feel that I am a person of worth, at least on an equal plane with others') frequently load on one dimension, the negative on another ('At times I think I am no good at all'). Kohn and Schooler *et al.* (1983) have opted to keep these factors separate, calling one self-confidence,[3] the other self-deprecation. (Also see Kaplan and Pokorny, 1969; Carmines and Zeller, 1979.) In our work (with the 'translation' of the Rosenberg self-esteem scale for younger children), we have used a LISREL measurement model and kept all of the items in one scale; even though the two positively worded items had considerably lower loadings than the four negative items, all loadings were significant. There was no indication that a second factor was necessary in order adequately to represent the data (Simmons *et al.*, 1987). Our concern is that we measure evaluation of the *self*, rather than a positive or negative orientation in general. We are attempting to avoid an acquiescence response set. (See Hoge and McCarthy, 1983, 1984 for a similar approach.) It is important for future studies to include positive and negative attitudes toward the self and toward other issues in the same factor analysis to see if one can distinguish between attitudes toward the self and toward other objects, as well as between positive and negative orientations.

While the considerations above appear to be measurement issues, they also bear heavily on the conceptualisation of self-esteem. The question is whether an overall global self-evaluation can be investigated, or whether positive and negative self-attitudes have to be considered separately. Bradburn and Caplovitz (1965) in studying happiness show that the frequency of positive feelings and the frequency of negative feelings vary somewhat independently. Yet individuals still appear capable of an overall judgment of happiness, and we suggest a similar pattern for self-esteem.

Adolescence and self-esteem: General theories and overall empirical findings

Entry to a new period in the life-course may challenge the self-image, particularly individuals' self-evaluations, as they attempt new tasks in which they can succeed or fail, as they alter their self-values and the areas which are important for overall self-esteem, and as they confront new significant others against whom they rate themselves and about whose judgments they care. Substantial controversy has been generated within the behavioural sciences concerning the difficulty of adolescence as a transitional period in the life-course. On the one hand, there are those who characterise the period as an exceptionally stressful period. On the other hand, many investigators see the supposed tumult of adolescence as just that, supposed and mythical.

Hall (1904) originally described the adolescent years as ones of 'storm and stress'. Later Erikson (1959; 1968) characterised adolescence as a time of identity crisis, in which the youngster struggles for a stable sense of self. Psychoanalysts, such as Blos (1962; 1971) and Anna Freud (1958), have suggested that puberty sparks a resurgence of oedipal conflicts for the boy and preoedipal pressures for the girl (see Barglow and Schaefer, 1979). According to Elkind (1967), cognitive processes also contribute to adolescent difficulty. Adolescents become cognizant that others are formulating opinions of them, but they are unable to differentiate their own self-preoccupations from the thoughts of this imaginary audience (adolescent 'egocentrism'). They concentrate on their own faults and believe that these faults are as evident to others as to themselves.[4]

From the sociological point of view, adolescence has traditionally been described as a period of physical maturity and social immaturity (Davis, 1944). Because of the complexity of the present social system, children reach physical adulthood before they are capable of functioning well in adult social roles. The disjunction between physical capabilities and socially allowed independence and power and the concurrent status-ambiguities are viewed as stressful for the self-image of the adolescent.

Yet many investigators claim that for most youngsters these years are not marked by stress or turmoil (Offer and Offer, 1975; Offer *et al.*, 1981; Haan, 1977; Petersen and Taylor, 1980; Savin-Williams and Demo, 1983; Dusek and Flaherty, 1981). Wylie (1979) in reviewing studies in this area concludes there is no patterned, consistent relationship of age to self-esteem, and no pattern across studies of increasing negative self-esteem in adolescence. In fact, more recent reviews of large-scale longitudinal studies report a consistent rise, not a drop, in self-esteem as children move from early to late adolescence (McCarthy and Hoge, 1982; O'Malley and Bachman, 1983).[5] In addition to concern over what happens *during* adolescence, there is some controversy over the fate of self-esteem in the transition between childhood and early adolescence. Some studies show no age difference (Yamamoto *et al.*, 1969; Attenborough and Zdep, 1973; Coleman, 1974), but others indicate negative changes near or upon entry to adolescence, that is, in Grades 6, 7 or 8 (age 12 to 13) compared with earlier (Piers and Harris, 1964; Katz and Zigler, 1967; Jorgensen and Howell, 1969; Trowbridge, 1972; also see Harter, 1983).

These studies vary in their methodology. The longitudinal studies that show a rise in self-esteem during adolescence are large-scale and probably can be trusted (O'Malley and Bachman, 1983). However, many of the studies comparing children with early adolescents are not as compelling. All are cross-sectional; some have small samples (Piers and Harris, 1964; Katz and Zigler, 1967; Bohan, 1973). Only a few indicate they used random sampling (Katz and Zigler, 1967: a suburban sample; Yamamoto *et al.*, 1969: a suburban sample; Attenborough and Zdep, 1973: a national household sample).

A question also arises as to whether females differ from males in terms of their self-esteem in adolescence and in terms of their reaction to the entry to adolescence. Once again there is controversy in the literature. Wylie (1979) and Maccoby and Jacklin (1974) in their reviews of pre–college-age adolescents report no global self-image differences by gender. However, significantly lower female self-esteem is indicated in nationally representative samples by O'Malley and Bachman (1979) and Conger *et al.* (1977). The studies of early and middle adolescents reviewed by Maccoby and Jacklin (1974) do not, for the most part, involve the individual's own view of his or her self-esteem, and the studies of adolescents which Wylie reviews are not based on large random samples of children in large cities with the full class structure represented.

Our own large-scale, random-sample surveys in two large cities show that both preadolescent and adolescent girls score lower than boys on self-esteem as well as on many more specific aspects of self-evaluation, particularly aspects of body-image (Simmons and F. Rosenberg, 1975; F. Rosenberg and Simmons, 1975; Bush *et al.*, 1977; Simmons and Blyth, 1987).

The impact of major social and biological changes on adolescent self-esteem

The entry into and exit from adolescence both involve major changes. Many of the identity theories (e.g. Erikson, 1959) have dealt with issues involving preparation for exit from adolescence – choice of an occupation, a mate, an adult identity. However, there has not been a great deal of work on the effect of various types of exit from adolescence on self-esteem (Offer and Offer, 1975; Bachman and O'Malley, 1977; Mortimer and Finch, 1984; Offer and Sabshin, 1984). Recently, there have been some large-scale studies concerned with the self-image at *entry* to adolescence (Petersen, 1983, Chapter 9; Dornbusch *et al.*, 1981). Our own is one of these studies.

As noted earlier, much of the work on self-esteem in adolescence focuses on the linkage to other psychological constructs and to cognitive development (Harter, 1983). We focus instead on the major social and biological changes in adolescence and their effects on global self-esteem. Is there evidence of a linkage between physical change and psychosocial reaction, between social structure and self-image? Specifically, we have studied the impact of two of the major changes confronting adolescents: the impact of timing of pubertal development and the effect of transition into a new, large, impersonal school environment (Simmons *et al.*, 1979; Blyth *et al.*, 1983; Simmons and Blyth, 1987).

Method

In this 5-year longitudinal study in Milwaukee, eighteen elementary schools were randomly sampled. Within the schools sampled, all sixth-grade students were invited to participate, and parental consent was secured from 82 per cent of the sample or 924 students, 621 of whom were white. Survey instruments were administered to these students once a year from Grades 6 through 10 (with the exception of Grade 8) if they remained in the Milwaukee public school system. Physical measurements to determine pubertal timing were collected more frequently. Time of onset of menarche for girls and time of peak rate of height growth for boys were the indicators used. (It should be noted that children are cognizant of these indicators of pubertal change.) The data were collected between 1974 and 1979.

Puberty

Despite theories of adolescent 'storm and stress' which imply that pubertal changes will negatively affect self-esteem, being on or off time in pubertal timing (being an early, middle or late developer) has no significant impact by itself on global self-esteem for either our male or our female subjects (see Simmons and Blyth, 1987). Nor does recency of pubertal changes to the time of the interview have an effect. In fact, the effects of pubertal change are concentrated on a few variables rather than being widespread and global. In the self-image area early pubertal development does affect evaluation of body-image (positively for boys, negatively for girls), but not overall self-esteem. Thus, we can document no effect of biological change on overall self-esteem. Further research will be needed to determine whether hormonal measures would yield more effects than the more 'public' indicators of body-change used.

School change

Communities and societies differ in the way they structure the entry to adolescence, one of these involves the timing and type of school transitions. At some point urban children have to learn to cope with the large-scale organisational environments so typical of modern society. They have to be able to move out of the small, intimate contexts of childhood into the more impersonal organisational contexts characteristic of adulthood. The question is whether this transition in the United States is frequently too early and too sudden or 'discontinuous' for children's 'developmental readiness' (see Simmons *et al.*, 1973).

In a 'natural experiment' in the Milwaukee study, children who made the first such transition into a large junior high school in Grade 7 at age 12 or 13 were compared with children who at the same age and grade remained in a small, intimate elementary school – a kindergarten through eighth-grade school (K–8). Not only were they studied prior to and after the Grade 7 transition but both cohorts were compared upon entry to senior high school as well (in Grade 10 for the junior high cohort, in Grade 9 for the K–8 cohort).

Figure 12.1 presents the trend for self-esteem graphically over the 5 years of the study (Blyth *et al.*, 1983). For boys, regardless of school type, and for girls in the K–8 cohort, self-esteem rises fairly continually with age from Grade 6 (the 'last year of childhood') to early and then to middle adolescence. Girls, however, are vulnerable to the early junior high transition. Self-esteem declines for the junior high girls upon entry to the new school in Grade 7. Their self-esteem rises again between seventh and ninth grade as they become the oldest students in the junior high school. Yet, on average, the gain is not enough for them to catch up completely with the K–8 cohort. The advantage of the K–8 cohort over the junior high girls in Grade 9 occurs despite the fact that the K–8 girls have just made their first transition into a large, impersonal school (the 'senior high'). A first transition at this later age (Grade 9) does not appear to have the negative consequences for girls that were evident when the first school transition occurred at a younger age, i.e. in Grade 7.

In Grade 10, the junior high cohort switches schools again and shows another downturn in self-esteem compared with the K–8 girls, whose self-esteem is rising at the same age. Just as the junior high girls were starting to recover, they are hit, in effect, with a 'double whammy'. This group of girls appears to be at considerable risk, with lower self-esteem than any other group of boys or girls, though on average their self-esteem is higher in

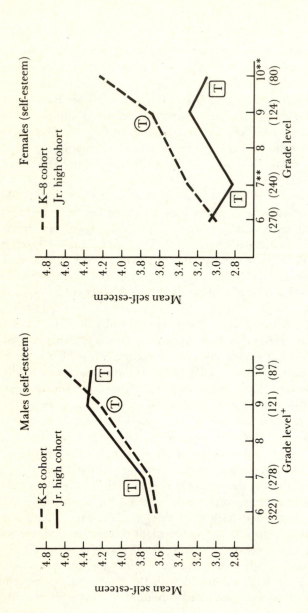

FIGURE 12.1   *Mean self-esteem from Grade 6 to Grade 10 by school type for each sex separately*

These graphs represent a trend analysis using the maximum number of cases available each year. The decreasing *N* for each grade level is due to sampling losses as noted in the text.

Levels of significance are based on one-way ANOVA's using school type as the factor and treating each grade level and sex separately. The degree of significance is indicated as follows: ☆, $p < .10$; ☆☆, $p < .05$; ☆☆☆, $p < .01$.

The symbol □ indicates a year of transition for the junior high cohort; ○ indicates a year of transition for the K–8 cohort.

†Children are generally aged 11 to 12 years in Grade 6, 12 to 13 in Grade 7, 13 to 14 in Grade 8, 14 to 15 in Grade 9 and 15 to 16 in Grade 10.

Reprinted with permission from D. A. Blyth, R. G. Simmons and S. Carlton-Ford, *Journal of Early Adolescence* (1983), 3(1–2), p. 110.

Grade 10 than in Grade 7. Thus, there is no support in these or any other of our Milwaukee data for a stress-inoculation hypothesis, for the idea that children benefit from having experienced early transitions at the time of later transitions. Rather there appears to be some evidence for a 'developmental readiness hypothesis', at least for girls. According to this hypothesis, environmental change will have negative effects only if it occurs in very early adolescence when the children lack the maturity to cope with it. In this study such negative effects persisted into middle adolescence, and the children did not recover rapidly or completely.

Independence

Not only do communities differ in the way they structure the entry to adolescence, but families vary as well. A major change in adolescence is the greatly increased independence from parental supervision. But families differ in the degree and timing of withdrawal from supervision. There has been little, if any, work on the impact of such independence on overall self-esteem. One might expect that increased independence would result in increased feelings of self-efficacy that would in turn translate into higher self-esteem. Our studies indicate that early independence from parental supervision prior to transition into junior high school related, if anything, to negative self-esteem after the transition (Simmons *et al.*, 1987). These results again support a developmental readiness hypothesis – the idea that children can be thrust too early into the rights and obligations of the new period in the life-course.

Delinquency

We have been discussing major biological, social, structural and beha-vioural changes that occur in adolescence. One of the clearest negative behavioural outcomes that occurs in adolescence is delinquency. Research has shown a correlation between low self-esteem and high delinquency. Questions have been raised as to whether delinquency causes low self-esteem or whether low self-esteem drives the child to delinquency in order to raise self-esteem (Kaplan, 1980; Rosenberg and Rosenberg, 1978). Our own findings suggest the former process at the time of entry to junior high school (Simmons *et al.*, 1987; also see McCarthy and Hoge, 1984).

The impact of cumulative change

Adolescence has been characterised as a time of ambiguous and 'discontinuous' change; that is, change that is sharp and sudden rather than gradual (Benedict, 1954; Davis, 1944). Entry to adolescence is also frequently a time of cumulation of change, a time when major life-changes all occur at once. In terms of the impact of cumulative change, Coleman (1974) has proposed a 'focal' theory of change, and in earlier publications we have developed similar propositions (Simmons *et al.*, 1979). According to these theories, adjustment is easier if the child goes through the various adolescent changes at different times rather than simultaneously. The attempt to cope with several major life-changes at the same time is expected to cause difficulty. More time to adjust gradually to one change before confrontation with another should be beneficial.

In order to test this hypothesis, children were classified as either having or not having experienced major changes (in or recently prior to Grade 7 entry) along the following dimensions: (1) entry into a junior high school rather than remaining in a K–8 school; (2) pubertal change close to Grade 7 entry (girls: onset of menarche within 6 months prior to the Grade 7 interview or up to 3 months later; boys: peak height growth prior to the Grade 7 interview); (3) early onset of dating; (4) geographical mobility since Grade 6; and (5) major family disruption since age 9 (death, divorce or remarriage of a parent).

Except for the change into junior high school, none of these changes by themselves affected self-esteem. For this analysis, children were categorised simply according to the number of changes they had experienced (see Simmons and Blyth, 1987). The number of changes was entered into a regression equation, and then it and its square were entered into a second regression equation (to test for curvilinear relations). For boys, there are no significant effects of cumulative change on self-esteem.

For girls, Figure 12.2 shows that the more changes they had experienced close to entry to adolescence, the lower their self-esteem. In terms of the size of the effects, we are talking about one-half of a standard deviation unit of self-esteem from one extreme to the other. In other words, the differences are sizeable.[6] Girls are more at risk at entry to adolescence if they have to cope with many changes simultaneously.

Conclusion

Although there may still be some controversy over the utility of global self-esteem as a theoretical construct and over its measurement, fruitful research using this concept and extant measures continues. Adolescence as a major new period in the life-course provides a very interesting research site for the study of multiple dimensions of the self-image and identity, including global self-esteem. In general, adolescence does not appear to be associated with a decrease in self-esteem for the majority of children. In fact, there is evidence of a general rise in self-esteem. However, adolescence

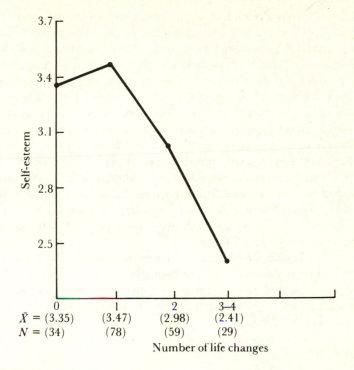

FIGURE 12.2   *Effect of number of life changes on female self-esteem (N = 200)*

does appear to have negative effects for the self-esteem of some children under particular circumstances (see Simmons *et al.*, 1987; Simmons and Blyth, 1987). Girls are more likely to show negative effects on entry to adolescence than boys, especially if change is marked by sharpness and discontinuity and occurs at too young an age (the 'developmental readiness' hypothesis) or coincides with too many other changes (the 'focal' theory of change).

'Arena of comfort'

Underlying both the 'developmental readiness' hypothesis and the 'focal change' hypothesis is the idea of an arena of comfort. If change comes too suddenly, that is, if there is too much discontinuity with prior experience, or if change is too early given the child's cognitive and emotional states, or if it occurs in too many areas of life at once, then the individual will experience great discomfort. Such children will not feel at one with themselves nor at home in their social environments.

If the child is comfortable in some environments, life-arenas and role-relationships, then discomfort in another arena can be tolerated and mastered. Children are less able to cope if at one and the same time they are uncomfortable with their bodies, due to physical changes; with family, due to changes in family constellation; with home, because of a move; with school, due to great discontinuity in the nature of the school environment; with peers, because of disruption of peer networks and changes in peer expectations and peer evaluation criteria, and because of the emergence of opposite-sex relationships as an important arena for success. There needs to be some arena of life or some set of role-relationships with which the individual can feel relaxed and comfortable, to which he or she can withdraw and become reinvigorated. In other words, it requires some energy and tension arousal to cope with those areas of life that are uncomfortable and that are changing. In order to maximise the expenditure of energy and avoid overstimulation, reduction of tension between challenges should be helpful.

We are not saying simply that a greater number of life-event stressors will result in more distress.[7] We are highlighting the multiplicity of arenas, role-relationships and role-identities in a person's life. At issue here, we hypothesise, is the absence of stressors in at least one significant sphere.

Girls versus boys

The apparent greater vulnerability of girls at entry to adolescence may be explained in part with the help of the self-image principles emphasised by Rosenberg (1979): Rosenberg emphasises the importance of the *reflected self* and of *social comparison* in determining self-esteem, as well as the importance of doing well in the areas one *values* (the principle of 'psychological centrality'). Our data suggest that in adolescence, at least in the 1970s, girls show an increased tendency over boys to place high value on body-image and same-sex popularity. It certainly is reasonable to think that the girls might be placed in increased jeopardy (1) because they value peer opinion more ('the reflected self'), especially in a new large school with many strangers, and (2) because they value body-image more at a time when the body is changing dramatically and social comparison along this dimension therefore becomes difficult. The fact that girls care more about body-image at the very same time as they are particularly dissatisfied with their looks helps to explain their lower global self-esteem (Simmons and Blyth, 1987; also see Rosenberg, Chapter 13).

Future Research

Linkages to other self-image dimensions

It would be very valuable for future research to investigate the causal interrelationships between self-esteem and the other dimensions of the self-image emphasised in this volume. Such work might be particularly helpful in explaining some of the findings detailed in this paper. Further research on the linkages to self-efficacy (Gecas and Mortimer, Chapter 17) and transient depersonalisation (Rosenberg, Chapter 13) might be especially fruitful. First, attention to the feelings of self-efficacy may help to explain why the self-esteem of boys and K–8 girls rises through adolescence. There is evidence that with maturation, the adolescent feels more competent and efficacious (see Damon and Hart, 1982; Selman, 1980; Rosenberg, in press; Brim, 1976). Feelings of self-efficacy may, in turn, work to produce higher self-esteem at the same time as other factors are threatening self-esteem. Feelings of greater control and power relative to their social and physical environment may have the same effect.[8] Children may also improve their interpersonal skills with age and be more capable of selecting peers and contexts that enhance self-esteem (Rosenberg, in press).[9]

Feelings of self-efficacy may also intervene to explain the 'developmental readiness' findings. Being thrust too early into the rights and obligations of a new period in the life-course, either because of school structure or because of premature withdrawal of parental supervision, may put the child in a situation he or she cannot handle. The result may be a reduced sense of self-efficacy and therefore less high self-esteem.

The process by which cumulative change affects self-esteem may also be clarified through inclusion of other self-image dimensions. We suggested that cumulative change results in feelings of discomfort. It is possible that these feelings of discomfort produce a sense of detachment from self, a sense of unreality. As one watches oneself in new and uncomfortable situations, one may feel what Rosenberg has called recurrent transient depersonalisation (Rosenberg, Chapter 13). This self-detachment or feeling of depersonalisation may negatively affect feelings of self-efficacy, which in turn negatively impact on self-esteem.[10] It is also possible that self-efficacy plays a further role. If one is involved at the same time in many new important situations and role-relationships, one might see oneself as generally ineffective. In other words, the inability to perform easily in multiple important new domains may generalise to an evaluation of self as inefficacious. Consequently, self-esteem may drop.

Cross-cultural research

Our study demonstrates an important connection between social structure and self-image: the self-esteem of children is affected by the way society structures the entry to adolescence. If one is interested in further studying this link between self-esteem and social structure, a cross-cultural examination of adolescent transitions in various modern societies would be valuable.[11]

Contemporary societies vary in the extent to which preadolescents and young adolescents are compelled to make major decisions. The age at which educational tracking decisions are made, the difficulty of switching tracks, the extent to which entry to the university track depends on test scores all should affect the child. If the 'developmental readiness' hypothesis has generalisability, we would expect increased difficulty for those young adolescents confronted by very early and important decision points.

Acknowledgment

This study was funded by National Institute of Mental Health Grant R01 MH30739 and a grant from the William T. Grant Foundation. In addition, the work of the author has been supported by a Research Development Award from the National Institute of Mental Health, No. 2 K02 MH41688. The University of Minnesota Computer Center has provided partial support to the author from the Supercomputer Institute.

Notes

1 See Harter (1983) for a review of the literature that categorises specific dimensions of self-evaluation.
2 The measurement used was a translation of the Rosenberg self-esteem scale for younger children (see Simmons *et al.*, 1979).
3 It should be noted that Rosenberg (1979) utilises the term 'self-confidence' to refer to self-efficacy. It probably would be better to use 'self-efficacy' or 'feelings of competence' (see Gecas and Mortimer, Chapter 17).
4 See Harter (1983) for a review of cognitive differences between adolescents and younger children.
5 Bowman (1974) shows this increase only in his longitudinal, not in his cross-sectional, samples.
6 These findings persist when self-esteem from the year before is controlled, and when socioeconomic status is controlled. The same

negative effect occurs for cumulative change when the K–8 and junior high cohorts are examined separately and the effects of all but school change are examined.

7 For studies of life events as stressors, see reviews by Zautra and Reich (1983), Tausig (1982) and Pearlin *et al.* (1981). Relatively few studies in the life-events area have dealt with normal adolescents (see Gad and Johnson, 1980; Padilla *et al.*, 1976; Gersten *et al.*, 1974, 1977; Newcomb *et al.*, 1981; Johnson and McCutcheon, 1980). Those few that have, by and large, do not focus on the normal, scheduled life-event changes of adolescence – the move into junior high, pubertal change, onset of dating (see Padilla's cross-sectional study of boys, 1976, for an exception).

8 Rosenberg (1985) shows that higher feelings of control over destiny correlate with self-esteem, although he does not investigate causal direction. Mortimer and Finch (1984) show that autonomy has been found to enhance the self-esteem of middle-adolescent boys. (Also see Franks and Marolla, 1976.) See Harter (1983) for a review of the literature on locus of control and self-esteem.

9 McCarthy and Hoge (1982) suggest that one reason for a rise in self-esteem in longitudinal data sets may be the importance of the motive to improve self-esteem. High self-esteem people are motivated to maintain high self-esteem and low self-esteem individuals are motivated to raise self-esteem. Therefore the mean level will improve with time (Rosenberg, in press). If this process is accurate, then self-esteem should rise regardless of the age-period being studied. The rise will not be due to anything special about the nature of adolescence.

10 Elliott *et al.* (1984) and Rosenberg (Chapter 13) discuss the impact of low self-esteem on depersonalisation, but we are suggesting a reciprocal relationship here.

11 Of course, classic studies by Ruth Benedict (1954) and Margaret Mead (1950) discuss the contrast between modern and preliterate societies in their treatment of adolescent age children and in the probable consequences of that difference.

References

Allport, G. W. (1961), *Pattern in Growth and Personality*, Holt, Rinehart & Winston: New York.

Attenborough, R. E. and Zdep, S. M. (1973), article in *Proceedings of the 81st Annual Convention of the American Psychological Association*, pp. 237–8.

Bachman, J. G. and O'Malley, P. M. (1977), 'Self-esteem in young men: A longitudinal analysis of the impact of educational and occupational attainment', *journal of Personality and Social Psychology*, 35(6), pp. 365–80.

Barglow, P. and Schaefer, M. (1979), 'The fate of the feminine self in normative adolescent regression', in M. Sugar (ed.), *Female Adolescent Development*, Brunner/Magel: New York.

Benedict, R. (1954), 'Continuities and discontinuities in cultural conditioning', in W. E. Martin and C. B. Stendler (eds), *Readings in Child Development*, Harcourt, Brace Jovanovich: New York.

Blos, P. (1962), *On Adolescence: A Psychoanalytic Interpretation*, Free Press: New York.

Blos, P. (1971), 'The child analyst looks at the young adolescent', *Daedalus*, Fall, pp. 961–78.

Blyth, D. A., Simmons, R. G. and Carlton-Ford, S. (1983), 'The adjustment of early adolescents to school transitions', *Journal of Early Adolescence*, 3(1–2), pp. 105–20.

Bohan, J. S. (1973), 'Age and sex differences in self-concept', *Adolescence*, 8, pp. 379–84.

Bowman, D. O. (1974), 'A longitudinal study of selected facets of children's self-concepts as related to achievement and intelligence', *The Citadel: Monograph Series*, no. XII, pp. 1–16.

Bradburn, N. M. and Caplovitz, D. (1965), *Reports on Happiness*, Aldine: Chicago.

Brim, O. G., Jr. (1976), 'Life-span development of the theory of oneself: Implications for child development', in H. W. Reese (ed.), *Advances in Child Development and Behavior*, vol. 11, Academic Press: New York.

Bush, D. E., Simmons, R. G., Hutchinson, B. and Blyth, D. A. (1977), 'Adolescent perception of sex roles in 1968 and 1975', *Public Opinion Quarterly*, 41(4), pp. 459–74.

Carmines, E. G. and Zeller, R. A. (1979), 'Reliability and validity assessment', *Sage University Paper*, Beverly Hills, Cal.

Coleman, J. C. (1974), *Relationships in Adolescence*, Routledge & Kegan Paul: Boston.

Conger, A. J., Peng, S. S. and Dunteman, G. H. (1977), *National Longitudinal Study of the High School Class of 1972: Group Profiles on Self-Esteem, Locus of Control, and Life Goals*, Research Triangle Institute: Research Triangle Park, N.C.

Damon, W. and Hart, D. (1982), 'The development of self-understanding from infancy through adolescence', *Child Development*, 53, pp. 841–64.

Davis, A. (1944), 'Socialization and adolescent personality', in *Adolescence, Yearbook of the National Society for the Study of Education*, vol. 43, Part I.

Dornbusch, S. M., Carlsmith, J. M., Gross, R. T., Martin, J. A., Jennings, D., Rosenberg, A. and Duke, P. (1981), 'Sexual development, age, and dating: A comparison of biological and social influences upon one set of behaviors', *Child Development*, 52, pp. 179–85.

Dusek, J. B. and Flaherty, J. F. (1981), 'The development of the self-concept during the adolescent years', *Monographs of the Society for Research in Child Development*, 46(4), serial no. 191.

Elkind, D. (1967), 'Egocentrism in adolescence', *Child Development*, 38, pp. 1025–34.

Elliott, G. C., Rosenberg, M. and Wagner, M. (1984), 'Transient depersonalization in youth', *Social Psychology Quarterly*, 47(2), pp. 115–29.

Epstein, S. (1973), 'The self-concept revisited: Or a theory of a theory', *American Psychologist*, 28, pp. 404–16.

Erikson, E. H. (1959), 'Identity and the life cycle', *Psychological Issues*, 1, pp. 1–171.

Erikson, E. H. (1968), *Identity: Youth and Crisis*, Norton: New York.

Fleming, J. S. and Courtney, B. E. (1984), 'The dimensionality of self-esteem: II. Hierarchical facet model for revised measurement scales', *Journal of Personality and Social Psychology*, 46(2), pp. 404–21.

Franks, D. D. and Marolla, J. (1976), 'Efficacious action and social approval as interacting dimensions of self-esteem: A tentative formulation through construct validation', *Sociometry*, 39(4), pp. 324–41.

Freud, A. (1958), 'Adolescence', *Psychoanalytic Study of the Child*, 13, pp. 255–78.

Gad, M. T. and Johnson, J. H. (1980), 'Correlates of adolescent life stress as related to race, SES, and levels of perceived social support', *Journal of Clinical Child Psychology*, Spring, pp. 13–16.

Gecas, V. (1972), 'Parental behavior and contextual variations in adolescent self-esteem', *Sociometry*, 35(2), pp. 332–45.

Gersten, J. C., Langner, T. S., Eisenberg, J. G. and Orzeck, L. (1974), 'Child behavior and life events: Undesirable change or change per se?' in B. S. Dohrenwend and B. P. Dohrenwend (eds), *Stressful Life Events: Their Nature and Effects*, Wiley: New York, pp. 159–70.

Gersten, J. C., Langner, T. S., Eisenberg, J. G. and Simcha-Fagan, O. (1977), 'An evaluation of the etiologic role of stressful life-change events in psychological disorders', *Journal of Health and Social Behavior*, 18, pp. 228–44.

Haan, N. (1977), *Coping and Defending: Processes of Self-Environment Organization*, Academic Press: New York.

Hall, G. S. (1904), *Adolescence: Its Psychology and Its Relations to Physiology, Anthropology, Sex, Crime, Religion and Education*, vols I and II, Appleton: New York.

Harter, S. (1983), 'Developmental perspectives on the self-system', in E. M. Hetherington (volume ed.), *Socialization, Personality, and Social Development* in P. H. Mussen (ed.), *Handbook of Child Psychology*, 4th ed., New York, John Wiley & Sons, pp. 275–385.

Hoge, D. R. and McCarthy, J. D. (1983), 'Issues of validity and reliability in the use of real–ideal discrepancy scores to measure self-regard', *Journal of Personality and Social Psychology*, 44(5), pp. 1048–55.

Hoge, D. R. and McCarthy, J. D. (1984), 'Influence of individual and group identity salience in the global self-esteem of youth', *Journal of Personality and Social Psychology*, 47(2), pp. 403–14.

Johnson, J. H. and McCutcheon, S. (1980), 'Assessing life events in older children and adolescents: Preliminary findings with the life events checklist', in I. G. Sarason and C. D. Spielberger (eds), *Stress and Anxiety*, Hemisphere: Washington, D.C., pp. 111–25.

Jorgensen, E. C. and Howell, R. J. (1969), 'Changes in self, ideal-self correlations from ages 8 through 18', *Journal of Social Psychology*, 79, pp. 63–7.

Kaplan, H. B. (1980), *Deviant Behavior in Defense of Self*, Academic Press: New York.

Kaplan, H. B. and Pokorny, A. D. (1969), 'Self-derogation and psychosocial adjustment', *Journal of Nervous and Mental Disease*, 149, pp. 421–34.

Katz, J. and Zigler, E. (1967), 'Self-image disparity: A developmental approach', *Journal of Personality and Social Psychology*, 5(2), pp. 186–95.

Kohn, M. L. and Schooler, C., with the collaboration of Miller, J., Miller, K. A., Schoenbach, C. and Schoenberg, R. (1983), *Work and Personality: An Inquiry into the Impact of Social Stratification*, Ablex Publishing Corporation: Norwood, N.J.

Maccoby, E. E. and Jacklin, C. N. (1974), *The Psychology of Sex Differences*, Stanford University Press: Stanford, Cal.

McCarthy, J. D. and Hoge, D. R. (1982), 'Analyses of age effects in longitudinal studies of adolescent self-esteem', *Developmental Psychology*, 18, pp. 372–9.

McCarthy, J. D. and Hoge, D. R. (1984), 'The dynamics of self-esteem and delinquency', *American Journal of Sociology*, 90(2), pp. 396–410.

Mead, M. (1950), *Coming of Age in Samoa*, New American Library: New York.

Mortimer, J. T. and Finch, M. D. (1984), 'Autonomy as a source of self-esteem in adolescence', Unpublished manuscript.

Murphy, G. (1947), *Personality*, Harper: New York.

Newcomb, M. D., Huba, G. J. and Bentler, P. M. (1981), 'A multidimensional assessment of stressful life events among adolescents: Derivation and correlates', *Journal of Health and Social Behavior*, 22, pp. 400–15.

Offer, D. and Offer, J. B. (1975), *From Teenage to Young Manhood: A Psychological Study*, Basic Books: New York.

Offer, D., Ostrov, E. and Howard, K. I. (1981), *The Adolescent: A Psychological Self-Portrait*, Basic Books: New York.

Offer, D. and Sabshin, M. (eds) (1984), *Normality and the Life Cycle: A Critical Integration*, Basic Books: New York.

O'Malley, P. M. and Bachman, J. G. (1979), 'Self-esteem and education: Sex and cohort comparisons among high school seniors', *Journal of Personality and Social Psychology*, 37(7), pp. 1153–9.

O'Malley, P. M. and Bachman, J. G. (1983), 'Self-esteem: Change and stability between ages 13 and 23', *Developmental Psychology*, 19(2), pp. 257–68.

Padilla, E. R., Rohsenow, D. J. and Bergman, A. B. (1976), 'Predicting accident frequency in children', *Pediatrics*, 58, pp. 223–6.

Pearlin, L. I., Lieberman, M. A., Menaghan, E. G. and Mullan, J. T. (1981), 'The stress process', *Journal of Health and Social Behavior*, 22, pp. 337–56.

Petersen, A. C. (1983), 'Pubertal change and cognition', in J. Brooks-Gunn and A. C. Petersen (eds), *Girls at Puberty*, Plenum: New York, pp. 179–98.

Petersen, A. C. and Taylor, B. (1980), 'The biological approach to adolescence: Biological change and psychological adaptation', in J. Adelson (ed.), *Handbook of Adolescent Psychology*, Wiley: New York, pp. 117–58.

Piers, E. V. and Harris, D. B. (1964), 'Age and other correlates of self-concept in children', *Journal of Educational Psychology*, 55(2), pp. 91–5.

Robinson, J. P. and Shaver, P. R. (1969), 'Measures of social psychological attitudes', Appendix B to *Measures of Political Attitudes*, Survey Research Center, Institute for Social Research, University of Michigan, Ann Arbor.

Rosenberg, F. R. and Rosenberg, M. (1978), 'Self-esteem and delinquency', *Journal of Youth and Adolescence*, 7, pp. 279–91.

Rosenberg, F. R. and Simmons, R. G. (1975), 'Sex differences in the self-concept in adolescence', *Sex-Roles: A Journal of Research*, 1(2), pp. 147–59.

Rosenberg, M. (1965), *Society and the Adolescent Self-Image*, Princeton University Press: Princeton, N.J.

Rosenberg, M. (1979), *Conceiving the Self*, Basic Books: New York.

Rosenberg, M. (1985), 'Self-concept and psychological well-being in adolescence', in R. Leahy (ed.), *The Development of the Self*, Academic Press: New York, pp. 205–46.

Rosenberg, M. (in press), 'Self-concept development from middle childhood through adolescence', in J. Suls and A. Greenwald (eds), *Psychological Perspectives on the Self*, vol. 3, Erlbaum: Hillsdale, N.J.

Rosenberg, M. and Simmons, R. G. (1972), *Black and White Self-Esteem: The Urban School Child*, Arnold and Caroline Rose Monograph Series, American Sociological Association, Washington, D.C.

Savin-Williams, R. C. and Demo, D. H. (1983), 'Conceiving or misconceiving the self: Issues in adolescent self-esteem', *Journal of Early Adolescence*, 3(1–2), pp. 121–40.

Selman, R. (1980), *The Growth of Interpersonal Understanding*, Academic Press: New York.

Simmons, R. G. and Blyth, D. A. (1987), *Moving into Adolescence: The Impact of Pubertal Change and School Context*, Aldine: Hawthorne, N.Y.

Simmons, R. G., Blyth, D. A., Van Cleave, E. F. and Bush, D. M. (1979), 'Entry into early adolescence: The impact of school structure, puberty, and early dating on self-esteem', *American Sociological Review*, 44(6), pp. 948–67.

Simmons, R. G., Carlton-Ford, S. L. and Blyth, D. A. (1987), 'Predicting how a child will cope with the transition to junior high school', in R. M. Lerner and T. T. Foch (eds), *Biological-Psychosocial Interactions in Early Adolescence: A Life-Span Perspective*, Erlbaum: Hillsdale, N.J.

Simmons, R. G. and Rosenberg, F. (1975), 'Sex, sex-roles, and self-image', *Journal of Youth and Adolescence*, 4(3), pp. 229–58.

Simmons, R. G., Rosenberg, F. and Rosenberg, M. (1973), 'Disturbance in the self-image at adolescence', *American Sociological Review*, 38(5), pp. 553–568.

Stryker, S. (1982), 'Symbolic interactionism: Themes and variations', in M. Rosenberg and R. H. Turner (eds), *Social Psychology: Sociological Perspectives*, Basic Books: New York, pp. 3–29.

Tausig, M. (1982), 'Measuring life events', *Journal of Health and Social Behavior*, 23, pp. 52–64.

Trowbridge, N. (1972), 'Self-concept and socio-economic status in elementary school children', *American Educational Research Journal*, 9(4), pp. 525–37.

Wells, L. E. and Marwell, G. (1976), *Self-Esteem: Its Conceptualization and Measurement*, vol. 20, Sage Library of Social Research, Sage Publications: Beverly Hills, Cal.

Wells, L. E. and Stryker, S. (in press), 'Stability and change in self over the life course', in P. B. Baltes, R. M. Lerner and D. L. Featherman (eds), *Life-Span Development and Behavior*, vol. 8, Erlbaum: Hillsdale, N.J.

Wylie, R. C. (1961), *The Self-Concept: A Critical Survey of Pertinent Research Literature*, University of Nebraska Press: Lincoln.

Wylie, R. C. (1974), *The Self-Concept: Vol. 1, A Review of Methodological Considerations and Measuring Instruments* (rev. ed.), University of Nebraska Press: Lincoln.

Wylie, R. C. (1979), *The Self-Concept Theory and Research: Vol. 2* (rev. ed.), University of Nebraska Press: Lincoln.

Yamamoto, K., Thomas, E. C. and Karns, E. A. (1969), 'School-related attitudes in middle-school age students', *American Educational Research Journal*, 6(2), pp. 191–206.

Zautra, A. J. and Reich, J. W. (1983), 'Life events and perceptions of life quality: Developments in a two-factor approach', *Journal of Community Psychology*, 11, pp. 121–32.

13 Depersonalisation: The loss of personal identity

Morris Rosenberg

The aim of this chapter is to identify certain factors that foster the experience of depersonalisation. Although the term 'depersonalisation' is used in several different ways in the literature, the meaning that concerns us here is the loss of a sense of personal identity, characteristically accompanied by a sense of unreality. Campbell (1981, p. 163) defines depersonalisation as 'a nonspecific syndrome in which the patient feels he has lost his personal identity, that he is different and strange and unreal'. Webster (1985, p. 340) defines depersonalisation as 'a psycho-pathological syndrome characterized by loss of identity and feelings of unreality and strangeness about one's own behavior'. In Bleuler's (1950) classic description of the condition, depersonalisation is described as the feeling that one is not oneself. A patient may do something but think that someone else is doing it; or the patient may feel that what is happening to him or her is happening to someone else. Depersonalised people may experience themselves as separated, detached or disconnected from themselves, as onlookers of their own actions.

In speaking of depersonalisation, it is essential to distinguish what DSM-III (American Psychiatric Association, 1980) identifies as the Depersonalization Disorder, which is a recognised clinical entity, from symptomatic, episodic or transient depersonalisation. As a clinical entity, the Depersonalization Disorder is a serious psychopathological condition that may last for years and is seriously disabling. In contrast, 'The symptom of depersonalization, even if recurrent ... does not cause any social or occupational impairment' (American Psychiatric Association, 1980, p. 260) or, at most, minimal impairment. Furthermore, it is not necessarily psychologically distressing. It is the phenomenon of episodic or symptomatic depersonalisation that we propose to explore in this paper.

Identity

The proposition we shall advance is that events or circumstances that undermine, threaten or challenge one's sense of identity will foster the experience of episodic depersonalisation.

The concept of identity, unfortunately, is an extraordinarily elusive and slippery one. Although Erikson (1959) provided sensitive descriptions of various features of identity, he refused to commit himself to a precise definition, preferring to use the term in different senses to reflect the particular feature under discussion. In the literature, the meanings that have been assigned to the term 'identity' have been many and varied. Writers have used the term to refer to: (1) the sense of continuity (Erikson, 1959; Hart *et al.*, Chapter 8; Levita, 1965); (2) distinctiveness, uniqueness or separateness (Cowan, 1978; Hart *et al.*, 1984; Levita, 1965); (3) group identification or ethnic identity (Driedger, 1976; Rovner, 1981; Sarbin and Scheibe, 1983); (4) social role configurations (McCall and Simmons, 1978; Stryker, 1980; Thoits, 1983); (5) authenticity, essence or real self (Wheelis, 1958); (6) situational roles (Alexander and Wiley, 1981; Goffman, 1963, 1969; Blumer, 1969); (7) efficacy, volition or personal agency (Bandura, 1978, 1980; Hart *et al.* 1984); (8) stability of values and sense of life meaning (Wheelis, 1958); (9) self-conception (Shibutani, 1961); (10) the distinguishing character of an individual (Webster, 1985).

For present purposes, the definition that we judge to be most useful is that offered by William James (1950). The essential characteristic of personal identity, according to James, is the 'consciousness of personal sameness'. In his view, 'there is nothing more remarkable in making a judgment of sameness in the first person than in the second or third, . . . The sense of our personal identity, then, is exactly like any one of our other perceptions of sameness among phenomena' (James, 1950, pp. 331, 334). Erikson (1959), too, equates identity with 'inner continuity and sameness'. Piaget (1968) contends that an essential precondition for the development of identity is the awareness of 'object permanence'.

What constitutes sameness, of course, is far from clear. Nothing in nature, including ourselves, is ever exactly the same from one moment to the next. No one steps into the same river twice. It is thus not actual sameness but the *sense* of sameness that is reflected in the concept. I think that I am the 'same' person today as yesterday even though in the interim my bone marrow has manufactured thousands of new red blood corpuscles while thousands of dead cells have passed out of the system. Similarly, I say that I am at the 'same' university this year as last despite major changes in the student body and perceptible changes in the faculty, administration, physical plant, and so on. James's (1950) concept of identity, then, refers not to actual sameness but to the perception or experience of sameness.

We have suggested that transient depersonalisation entails the momentary loss of the sense of identity. If identity is based on the feeling of personal sameness, then those events, conditions or circumstances that threaten one's sense of personal sameness would be expected to foster depersonalisation.

What factors, then, represent threats to personal sameness? The two types of events or experiences on which we shall primarily focus are the following:

1. Violations of self-expectations. The self-concept may be viewed largely as a system of self-expectations. When these expectations are met, the sense of identity tends to be firm and secure. When they are violated, however, the sense of personal sameness is called into question and the feeling of transient depersonalisation may be aroused.
2. Experiences of self-change. Change in the self, in whole or in part, may challenge the sense of personal sameness and thus produce feelings of depersonalisation.

Sample and measure

The data for this report are based on a study of a probability sample of 1,988 school pupils from Grades 3 to 12 in twenty-five Baltimore City schools. Most pupils were between 9 and 18 years of age, (Details concerning sample selection are presented in Rosenberg and Simmons, 1972.) Personal interviews were conducted in school after class hours.

In the course of these lengthy interviews, respondents were presented with the following five questions:

1. When talking to other people, Sam (Joan) sometimes feels that this isn't really happening to him, that this isn't real. How often do you feel like this?
2. When you're doing something, do you ever feel like you're in a dream, like it isn't real?
3. A kid told me: 'Sometimes I'm talking to someone and all of a sudden I wonder what they're thinking, and I look at myself and feel kind of funny.' Do you ever feel like this?
4. When you're doing something, do you ever think to yourself: 'This can't be happening to me'?
5. When playing or doing something, Bill (Susan) sometimes feels like he is looking at himself – almost like it isn't really him doing it. How often do you feel like this?

Except for names and pronouns, the questions were the same for boys and girls. In order to reduce response set, these items were scattered across the interview schedule. Cronbach's alpha (Cronbach, 1951) was .664.

Of the five items in the depersonalisation scale, the proportion giving the depersonalisation response ranged between 34 and 67 per cent. These data suggest that many – probably most – people have at some time or other experienced a depersonalisation episode and that they recognise it as a feature of their experience.

Following item 5, respondents were asked, 'Can you tell me a time when you felt like you were looking at yourself doing something – almost like it wasn't really you doing it?' In response to this question, 64 per cent said 'No' and 36 per cent said 'Yes'. Of the 36 per cent who said 'Yes', only 3 per cent said that it happened 'very often', 20 per cent that it happened 'sometimes' and 12 per cent that it happened 'not very often'.

These 36 per cent were asked to describe an instance in which this had occurred to them. Of this number, exactly half (18 per cent) identified at least one specific occasion during which they experienced episodic depersonalisation.

We shall focus first on the specific incidents cited and then turn to analyses involving the five-item scale.

Violation of self-expectation

In the course of development, people build up ideas of what they are like – what they look like, how they typically behave, what their realms of competence are, how they characteristically feel, and so on. These self-expectations constitute a major component of their self-concepts. When their behaviour, appearance, feelings, etc., match these self-expectations, the sense of personal sameness is maintained and the feeling of identity is secure. But when behaviour is inconsistent with or contradictory to these self-expectations – when the individual is not 'the same' as usual – then the sure sense of identity is threatened.

To take a hypothetical example, if I were to step out on the tennis court and effortlessly defeat a tennis champion, this experience would so grossly contradict my self-expectation that I would probably have the feeling that this was not real, that it was a dream, that it could not be happening to me. The sense of personal sameness thus depends on whether one's behaviour, feelings, abilities, etc., are essentially consistent with what one has come to expect of oneself.

In examining the specific incidents of depersonalisation cited by our respondents, we found that the overwhelming majority involved violations of self-expectations. These pupils almost invariably cited events in which their behaviour surprised them, contradicting their views of what they believed they were like. Some sense of the events that precipitated the depersonalisation experience can be conveyed by describing some of the types of expectations that were violated.

Efficacy expectations

Bandura's (1978; 1980) concept of efficacy refers to people's expectations concerning their own abilities. In this study, depersonalisation was often reported when efficacy self-expectations were violated. This occurred not only when the individual fell short of his or her self-expectations but, even more frequently, when they surpassed them. Thus, asked to cite an occasion when 'you felt like you were looking at yourself doing something – almost like it wasn't really you doing it', respondents cited the following examples of incidents that aroused the depersonalising experience: 'I could never reach the punch ball. One day I did and had a home run'; 'When I built something creative better than planned – a strobe light'; 'Taking the driver's test – I parked the car without banging into anything'; 'Sometimes answering a question in school wrong'; 'When I had a car accident, I couldn't believe I was that stupid'. Whether individuals exceed or fall short of their anticipated performances, they surprise themselves, and this surprise arouses momentary feelings of depersonalisation.

Physical appearance expectations

One of the strongest systems of self-expectations is one's physical appearance. Anyone who has looked in the mirror the morning after a night of carousing and seen a haggard, tousle-haired, heavy-lidded stranger staring back at him has had momentary doubts about his identity. Similar feelings may be aroused when we look at old photographs of ourselves or when we dress in strange clothes, try new hair-dos, transform our skin tone or facial features with stage make-up. A girl in her first party dress or a boy in his first suit may experience herself or himself as a stranger when gazing at the image in the mirror.

Thus, one girl reported the experience of unreality 'when I first started wearing make-up'. Another said, 'When I look in the mirror'. One incident cited by a girl in which she experienced a feeling of unreality was when 'I was looking in the mirror and combing my hair'. When the physical self one perceives is different from the self one expects to perceive, the sense of personal sameness is undermined, increasing the likelihood that one will experience depersonalisation.

Personality expectations

This term is used to describe traits or dispositions of the individual other than those involving competence or efficacy. People may tend to think of themselves as cheerful, energetic, optimistic, generous. When they behave in ways that differ from these self-expectations, however, they may experience doubts about who they are. Thus, in describing a depersonalising experience, one youngster cited an incident of 'fighting for my brother to help him, because I don't like to fight'. Another could not understand his behaviour when 'I pushed a girl down in the street because she hit me'. 'A little boy was standing in the street and a car was coming. I pulled him out of the way.' In each case the youngsters felt that they were not themselves when performing this behaviour, and this was accompanied by a mild sense of unreality.

Role expectations

Stryker (1980) has described social roles as systems of social expectations. When individuals internalise certain social positions or statuses as components of their social identity, they simultaneously internalise the behavioural and other expectations associated with these positions.

In a number of cases our respondents reported experiencing episodic depersonalisation when they violated role standards. One youngster reported that it felt as if it was not really him 'When I was on a roller coaster with mostly grownups and it seemed strange that I could do it because I was so young'. 'Once when I was playing baseball, I didn't think it was me because it wasn't ladylike.' Part of what we expect of ourselves is based on the social expectations associated with a given status; and, in violating the role expectations, we simultaneously contradict our self-expectations. Transient depersonalisation may be one consequence of this experience.

Physiological and physical expectations

Although the self-concept is characteristically viewed as a cognitive structure (a set of ideas that the individual has about himself or herself), it might also be viewed more broadly as 'the totality of the individual's thoughts and feelings with reference to [the] self as an object' (Rosenberg, 1979). So conceived, the self-concept would include physiological and physical states. The individual comes to expect certain feeling states of himself or herself: tired in the morning, bouncy in the evening, excited at ball games, and so on. But when we encounter unfamiliar physiological or physical experiences, our self-expectations are challenged and our secure, implicit notions of our identity may be undermined.

What conditions arouse such unexpected physiological states? One of these is the action of chemical agents, especially when experienced for the first time. Thus, one youngster reported feelings of depersonalisation: 'When I was out drinking and I got sick, I couldn't believe it was me'. Another also referred to 'the time I got drunk. I had never gotten drunk before'.

Unaccustomed physical sensations may also bring on depersonalisation. A hospital patient subjected to the prods, pricks and probes in unexpected parts of the anatomy that are a normal aspect of hospital routine may experience the feeling of self-detachment. One adolescent subjected to such violation of the self adopted an attitude that he was a separate body, a detached onlooker of the events happening to him. Another incident was cited by a girl who reported that she was 'skating and my sister was helping me, but she let me go and I was gliding by myself'. Another experienced depersonalisation when he was suffering from a middle-ear infection and heard sounds that reverberated like a chord.

An important component of the self-concept, then, is the individual's system of self-expectations – expectations concerning one's traits, appearance, feelings, etc. The question is: why do people violate their self-expectations? At least three reasons may be suggested. The first reason, obviously, is that the organism does not meekly bow to the commands of the self-concept. As George Herbert Mead (1934) stressed in his discussion of the self, there is a radical distinction between the self as object (the 'me') and the self as subject (the 'I'). The 'I' is the spontaneous, unpredictable, unanticipated component of the personality; the 'me' is the internalised attitudes of the community as a whole toward the self. It is the self-as-subject that, at the instant of action, hits the baseball squarely for a home run, the self-as-object that experiences surprise at the feat and feels pride. Thus, the main anchor in the shifting sea of experience – the self-concept – is most endangered by the unexpected, unpredictable, spontaneous features of personality. Nothing is more central to our concerns than having the secure knowledge of what we are like, of possessing the confident feeling that we know what to expect of ourselves. And nothing more threatens and undermines this valued structure than ourselves – the organism or self-as-subject. Hence, people inevitably surprise themselves, calling into question their sense of personal sameness, and, on occasion, experiencing momentary depersonalisation feelings.

The second reason why the knowledge of who and what we are can never be perfectly secure is that we actually constantly change. If we are to retain a sense of identity it must rest on continuity rather than on actual sameness. If our self-concept were finally established for good and all, providing a secure sense of identity, it would soon be outmoded and dysfunctional.

Third, new experiences produce behaviour for which no precedent is available. No human being is immune to the course of events that may call forth responses that violate self-expectations. In a sudden emergency, I am called upon to take charge of my military unit; suddenly I find myself making decisions and giving orders and, in the process, wondering whether this is me and whether this is real. Or I may have this feeling when I am frantically driving an automobile accident victim to the hospital. Life events inevitably place us in situations where we grossly violate our self-expectations. Such events are likely to foster episodic depersonalisation. It is also possible that sudden role changes – marriage, motherhood, entering college – may foster depersonalisation, although, because these are expected changes, characterised by 'anticipatory socialization' (Merton, 1968), they may be experienced as part of a continuous self.

Other depersonalisation events

Although the events that precipitated the depersonalisation experience most often involved the violation of self-expectations, certain other events also produced this effect.

In a number of cases these pupils reported experiencing depersonalisation under conditions of *public performance*. Instances when the youngsters felt as if they were detached observers of their own actions were the following: 'When I was playing piano on stage'; 'When I accepted my trophy for dancing'; 'I was singing with a band'; 'I was in a play at the Spotlight Theater'. One girl reported the experience when seeing herself on television. One youngster reported feelings of unreality 'when I'm giving a book report'.

Feelings of depersonalisation are also associated with events involving a *failure in self-attribution*. In general, we believe that failure in self-attribution is an exceptional experience. Although people may subsequently acknowledge that they have erred, at the instant of action most people's behaviour makes sense to them. There are occasions, however, in which self-attribution fails. The individual is unable to assign cause, motive, intention, etc., to his or her own behaviour. Forces in the organism or the unconscious produce behaviour that is baffling and incomprehensible to the individual himself or herself.

For example, one girl reported feelings of depersonalisation when 'I told my boyfriend I wouldn't babysit for someone and I told my cousin I would'. This girl was totally at a loss to understand why she had given contradictory information to her boyfriend and her cousin. Another experienced depersonalisation on an occasion when he was 'talking with people and realise I'm not making any sense'. Another reported that 'Once I talked to myself'. One youngster replied that 'A girl was trying to make friends [with me], and I was thinking about something else, so I finally hit her in the stomach'. These youngsters observe their own behaviour and find it completely incomprehensible. When people behave in ways for which they can assign no cause – behaviour that appears to be independent of their own will, intent or volition – they are apt to have feelings of doubt about their identity.

Although our data did not provide any instances of the phenomenon, we believe that depersonalisation is also likely to be experienced when other people *fail to validate the self-concept*. For example, we would expect depersonalisation to be a common response in cases of mistaken identity. If other people insisted, for example, that we were an escaped criminal or an incognito movie star, we might develop momentary uncertainty about who we were, with accompanying feelings of unreality. We might even have this response if other people attributed to us qualities that we were convinced that we lacked (e.g. insisted, contrary to our self-concepts, that we were highly creative). Such interpersonal evidence would challenge our sense of personal sameness or identity.

Finally, people may experience events that are so improbable or outlandish that they feel the events cannot be happening to them and that the experience is unreal. Among instances reported to us, in other work, are the following: finding oneself in the midst of a bank robbery; arriving at Kennedy Airport from Africa but, because one's papers are not in order, being sent back on the next plane; watching as two KGB agents ransacked one's room in a Soviet hotel; being lost in a strange city; finding oneself in a country where no one spoke one's language.

Like the violation of self-expectations, the experiences of public performance, failure in self-attribution, lack of interpersonal validation and involvement in outlandish events are usually exceptional experiences in the individual's life. Depersonalisation is thus apt to be associated with unexpected, unfamiliar, nonroutine life experiences. The sense of identity, then, can never be absolutely secure since no human being is ever completely immune to exposure to the unexpected.

There are, of course, many other influences, dispositional and situational, that may foster depersonalisation. Several of the self-concept dimensions that may exercise this influence have been discussed by Elliott *et al*. (1984).

The experience of self-change

Change in the self, it is obvious, poses a threat to the sense of personal sameness. Yet such change – in appearance, abilities, interests, values – are an inevitable part of life. School pupils are probably more aware of and sensitive to such changes in themselves than adults, in part, at least, because the changes that occur are often so rapid and so visible to others.

(The frequent comment 'My, how you have grown' or 'I can hardly recognise you' inevitably calls such change in self to their attention.) Thus, any change in the self, constituting a threat to personal sameness, would be expected to increase the likelihood of depersonalisation.

In order to examine this question, we focused on five indicators of experienced change. Two of these dealt with physical change (whether their looks had changed much in the past year and whether they experienced difficulty adjusting to their changed appearance) and three to unspecified change (how much they had changed in the past year, whether these changes had surprised them and whether they felt different from when they were younger).

Each of the change items was significantly related to the five-item depersonalisation index beyond the .001 level. The correlations ranged between .1053 and .2813. The strongest association was with the item 'I can't get used to my new looks' ($r = .2813$). This suggests that it is not simply change in the self that is the problem but the difficulty of integrating the change into a revised self-concept.

The second change item that showed a clear association with depersonalisation was the question 'Have any changes about yourself surprised you?' ($r = .2530$). This finding is consistent with our observation that it is not change *per se* but *unexpected* change that threatens the sense of personal sameness. If changes occur that are consistent with one's self-expectations, then the sense of identity may remain secure. But if the changes are startling or unexpected, then it may be difficult to integrate them smoothly into a revised view of oneself.

In addition to these specific changes, it is relevant to consider people's general tendency to experience self-concept change. Some people's self-concepts are generally volatile and variable, fluctuating from moment to moment and situation to situation, whereas other people's self-concepts are firm and stable. People with shifting self-concepts, we expect, would be less likely to have a sure sense of their identity.

In order to examine this question, a seven-item 'stability of self-concept' measure (alpha = .649) was constructed. (Illustrative items: 'A kid told me: "Some days I like the way I am. Some days I do not like the way I am." Do your feelings change like this?'; 'A kid told me: "Some days I think I am one kind of person, other days a different kind of person." Do your feelings change like this?')

Consistent with expectations, youngsters whose self-concepts are highly volatile were more likely to score high on the five-item depersonalisation measure ($r = -.3550$, $p < .001$). People whose thoughts and feelings about the self tend to shift from day to day or moment to moment obviously experience a threat to personal sameness. The secure sense of identity is undermined, producing recurrent experiences of episodic depersonalisation.

Depersonalisation among adolescent boys and girls

Although sociodemographic variables show little association with depersonalisation, there is one interesting exception: girls are somewhat more likely than boys to report feelings of depersonalisation. The relationship, though modest ($r = -.0870$), is statistically significant at the .001 level.

This sex difference, however, is not the same at all ages. Between the ages of 8 and 11, there is little difference between boys and girls. Starting with age 12, however, and reaching a peak at age 13, the depersonalisation scores of girls rise sharply while the boys' scores remain unchanged. Between the ages of 12 and 16, 29 per cent of the girls rank high on the depersonalisation scale compared with 19 per cent of the boys. At the lower end of the scale, the differences are still larger: 40 per cent of the boys are low compared with 26 per cent of the girls ($r = -.1449$, $p < .001$). For 17- to 18-year-olds, the relationship of gender to depersonalisation is weak and not significant.

Between the ages of 12 and 16, then, girls are undergoing certain experiences that enhance their risk of episodic depersonalisation. What are these experiences? An exploration of this question indicates that adolescent girls are much more likely than boys to report that they have difficulty in adjusting to their changed body images. In response to the question 'A kid told me: "I can't get used to my new looks." Do you ever feel like this?' girls were three times as likely as boys to say that they did ($r = -.1909$, $p < .001$). Change, even physical change, as such does not itself necessarily threaten one's identity as long as the change can be smoothly incorporated into a continuous self-concept. But if, for some reason, the individual has difficulty incorporating the change into a revised self-concept structure, then he or she may experience depersonalisation.

Incidentally, it is not the experience of change in general but of physical change in particular that distinguishes adolescent boys and girls. In response to the questions dealing with unspecified change – how much they had changed in the past year, whether they felt different from when they were younger or whether changes had surprised them – the responses of the adolescent girls and boys were similar.

In addition to the problem of physical change, 12- to 16-year-old girls are more likely than boys to experience depersonalisation because their self-concepts are much more volatile at this age (Rosenberg, 1986). Even among 8- to 11-year-olds, girls' self-concepts are somewhat more unstable than boys', but between the ages of 12 and 16, the gap widens substantially. At this age, girls are more apt to report that their ideas about themselves seem to change from day to day and even moment to moment ($r = -.1764$, $p < .001$). Such self-concept fluctuation clearly undermines the sense of personal sameness and fosters episodic depersonalisation.

Summary

The aim of this chapter has been to attempt to improve our understanding of the phenomenon of episodic depersonalisation. Since depersonalisation involves the momentary loss of the sense of identity, usually with accompanying feelings of unreality, circumstances that challenge the sense of identity would be expected to foster depersonalisation. Following William James (1950), we have adopted the view that threats to the feeling of personal sameness tend to undermine the secure sense of identity.

What seems apparent from these data is that to an important extent the self-concept consists of a system of self-expectations. These self-expectations form the foundation for decision and action. But they are subject to three major threats. The first is the spontaneous, unpredictable features of the organism, whose behaviour, by definition, can never be completely foreseen. The second is the unpredictability of events that may elicit responses from the self that contradict the established self-concept. The third is the reality of change that characterises all life and that, in time, renders any fixed system of self-expectations obsolete. These factors may threaten the feeling of personal sameness, weaken the sense of identity and arouse the feeling of transient depersonalisation. At certain life stages, especially early adolescence, the sense of change is apt to be high, and this may produce the momentary experience of identity loss. Because of their greater self-concept volatility and difficulty in adjusting to changing physical appearance, girls are more likely than boys to undergo such experiences at this age.

Acknowledgment

The preparation of this paper was funded by Grant MH39710 from the National Institute of Mental Health.

References

Alexander, C. N., Jr. and Wiley, M. G. (1981), 'Situated activity and identity formation', Chapter 9 in M. Rosenberg and R. H. Turner (eds), *Social Psychology: Sociological Perspectives*, Basic Books: New York.

American Psychiatric Association (1980), *Diagnostic and Statistical Manual of Mental Disorders*, 3rd ed., American Psychiatric Association: Washington, D.C.

Bandura, A. (1978), 'The self in reciprocal determinism', *American Psychologist*, 33, pp. 344–57.

Bandura, A. (1980), 'The self and mechanisms of agency', in J. Suls (ed.), *Psychological Perspectives on the Self*, vol. 1, Erlbaum: Hillsdale, N.J.

Bleuler, E. (1950), *Dementia Praecox or the Group of Schizophrenias*, International Universities Press: New York (Monograph Series on Schizophrenia, no. 1, trans. from German edition, 1911).

Blumer, H. (1969), *Symbolic Interactionism: Perspective and Method*, Prentice-Hall: Englewood Cliffs, N.J.

Campbell, R. J. (1981), *Psychiatric Dictionary*, 5th ed., Oxford University Press: New York.

Cowan, P. (1978), *Piaget with Feeling*, Holt, Rinehart & Winston: New York.

Cronbach, L. J. (1951), 'Coefficient alpha and the internal structure of tests', *Psychometrika*, 16, pp. 297–334.

Driedger, L. (1976), 'Ethnic self-identity: A comparison of in-group evaluations', *Sociometry*, 39, pp. 131–41.

Elliott, G., Rosenberg, M. and Wagner, M. (1984), 'Transient depersonalizaion in youth', *Social Psychology Quarterly*, 47, pp. 115–29.

Erikson, E. H. (1959), 'Identity and the life cycle: Selected papers', *Psychological Issues*, 1, pp. 1–171.

Goffman, E. (1963), *Stigma: Notes on the Management of Spoiled Identity*, Prentice-Hall: Englewood Cliffs, N.J.

Goffman, E. (1969), *Strategic Interaction*, Ballantine Books: New York.

Hart, D., Maloney, J., Damon, W. (1984). The meaning and development of identity', paper presented at the International Interdisciplinary Conference on Self and Identity, Cardiff, Wales.

James, W. (1950), *The Principles of Psychology*, vol. 1, Dover: New York.

Levita, D. de (1965), *The Concept of Identity*, Basic Books: New York.

McCall, G. J. and Simmons, J. L. (1978), *Identities and Interactions*, rev. ed., Free Press: New York.

Mead, G. H. (1934), *Mind, Self, and Society*, University of Chicago Press: Chicago.

Merton, R. K. (1968), *Social Theory and Social Structure*, enlarged edition, Free Press: New York.

Piaget, J. (1968), *Six Psychological Studies*, Vintage Books: New York.

Rosenberg, M. (1979), *Conceiving the Self*, Basic Books: New York.

Rosenberg, M. (1986), 'Self-concept from middle childhood through adolescence', in J. Suls and A. G. Greenwald (eds), *Psychological Perspectives on the Self*, vol. 3, Erlbaum: Hillsdale, N.J., pp. 107–36.

Rosenberg, M. and Simmons, R. G. (1972), *Black and White Self-Esteem: The Urban School Child*, Arnold and Caroline Rose Monograph Series, American Sociological Association: Washington, D.C.

Rovner, R. A. (1981), 'Ethno-cultural identity and self-esteem: A reapplication of self-attitude formation theories', *Human Relations*, 34, pp. 427–34.

Sarbin, T. R. and Scheibe, K. E. (eds) (1983), *Studies in Social Identity*, Praeger: New York.

Shibutani, T. (1961), *Society and Personality*, Prentice-Hall: Englewood Cliffs, N.J.

Stryker, S. (1980), *Symbolic Interactionism*, Benjamin/Cummings: Menlo Park, Calif.

Thoits, P. A. (1983), 'Multiple identities and psychological well-being: A reformulation and test of the social isolation hypothesis', *American Sociological Review*, 48, pp. 174–87.

Webster's Ninth New Collegiate Dictionary (1985), Merriam-Webster: Springfield, Mass.

Wheelis, A. (1958), *The Quest for Identity*, Norton: New York.

14 Changing definitions of self for young women: The implications for rates of violence

Diane Mitsch Bush

Social change and gender differences in the experience of adolescence

There is ample evidence that adults' attitudes toward female gender roles have changed over the past two decades (Thornton *et al.*, 1983; Cherlin and Walters, 1981). On the basis of these findings, the assumption appears to follow that adults are now communicating less sex-typed expectations to children. Therefore it is often assumed that children are now experiencing adolescence in less gender-specific ways. There are two problems with this simple convergence model: (1) it overstates the amount and kind of change that has taken place in the sex-gender system (Rubin, 1981; see also Chodorow, 1978); and (2) it assumes that adults' 'non-traditional' beliefs about 'appropriate' gender roles get translated into gender convergence of children's beliefs about the self and social world and into behavioural convergence as well.

With regard to the first problem, closer scrutiny of available panel data on adults' attitudes reveals a more marked shift toward egalitarian attitudes about women's roles in the economy and policy than in the home (Mason *et al.*, 1976; Thornton *et al.*, 1983). However, the actual division of labour in households appears to have changed little over the period in question (Bush, 1985), and women in the public sphere remain segregated in low-paying, low-status jobs (Stallard *et al.*, 1983; Bush, 1985; Siltanen and Stanworth, 1984).

Women's participation in the public sphere and the attitudes of both women and men continue to reflect a social organisation of gender based on the principle that women's primary responsibility lies in the domestic sphere (Rosaldo, 1974). Thus, it is not surprising that studies of current cohorts of adolescents reveal sex-typed attitudes and traditional gendered stereotypes about future expectations (Bush *et al.*, 1978; see Bush, 1985, for summary). It is in any case a mistake to assume that if adults' attitudes about gender become less stereotyped, then girls' and boys' beliefs and behaviours will converge. We cannot begin to understand how adolescent boys and girls construct gender-specific selves by looking only at the content of adolescent socialisation, although gender-specific content is an important piece of the puzzle. We must also turn our attention to possible gender-specific processes.

One key to understanding the interaction of gender-specific content and processes of socialisation is gender intensification in early adolescence (Hill and Lynch, 1984). A wide variety of theory and findings shows that sex-typed beliefs, behaviours and expectations become more pronounced during early adolescence (ages 12 to 16), especially for girls (Maccoby and Jacklin, 1974; Huston-Stein and Higgins-Trenk, 1978; Weitzman, 1979; Block, 1978; Bernard, 1975). Passivity, dependence, nurturance, an increased emphasis on popularity, a decrease in mathematical achievement and a lowering of occupational aspirations either emerge or intensify in girls during early adolescence (Maccoby and Jacklin, 1974; Block, 1978; Weitzman, 1979; Bush *et al.*, 1978; Rosen and Aneshensel, 1976). Our prior research (Bush *et al.*, 1978; Simmons *et al.*, 1979), using longitudinal data, finds that girls' self-image drops dramatically from ages 12 to 13, and that looks and popularity become more valued at the expense of achievement. During adolescence girls begin to exhibit traits convergent with the traditional female role located in the domestic sphere (Rosaldo, 1974).

Content and outcomes of gendered development in adolescence

How does the content of socialisation experience change in early adolescence to produce such marked changes? The gender-intensification hypothesis (Hill and Lynch, 1984; Block, 1978) argues that demands placed on adolescent girls change from those placed on girls earlier and differ considerably from those placed on boys. Parents, peers and teachers are all said to begin to require behaviours consistent with preparation for the traditional wife/mother role (Bernard, 1975; Hill and Lynch, 1984). Traditional parents repond to girls' reproductive maturity by protecting girls and emphasising dependent, passive behaviours (Baumrind, 1975; Huston-Stein and Higgins-Trenk, 1978; Weitzman, 1979). Rosen and Aneshensel (1976) show that perceived parental restrictions *and* involvement in a number of dating relationships led adolescent girls to be overly compliant so as to conform to perceived sex-role expectations. Baumrind (1975) concurs.

The content of adolescent socialisation for girls is fraught with discontinuity and conflict. Girls appear to discover that they are 'supposed to' be concerned with boys and that boys expect them to act in traditionally female ways (Best, 1983; Simmons *et al.*, 1979). Yet at the same time, they begin to realise that these 'feminine' behaviours are devalued in the world of boys, as well as in the adult public sphere (Broverman *et al.*, 1972; Siltanen and Stanworth, 1984). Thus, the content and outcomes of gender socialisation for the sexes correspond to the ideology of private/public duality (Rosaldo, 1974): women's sphere is the private sphere of domesticity oriented around nurturance and dependence upon public man. In contrast, the public, male sphere is said to require independence, instrumentality and competition, according to the ideology of separate, gendered spheres (Siltanen and Stanworth, 1984; Bush, 1984).

Processes of gender socialisation

Content alone does not account for sex differences in cognition or behaviours, including violent ones, even though much theory and most research explore only content. Chodorow (1978), Gilligan (1982) and Bem (1981; 1983) have extended, respectively, psychoanalytic theory, cognitive-developmental theory and a synthesis of cognitive-developmental and social learning theory in attempts to link content and/or outcomes of socialisation to processes of gender socialisation. Briefly, Chodorow (1974; 1978) centres her theory around the fact that women are the primary caretakers for children within the domestic sphere. This family structure and the associated public–private duality in the larger social structure lead to different processes and outcomes of socialisation for boys and girls. This is Chodorow's major point of departure from psychoanalytic theory and from the functionalist tradition upon which she draws. She utilises feminist theory from cultural anthropology, especially Margaret Mead (1949), Rosaldo and Ortner (Rosaldo, 1974), to argue that the social structure extant in virtually all societies which relegates women to the private sphere also renders them socially and politically subordinate to men in the public sphere. This process is intensified in advanced capitalist societies because of the more marked structural and ideological separation between the family sphere and the public spheres of the economy and the state (Chodorow, 1978, pp. 179–81). Thus, the feminine qualities of nurturance and interpersonal connectedness become devalued at both the interpersonal and cultural levels as well as in social theory itself.

Because the mother is present within the everyday world of the child and because she sees the daughter as similar to herself, girls develop by personal identification. This process of role learning is characterised by expressive interaction and acceptance, resulting in a self and gender-role identity marked by affiliation and intimacy. In contrast, boys' gender-role development revolves around separation from maternal attachment and positional identification with a largely invisible male role model due in part to the public/private split. Since the father is not as readily available for interaction, male role learning tends to be more abstract and formal, often gleaned from cultural, not personal, images. Boys begin to have a stereotypic conception of masculinity, and the development of gender identity is characterised by proscriptions, which warn against being 'soft' or 'sissy'. Research indicates that boys' self-definition centres on 'not-being-feminine' in adolescence (Stericker and Kurdick, 1982; Bush *et al.*, 1978), girls' self-definition resides in relations, especially heterosexual ones (Simmons *et al.*, 1979). and boys are far less likely than girls to be androgynous (Stericker and Kurdick, 1982). In early adolescence, both the process and content of socialisation centre on affiliation for girls and separation for boys.

Gilligan (1982) links these same gender differences in socialisation processes to distinctive patterns of moral development for boys and girls. She specifically extends Chodorow's analysis to adolescence and early adulthood. She illustrates that male development follows Erikson's (1950) stage sequence: 'identity versus role confusion' is completed, then 'intimacy versus isolation' is tackled. However, for girls intimacy and identity are not separate stages. Therefore Gilligan (1982, p. 8) maintains that 'male gender identity is threatened by intimacy while female gender identity is threatened by separation'.

Associated with this difference in process is Gilligan's (1982, p. 173) insistence that 'men and women speak different languages that they assume are the same'. This results in misunderstanding between women and men, but, more importantly for our purposes here, it reveals that theory and research should explore the meaning of women's and men's worlds if we are to grasp the processes by which selves are constructed. She finds that affective ties and concern for others – an essential connectedness – are the bases for girls' moral judgments. Girls see morality as a way to solve conflicts so that no one is hurt. For boys, fairness and individual autonomy are the bases for moral judgments. Moral decisions are arrived at by impersonally applying a system of rational, abstract principles to conflicts in order to deduce solutions; separation is the basis for such decisions.

Gilligan does not emphasise cohort differences in vocabularies of meaning. Given recent changes in women's definitions of self discussed above, it is conceivable that the meanings of independence and competence may begin to entail an integration of attachment and separation. Thus the adolescent girl who eschews the traditional passive-dependent role may not reject connectedness with others. Gilligan's interviews with young adults in the early 1970s suggest that the process of moral development for women is characterised by reconciling needs of self and other by rooting the identity in personal, concrete relationships. This process appears to be a crucial element in the construction of self for young women.

Bem's (1981; 1983) gender-schema theory begins with the related propositions that cultural definitions of female and male extend to a wide variety of attributes, behaviours and beliefs not directly linked to sex differences in anatomy and reproductive functions and that the child learns to process new information in terms of this diffuse, heterogeneous network of sex-related associations, i.e. according to a gender schema (Bem, 1981, pp. 354–6; 1983, pp. 603–4). Both the social world and the self get assimilated into the gender schema so that the child narrows her or his universe of possible beliefs and behaviours.

Bem (1983), like many feminist social scientists, maintains that the depth and breadth of the male–female dichotomy in culture accounts for the centrality of the gender schema. Although she concludes that children would be less sex-typed if the extent of cultural links between sex and other attributes, beliefs and behaviours were limited, she does not speculate upon the content of current or alternative gender schemata. If we integrate her insights with those of Gilligan, we may speculate that as the boundaries of women's roles have widened to some extent, new role definitions have incorporated elements of both 'masculine' and 'feminine' rather than rejecting 'the feminine' (see Gilligan, 1982; Chodorow, 1978; Ehrenreich, 1983; Eisenstein, 1981, for related speculations). If the gender schema has changed in such a fashion, we would expect adolescent girls in the mid-1970s to be less sex-typed in some beliefs and behaviours.

In contrast, the logic of Chodorow's theory implies that there will be little change in women's and men's needs and capacities, and therefore in their respective statuses and roles, until the structure of the domestic and the public spheres changes. She argues that the fact that women are responsible for child-rearing within the historically specific structure of the nuclear family in contemporary capitalist societies reproduces both family structure and the larger social organisation. Both structures are predicated upon, and reproduce, a feminine self characterised by nurturance, dependence and connection and a masculine self characterised by competitiveness, independence and separation from others. Therefore, until men take an active and equal role in parenting and women participate equally in the public sphere, this family structure will continue to produce two distinct sets of experiences for girls and boys. Chodorow contends that these two distinct experiences reproduce new generations of men who have both the capacity and the need to define self in relation to the impersonal, competitive world at the bureaucratic workplace. Likewise, these disparate experiences rooted in family structure reproduce women who have the need and capacity to define self largely in terms of others. Chodorow stresses that social reproduction of such dichotomous male and female selves is not the result simply of content of socialisation nor of intent in socialisation. Rather, it is due to gendered processes of socialisation.

Gender, social change, socialisation and violence

The implications of change and consistency in the social organisation of gender in capitalist societies and in gendered socialisation may be clarified by examining work on gender equality and changes in rates of violence. One position is that as women reject traditional gender role definitions of the female self, women's approval of violence and participation in violence will resemble those for men (Adler, 1975; Kelley, 1977). In contrast, theory and empirical evidence indicate that women who have constructed non-traditional identities will be less likely to approve of or engage in violence than traditional women (Richardson *et al.*, 1980; Bush, 1983) or men (Gilligan, 1982; Boulding, 1984). To gain insight into these contradictory predictions I will now examine the assumptions and evidence which underlie them, with emphasis on the bases for existing sex differences in violence as well as associated cognitions and behaviours. This line of enquiry will lead us back to consideration of both content and processes of socialisation.

Current gender differences in violence

The debate on changing definitions of self for women and their implications for changing rates of violence is located in the study of gender differences. Of the relatively small number of empirically validated gender differences in personality, beliefs and behaviour (Maccoby and Jacklin, 1974; Parsons, 1980), the most striking is the difference in violent behaviour and beliefs (Maccoby and Jacklin, 1974; Parsons, 1980; Freize *et al.*, 1978). If violence is defined as the intentional physical injury of human beings (Bush, 1984; see Blumenthal *et al.*, 1972, Tilly, 1978, and Graham and Gurr, 1979, for discussion of the concept) rather than the more diffuse set of beliefs and behaviours grouped under the rubric of aggression, there is a clear difference between the sexes. From infancy through adulthood, males exhibit higher rates of violence than do females (Parsons, 1980; Maccoby and Jacklin, 1974). Whether in the domestic sphere (Breines and Gordon, 1983) or in the public sphere, men are more likely to engage in violent behaviour than women (Ruddick, 1983; Elshtain, 1983). It is possible that this observed gender difference is actually a sex difference, that it is due to biological differences between males and females. Both the complexity of the human cortex and the enormous amount of within-sex variation cast doubt on this explanation. However, it cannot be ruled out until research on hormone effects (see Baker, 1980, for a useful review and Parsons, 1980; Petersen, 1980), brain lateralisation (see Parsons, 1980; Sayers, 1981; De La Coste and Holloway, 1982) and genotype–phenotype interactions generally (Lewontin, 1983) advances further. It is unlikely that the effect of biology is a direct one; to the extent that gender differences in human violent behaviour are affected by biology, the effect is mediated socially (Parsons, 1980; Sayers, 1981). Anthropologists (Rosaldo, 1974), psycho-endocrinologists (Baker, 1980; Petersen, 1980) and biologists (Lewontin, 1983) argue that biology becomes socially constructed; that construction then determines attributes, beliefs and behaviours. One way in which biological sex differences are socially interpreted and constructed as gender is through socialization.

It is assumed that there is a parallel gender difference in approval of violence. Research abounds on differences in violent behaviour, but there is little on sex differences in attitudes toward violence, nor on how sex differences in socialisation may lead to approval of violence. What research there is concentrates on men (Blumenthal *et al.*, 1972; Ball-Rokeach, 1973). Blumenthal *et al.* (1972) examined antecedents of approval for violence among American men ($N=1374$). The majority of their respondents approved of violence when it was a means to a desired end. Moreover, a constellation of values corresponding to traditional masculine values – valuing bravery, retributive justice and the physical ability to defend oneself and win – are associated with greater approval of violence in their sample. Contrary to subculture theory (for other disconfirming evidence see Ball-Rokeach, 1973; Smith, 1979), the Blumenthal study emphasises that these values are a central component of American culture. Similarly, Graham and Gurr (1979) concentrate on what they call 'aggressive masculinity' as a core component of American culture which contributes to the high rates of violence in the United States relative to other industrialised countries.

These results are consistent with studies of 'the gender gap' in the United States. Recent research reveals that men are more likely than women, both currently and historically, to approve of organised violence (i.e. military expenditures, strategies and actions) as a solution to political conflict (Goertzel, 1983; Boulding, 1984). This gender difference in beliefs may be linked back to the social organisation of gender into public and private spheres. Elshtain (1983) argues that the public–private split has created two polar types: the 'beautiful soul' and 'the just warrior'. The beautiful soul resides in the private sphere, upholding the essence of all that is pure and good and opposed to all that is violent, while the just warrior defends both private and public use of violence. (See Bush, 1984, for discussion of this and other theoretical frameworks oriented around women, men, the public–private split and violence.) In a similar vein, Ruddick (1983) maintains that this separation of spheres corresponds to two distinctive cognitive styles: the abstract and the concrete. The concrete is well-suited to the demands of the domestic sphere; it focuses on the personal and the detailed, whereas the abstract style is depersonalised and oriented around generalisation. The latter style makes it possible to create an abstract enemy and then kill him or her. In contrast, such a creation is exceedingly difficult within the concrete style (see also Kelman, 1973) because the enemy is viewed in more personal terms. Ruddick's conception is similar to both Gilligan's (1982) and Chodorow's (1978, discussed above), in that she contends that the concrete style is more characteristic of women and the abstract style is more characteristic of men in industrial societies.

Gender equality and violence

Various conceptualisations of gender differences in approval of violence all utilise, either implicitly or explicitly, woman's location in the domestic sphere and her statuses of wife and mother as an explanation for women's disapproval of violence and for women's lower rates of violent behaviour. Many discussions of gender equality view women's participation in the public sphere as the essence and operationalisation of equality. Anti-feminist, non-feminist and some avowedly feminist conceptions of gender equality focus on women leaving the home and competing 'like a man in a man's world' as the *sine qua non* of gender equality (see Bush, 1984, for further discussion of this issue). Thus, the contention that equality for women will spell higher rates of violence in society is based on the assumption that 'equality' means 'being the same as men'.

The implications of this assumption can be seen in both theory (Adler, 1975) and policy (Kelley, 1977) statements on women and crime. Adler (1975) maintains that as women gain equal opportunity and shed traditional female roles, their patterns of criminal behaviour, especially violence, will resemble those of men. She states that:

> The phenomenon of female criminality is but one wave in the rising tide of female assertiveness. A wave which has not yet crested and may even be seeking its level uncomfortably close to the high water mark set by male violence (Adler, 1975, p. 1).

Women's behaviours will become like men's because there exists a 'gradual but accelerating social revolution in which women are closing many of the gaps that have separated them from men. The closer they get, the more alike they look and act' (Adler, 1975, p. 30). It is beyond the scope of this chapter to assess the argument that women are actually rapidly closing social and economic gaps between themselves and men, but virtually all the research on income, especially the literature on single-parent households and the feminisation of poverty, questions this assertion (Stallard *et al.*, 1983). As discussed above, there is an abundance of research that shows considerable change in women's attitudes toward traditional female roles over the past fifteen years (Mason *et al.*, 1976; Cherlin and Walters, 1981; Thornton *et al.*, 1983); women appear to reject traditional stereotypes about their participation in the workplace and the polity. Adler argues that these changes in sex-role expectations are a move toward acceptance of masculine norms and values, which includes approving of and engaging in violence.

So far the quantitative evidence on crime rates over the past fifteen years does not support Adler's theory (Simon, 1983). Although female rates for property crime have doubled during this period, there has been no concomitant increase in rates of violent crime (Simon, 1975; Bowker, 1978). How can we explain these data in light of Adler's theory? Either there is an insufficient time lag between the attitudinal changes and behavioural effects or the theory itself is invalid.

With regard to the first alternative explanation, most of the change in women's sex-role attitudes appears to have taken place in the mid-1970s (Mason *et al.*, 1976; Cherlin and Walters, 1981; Thornton *et al.*, 1983), so it is possible that these changes are not yet reflected in rates of violent crime. As successive cohorts mature in this milieu, it is possible that non-traditional sex-role expectations for women might result in higher rates of violence. If such a trend is on the horizon, research on adolescents might uncover it. There are anecdotal accounts of such convergence for current cohorts of teenage boys and girls (Bowker, 1978, p. 21), but very little systematic work on convergence regarding violence (Smart and Smart, 1978; Bowker, 1978). There is evidence on the link between girls' gender role expectations and delinquency generally, but that research shows no relationship between non-traditional gender roles and delinquency (Giordano and Cernkovich, 1979).

I argue that, even if rates of violent crime by women had increased during the 1970s, interpreting such an increase as support for Adler's theory might lead to the ecological fallacy. Instead, what we need is research which compares women and/or girls who have rejected traditional sex-role expectations with those who accept traditional role expectations to see if the former are, in fact, more violent. Given Adler's assumption that adherence to traditional male values is a determinant of violence, then research should show that men who value such traits are indeed more approving of, and more likely to engage in, violence. I have discussed studies which show just such a relationship for men (Graham and Gurr, 1979; Ball-Rokeach, 1973; Blumenthal *et al.*, 1972).

If men who adhere most to traditional male sex-role expectations are more likely to approve of and/or to engage in violence, then it seems to follow that as girls and women move away from traditional sex roles – as they assert themselves and compete in previously male-dominated social settings – such equality will spell greater approval of violence and more violent behaviour. However, two studies which examine this question directly find no such relationship between non-traditional sex-role attitudes and violence. Indeed, Richardson *et al.* (1980) found that women who are non-traditional in gender-role attitudes are less likely to respond violently to experimentally induced frustration than are traditional women. My own research shows no difference between girls with traditional orientations and non-traditional girls in levels of approval of violence (Bush, 1983). Girls who have rejected traditional gender-role presumptions are not more similar to boys in their attitudes toward violence. Neither of these studies is consistent with Adler's hypothesis.

How can we explain these findings in light of Adler's theory? She maintains that, as women become socially, politically and economically more equal to men, they will be more similar to men in beliefs and behaviour. Richardson's findings imply that non-traditional women are even less violent than traditional women, who are, in turn, less violent than men. She explains her data with the assertion that women who are non-traditional in sex-role attitudes are more liberal overall – one component of liberalism is pacifism. My research suggests that girls who have rejected traditional gender-role expectations do not take on traditional male traits and values. Rather, it is possible that these girls have rejected a central component of traditional gendered ideology suggested by both Ruddick and Elshtain (above): that 'masculine' ways of solving disputes are preferable, especially in the public sphere. Both Ruddick and Elshtain characterise western gendered ideology and structure of separate spheres as legitimating certain forms of violence, especially war. Elshtain's 'beautiful soul/just warrior' distinction implies that women value nurturance, compassion and tenderness in the private sphere while accepting, even endorsing, violence in the public sphere.

From Adler's perspective, women would simply adopt the 'just warrior' stance (Elshtain, 1983) and the abstract style (Ruddick, 1983) as they participated in the economy and polity. Richardson's work implies that non-traditional women might bring pacifist values into the public sphere, perhaps resulting in less violence. I argue that rejection of traditional female gender roles does not necessarily imply rejection of all traditional female values by the individual young woman. Instead it may mean that she infuses the traditional 'masculine' emphasis on competition, on independence, which often translates into rejection of connection (Bakan, 1966), and on separation with the traditional feminine values of nurturance, closeness and connection. Gilligan's (1982) research on adolescent girls and young women implies that competence and independence for high-achieving females are often based in connection with and concern for others. Gilligan's and Richardson's findings, as well as my own, suggest that the problem with Adler's theory is that she assumes that equality for women means becoming the same as men.

I argue that girls who value non-traditional sex-role traits will be no more likely to approve of violence than girls who value traditional traits, and it is possible that they will be less likely to approve of violence. Furthermore, the issues of causation and attitude change have not been adequately addressed in prior research. A connection between changes in attitudes about desirable traits for women and changes in rates of violent behaviour or approval of violence has been assumed, not tested. Also most tests have utilised cross-sectional data which do not warrant inferences about change in attitudes or behaviour (see Duncan, 1980, and Markus, 1979, for discussion of methodological problems encountered when studying change). Most research on this question has examined arrest rates over the period in which attitudes toward women's roles have changed and concluded that any change in arrest rates is due to changes in attitudes (Simon, 1975; Adler, 1975). Giordano and Cernkovich (1979) have pointed out the pitfalls of this approach, most notably the way it oversimplifies the concepts of 'sex role' and 'women's liberation'. But perhaps more importantly, this approach does not test for a relationship between non-traditional attitudes and deviance. Among the studies that do examine the question empirically (Giordano and Cernkovich, 1979; Jensen and Eve, 1976), all are cross-sectional in nature and deal with crime or delinquency generally, not violence or attitudes about violence. The cross-sectional studies are limited in that, even if they find a relationship, the causal direction is not known. In addition, the dependent variable here is change in attitudes; cross-sectional data do not allow conclusions about attitude change. Therefore, it seems that a longitudinal study which examines how adolescents' sex-role orientations are related to approval of violence would be a step toward understanding this issue.

From the preceding discussion, two questions emerge which require investigation using longitudinal data:

1. Do the same variables influence approval of violence in the same way for adolescent girls and boys?
2. Do adolescent girls who value non-traditional sex-role traits approve of violence more than traditional girls?

The first question stems directly from the positions discussed earlier; it asks whether and how the content and processes of socialisation differ during a crucial developmental period. The second question moves to the heart of the issue. An answer to it requires not only that we compare the impact of violence, but that we explore the meaning of such expectations.

The data used to examine these hypotheses came from a longitudinal study conducted in the Milwaukee public schools from 1974 to 1979. A cohort was followed from Grade 6 through Grade 10. Eighteen schools were sampled; all the children in each school were asked to participate. Parental permission was secured from 80 per cent. Because of length limitations on the interview, the questions on violence were administered to a random half

TABLE 14.1   *Means and standard deviations for items for approval of violence, perceived parental encouragement, importance of bravery, instrumental–interpersonal orientation and school context of violence*

	Approval of violence	Parental encourage-ment[b]	Value of bravery[c]	Inter-personal–instrumental orientation[d]	School context of violence[c]	
	X (SD)	X (SD)	X (SD)	X (SD)	X (SD)	N
6th Grade						
Boys	2.57 (1.05)	2.57 (1.06)	3.28 (0.72)	0.76 (0.43)	35.13 (14.38)	53
Girls	2.20 (1.08)	2.49 (1.05)	3.09 (0.77)	0.71 (0.46)	34.99 (14.89)	65
Both	2.36 (1.08)	2.52 (1.05)	3.18 (0.75)	0.73 (0.45)	35.05 (14.60)	118
7th Grade						
Boys	2.85 (0.85)	2.56 (0.93)	2.83 (0.89)	0.87 (0.34)	24.22 (11.74)	53
Girls	2.42 (1.00)	2.18 (1.07)	2.85 (0.75)	0.71 (0.46)	22.38 (13.38)	65
Both	2.61 (0.96)	2.35 (1.02)	2.84 (0.82)	0.78 (0.42)	23.21 (12.65)	118
9th Grade						
Boys	2.96 (0.73)	2.32 (0.80)	2.89 (0.61)	0.85 (0.36)	29.43 (18.78)	53
Girls	2.55 (1.06)	2.03 (0.98)	2.80 (0.79)	0.83 (0.38)	30.45 (20.21)	65
Both	2.74 (0.95)	2.16 (0.91)	2.84 (0.72)	0.84 (0.37)	29.99 (19.51)	118
10th Grade						
Boys	3.02 (0.87)	2.30 (0.97)	2.06 (0.66)	0.87 (0.34)	20.25 (7.35)	53
Girls	2.42 (1.13)	1.97 (0.92)	1.97 (0.86)	0.89 (0.31)	19.31 (13.53)	65
Both	2.69 (1.06)	2.12 (0.95)	2.01 (0.78)	0.88 (0.32)	19.73 (11.21)	118

[a] Item wording: 'If somebody was giving a kid a hard time and that kid hit this other person to make them quit, would that be: really OK, kind of OK, not really OK, or not at all OK?' The item was recoded so that higher values indicate more approval.

[b] Item wording: 'How important do your parent(s) think it is for you to use your fists to defend yourself? Do your parent(s) think it is: very important, somewhat important, not very important, or not at all important?' The item was recoded so that higher values indicate more approval.

[c] Item wording: 'How important is it for a person to be brave? It is: very important, somewhat important, not very important, or not at all important?' The item was recoded so that a higher value indicates more importance.

of the sample in Grade 6 and a random half of that sample in Grade 7. Due to this factor and attrition in Grades 9 and 10, the longitudinal sample for this research is 118: 53 boys and 65 girls.

The measures used are listed in Table 14.1. The four category items are recoded so that higher values indicate more approval of violence, greater parental encouragement or a greater value placed on bravery. Responses to the interpersonal–instrumental item are coded into a dummy vector such that the two non-traditional (for females) responses are assigned a value of '1' and the traditional interpersonal preference is assigned a value of '0'. School context was tapped by constructing a school score based on the proportion of children in each school who answered in the affirmative to the item 'Is this school a dangerous place where other kids hit you or take things from you?'

Findings

Table 14.1 shows means and standard deviations for each grade by sex. In each grade, boys approve more of violence than do girls. Approval levels increase for boys from Grade 6 to Grade 10, while they decrease for girls from Grade 6 to Grade 10.

Boys' and girls' responses about parental encouragement are virtually identical in Grade 6; boys are slightly more likely to report greater parental encouragement of violence. This same pattern maintains through Grade 10 with the sex difference increasing somewhat. Both sexes report that parental encouragement diminishes from Grade 6 to Grade 10.

Responses to the bravery item show a pattern similar to that for parental encouragement, but the sex difference in responses is less. Boys place a slightly higher value on bravery in Grade 6 than do girls; this difference diminishes in Grade 7. Both sexes value bravery less in each successive grade.

In Grade 6 boys place slightly greater value on instrumental traits than do girls. This gap widens in Grade 7 and drops almost to zero in Grades 9 and 10. The pattern of change from Grade 6 to Grade 7 is consistent with the gender-intensification hypothesis (Hill and Lynch, 1984) as well as with literature on sex differences (Maccoby and Jacklin, 1974; Weitzman, 1979).

Scores on school context of violence drop in Grade 7, rise in Grade 9

---

[d] Item wording: 'Which is most important for you: being able to do things for yourself, being well-liked, or being best at the things you do?' A dummy variable was created so that independence and competence (do things for yourself, being best at the things you do) were coded '1' and interpersonal orientation (being well-liked) was coded '0'.

[e] Each school was assigned a score based on the proportion of respondents in the school who responded that their school was 'a dangerous place' (see text for further discussion).

TABLE 14.2   *Regressions of approval for instrumental violence[a] in Grades 6, 7, 9 and 10 on parental encouragement, value placed on bravery, instrumental–interpersonal orientation and earlier approval of violence by sex[b]*

	Parental encouragement	Value of bravery	Instrumental–interpersonal orientation	School context of violence	Approval of violence $(t-1)$	Constant	R^2	N
6th Grade								
Boys	.047	.014	.271	.004		2.046	.016	53
	(.157)	(.239)	(.358)	(.010)				
Girls	.366[d]	.232	−.325	.002		0.728	.186	65
	(.137)	(.170)	(.284)	(.009)				
Both	.195	.132	.016	.004		1.297	.067	118
7th Grade								
Boys	.354[d]	.046	−.011	.012	.264[c]	0.868	.281	53
	(.129)	(.135)	(.317)	(.009)	(.105)			
Girls	.222[c]	−.062	−.199	.004	.434[d]	1.282	.366	65
	(.109)	(.149)	(.229)	(.008)	(.104)			
Both	.302[d]	−.019	.123	.006	.362[e]	1.051	.338	118
	(.081)	(.100)	(.178)	(.006)	(.072)			
9th Grade								
Boys	−.130	.417[d]	−.376	−.001	.509[e]	0.966	.498	53
	(.110)	(.139)	(.223)	(.004)	(.009)			
Girls	−.077	.604[e]	−.091	−.004	.335[d]	0.427	.379	65
	(.120)	(.146)	(.294)	(.006)	(.121)			
Both	−.086	.535[e]	−.186	−.002	.425[e]	0.526	.414	118
	(.083)	(.102)	(.190)	(.004)	(.078)			
10th Grade								
Boys	.265[d]	.157	−.495	.026[c]	.656[e]	0.056	.433	53
	(.101)	(.154)	(.281)	(.013)	(.139)			
Girls	.212	.003	−.173	−.010	.456[e]	1.174	.246	65
	(.152)	(.166)	(.415)	(.009)	(.131)			
Both	.281[d]	.112	−.370	−.002	.524[e]	0.791	.315	118

[a] See item wording in Table 14.1.
[b] Coefficients are unstandardised regression coefficients; standard errors are in parentheses.
[c] $p \leq .05$
[d] $p \leq .01$
[e] $p \leq .001$

(although not to the sixth-grade level) and decrease in Grade 10. There is a minimal sex difference in each grade; since these are composite school scores, the reason for the sex difference is not readily apparent. It could be that schools with a higher proportion of boys are perceived to be more dangerous. These data are merely suggestive in this regard. The decrease in scores from Grade 6 to 7 and from Grade 9 to 10 is more notable. We must remember that these are perceptions of danger; thus, any change could be due either to a real change in violence or to a heightened or lessened awareness of danger. One argument for the decrease from Grade 6 to 7 is that children have heard rumours about how violent junior high is; when they enter junior high, they find that the situation is not as drastic as rumour had suggested. Another argument is that children become desensitised to violence and therefore perceive less danger. The data analysed here do not allow us to choose between these explanations.

Table 14.2 shows the results of regressing attitudes toward violence on parental encouragement, value placed on bravery, instrumental–interpersonal orientation and school context of violence for each grade. Regressions are estimated separately for boys, girls and both sexes combined. The pooled estimates for both sexes may be used as a yardstick for evaluating differences between sexes. Approval of violence in the preceding grade is a lagged variable which in effect controls for the earlier score on approval of violence.

Scrutiny of the coefficients for parental encouragement of violence for Grade 6 reveals no impact for boys and a positive impact for girls. In Grade 6, girls who report that their parents encourage them to fight back physically are more approving of violence. In Grade 7, parental encouragement has a positive impact for both sexes, but in Grade 9 there is no effect. By Grade 10, parental encouragement has a significant positive effect on approval of violence only for boys.

Valuing bravery has no impact upon approval of violence in Grades 6, 7 or 10. In Grade 9, it has a positive effect upon approval of violence for both sexes. The ninth-grade results are consistent with previous research; however, the lack of significant effects in other grades is curious.

School context has no impact upon approval of violence except for tenth-grade boys. For this group, the more violent the school context, the more likely boys are to approve of violence.

None of the coefficients for instrumental–interpersonal orientation is significant. However, all signs are negative, except for sixth-grade boys. Girls who value competence or independence rather than the traditional trait of popularity are no more likely to approve of violence than girls who value a traditional trait; indeed, the signs imply that they are somewhat (not significantly) less likely to have positive attitudes toward violence.

In summary, the impact of parental encouragement, value of bravery, instrumental–interpersonal orientation and school context upon attitudes toward violence do not appear to differ significantly by sex. The exceptions to this finding are the sex difference in the impact of parental encouragement in Grades 6 and 9 (positive, significant for girls in Grade 6, for boys in Grade 10) and in the positive impact of school context upon approval of violence for tenth-grade boys.

With regard to the second research question, girls who value instrumental traits are no more likely to approve of violence than girls who value interpersonal traits. The signs of coefficients imply a trend in the opposite direction.

Discussion

In both Grade 6 and Grade 7, girls who report parental encouragement of violence are more likely to approve of violence. This would seem to point to non-traditional parental expectations as a determinant of approval of violence for girls. This fits well with Adler's argument. However, this interpretation does not fit with the data on bravery or instrumental orientation. One reason for this apparent inconsistency may lie in the assumption that parents who encourage daughters to defend themselves physically also present non-traditional sex-role expectations. The regression results militate against making such an assumption. Furthermore, consideration of zero-order correlations between parental encouragement and the dummy variable for instrumental–interpersonal orientation cast doubt on both the assumption and its implications (Grade 6: $r = .207$; Grade 7: $r = -.016$; Grade 9: $r = .140$; Grade 10: $r = .097$).

One explanation for the inconsistency of these findings, again particularly that between parental encouragement and instrumental–interpersonal orientations and value of bravery, is that the process whereby parents and others socialise adolescent sex-role expectations may not be explicit. These findings then provide us with more questions than answers about sex differences in socialisation, but they do focus our questions on the process, not only the content. No distinct patterns of sex differences in socialisation as measured here account for the sex differences in approval of violence.

Boys and girls in this sample do not seem to differ dramatically in their interpersonal–instrumental orientations. Yet they do differ in their approval of violence. Not surprisingly, then, neither valuing independence nor valuing competence has a significant effect on approval of violence for girls. Girls who value independence or competence over popularity may be said to have a non-traditional orientation along the interpersonal–instrumental dimension. They are no more likely to approve of violence than are girls who value popularity. This finding is contrary to the assertion that non-traditional females will hold attitudes toward violence which resemble males' attitudes. However, it should be noted that boys in Grades 9 and 10 who value independence over popularity (and are therefore 'traditional' in one sense) do not approve of violence more than other boys; indeed, the trend is in the other direction.

At first glance the argument seems to fly in the face of theory on the sex differences in processes of socialisation (Chodorow, 1978; Gilligan, 1982).

Gilligan argues that females' tendency to eschew violence as a solution to problems comes from their distinctive patterns of development which emphasise connectedness and concern for others, whereas the process for boys results in separation and a concern for logic in problem solving which would lead to approval or instrumental violence. If girls value competence and independence more than popularity, it would seem to follow that they are less concerned with others, and thus violence is acceptable. Yet I find no difference between instrumentally oriented and socioemotionally oriented girls.

Obviously the answer to this question depends upon what competence and independence mean. If Gilligan (1982) is correct about the effects of personal identification, then 'being able to do things for yourself' or 'being good at the things you do' may mean something very different for adolescent girls from what 'independence' or 'competence' mean for adolescent boys. In particular, girls' definitions of competence and independence may include concerns with not hurting others while succeeding or being independent. My data do not speak to this issue in any direct way, but the findings certainly suggest further consideration of these questions of what non-traditional sex-role attitudes signify for girls who hold them. The point is that we must be careful not to oversimplify the meaning of changing sex-role definitions. To say that some women have questioned and begun to reject traditional women's roles does not mean that the alternative is the traditional male role (Rosaldo and Lamphere, 1974; Rossi, 1983, 1984; Gilligan, 1982; Ruddick, 1983).

Shortcomings in this analysis point out the need for a methodology that gets at the development of meanings of self and other for the sexes. Asking a series of identical, closed-ended questions of a longitudinal sample of both boys and girls provides a basic yardstick for comparison, but it ignores the richness and depth of both similarity and difference. A combination of survey and in-depth case-study techniques might be optimal, bearing in mind constraints placed on research and researchers (see Honess and Edwards, Chapter 16, for an example of the possibilities with in-depth case studies). Using a subsample of a larger panel for in-depth interviews seems to be a necessity for getting at questions of gendered development.

This research and that reviewed above imply that gender equality may lead to lower rates of violence in society. In particular, it is possible that gender equality may result in a devaluing of the extremes of traditional masculine and feminine roles and a less extensive male–female dichotomy (Bakan, 1966; Gilligan, 1982). One outcome of such change might be a lower incidence of wife-battering because there were less passive, less dependent women and less competitive, less aggressive men (see Straus *et al.*, 1980; Thorne, 1982; Breines and Gordon, 1983; Schechter, 1982; Morgan, 1981; Bush, 1984) coupled with a blurring of the public/private split in both ideology and social structure. Less emphasis on competition, hierarchy, aggressiveness and separation may enable us to deal more effectively with the threat of nuclear war. This line of reasoning is quite similar to Kelman's (1973) earlier analysis: if we are able cognitively to dehumanise others, to construct abstract enemies, then we are more likely to wage war against them. This suggests that we must begin to understand the essence of connectedness – of how both sexes may develop a self and an identity separate enough to be individual but connected enough to be empathetic.

But we must also grasp the limitations imposed upon such selves and upon an understanding of them by seemingly impenetrable social structures of inequality and domination which contribute to violence (Gramsci, 1971; Therborn, 1980; Zaretsky, 1976; Young, 1981; McIntosh, 1978; Piven, 1984). Recent theory and research on women and men, such as that discussed in this chapter, focus our attention on the inadequacies of previous research and methodology (Chodorow, 1978; Gilligan, 1982; Siltanen and Stanworth, 1984). Theories and methodologies which used the male experience of socialisation as the model not only failed to explain women's experience, but treated it as inferior. Just as earlier work either left women out or created misogynist accounts of female identity and self, current work (including the analysis reported here) tends to assume that the process of socialisation does not differ by race or class. This assumption may be a valid one, but we will not know until we explore the process and the meaning of socialisation from the perspective of people who occupy a variety of positions in the social structure. Gender, class and race all place limits upon the number and kinds of socialisation experiences available to the individual. Without an understanding of these limits, we will continue to study the individual and the social structure as separate, failing to comprehend equality, social change or violence.

Acknowledgment

Data collection for a portion of this research was funded by NIMH Grant R01 MH30739 and a grant from the William T. Grant Foundation. Data analysis was funded by a Faculty Research Grant from Colorado State University. I gratefully acknowledge Steven Pratt's able research assistance. Many thanks to Diane English for her expertise in manuscript preparation.

References

Adler, F. (1975), *Sisters in Crime*, McGraw-Hill: New York.
Bakan, D. (1966), *The Duality of Human Existence*, Rand McNally: Chicago.

Baker, S. W. (1980), 'Biological influences on human sex and gender', *Signs: Journal of Women in Culture and Society*, 6(1), pp. 80–96.

Ball-Rokeach, S. J. (1973), 'Values and violence: A test of the subculture of violence thesis', *American Sociological Review*, 38, pp. 736–49.

Baumrind, D. (1975), 'Early socialisation and adolescent competence', in S. E. Dragastin and G. H. Elder, Jr. (eds), *Adolescence in the Life Cycle: Psychological Change and Social Context*, Hemisphere Publishing: Washington, D.C., pp. 117–42.

Bem, S. L. (1981), 'Gender schema theory: A cognitive account of sex typing', *Psychological Review*, 88(4), pp. 354–64.

Bem, S. L. (1983), 'Gender schema theory and its implications for raising gender-aschematic children in a gender-schematic society', *Signs: Journal of Women in Culture and Society*, 8(4), pp. 598–616.

Best, R. (1983), *We've All Got Scars*, Indiana University Press: Bloomington.

Bernard, J. (1975), 'Adolescence and socialization for motherhood', in S. E. Dragastin and G. H. Elder, Jr. (eds), *Adolescence in the Life Cycle: Psychological Change and Social Context*, Hemisphere Publishing: Washington, D.C., pp. 227–52.

Block, J. H. (1978), 'Another look at sex differentiation in the socialization behaviors of mothers and fathers', in J. Sherman and F. Denmark (eds), *Psychology of Women: Future Directions of Research*, Psychological Dimensions: New York.

Blumenthal, M. D., Kahn, R. L., Andrews, F. M. and Head, K. B. (1972), *Justifying Violence: Attitudes of American Men*, Institute for Social Research, University of Michigan: Ann Arbor.

Boulding, E. (1984), 'Focus on: The gender gap', *Journal of Peace Research*, 21(1), pp. 1–3.

Bowker, L. H. (1978), *Women, Crime, and the Criminal Justice System*, D.C. Heath: Lexington, Mass.

Breines, W. and Gordon, L. (1983), 'The new scholarship on family violence', *Signs*, 8(3), pp. 490–531.

Broverman, I. K., Vogel, S. R., Broverman, D. M., Clarkson, F. E. and Rosenkrantz, P. S. (1972), 'Sex-role stereotypes: A current reappraisal', *Journal of Social Issues*, 28(2), pp. 58–78.

Bush, D. M. (1983), 'Adolescent girls and attitudes toward violence: In the same voice or in another?' Paper presented at the Thematic Panel on Gender, Age, and Deviance at the Annual Meeting of the American Sociological Association, Detroit.

Bush, D. M. (1984), 'The hearth, the market, and guns: A new look at the public–private duality and sex differences in violence', Paper presented at the Western Social Science Association Meetings, San Diego, California.

Bush, D. M. (1985), 'The impact of changing gender role expectations upon socialization in adolescence: Understanding the interaction of gender, age, and cohort effects', in A. C. Kerckhoff, *Research in the Sociology of Education and Socialization*, vol. 5, JAI Press: Greenwich, Conn.

Bush, D. M., Simmons, R. G., Hutchinson, B. and Blyth, D. A. (1978), 'Adolescent perception of sex roles in 1968 and 1975', *Public Opinion Quarterly*, 41(1977–78), pp. 459–74.

Cherlin, A. and Walters, P. B. (1981), 'Trends in United States men's and women's sex-role attitudes 1972 to 1978', *American Sociological Review*, 46(4), pp. 453–60.

Chodorow, N. (1974), 'Family structure and feminine personality', in M. Z. Rosaldo and L. Lamphere (eds), *Women, Culture, and Society*, Stanford University Press, Stanford, Calif., pp. 43–56.

Chodorow, N. (1978), *The Reproduction of Mothering: Psychoanalysis and the Sociology of Gender*, University of California Press: Berkeley.

De La Coste-Utamsing, C. and Holloway, R. (1982), 'Sexual dimorphism in the human corpus callosum', *Science*, 216, pp. 431–2.

Duncan, O. D. (1980), 'Testing key hypotheses in panel analysis', in K. Schuessler (ed.), *Sociological Methodology 1980*, Jossey-Bass: San Francisco, pp. 279–89.

Ehrenreich, B. (1983), *Hearts of Men: American Dreams and the Flight from Commitment*, Anchor-Doubleday: New York.

Eisenstein, Z. R. (1981), *The Radical Future of Liberal Feminism*, Longman: New York.

Elshtain, J. B. (1983), 'Beautiful souls and just warriors: Reflections on men, women, war and cultural image', Paper presented at the Thematic Panel on Gender and Politics at the Annual Meeting of the American Sociological Association, Detroit.

Erikson, E. H. (1950), *Childhood and Society*, Norton: New York.

Freize, I. H., Parsons, J. E., Johnson, P. B., Ruble, D. N. and Zellman, G. L. (1978), *Women and Sex-Roles: A Social Psychological Perspective*, Norton: New York.

Gilligan, C. (1982), *In a Different Voice: Psychological Theory and Women's Development*, Harvard University Press: Cambridge, Mass.

Giordano, P. C. and Cernkovich, S. A. (1979), 'On complicating the relationship between liberation and delinquency', *Social Problems*, 26(4), pp. 467–81.

Goertzel, T. R. (1983), 'The gender gap: Sex, family income and political opinions in the early 1980s', *Journal of Military and Political Sociology*, 11(2), pp. 209–22.

Graham, H. D. and Gurr, T. R. (1979), *Violence in America*, rev. ed., Sage: Beverly Hills, Calif.

Gramsci, A. (1971), *Selections from the Prison Notebooks*, ed. and trans. Q. Hoare and G. Nowell-Smith, International: New York.

Hill, J. P. and Lynch, M. E. (1984), 'The intensification of gender-related role expectations during early adolescence', Chapter 10 in A. C.

Petersen, *Girls at Puberty: Biological and Psychological Perspectives*, Plenum Press: New York.

Huston-Stein, A. and Higgins-Trenk, A. (1978), 'Development of females from childhood through adulthood: Career and feminine orientations', in P. B. Baltes (ed.), *Life-Span Developmental Psychology*, vol. 1, *Development and Behavior*, Academic Press: New York, pp. 257–96.

Jensen, G. and Eve, R. (1976), 'Sex differences in delinquency', *Criminology*, 13, pp. 427–48.

Kelley, C. J. (1977), 'Message from the Director', *FBI Law Enforcement Bulletin*, 46, pp. 1–2.

Kelman, H. C. (1973), 'Violence without moral restraint: Reflections on the dehumanization of victims', *Journal of Social Issues*, 29, pp. 25–61.

Lewontin, R. C. (1983), 'The corpse in the elevator', *New York Review of Books*, 29(21–22), pp. 34–7.

Maccoby, E. E. and Jacklin, C. N. (1974), *The Psychology of Sex Differences*, Stanford University Press: Stanford, Calif.

Markus, G. (1979), *Analyzing Panel Data*, Sage: Beverly Hills, Calif.

Mason, K. O., Czajka, J. A. and Arber, S. (1976), 'Change in U.S. women's sex role attitudes', *American Sociological Review*, 41(4), pp. 573–96.

McIntosh, M. (1978), 'The state and the oppression of women', in A. Kuhn and A. M. Wolpe (eds), *Feminism and Materialism*, Routledge & Kegan Paul: London, pp. 254–89.

Mead, M. (1949), *Male and Female: A Study of Sexes in a Changing World*, Morrow: New York.

Morgan, P. (1981), 'From battered wife to program client: The state's shaping of social problems', *Kapitalistate*, 9, pp. 17–40.

Parsons, J. E. (ed.) (1980), *The Psychology of Sex Differences and Sex Roles*, Hemisphere Press: Washington, D.C.

Petersen, A. C. (1980), 'Biopsychosocial processes in the development of sex-related differences', in J. E. Parsons (ed.), *The Psychology of Sex Differences and Sex Roles*, Hemisphere Publishing: Washington, D.C., pp. 31–3.

Piven, F. F. (1984), 'Women and the state: Ideology, power and the welfare state', *Socialist Review*, 74, pp. 11–19.

Richardson, D., Vinsel, A. and Taylor, S. P. (1980), 'Female aggression as a function of attitudes toward women', *Sex Roles*, 6(2), pp. 265–71.

Rosaldo, M. Z. (1974), 'Women, culture, and society: A theoretical overview', in M. Z. Rosaldo and L. Lamphere (eds), *Women, Culture, and Society*, Stanford University Press: Stanford, Calif., pp. 17–42.

Rosaldo, M. Z. and Lamphere, L. (eds) (1974), *Women, Culture, and Society*, Stanford University Press: Stanford, Calif.

Rosen, B. C. and Aneshensel, C. S. (1976), 'The chameleon syndrome: A social psychological dimension of the female sex role', *Journal of Marriage and Family*, May, pp. 605–17.

Rossi, A. S. (1980), 'Life-span theories and women's lives', *Signs*, 6, pp. 4–32.

Rossi, A. S. (1983), 'Beyond the gender gap: Women's bid for political power', *Social Science Quarterly*, 64(4), pp. 718–33.

Rossi, A. S. (1984), 'The Presidential Address: Gender and parenthood', *American Sociological Review*, 49(1), pp. 1–18.

Rubin, L. (1981), *Women of a Certain Age: The Mid-life Search for Self*, Harper and Row, New York.

Ruddick, S. (1983), 'Preservative love and military destruction', in J. Trebilcot (ed.), *Mothering: Essays in Feminist Theory*, Littlefield, Adams: Totowa, N.J.

Sargent, L. (ed.) (1981), *Women and Revolution: A Discussion of the Unhappy Marriage of Marxism and Feminism*, South End Press: Boston.

Sayers, J. (1981), *Biological Politics*, Tavistock: London.

Schechter, S. (1982), *Women and Male Violence: The Visions and Struggles of the Battered Women's Movement*, South End Press: Boston.

Siltanen, J. and Stanworth, M. (1984), *Women and the Public Sphere: A Critique of Sociology and Politics*, St. Martin's Press: New York.

Simmons, R. G., Blyth, D. A., VanCleave, E. and Bush, D. M. (1979), 'Entry into early adolescence: The impact of puberty, school structure, and early dating on self-esteem', *American Sociological Review*, 44(6), pp. 948–67.

Simon, R. J. (1975), *The Contemporary Woman and Crime*, National Institute of Mental Health: Washington, D.C.

Simon, R. J. (1983), 'Women and crime: Another look', Paper presented at the Thematic Panel on Gender, Age, and Deviance, at the Annual Meeting of the American Sociological Association, Detroit.

Smart, C. and Smart, B. (1978), *Women, Sexuality, and Social Control*, Routledge & Kegan Paul: London.

Smith, M. (1979), 'Hockey violence: A test of the violent subculture hypothesis', *Social Problems*, 27(2), pp. 235–47.

Stallard, K., Ehrenreich, B. and Sklar, H. (1983), *Poverty in the American Dream: Women and Children First*, Institute for New Communications: New York.

Stericker, A. B. and Kurdick, L. A. (1982), 'Dimensions and correlates of third through eighth graders' sex-role self-concepts', *Sex Roles*, 8(8), pp. 915–29.

Straus, M. A., Gelles, R. J. and Steinmetz, S. K. (1980), *Behind Closed Doors: Violence in the American Family*, Anchor-Doubleday: Garden City, N.Y.

Therborn, G. (1980), *The Power of Ideology and the Ideology of Power*, Verso: London.

Thorne, B. (ed.) (1982), *Rethinking the Family: Some Feminist Questions*, Longman: New York.

Thornton, A., Alwin, D. F. and Camburn, D. (1983), 'Causes and consequences of sex-role attitudes and attitude change', *American Sociological Review*, 48(3), pp. 211–27.

Tilly, C. (1978), *From Mobilization to Revolution*, Addison-Wesley: Reading, Mass.

Weitzman, L. J. (1979), *Sex-Role Socialization: A Focus on Women*, Mayfield: Palo Alto, Calif.

Young, I. (1981), 'Beyond the unhappy marriage: A critique of the dual systems theory', in L. Sargent (ed.), *Women and Revolution: A Discussion of the Unhappy Marriage of Marxism and Feminism*, South End Press: Boston, pp. 43–70.

Zaretsky, E. (1976), *Capitalism, the Family, and Personal Life*, Harper & Row: New York.

15 Personal projects and fuzzy selves: Aspects of self-identity in adolescence

Brian R. Little

Introduction: Personal projects and action theory

Personal projects are extended sets of personally relevant action that can range from highly circumscribed behaviours such as 'putting out the cat' to extensive enterprises such as 'coping with my cancer' or 'sailing the Atlantic'. They can be solitary pursuits or communal undertakings, one-shot affairs or lifelong commitments, self-generated expressions of one's deepest aspirations or imposed demands that are profoundly resented. Such projects would seem to embody both the mundane and magnificent features of daily lives and they have been proposed as new units of analysis for research in personality and social and interactional psychology (Little, 1983; in press). They can be examined empirically by the use of Personal Projects Analysis (Little, 1983), which is a generalised methodology for eliciting, rating and examining the hierarchical and contextual properties of individuals' personal project systems. In this chapter I wish to explore the use of the project analytic perspective to examine the daily pursuits of adolescents and to develop a line of argument about self-identity and the nature of alienation in adolescents.

In a recent review of developments in personality and environmental psychology (Little, 1987), it was suggested that a conative revolution is under way in diverse areas of psychology and that the central feature of this revolution is the displacement of purely cognitive, behavioural or affective units of analysis by units emphasising extended forms of intentional action. Although purposive behaviour has long flourished as a central concern in social science and even in the golden years of behaviourism under the aegis of Tolman, it has never dominated psychological research in the fields of personality and social psychology, despite its central relevance to the classical issues in those fields. While a systematic psychological theory of intentional action has yet to take hold, there is a congeries of approaches and conceptual frameworks sharing a number of key features which can be identified as psychological action

230

theory, and this emerging perspective would seem to offer a common home for those working within a conative framework (see, for example, Binkley *et al.*, 1971; Davidson, 1971; Harré, 1979).

Two aspects of an action theory approach to human personality can be identified, each of which is concerned with the contextual framework within which action is embedded. The first we might call the intentional context of action; the second, the ecological context.

Intentionality would seem to be the defining attribute of action, in contrast with mere behaviour, though this is an issue which has generated considerable controversy within analytic philosophy. The intentional context of action can be regarded as the subjectively construed purpose for which action is undertaken. For example, in the project 'put out the cat' noted above, the intentional context of that action might be the fact that the boy putting out the cat intended to prevent feline infelicities from occurring on the rug. On the other hand, he may have been explicitly instructed by his mother to 'put out the cat' at nine o'clock sharp, and his intention is simply to obey. More interestingly, he might well have been told by his mother not, under any circumstances, to put out the cat (as she had just been spayed and was to convalesce indoors for a day or two). *Now*, the intentional context of his action becomes particularly critical in attempting to understand and explain the teenager's action. We shall explore, in a later section, just how the intentional context of an action can be approached methodologically. For now, it will suffice to note that the defining attribute of intentionality can be seen to be the extent to which the question 'Why?' can be legitimately answered regarding a particular action (see, for example, Anscombe, 1963).

The ecological context of an action or the nature of the situation or historical context within which an action is embedded is also accorded importance in contemporary action theories. Indeed, the case can be made that an action cannot be interpreted validly without an understanding of the situational context in which it occurs. For example, the project 'to cope with my cancer' may be profoundly influenced by the presence or absence of social supports, of economic resources, even of an atmosphere of encouragement within the environment of the suffering person. McIntyre (1981), in particular, has been insistent that an understanding of the history of the milieu which engulfs action is central to an interpretation of that action.

To the intentional and ecological contexts of action, I wish to add a third contextual influence, one which might be called the systemic context of action. The central idea here is that people are not normally involved in single actions or one project only, but are simultaneously engaged (at least in the sense of having a continuing commitment to) a whole set of pursuits and activities. Thus the teenager putting out the cat may also be simultaneously engaged, with differing levels of focal attention, in talking to his girlfriend on the phone, thinking about his history test, getting over the fight he lost in the school yard that morning and tensing his right bicep in an effort to appear more hunk-like and attractive to Emma (who does *not* happen to be the person he is talking to on the phone). Our assumption is that these different personal projects form a project *system*, such that pressures and commitments in one part of the system have ramifications for others and that conflict, trade-offs, potentiation, subordination and other systemic properties come into play when interpreting and explaining any given action. For example, the meaning of the action 'impress Emma' is interpreted quite differently when juxtaposed to the project 'keeping Nancy as a girlfriend', in contrast with a project like 'find someone who likes me'. In short, personal projects and actions generally are part of a system of commitments and concerns. The systemic nature of the embeddedness of projects must figure in our explanations of personal pursuits.

To summarise, personal projects can be regarded as units of analysis for the study of action in context. Three contexts can be discerned: the intentional context, in which the reasons or purposes underlying the crying out of projects are adduced, the systemic context, in which relations with other projects are examined, and the ecological context, in which the surrounding milieu is taken into account. Each context needs to be included in attempting to explain the personal projects of individuals. We shall turn now to the rather demanding methodological implications of this conclusion.

Personal Projects Analysis as a methodology for action theory

The central task of this chapter is to show how Personal Projects Analysis can be used to operationalise the concerns outlined above. While I shall draw from some of the empirical studies that my students and I have been involved in over the past few years, the primary purpose is to illustrate the methodological scope of Personal Projects Analysis in the context of trying to understand aspects of identity formation during adolescence, particularly late adolescence.

Project elicitation: What do adolescents think they're doing?

The initial task in Personal Projects Analysis (PPA) involves the elicitation of an individual's current personal projects. Our Kellian roots will be apparent (see Little, 1972; 1976) in the approach we take to this question, which is essentially a credulous one: we ask the individuals directly to write down their current personal projects. We are under no illusion that what emerges from this will be a dump of *all* the current concerns, commitments, pursuits and passions of the respondent. But we are convinced that what does emerge from this first stage is sufficiently rich to serve as the initial probe of an individual's current projects. A detailed copy of the instructions for the elicitation phase together with the rating instructions is available from the author. It should be noted that Personal Projects Analysis is *not* a fixed test, but a generalised assessment methodology, and that it is designed to be a flexible vehicle for appraising diverse aspects of human conduct. For some investigators, the initial project listing may be too broad a sampling of the respondent's projects. They may prefer to restrict the elicitation procedure to academic projects only, or to those involving problematic interpersonal relations. For illustrative purposes, however, I wish to focus on the broad-band elicitation procedure we use most frequently in our own work, without suggesting that more focalised elicitation procedures may not be useful.

When we ask adolescents what kind of personal projects they are engaged in, how do they respond? As part of an extensive sampling of personal projects across the lifespan (Little *et al.*, 1982) an analysis of the personal projects of 600 adolescents was undertaken. Here is a sampling of some of the personal projects they listed:

riding my new windsurfer this
  summer

finding the perfect girl

trying to understand and help my
  family and friends

stop smoking

learning to be a better marksman
  for next duck-hunting season

trying to keep gas tank full

picking up girls

cruising Carling

finish my computer assignment

a trip to Quebec City

getting along with as many people
  as I can

parties during break

what to do in the future

lose some weight

try to get Susan to notice me

quit smoking

going for a cigarette once in a while
  behind your parents' back

phoning up guys

getting my ring from boyfriend

getting driver's licence!

control my feelings of immense
  dislike toward my friend's friend

party a lot

trying to increase my social life
  (which includes someone special
  of the opposite sex)

taking Tai Kwon Do

getting involved with a girl

party!

trying to understand quadratic
  equations

trying to attract a guy

working with mentally disabled
  children

make the dinners at home

finish my sewing of a jacket	do Christmas baking
try to be more patient	try to control my temper

Projects elicited at this stage of PPA are phrased idiosyncratically. It is in this form that the respondent proceeds, in later stages of PPA, to provide dimensional ratings and contextual information about his or her projects. For purposes of counselling and clinical work and for ideographic purposes, it is desirable to examine the projects in their original idiosyncratic form. They provide specific, subjectively phrased and ecologically representative units of analysis linking individuals with their milieu, and provide distinguishing information about both. For purposes of making group comparisons, however, such as the difference between depressed and non-depressed adolescents, or the distinctive project characteristics of highly successful students, it is possible and desirable to seek through content analysis generic categories of project which recur with a given group of respondents. In the case of the adolescent data, for example, we have found that a 21-category system allows us to code reliably 97 per cent of projects. Table 15.1 presents these categories and the frequency with which they appear in the protocols of a random sample of 234 adolescent respondents, whose ages ranged from 13 to 18 years. It is apparent from Table 15.1 that

TABLE 15.1 *Categorisation of projects of 234 adolescents: Absolute, cumulative and relative frequencies*

Absolute frequency	Category of project	Cumulative frequency (%)	Relative frequency (%)
325	interpersonal	13.9	13.9
302	academic	26.7	12.9
276	recreational	38.5	11.8
164	finance–legal	45.5	7.0
151	health–body	52.0	6.4
130	cultural–aesthetic	57.5	5.5
114	sports	62.4	4.9
113	estate	67.2	4.5
110	intrapersonal	71.8	4.6
87	family	73.5	3.7
86	drinking/drugs	77.2	3.7
70	occupational	82.2	3.0
68	vocational	85.1	2.9
67	boy/girlfriend	88.0	2.9
41	hobbies	89.7	1.7
39	reading	91.4	1.7
36	sex	92.9	1.5
35	vacations/trips	94.4	1.5
30	metaprojects	95.7	1.3
13	spiritual	96.3	0.6
12	community	97.4	0.5

adolescents' projects are largely focused on interpersonal relationships, school work, recreation, finance–legal business and health and body projects. These categories account for over 50 per cent of all projects. When opposite-sex relationships, community and family projects are included in the interpersonal category, it alone accounts for 21 per cent of all projects listed. It should also be noted that there were relatively high frequencies of reported sex and drinking/drug pursuits mentioned by these adolescent respondents, suggesting that the elicitation format pulls out not only formalised projects, but also the more informal and pleasurable, if often illicit, preoccupations of youth. The very high frequency of projects involving others, particularly peers, accords with the findings of Csikszentmihalyi *et al.* (1977), who showed that interpersonal activities figured largely in the daily activities of teenagers.

Project ratings: How's it going?

It is instructive to consider for a moment the similarities and differences between personal project and other units of analysis which might be used to explore the daily pursuits of adolescents. For example, in the Csikszentmihalyi *et al.* study, students were paged by a remote-control beeper and asked to report what they were engaged in at the time of paging. This is similar to time-budget studies, in which specific acts are recorded in terms of the time spent on them over a specified period. Personal projects are similar to these techniques in that they elicit information about ongoing activities. However, projects may be (though there is no constraint that they *must* be) phrased at a more molar and integrative level. When paged at ten o'clock at night, for example, a teenager may report he's sitting alone in his room listening to records. Were he to be writing about or recording his personal projects he might, instead, say that he was trying 'to cope with' the imminent loss of his girlfriend. Both the micro-behavioural and macro-intentional aspects of human conduct need to be included in a full accounting of adolescent action and, as we shall see, it is particularly important that these different levels of analysis be commensurable.

Some of the beeper methodologies involve a second stage of analysis when respondents provide ratings of their current pursuits on appropriate dimensions (e.g. how enjoyable it is, or how stressful). In PPA, such ratings form the initial assay of the primary context of projects mentioned above. By getting adolescents to rate each of their projects on a set of provided dimensions it is possible to gain an appreciation of the primary context in which they are embedded. (We have also explored in some depth the relationship between our provided dimensions and respondents' own personal constructs about their projects. This research falls outside the scope of the present chapter.) It will be recalled that the primary context of a personal project is the set of associated ideas, values or general constructs which give it meaning for the individual. If the project elicitation phase of PPA involves the psychometric equivalent of the everyday question 'What are you up to?', the dimensional ratings are the equivalent of the question 'How's it going?'. To date, we have used dozens of different dimensions to evaluate how respondents view their personal projects. Most frequently we have used a core group of sixteen dimensions, though these are often augmented by dimensions which are created *ad hoc* for a given study. On both theoretical and psychometric grounds, we can group these dimensions in five categories. The first category involves *project meaning*. Here we inquire into how enjoyable, how important, how consistent with one's values and how reflective of one's 'true self' the respondent views each of the projects that have been listed. The second category, *project structure*, refers to the extent of each project's self-initiation, own control, time pressure, and its positive and negative impact on other projects. The third category, *project community*, refers to the extent to which projects are visible to others (versus concealed or unexpressed) and the extent to which they are felt by the respondent to be valued by significant others. Category four, *project competency*, contains a pair of dimensions dealing with progress to date and anticipated outcome of each project. The final category is focally concerned with *project stressfulness* and includes ratings on dimensions of stress, challenge and difficulty. (Factor analytic investigations have generally supported the presence of these categories, though the specific dimensions which emerge differ from study to study.) In brief, the dimensions when taken together enable us to answer the questions: What kind of pursuits of adolescents seem to provide the greatest sense of meaning for them? Which are the most manageable? For which do they seem to get the greatest support? What projects seem to give adolescents the greatest feeling of efficacy? In what types of pursuits are they most hassled and experience the greatest stress? At the individual level it is possible to answer these questions by reference to specific projects, an appraisal that may lead to specific counselling or clinical interventions about which projects might be reformulated, enhanced or perhaps abandoned. At the level of group comparisons the categories depicted in Table 15.1 can be analysed on each dimension as depicted in Table 15.2 It is apparent from Table 15.2 that, for the respondents in our sample, the most meaningful projects are those involving interpersonal relationships, while the least meaningful are academic and estate projects. Most beleaguered parents will not be surprised to find that projects like 'clean your room' and 'do your homework' are grimly endured while 'going out with friends' are eagerly pursued. In a later section we shall examine in more detail the self-identity dimension, as it can be seen to tap directly into concern about identity and conceptions of self in adolescence.

TABLE 15.2 *Mean project dimension score by category of activity*

	IMP	ENJ	SELF	VALU	TIME	OUTC	PROG	CONT	INT	VIS	OTHV	DIFF	STRE	CHAL	POS	NEG
Intrapersonal	8.19	5.96	7.40	8.57	6.68	6.25	5.21	7.61	7.97	3.29	6.43	6.52	6.48	7.62	7.31	2.49
Vocational	8.18	5.81	6.32	7.91	5.19	6.33	3.56	5.51	6.66	5.43	7.05	7.51	6.72	7.88	7.34	3.10
Occupational	7.59	6.24	7.46	7.88	6.87	7.44	7.30	7.25	7.81	5.61	6.44	4.91	5.53	6.77	6.75	4.25
Estate	6.42	5.25	6.04	8.58	5.35	7.11	6.23	6.62	6.43	5.13	5.65	4.49	4.36	5.35	5.96	3.23
Family	8.20	6.23	7.36	7.59	5.63	6.57	5.54	5.94	7.68	5.22	6.64	5.95	6.18	7.00	6.69	4.78
Spiritual	8.53	8.61	8.85	9.00	5.67	6.69	5.38	7.61	4.77	5.23	7.31	5.46	6.23	5.92	8.77	1.23
Health–body	8.07	5.69	6.99	7.22	5.94	6.30	4.81	7.52	7.65	4.52	5.78	5.87	5.25	7.22	6.36	2.93
Community	8.83	9.42	9.75	9.27	8.58	7.92	8.42	8.17	7.33	4.58	7.00	5.42	4.17	7.42	8.75	3.85
Finance–legal	7.56	6.61	6.68	7.11	5.50	7.05	5.27	7.50	7.82	5.38	5.97	5.62	5.08	5.79	5.82	3.0
Metaprojects	7.77	6.73	6.90	7.70	6.00	7.07	5.51	7.07	8.60	4.77	6.77	6.83	5.41	7.33	7.47	2.48
Cultural	7.45	8.55	8.22	7.63	6.44	7.68	7.14	8.00	8.22	6.12	6.17	3.07	2.28	5.69	6.55	2.47
Reading	6.64	7.56	6.15	5.82	4.82	7.51	6.28	8.62	7.18	4.05	4.95	2.67	2.69	4.08	6.33	3.56
Academic	8.31	3.59	5.65	7.70	5.66	6.78	4.91	7.45	5.44	5.92	7.47	7.32	7.61	7.67	6.32	4.66
Interpersonal	8.03	8.59	7.90	7.30	6.60	7.71	7.01	7.36	7.79	6.23	6.55	3.15	3.32	5.62	6.53	3.16
Boy/girlfriend	9.24	9.18	8.45	8.20	7.04	7.93	7.22	7.15	7.72	6.19	7.12	3.84	4.13	6.62	6.86	4.10
Sex	9.22	9.19	8.63	8.17	7.08	8.17	7.18	7.11	8.08	5.44	7.27	2.39	3.69	7.50	7.45	2.46
Drinking/drugs	7.72	9.10	7.63	5.97	7.04	8.43	7.59	8.01	7.93	6.85	5.10	2.29	2.20	4.47	5.62	4.36
Recreation	7.16	8.77	7.95	6.94	6.34	7.72	6.78	7.79	7.20	6.36	5.15	3.38	2.95	5.66	6.10	2.89
Hobbies	7.22	8.22	8.10	7.41	5.37	7.39	6.60	8.15	7.34	4.73	5.33	4.43	2.90	6.83	6.65	2.33
Vacations	7.63	9.14	7.34	7.86	5.26	8.26	5.79	7.44	7.00	6.03	7.43	3.91	2.20	6.21	6.40	2.60
Sports	7.59	8.64	8.14	8.04	6.91	8.02	7.83	8.18	8.15	6.73	6.34	3.01	4.13	7.47	7.00	2.85

IMP is Project Importance; ENJ, Enjoyable; SELF, True-self; VALU, consistent with values; TIME, Time Pressure; OUTC, Anticipated Outcome; Progress; CONT, own Control; INIT, own Initiation; VIS, Visibility to others; OTHV, Valued by others; DIFF, Difficulty; STRE, Stress; CHAL, Challenge; POS, Positive Impact on other Projects; NEG, Negative Impact.

The most manageable personal projects of the adolescents in our sample, at least in terms of the sense of control and time pressure, were projects dealing with community action, sports and drinking and drug use. One explanation for this may be that it is likely that these pursuits may be locked into timetables that are imposed from without and which are thus seen as obligatory (e.g. Boys' Club meetings are held on Thursdays at three, football practice is every Monday after school and Saturday nights are 'for going out to the pub'). In contrast, academic projects (these are largely related to studying for exams, completion of essays, etc.) were seen as largely initiated by others and uncontrollable. Vocational and spiritual projects were also low on structural categories, though this was due to the spiritual projects being perceived as very low on initiation and vocational projects as very low on controllability.

Those project categories rated highest on a sense of community were vocational and academic projects, both highly visible and both involving adult groups (parents and teachers, respectively) who were seen as viewing the projects as important. The lowest project categories on community were intrapersonal pursuits and reading, each of which is largely a personal, private concern. The projects most likely to be seen by adolescents as being carried out competently are community, drinking/drug and sexual pursuits, suggesting that these activities may be attractive, in part, because they are ones in which adolescents experience some success and sense of accomplishment. In marked contrast, both vocational projects (e.g. 'planning a career') and health–body projects (e.g. 'losing weight') were seen as being unsuccessful to date and unlikely to be successful in the future relative to other categories. Clearly, pursuits relating to love and friendship seem better able to generate a sense of efficacy in contemporary Canadian adolescents than those relating to the world of work, an issue of considerable relevance to those theorists of Eriksonian persuasion who recall the critical role played by work roles in establishing a sense of personal identity in his early formulation of identity theory. Finally, the most stressful projects were those relating to academic and job prospects, while those least stressful were those concerned with drinking/drugs, reading and cultural pursuits (often represented by rock concerts) and sexual activities, providing at least some support for the notion that drugs and sex and rock'n'roll are key stress-reducers in adolescence, though rock'n'roll or an occasional good book actually outranked sex on this category!

Together, the results expand upon and provide emphasis for the data on frequencies of personal projects discussed above. The critical positive role of interpersonal projects (ranging from sexual pursuits to community service), as well as those recreational activities, like drinking, normally carried out in informal groups, are seen as the most positive. Indeed, if we form a composite of the five dimensions, assuming that meaning, structure, community and competency are positive dimensions and stress is negative, the overall highest categories are sex, drinking, community, interpersonal, boy/girl and sports, while health, academic and particularly vocational projects are seen as the most negative.

Predicting well-being with personal projects dimensions

One of the strategies we have adopted in the projects perspective is to examine the relationship between overall project dimension scores (i.e. the sum of ratings on dimension across an individual's projects) and various outcomes or dependent variables. We anticipate, for example, that variables such as subjective well-being, depression or stress would be predictably related to dimension scores. Several examples of studies exploring these relationships within a projects framework can be briefly noted. Palys and Little (1983) have shown that project dimensions of enjoyment and visibility are significantly higher for those showing high life satisfaction compared with individuals low in satisfaction. Oke (1985) has shown that project system stress is a key factor predicting depressive affect and Collette (1985) has shown that project stress also predicts independently measured stress levels.

It is important to note that, unlike orthodox assessment approaches to well-being and mental health, the project analytic appraisal of an individual's life does not stop at depicting him or her as, say, depressed or stressed, but provides information about the *specific* undertakings and pursuits which generate depression or feelings of stress. Thus, projects are psychometrically equivalent to items in orthodox inventories in that they serve as the units over which dimensional ratings are aggregated for purposes of ascribing predicates such as hassled or low sense of control. However, they also have an ontological status of their own, i.e. they are often real events in space and time which can be interfered with, reformulated, traded off, abandoned, fortified or down-graded so as to effect changes in the respondent's life.

The triple contexts of personal projects

The three contexts developed in my first section were said to pose some challenging problems for the assessment methodologist. I now wish to introduce three of the techniques we have been exploring over the past few years which exemplify the kind of approach we recommend to the appraisal of human action in its natural context.

Primary context: Laddering techniques. The dimension ratings contained in the second phase of PPA may give some initial indication of the kind of primary context within which a given project is embedded, but they do so only obliquely. A more direct and systematic approach to assessing context features at the level of the single project is through the use of a technique we call project laddering.

Laddering is a methodological tool explicitly based on the assumption that personal projects represent middle-level units of analysis and are logically and functionally placed between molecular acts at a subordinate level and molar values, accounts, goals and concerns at the superordinate level. Thus, just as the new generation of cognitive psychologists have explored the hierarchical structure of object taxonomies, similar exploration within action units is a focal aspect of project analytic work.

We assume that a project's subordinate and superordinate linkages can be accessed most appropriately by asking the respondent to account for *how* the project will be enacted and *why* it is being undertaken. (In the laddering procedure, the project is placed in the centre of the page and the respondents answer the 'How' question by listing to the *right* of the project the different levels of acts needed to accomplish it. They answer the 'Why' question, similarly, by listing answers to the left of the project. Accordingly, we often refer to left and right laddering as a shorthand expression for this procedure.) The former question generates at least one and possibly several ladder rungs of action in the service of the project. For each of these acts, in turn, it is possible to ask 'how' *they* are to be performed. Our goal here is to continue right laddering until a project is either anchored in a set of what we call *schedulable acts* (i.e. they can be literally scheduled into a particular place and time slot of up to 20 minutes' duration) or until the individual is unable to specify more molecular acts through which the project can be accomplished. We anticipate that individuals will show characteristic ways of phrasing their personal projects, so that some phrase at a highly molecular level (e.g. 'returning my library books') while others will phrase at a more molar level ('get organised').

The left-laddering procedure, which accesses superordinate accounts as to why a project is being engaged in, is a methodological probe based explicitly on philosophical treatments of intentionality. Anscombe (1963), in particular, is clear about the constituent conditions for ascribing intentionality to an action. Just as with right laddering, the left-laddering procedure begins with a query as to why each listed personal project is being undertaken, and, as with the subordinate action level, one or several superordinate accounts may be given in response to this initial question. These 'why' answers, which generically can be regarded as accounts (Harré, 1979), can in turn be queried, and each response represents an additional ladder rung removed from the initial project. We continue probing with successive 'whys' until a *terminal account* is given, that is, an account which does not require an additional reason for its being undertaken (equivalent to a Rokeachean terminal value).

When both laddering procedures have been completed for an individual project, it is possible to see the hierarchical framework within which that project is embedded. It is possible to count the ladder rungs between the initially formulated project and its two termini in order to determine, in an ipsative sense, whether the project is primarily phrased at a molar or a molecular level of analysis. Some individuals appear to phrase their projects largely in specific molecular acts ('go to church on Sunday') while others phrase them at a considerably more comprehensive level ('explore my religious convictions'). Adopting a word-processing metaphor we might say the molecular individuals have their projects right-justified, i.e. stacked over to the right-hand ladder side, while the individuals adopting the more molar phrasing level are left-justified. If we look at molecular acts as pragmatic, accomplishable means and molar accounts as valued ends, then project systems pitched primarily to the right are likely to facilitate achievement of structure and competency in individuals' daily pursuits, but with a possible scarcity of meaning. Such individuals are likely to be adolescents who complain about just going through the motions. On the other hand, those who are left-justified are more likely to have their daily lives full of meaning but perhaps, if they are not linked to molecular acts, difficult to structure and co-ordinate. In short, the laddering procedures can be involved to explore psychometrically the trade-offs we enact on our projects in daily life between meaningfulness and accountability.

Secondary context: Cross-impact matrices. The chief goal of secondary contextural analysis in projects methodology is to discover the content and nature of the *system* of projects of which the focal project is a member. This can be explored by taking the focal project and examining the extent to which it is seen to have an impact upon each of the other projects listed by the respondent. It should be noted that an exhaustive listing of all the projects or incipient activities of an individual is probably unachievable but it *is* possible to gain an understanding of a person's major projects by performing a *project dump*, i.e. a listing of each project at different stages of completion from inception to termination, with prompts to consider different categories of project. Then, the following procedure can be used to gauge the interrelations among projects. Respondents' projects are presented in the form of a cross-impact matrix and, starting with row 1, the respondent indicates whether project 1 helps, hinders or is independent of project 2, project 3 and so on. (Respondents indicate by a ++ if a project strongly facilitates the accomplishment of another project, a + for facilitating, 0 for no relation, − for hinders and −− for strongly hinders.) Project impact may well be asymmetrical, and some projects may be critical for the system in that they are major sources of conflict. Moreover, some systems, as a whole, may be conflict-ridden (see Little, 1983) and normative scores on overall project conflict can be easily assessed via the cross-impact matrix. Although cross-impact scores have not been examined with adolescent subjects, two columns on the rating matrix provide a hint of the secondary context of different projects. The analysis of the positive and negative impact ratings of each project on the others indicates that spiritual and community projects were felt to provide the greatest overall support for other projects, while family and academic projects were rated as having the highest negative impact. Further exploration with the cross-impact matrix would enable us to determine both the specific form of the positive and negative impact and the type of projects which receive such impact.

Tertiary context: Joint cross-impact matrices and open columns. The measurement of systematic links between personal projects within an individual's personal project system can be generalised to the measurement of dyadic or higher-order project systems through use of a joint cross-impact matrix.

Another route into studying the tertiary or ecological context of personal projects is by examining what we call the Open Columns of PPA. These are columns in which the respondent lists 'with whom' and 'where' projects are undertaken. Several indices can be calculated from these columns, including measures of focal and diffuse interdependency (see Palys and Little, 1983), which taps whether individuals include a broad range of associates in their projects or concentrate on one or two intensely involved others. These open columns also allow for more truly ecological measurement to be incorporated systematically into project assessment. For example, the actual distance between project locations for a given project system might be a key factor in the overall hassle experienced by an adolescent, a hassle that could be easily overcome by more efficient means of transportation, etc..

To summarise, the last three sections have shown how the triple contexts within which personal projects are embedded may be operationalised by personal projects methodology. The measurement of the primary context through laddering allows us to discern the superordinate and subordinate anchors within which projects are constructed and enacted. The appraisal of the secondary context through systematic measurement of the reciprocal impacts between projects allows us to lay bare the inevitable trade-offs that are involved when we are committed to, or attracted to, more than one thing, while tertiary contextual analysis reminds us that projects can have impacts upon the ecosystem in which the individual is embedded and that ecosystem constraints and resources (see Little and Ryan, 1981) are important foci for assessment throughout the lifespan.

Fuzzy selves and personal projects: A proposal

In this concluding section, I would like to focus on a specific dimension of meaning in PPA of particular relevance to the theme of this volume. This is the self-identity column, which asks respondents to indicate to what extent the project they are rating is prototypical of them, i.e. is 'truly' or 'typically' them.

We suspect that some acts in which an individual, George, engages are seen by him to be peculiarly Georgian, while others are seen as being phoney, involving disingenuous conduct or as alienating in an even deeper sense. Indeed we might even see this as a possible route into understanding the nature of the self-concept. We might suppose that selves, like so many other categories being explored by cognitive psychologists at present, are really fuzzy sets, with the elements comprising acts and images varying in their degree of prototypicality to a core conception of self (see, for example, Buss and Craik, 1984; Cantor and Mischel, 1979). Thus, for one teenager, a given project may be an exemplar *par excellence* of his conception of who he truly is, while the same project for another may be peripheral to the self-prototype. If this is so, we should anticipate that acts or projects which are seen as highly self-prototypical should be encoded and operated upon in a more efficient and articulated fashion than those which are low on self-prototypicality. Moreover, it can be suggested that adolescents who have very few self-prototypical projects in their systems will be at risk for the development of alienation or depression. We are currently exploring these hypothesised relationships with a large group of adolescents, and the early returns suggest that while depression is moderately related to the lack of self-prototypical projects, life satisfaction is strongly related to the presence of such projects.

We are also exploring the correlates of self-prototypical projects with other project dimensions and with project content in adolescents. The self-identity column appears to be a central dimension in PPA in that it shows significant correlations with each of the positive project dimensions (e.g. enjoyment, value congruency) and (negatively) with each of the negative dimensions (e.g. stress, difficulty). With respect to content, the project categories rated highest in self-prototypicality by adolescents are community, spiritual, sex and boyfriend/girlfriend relations, a set which we met earlier as having the highest score on project meaning. (However, this is partly an artefact due to inclusion of self-prototypicality in the meaning cluster.) The projects scoring lowest in self-identity for adolescents are those related to school work (academic projects and reading). Again, it appears that what is most self-prototypical for adolescents is that set of projects involving interpersonally intimate or nurturant themes, rather than isolated, self-focused pursuits. Explorations of individual differences, ecosystem correlates and developmental trends in these relationships are high on the list of agenda topics for project analytic research.

In conclusion, we have presented the case for using personal projects as units of analysis for the exploration of self-identity in adolescents and projects methodology as a flexible framework for examining the triple contexts of mundane activity. The data generated by projects analysis are sufficiently rich to capture the complexities of adolescents pursuing their goals through alternative project paths; but they are also pointing to recurring themes, such as the pursuit of intimacy, which tap into the deeper structure of 'muddling through'.

References

Anscombe, G. E. M. (1963), *Intention*, 2nd ed., Blackwell: Oxford.

Binkley, R., Bronaugh, R. and Marras, A. (eds) (1971), *Agent, Action, and Reason*, University of Toronto Press: Toronto.

Buss, D. M. and Craik, K. H. (1984), 'Acts, dispositions, and personality', in B. A. Maher and W. B. Maher (eds), *Progress in Experimental Personality Research: Normal Personality Processes*, vol. 13, Academic Press: New York.

Canter, N. and Mischel, W. (1979), 'Prototypes in person perception', in L. Berkowitz (ed.), *Advances in Experimental Social Psychology*, vol. 12, Academic Press: New York.

Collette, D. (1985), 'Personal Projects Analysis: An index of individual differences moderating the effects of life stress', Unpublished bachelor's thesis, Carleton University, Ottawa.

Csikszentmihalyi, M., Larson, R. and Prescott, S. (1977), 'The ecology of adolescent activity and experience', *Journal of Youth and Adolescence*, 6(3), pp. 281–94.

Davidson, D. (1971), 'Agency', in R. Binkley, R. Bronaugh and A. Marras (eds), *Agent, Action, and Reason*, University of Toronto Press: Toronto.

Harré, R. (1979), *Social Being*, Blackwell: Oxford.

Little, B. R. (1972), 'Psychological man as scientist, humanist and specialist', *Journal of Experimental Research in Personality*, 6, pp. 95–118.

Little, B. R. (1976), 'Specialization and the varieties of environmental experience: Empirical studies within the personality paradigm', in S. Wapner, S. B. Cohen and B. Kaplan (eds), *Experiencing the Environment*, Plenum: New York, pp. 81–116.

Little, B. R. (1983), 'Personal projects: A rationale and method for investigation', *Environment and Behavior*, 15, pp. 273–309.

Little, B. R. (1987), 'Personality and the environment', in D. Stokols and I. Altman (eds), *Handbook of Environmental Psychology*, Wiley: New York.

Little, B. R., Lavery, J., Carlsen, N. and Glaven, G. (1982), 'Personal

Projects Analysis across the life-span', Unpublished report to SSHRC, May 1982.

Little, B. R. and Ryan, T. J. (1979), 'A social ecological model of development', in K. Ishwaran (ed.), *Childhood and Adolescence in Canada*, McGraw-Hill: Toronto.

MacIntyre, A. (1981), *After Virtue: A Study in Moral Theory*, Duckworth: London.

Oke, L. (1985), 'A Personal Projects Analysis of depression', Unpublished bachelor's thesis, Carleton University, Ottawa.

Palys, T. S. and Little, B. R. (1983), 'Perceived life satisfaction and the organization of the personal project systems', *Journal of Personality and Social Psychology*, 44, pp. 1221–30.

16 Qualitative and case-study research with adolescents

Terry Honess and Anne Edwards

The general proposition is advanced (see Campbell, 1984) that the qualitative understanding informing any research endeavour cannot simply be replaced by a quantitative analysis. In this chapter, the proposition is addressed through the need to distinguish between 'statistical' and 'analytic' inference. The former mode of inference is particularly suitable for survey methods, which involve large numbers of respondents. The latter is suitable for case study work, which typically involves intensive work with relatively few respondents and relies largely on qualitative interpretation. Recent studies of the adolescent in school and at home (e.g. Kitwood, 1980; Griffin, 1985; Wallace, 1986) show an increased concern with relatively neglected qualitative research. However, it can still be argued that even an explicit concern with qualitative work is still largely rendered merely as illustration for researchers' particular interpretations.

Moreover, there still exists a methodological hiatus between intensive and extensive forms of analysis. This chapter describes part of a research project on adolescent identity which seeks to address this problem. It will discuss what constitutes the kind of 'case study' methodology which allows a more systematic interpretation of qualitative data. We shall also seek to show how this allows access to the dynamic that obtains between individual and culture (particularly important for overcoming the personal versus social identity dichotomy), yet can be integrated with more extensive sampling. Before proceeding to our own research it is necessary to clarify what is meant by the different inference procedures introduced here and to elaborate further on the meaning of 'case studies'.

Statistical versus analytic inference

As Campbell (1984) argues in his article 'Can we be scientific in applied social science?', much social research is based on quantifiable measures of supposedly key variables and, in outcomes studies, on quantification of particular criteria, which some researchers argue more readily serves the need for accountability. In seeking to generalise and draw conclusions from this kind of work, researchers typically seek to show that the sample in their study is one that is unbiased and representative of the particular population that is of interest. Assuming their sample is representative in this way, they can reasonably conclude that the incidence and co-incidence of particular characteristics reflect their occurrence in the wider population. Campbell's call is to recognise the qualitative grounding for the interpretation of such conclusions: in order to explicate the reasons for any particular quantitative findings, the researcher needs to go beyond statistical inference either to explicit theory or more usually to an implicit common sense, often informed by what Campbell describes as 'situation specific wisdom'. Hence, conclusions and explanations are not themselves grounded in 'representativeness' at all. In short, we argue, statistical inference is often elided with analytic inference.

Turning now to the study of a single case, whether this case is a particular individual or one particular institution or whatever, it is certainly true that one could rarely claim that this one case was 'representative' in the statistical sense of some larger population. Indeed, if one analyses the demise of case study in personality and developmental theory, one finds that the problem of generalisation appears to have been the most telling (for example, see Runyan's, 1983, analysis). However, the criticism cannot be a convincing one; it is simply that generalisation from a single case proceeds through an analytic rather than a statistical inferential procedure. Thus, detailed studies of individual cases must be judged in terms of their explanatory power (see discussion below of the different types of case study), not in terms of their 'typicality' (see Mitchell, 1983). In essence, a search for a 'typical case' can be misguided in so far as it confuses the two modes of inference. Indeed, explanatory principles may be clearest in atypical cases that are thought to bring these into sharp relief, a principle long recognised by many of those influenced by the Chicago School, not least the ethno-methodologists.

The distinction introduced here has been discussed at length, much earlier, by Znaniecki (1934) in terms of what he called enumerative versus analytic induction. It periodically reappears in the sociological literature (e.g. Becker, 1968) and quite frequently in the social anthropological literature (e.g. Gluckman, 1961). Probably the distinction most familiar to psychologists and which comes closest to that discussed here is that of Bakan (1968), who sought to distinguish 'general propositions', i.e. those presumably true of all members of a class, from 'aggregate propositions', i.e. those presumably true only of the class considered as an aggregate. Notwithstanding these regular reminders, it is evident that much research, whether avowedly 'applied' or not, blurs the distinction (as comments by Campbell, 1984, with regard to applied research, clearly illustrate). What then does a case study perspective involve, and why has there been a waxing of interest in this mode of research?

Case study and situation analysis

Most definitions of the case study method explicitly involve the idea of generalisation through analytic inference. Thus, Becker (1968) describes 'the case study as an attempt to arrive at a comprehensive understanding of the group under study. At the same time, the case study attempts to develop more general theoretical statements about the regularities in social structure and process'. Definitions such as this have been systematised by Eckstein (1975), a political scientist much influenced by the social anthropologist, Gluckman (1961). Eckstein distinguishes five categories of case study. First, he talks of 'configurative ideographic' studies that are largely descriptive, which may provide theoretical insights but do not necessarily lend themselves to direct theoretical interpretation. In this tradition one sees a concern, with respect to adolescents, with allowing these young people 'to speak for themselves' (e.g. Griffin's work, 1985, on 'typical girls'). Second, there is the 'disciplined configurative' study which is largely concerned with the application of principles, so that any 'theory' determines the form of interpretation. This is arguably the most common, where investigators use cases to illustrate a theoretical position; the ethnographic work of Willis (1978), with young males, is close to this type.

The third use, within which the research to be described here is best situated, is what Eckstein calls 'heuristic cases', which are involved in generating theory. Fourth, Eckstein talks of 'plausibility probes', where cases are specifically selected to test interpretative paradigms (e.g. the selection of atypical cases often falls into this category). Finally, he talks of 'critical case studies', which may be construed as a critical test for particular theories (rarely used by psychologists). It should be evident from the range of possibilities syggested by Eckstein that there can be no standard procedures for a case study strategy, since a procedure will depend on the questions that particular investigators ask and the particular grounding that they are coming from.

Notwithstanding the variety of different aims for which a case study perspective can be evolved, there is a further theme that constantly recurs, that is, a concern with subjectivity. Van Velsen (1967) is typical of the social anthropologists who argue for greater emphasis on the choice-taking of actors, which, he argues, requires a detailed and intimate familiarity with those actors on the part of researchers. Here, particular cultures *per se* are not seen as the object of analysis; rather, the focus is on personal negotiations within social *processes*. More recently, the sociologists Bertaux and Kohli (1984) argued for the explicit acknowledgment that 'social structures are a result of sociohistorical processes in which action, and therefore subjectivity, is playing its part'.

The central theme of the remainder of this chapter is the study of individual lives, with particular emphasis on the methodological features of such work. An early detailed analysis of 'what makes a conceptualisation valid' is that of Allport (1942), who focuses on 'feelings of subjective certainty', 'conformity with known facts', 'mental experimentation', 'predictive power', 'social agreement' and 'internal consistency'. These features appear in more recent reviews: Yin (1984) and Bromley (1986) provide helpful summaries that largely cover American and British work, and Bertaux and Kohli (1984) provide a review of current research in continental Europe. By way of illustration, we will draw particularly on this last review to discuss French and German trends since these are relatively less well known to English-speaking social scientists. Such research appears to be especially strong in West Germany, presumably influenced by the interpretative sociological tradition of that country.

Schutze (1976; 1980; cited in Bertaux and Kohli, 1984) is representative of those who seek to develop the 'narrative interview', a method that involves a detailed analysis of the structure of interview texts and which has a clear affinity with the conversation analysis of the ethno-methodologists (see Heritage, 1984). Following this, there is a concern to identify typical cases and relevant theoretical categories, drawing on the Glaser and Strauss (1967) propositions from grounded theory. The second broad tradition in West Germany is exemplified in the work of Oevermann *et al.* (1979; cited in Bertaux and Kohli, 1984) and 'objective hermeneutics'. Essentially, interview/text interpretation is as extensive as possible – all possible meanings of a text are identified and all known information that may be germane to such interpretation (which is likely to move beyond the text itself) is exploited. This material is designed to help generate underlying rules in sociological terms, 'assuming a rational orientation to social goals with psychological interpretations only being offered as a last resort'. With the exception of its emphasis on exclusively sociological interpretations, the work on hermeneutics is of much interest in so far as it has clear affinity with Allport's work in the 1930s and 1940s (who in turn acknowledges the 'large literature on understanding' in the German language). Moreover, it will be seen to be the perspective which, along with that of Bertaux (see below), is closest to the authors' research programme.

Workers within the life-history orientation in France are much influenced by the all-pervasive structuralist tradition of that country. Hence, Bertaux (1976; cited in Bertaux and Kohli, 1984) takes it as axiomatic that lives do not bear an inner logic but are determined by 'the historical movement of sociostructural relationships'. However, for Bertaux, it is this that makes the study of individual lives particularly interesting in so far as one can see in the ordinary practices of everyday life the constraining effects which allow for a particular form of life to develop. These then become the object of a sociological enquiry whether it is based on a structuralist conception of society or not. Thus, Bertaux argues that we should collect life histories for a particular milieu with a focus on practice, not on perceptions or feelings, and that we can infer from these practices the pattern of sociostructural relationships that are generating or constraining them. He seeks to do this through a process of 'saturation'. Here, members of a research team must move from case to case to modify questions along the way until eventually the researcher or researchers find that subsequent cases 'confirm' a particular interpretation. 'Saturation' is a feature that is common to almost all paradigmatic statements of what constitutes case-study methodology (see Glaser and Strauss, 1967, pp. 60–5), although Bertaux's de-emphasis of perceptions and feelings is not one that we share.

Research programme: School-leavers' coping strategies and identity development

A brief outline of the programme is first provided; we then seek to show how a stress on participant interviewing, with subsequent interpretation of qualitative material, acts as a corrective, as well as a basis for theoretical development, in seeking to understand adolescent identity. Finally, it will be shown how a case-study approach operates within such a context. The study is a longitudinal one concerned with the 'coping strategies and identity development' of poorly qualified young school-leavers in Wales. The young people were first contacted in the year prior to their leaving school, at age 15 years. An early conceptual guide for interview analysis was Harré and Secord's (1972) analysis of social life as the blocking or exercise of personal powers and the succumbing to, or overcoming of, personal liabilities. This appeared to be helpful in so far as it characterised an individual's possibilities for movement in a way that could be seen to be enhanced or limited by particular environmental contingencies. Moreover, it appeared to meet the need articulated by Lazarus (1978): 'To think fruitfully of stress and coping these must be seen as a special kind of transaction between a person of a particular sort i.e. with plans, commitments, hidden agendas and belief systems and an environment with its own characteristics, e.g. demands, constraints and resources'.

Hence, the system which yielded data of the form summarised in Figure 16.1 was evolved. Such a system does allow a description of person characteristics, and we assumed (and to some extent still do) that particular features of these person/environment characteristics were key identity elements for individuals, without which there could be no *identity position*. For any individual, these themes are of course expressed in particular forms and in particular contexts as environmental enabling conditions, e.g. (i) 'circumstances' – the liability of being easily distracted may be overcome if an individual is given a quiet place to work, but if the

Personal enabling conditions

Powers (blocked or expressed)	*Liabilities (prone to or mastered)*
Learning	Powerlessness
Loyalty to friends	Having a temper
Skill at sports	Feelings of isolation
Growing up	Severe worries about jobs
Determination	Unattractiveness

Social/external enabling conditions (affecting blocking, expressing, succumbing and mastery

Circumstances	*Interpersonal network*	*Subculture*
YTS (Youth Training Scheme)	Mother	The 'boys'
Job	Father	Opportunity for 'obbles'
Living at home	Other family	(Work in 'black' economy)
Occupation of parents and siblings	Boy/girlfriend	Local history of unemployment
Availability of sports facilities	Friends	Pressure for early marriage
School support	Former teachers	
Lack of money	Neighbours	

FIGURE 16.1 *Enabling conditions for action (coping) – Examples of General Categories*

bedroom is shared by younger siblings . . .; (ii) 'interpersonal network' – 'I feel I could do well in my exams, but Mum says it's just a waste of time because I haven't got the head for them'; (iii) 'subculture' – different 'coping' patterns are relatively strongly expressed in different communities (see Honess and Edwards, in preparation, on 'interdependent' and 'independent' styles of accommodation in town and valley children).

The examples in Figure 16.1 are drawn from a sample of 160 children, 40 from each of four schools, two in Cardiff (town children) and two from mid-Glamorgan (valley children). All of these children were interviewed individually, prior to their leaving school. Eighty were also re-interviewed approximately one year later. In both sessions, we sought to explore current state, expectations and actual changes with regard to employment, organisation of time, relationships with parents and friends and self-perceptions (full details of the schedules and coding schemes employed are available from T. Honess). In addition, 24 young people, 6 from each of the four schools (the *case-study* sample) were seen for a further series of interviews, using a variety of different techniques, and at least one parent of each of these young people was also interviewed.

How then has a concern with qualitative understanding (based on the relatively open-ended interview schedules) and the case studies themselves affected the evolution of this project? We shall show how a concern with the individual case uniquely allows examination of the (often conflicting) personal negotiations that characterise an identity development. However, we begin with three illustrations of the way in which a concern properly to represent open-ended data, from a number of different respondents, leads to the evolution of a minimally pre-emptive category set (the 'heuristic' strategy discussed earlier).

(1) Which statements should be elicited and/or which should be coded in order properly to reflect an identity position? There will be widespread agreement that 'I am a generous person' should be included, but what about 'I always play soccer on Thursday nights', where the emphasis given suggests much importance in the sense of satisfaction derived? Our pilot schemes focuses too much on personality descriptors and conscious self-images, which proved to be unwarranted, reflecting assumptions carried over from more structured interview methods (see Turner, 1987, and Yardley, 1987, for related critiques). Much of one's common-sense 'feel' for some individuals is lost if one only considers the more conscious self-images that are presented in an interview. Indeed, the broad, yet detailed, self-descriptions we elicited gave strong support to Turner's contention that identity establishment is often a matter of indicating realms (which may be particular activities) within which a person feels comfortable.

(2) To what extent is it possible to separate personal and social processes, in particular personal and social 'enabling conditions'? We have sustained the distinction to aid the development of a coding scheme, but in considering the detail of particular decisions made by respondents, it has become clear that different situations can be seen to 'call out' particular accommodation styles, which themselves define the social milieu in a new way. Hence, a too-ready acceptance of the division could lead to inappropriate inference. For example, our data, along with that of others in the unemployment literature suggest that those with a relatively 'internal' locus of control (a particular personal style) are more likely to be in paid employment. In addition, we find that valley children are lower on this style, but higher on an interdependent style (concerned with quality of relationship), one that is rarely discussed in the literature. Should valley children be encouraged to adopt a more internal style? Perhaps, but one needs to acknowledge that employment opportunities are fewer here (a particular social constraint), and hence their style may be appropriate to their particular context.

(3) It is often assumed that 'independence' is an important identity achievement, yet how does one identity this? The qualitative data forced a correction to the commonly held assumption that the maturation process necessarily entails increasing autonomy and independence from others. In

practice, there proved to be problems in coding descriptions of relationships and actions that were interdependent on and with others. The final scheme (see below) picks up a number of these joint actions which can be of a negative kind, for example, overcontrol by others or relative lack of desired response from others. In contrast, interdependence, which involves relating *with* others, can be of a positive kind where power is shared in a way that is considered appropriate by both parties. In essence, then, the derived coding scheme does not only, or always, value 'independence' positively.

The above examples illustrate, at the very least, the important heuristic values of working with qualitative material. In the remainder of this paper, the construction of one particular case, that of 'Jane', a Cardiff girl, will be discussed. As well as allowing a consideration of the dynamics of the socialisation process, it will allow us to illustrate the application of the coding scheme introduced above. Arguably, the most important prescription for case-study construction (see Bromley, 1986, for more detailed consideration) is that there ought to be critical enquiry into the internal coherence, logic and external validity of the whole network of the argument that the researcher develops. This concern relates to the sociological concept of 'triangulation', which in this project is reflected in the use of different interview methods (see Honess and Edwards, 1984, for a summary of these) as well as the 'network' of evidence from the different perspectives of the researchers, the adolescent and the parents.

Finally, the explicit tie with the 'narrative' constructions introduced earlier (and in several chapters of the present text) needs to be reiterated. The 'logic' of the researchers' interpretation is at least partly parasitic on the coherence of the story that is constructed. In its simplest form the story can be seen to comprise the narrative which answers the question 'and then what happened?' and themes which provide a response to the question 'why did it happen?' It is these themes which provide what Hillman (1975) describes as personal plots or unifying elements in life stories. For present purposes we shall discuss just one part of Jane's 'story', her changing relationship with her parents, since this includes themes generally seen as important by adolescents because they relate to the almost universal wish to come through the rites of passage that confer the status of 'adult'. We will give summaries of all Jane's responses that relate to her parents and her boyfriend. In addition, we shall give extracts from the interview with her mother.

The case of 'Jane'

Jane's first general interview ('general' in the sense that the interview schedule was used with the extensive as well as the case-study sample) took place two months prior to her summer school leaving. Her second general interview took place ten months after she left, and the interview with her mother took place shortly before this.

General interview 1

The interviewer's impressions of Jane while she was at school were of a girl primarily concerned with 'mucking about' and 'playing practical jokes'. She appeared immature and tomboyish, and was generally treated with amused tolerance by the staff. Twenty-nine 'self' statements were extracted from Jane's script (the average for the full sample of 160 young people on this interview is 26). Twenty-two were positive (+ve) and 7 were negative (−ve). Four involved an internal attribution (I) and 14 an external attribution (E), 5 involved a quality that required the recognition of others to allow its expression, e.g. Jane's 'I like playing practical jokes on the teachers' (OF), 2 statements reflected a positive interdependent relationship (C), 4 denoted a relationship experienced as overcontrolling by the other (Co); there were no references to a relationship in which there was an experienced lack of response from the other (Cl). Summaries of all the mother- and father-context responses only follow (it should be noted that all parts of the script are used to help code any one statement).

Comments on Mother: I get on fine with her except for her bossing me (−ve/Co); I think I'll probably work with my mother for a while until I get a job (+vef/C); I'll still get my pocket money (+vef/C); we've got so many animals, working with animals is something I've always wanted to do . . . mother would love to see me working with animals (+ve/E); I don't get much privacy in my house (because Mum is at home mainly), it's important if you want it . . . it doesn't worry me (−ve/Co).

Comments on Father: Hardly ever at home, we get on fine (+ve/E); was very pleased when I got this Saturday job (+ve/E).

Inferences from general interview 1: The only overcontrolling responses in the full script are attributed to Mum, although these were heavily qualified in such a way as to suggest that they were not important and were therefore overcome, 'mastered'. The two positive relational attributions for Mum were both of a relatively unusual type (coded f), where the respondent is referring to some future time, when circumstances may have changed. In these two instances, Jane is anticipating Mum's help with a back-up employment prospect (although not her first choice for a job), plus continued financial support (still called pocket money) − an important consideration for many young people, not least Jane, who incidentally referred to her three different savings accounts. Neither of the father attributions are coded in relationship terms; both were characterised by a sense of the father's general absence, and later interviews confirmed the impression that father was not an important figure. Other significant figures at this time were a same-sex friend and Jane's grandmother, not discussed here.

General interview 2

The interviewer noted that Jane had grown around three inches, had lost weight and appeared more self-confident. She still wore no make-up, generally wore jeans or cords for the interviews around this period, and no longer appeared to present herself as a child preoccupied with 'mucking about'. Questions in this interview solicit information on what has happened in the intervening period in all aspects of the young person's life (especially focusing on blocks and on enablements of personal, family and cultural types). It also allows re-presentation of parts of what the respondent said first time around to encourage accounting for both consistencies and inconsistencies. Jane's interview produced 91 'self' statements, of which 58 were +ve and 37 −ve; these broke down into 34 E, 22 I, 23 C, 11 Co and 5 Cl. Once again we focus on the parent contexts.

Comments on Mother: She just let me get on with the job hunting (−ve/Cl); used to nag me (−ve/Co); always asking me to do the washing up or ironing . . . didn't have to do it in school (−ve/Co); similar items repeated and 'I just don't do it, can't be bothered' ('mastery'); made me feel really guilty because I didn't want to be a bridesmaid (for her sister's wedding) (−ve/Co); my mother wouldn't let me stay out late before but now she thinks I'm old enough to look after myself (+ve/C) . . . I tell her I'm going down my friend's house, and shoot off with my boyfriend, just to stay out, to get away from the nagging (−ve/Co again, but 'mastered' through avoidance); haven't really asked her about jobs . . . as long as I'm having a job that's alright (−ve/Cl); she doesn't boss me a lot now, better than last year (+ve/C); she shows me up sometimes, most of the time actually . . . I'm hardly ever there (−ve/Co); change when my sister got married, she's wanting to get me married off I think. That's why she's been so kind (−ve/Co); ditto, she's waiting for me to leave home so she can move to a smaller house (−ve/Co); avoidance theme repeated several times: the only time I'm really in is when I'm coming in to go to bed, I see them [mother and father] even less now; didn't work [referring here to possible employment with nurse mother] with my mother, she just lent me money and that, just didn't get around to it (−ve/E); I wouldn't mind leaving home, I'd have my freedom then, feel a bit restricted, times I've got to be in by (−ve/Co); this is qualified by 'I'd like to leave home but it's not really bothering me'; money is quite important, got to buy clothes and save, still get money from my mother (+ve/C); I get in a bad mood when my mother's going on at me (−ve/Co); important that you have privacy, Mum's giving me more now (+ve/C).

Comments on Father: Haven't really talked to him about my job (−ve/Cl); he's alright, hardly ever in, down the pub (−ve/Cl).

Inferences from general interview 2: There are only two references to father, and, as in the first interview, these are typified by his absence. However, his lack of interest is acknowledged more clearly, hence the −ve codings. There is no evidence that this is particularly damaging; he is simply a relatively unimportant figure. The strongest theme that permeates references to mother are encapsulated in the overcontrolling (−ve/Co) code. In contrast to the first interview the significance of this is not minimised. Jane's primary strategy is to keep out of the house and not to accede to what are experienced as unreasonable controls. There is also some acknowledgment of mother's accommodation of Jane's expressed wish for more control (but only two +ve/C codings that didn't relate to money). Of Jane's two future positive codes from the first interview, one expectation is not confirmed. With respect to job search she simply experiences nagging, but would have welcomed appropriate assistance, hence the lack of response (−ve/Cl) code. With respect to financial support, her expectations are entirely confirmed since her mother continues to provide this. With the advantage of hindsight, Jane observes that things are better now with regard to the relationship with her mother.

Consistent with the overall picture of the mother–daughter relationship, there is little manifest interdependence, where both parties are contributing to the relationship in a way that both feel comfortable with. However, given the avowed methodological concern with internal consistency, we must now examine this interpretation against evidence from other parts of Jane's interviews. First, what does the mother have to say about Jane?

Interview with mother

The issue most frequently raised by the mother can be seen to be related to Jane's gender socialisation: 'I think she does her own thing to a certain degree, but is still aware that there are certain . . . um, standards and rules, laid down for men and women, and you don't step over, as much as you want to'. The mother clearly saw this as a very significant issue for Jane: 'Jane would probably be quite happy as a commando in the SAS . . . the army would probably suit her'. Mother reported that Jane had thought about it, but not tried because of 'the male/female thing – women don't join the army'. Indeed, mother herself described 'mixed feelings' here, since when she was 17 she had had the same idea, but 'I think I'm still of the old-fashioned school, that girls don't join the army. But again, I haven't said this and it's up to her entirely'. Also, 'she's the only girl in the motor bike team . . . somebody will laugh and say, "that's typically Jane"', and 'I don't think you'll ever get Jane as a chambermaid or a cook!'

Mother then proceeded to pursue in some detail what she regarded as the closely related issue that 'Jane has got to straighten herself out', with regard to what she intended to do: 'You know, Jane would be quite happy if I rang up and went for the interviews and filled in the application forms and got her the job . . . but she's not prepared to push' (although mother appeared to be dismissive of one of Jane's attempts at letter-writing for a job). In sum, 'I don't think Jane knows who she is at the moment, or where she is going', and again mother observes, 'She still feels hampered by . . . the views on what girls "should" and "shouldn't" do'. However, mother also indicated at several different times in the interview that she and Jane never talked about any of this, e.g. 'Jane never discusses anything'.

This script, then, clearly concords with Jane's account in several ways. Little practical support is given to Jane's job search, although mother's position is that it is in Jane's interests for Jane herself to decide what to do and take the necessary action. There is a clear awareness of Jane's sense of conflict over gender expectations, which the mother has some sympathy with, but an overriding message from her is that Jane needs to sort herself out. From the mother's perspective, an acceptance of normal gender expectations would appear to be an important route to this end. She sees Jane's problem here as just a 'stage', typical of all adolescents. Moreover, this 'tough guy' image is something Jane will grow out of. Hence, maternal pressure is evidently toward a 'traditional' socialisation, but it is not an issue they have overtly discussed. The issue is patently a problematic one for Jane. We have seen that she was, for example, a keen and skilled motor cycle rider for a period, and clearly disliked wearing 'feminine' clothes: 'I didn't want to be a bridesmaid [for her sister's wedding], probably because of the dress. When I saw it, all frills and everything, I felt really ill' (this was not related to her relationship with her sister, with whom Jane got on quite well). To clarify these issues still further, we finally turn to one of the interview techniques that was used only with the case-study sample.

Social Identity Inventory: Further interview with Jane

The Social Identity Inventory is designed to provide information on the personal meaning and ramifications of membership of particular groups or groupings (e.g., 'we the girls are . . .' and 'they the girls are . . .'). It is a modified form of the procedure developed by Zavalloni (1971; see Honess,

1987, for details of procedure and the results from all the case-study sample). The groups or groupings under consideration in this project were 'girls' (or 'boys'), 'school-leavers', 'people in one's neighbourhood' and a fourth grouping supplied by the respondent (in Jane's case, this was 'pub goers'). Responses to the first two of these stimulus groups are discussed here.

Prior to leaving school, general characteristics, such as friendly, shy and kind, were elicited in relation to the 'girls' prompts, and these need not be discussed further here. Her second social identity inventory (8 months after leaving school) revealed a changing set of characteristics through which she identified with the 'girls' – 'soft', 'too easy-going', 'determined' and 'not spoilt enough' (all positively valued, except 'determined', which was given a neutral valuation). She also ascribed 'independence' to girls, but did not identify with this and gave it a neutral valuation. When elaborating her answers (see Honess, op. cit., for details of prompts), the 'soft' and 'spoilt' answers related to boys and buying drinks; 'soft' – 'give in easily to [men's] needs' – emanated from reference to giving in to buying the drinks; although it was generally qualified with 'I stand up to him [Dave, Jane's boyfriend]'. Also, 'the boys should buy all the drinks, we deserve to be spoiled a bit more'.

With regard to the school-leavers group, there was a little less identification at the time of the second testing. Nevertheless, there was strong identification at this time with the negatively valued 'unhappy on the dole'. The 'we' prompt for school-leavers also elicited 'too dependent', negatively valued, but a characteristic she did not identify with. The 'they' prompt produced 'not dependent enough', with a neutral valuation, but also not identified with. In elaborating her answers here, Jane expanded on the '*too* dependent' prompt and appeared to 'own' part of this feeling in focusing on dependence on parents for money. For the 'they' prompt, Jane's elaboration was 'not dependent enough on their parents, should try to get more money out of their mother, it's up to them'. It can be seen that the dependency theme is revisited in the context of the identity inventory interview, and it is to a summary of our understanding of this theme in Jane's life that we now turn.

Summary of inferences from all interviews

The overall theme for the father is one of his absence, and Jane has been and continues to be relatively uninfluenced by him and relatively independent of him. The picture of Jane's relationship with her mother reflects a general move from dependence on her to an independence from her, but one that is negatively achieved in the sense of Jane's increasing avoidance. The exception is in the area of Jane's financial dependence on her mother. However, this 'avoidance' interpretation needs qualification. It will be apparent that Jane spent a great deal of time talking about her mother, and she acknowledges close family ties, with the mother possibly being experienced as 'overprotective' as well as 'overcontrolling'. Mother herself clearly expresses much exasperation with Jane. A particular point of tension had been mother's perception of Jane's immaturity, particularly as this related to the lack of 'femininity', an issue that was partly being 'resolved' in so far as she became engaged to be married shortly after the time of the interview with the mother.

There had not, however, been a simple switch in key figures for Jane, e.g. from mother to boyfriend, in that the relationship with 'Dave' (not detailed in this paper) was one in which Jane felt an equal partner, although she still used her avoidance strategy when he was in especially bad moods. Nor could it be said that Dave was a compensation for her work life and therefore an equally acceptable route to adulthood. Jane reported that her new Government Training Scheme placement in an outdoor pursuits shop (where a bonus was that she could wear trousers to work) afforded the most satisfaction in her life.

Conclusions

In so far as psychological case-study method involves different sources of information collected over a period of time, we have tried to show how the contradictions and problems that beset a particular life must be understood as constituting part of the *process* of personal transition. For example, it is commonly assumed (e.g. Mungham, 1976; Brake, 1980) that marriage is crucial for working-class young women's rite of passage to adulthood, and that it is therefore generally desired by young women. Jane's early engagement to be married lends superficial support to this, but her personal 'negotiations' suggest that this is in no sense a smooth transition. Rather, the engagement might be seen as part of her attempt to create a context in which she can experience a degree of resolution of the manifest conflict that she has experienced concerning 'dependency' and what it is that young women are 'supposed' to do.

As it stands, Jane's 'case' is most readily seen as one of Eckstein's 'heuristic' types, in so far as it suggests a number of hypotheses relating to young women's identity development. These could be examined by switching to larger-scale quantitative studies, or through persisting with case studies and asking such questions as 'Are similar patterns repeated in subsequent cases?' 'Which features of the case are relatively invariant?' 'Which are idiosyncratic?' 'Can similar family dynamics lead to different outcomes?' and so on. In the project described here, both strategies were followed. In addition, it has been shown how the detailed study of cases has enhanced the development of a more sensitive analysis of the extensive sample, and continues to assist in facilitating interpretation of the extensive work. The argument developed in this chapter is, therefore, that qualitative methods should not be seen merely as a pilot stage before 'proper' research begins. Rather, they implicate their own equally defensible and publicly communicable research assumptions and logic. Moreover, in the field of identity research they are regarded as an indispensable complement to quantitative methods.

Acknowledgment

The support of the Economic and Social Research Council (Ref. C0023/0072) is gratefully acknowledged.

References

Allport, G. W. (1942), *The Use of Personal Documents in Psychological Science*, SSRC: New York.

Bakan, D. (1969), *On Method: Towards a Reconstruction of Psychological Investigation*, Jossey-Bass: San Francisco.

Becker, H. (1968), 'Social observation and case studies', in D. L. Sills (ed.), *International Encyclopedia of the Social Sciences*, vol. 11, Macmillan: New York.

Bertaux, D. and Kohli, M. (1984), 'The life story approach: A continental view', *Annual Review of Sociology*, 10, pp. 215–37.

Brake, M. (1980), *The Sociology of Youth Culture and Youth Subcultures*, Routledge & Kegan Paul: London.

Bromley, D. (1986), *The Case Study Method in Psychology and Related Disciplines*, Wiley: Chichester.

Campbell, D. (1984), 'Can we be scientific in applied social science?', *Evaluation Studies*, 9, pp. 26–48.

Eckstein, H. (1975), 'Case study and theory in political science', in F. Greenstein and N. Polsky (eds), *Strategies of Inquiry*, Addison-Wesley: Reading, Mass.

Glaser, B. and Strauss, A. (1967), *The Discovery of Grounded Theory*, Weidenfeld & Nicolson: London.

Gluckman, M. (1961), 'Ethnographic data in British social anthropology', *Sociological Review*, 9, pp. 5–17.

Griffin, C. (1985), *Typical Girls?* Routledge & Kegan Paul: London.

Harré, R. and Secord, P. (1972), *The Explanation of Social Behaviour*, Blackwell: Oxford.

Heritage, J. (1984), *Garfinkel and Ethnomethodolgy*, Polity Press: Cambridge.

Hillman, J. (1975), 'The fiction of case history: A round', in J. B. Wiggins (ed.), *Religion and Story*, Harper & Row: New York.

Honess, T. (1987), 'Group membership and personal identity: School-leavers' changing perceptions', manuscript under consideration.

Honess, T. and Edwards, A. (1984), 'Poorly qualified school leavers' coping strategies and identity development', *Education Section Review*, 8, pp. 37–41.

Honess, T. and Edwards, A. (in preparation), 'Styles of accommodation: Poorly qualified school leavers' sense of self', in H. Bosma and S. Jackson (eds), *Coping and Self in Adolescence*, Springer Verlag: New York.

Kitwood, T. (1980), *Disclosures to a Stranger*, Routledge & Kegan Paul: London.

Lazarus, R. (1978), 'The stress and coping paradigm', Paper presented at the Oregon Conference on the Critical Evaluation of Behavioral Paradigms for Psychiatric Science.

Mitchell, J. (1983), 'Case and situation analysis', *Sociological Review*, 31, pp. 187–211.

Mungham, G. (1976), 'Youth in pursuit of itself', in G. Mungham and G. Pearson (eds), *Working-Class Youth Culture*, Routledge & Kegan Paul: London.

Runyan, W. (1983), 'Idiographic goals and methods in the study of lives', *Journal of Personality*, 51, pp. 413–37.

Turner, R. (1987), 'Articulating self and social structure', in K. Yardley and T. Honess (eds), *Self and Identity: Psychosocial Processes*, Wiley: Chichester.

Van Velsen, J. (1967), 'The extended case study method and situational analysis', in A. L. Epstein (ed.), *The Craft of Social Anthropology*, Pergamon Press: Oxford.

Wallace, C. (1986), 'From girls and boys to men and women', in L. Barton and S. Walker (eds), *Youth Unemployment and Schooling*, Open University Press: Milton Keynes.

Willis, P. (1978), *Learning to Labour*, Saxon House: London.

Yardley, K. (1987), 'What do *you* mean "Who am I?" Exploring the implications of a self-concept measurement with subjects', in K. Yardley and T. Honess (eds), *Self and Identity: Psychosocial Processes*, Wiley: Chichester.

Yin, R. K. (1984), *Case Study Research: Design and Methods*, Sage: Beverly Hills.

Zavalloni, M. (1971), 'Cognitive processes and social identity through focused introspection', *European Journal of Social Psychology*, 1, pp. 235–60.

Znaniecki, F. (1934), *The Method of Sociology*, Farrar & Rinehart: New York.

Part IV

Beyond adolescence – institutional demands and personal resolutions

17 Stability and change in the self-concept from adolescence to adulthood

Viktor Gecas and Jeylan T. Mortimer

This chapter addresses the issue of stability and change in the self-concept during an important segment of the life course, the transition from adolescence to adulthood. Conceptually, we distinguish between several dimensions of the self-concept; discuss the processes involved in their development; and consider how the distinguishing features of these two stages in the life course (adolescence and young adulthood) affect them. Wherever possible we marshal evidence, utilising published research and some new analysis to examine, illustrate and test some of our expectations.

We consider the self-concept to be a multidimensional phenomenon encompassing a broad range of psychological elements in terms of which individuals define themselves, such as attitudes, beliefs, values and experiences, along with their evaluative and affective components. These various aspects of the self-concept can be considered under two broad dimensions: identity and self-evaluation. The concept of identity focuses on the meanings constituting the self as an object, gives content, structure and continuity to self-conceptions and anchors the self to social systems. Self-evaluation refers to the value placed on the self-concept as a whole or on its particular components and is manifest in several evaluative experiences or outcomes (such as self-esteem). 'Identity' and 'self-evaluation' correspond to the meaning and value aspects of self-concept, the two basic components of symbols in general (Rose, 1962).

The concept of identity has had an interesting and complex history in the social sciences (see Weigert, 1983, for a review). In general, it refers to who or what one is; to the various meanings attached to oneself by self and others. There are several important types of identity that need to be distinguished for analytical purposes: role-identity; character; and existential identity. Role-identities refer to the structural features of group membership which individuals internalise and to which they become committed, e.g. various social roles (such as professor, parent, spouse), memberships (labour union, country club) and social categories (gender, age, race, etc.). Role-identities anchor the individual to social institutions and to various kinds of social networks, and in so doing often provide the ontological grounding for the individual. So important is this category of identity for sociological perspectives on the self that some sociologists even consider the concepts of identity and role-identity as synonymous (Stryker, 1980; Burke, 1980; McCall and Simmons, 1966). For example, in Stryker's (1980) structural version of symbolic interactionism, which he calls 'identity theory', identities are defined as 'parts of the self, internalized positional designations. They exist insofar as the person is a participant in *structured role relationships*' (p. 60, emphasis added). There is no question that role-identities are important, but there are also other important features on the identity landscape.

We use the concept 'character' or 'character identity' to refer to that group of identities characterised by dispositional and attributional terms. 'Character' refers to the qualities which the individual and others attribute to self, typically expressed in terms of values, beliefs and especially character traits (e.g. honest, industrious, brave, resourceful, religious). Alexander and Knight's (1971) concept of 'situated identity' is used in this way, to refer to the dispositioned imputations or character traits that others are likely to attribute to an actor on the basis of his or her actions in a particular social context. Identity-as-character emphasises the *kind* of person one is, whereas identity-as-role specifies *what* one is. Dispositional identities or character identities link the individual to the cultural–ideological domain via systems of values and beliefs as these are expressed in definitions of self. But, even more important, morality is most relevant to this feature of identity, since character traits are often cast in moral terms (see Backman, in press).

The symbolic interactionist emphasis on negotiating identities in social interaction is most appropriate to this category of identity. This is the aspect of self-concept which individuals are most likely to strive to protect in their self-presentations and impression-management strategies (Goffman, 1959). Interactionist concepts such as 'accounts' (Scott and Lyman, 1968), 'motives' (Mills, 1940) and 'disclaimers' (Hewitt and Stokes, 1975) refer to various explanations, justifications and excuses that individuals use in the service of presenting self as a certain kind of person – a morally acceptable person, a person who possesses the competencies expected in a given 'presented' self.

Clearly there is a connection between role-identities and character identities. Some role-identities become infused with characterological connotations or come to imply certain traits (e.g. the '*self-sacrificing* mother', the '*shrewd* businessman', the '*dutiful* son', etc.). There may also be a self-selection factor in that certain kinds of people seek out roles which have stereotypes compatible with their dispositional self-conceptions (Backman and Secord, 1968; Mortimer and Lorence, 1979a). But there is also a difference. Character traits, even if originally associated with a particular role-identity, tend to be more diffuse and less situation specific than are role-identities.

Existential identity is used here to refer to the individual's sense of uniqueness (e.g. personal name) and continuity. Our use of the concept is similar to Erikson's concept of 'ego-identity', which he described as 'the awareness of the fact that there is a selfsameness and continuity of the [self]' (1959). Existential identity is also similar to Goffman's conception of 'personal identity' (which he used to refer to the individual's uniqueness) and 'ego-identity' (i.e. 'the sense of existential continuity resulting from social experiences'; Goffman, 1963, p. 105). More than the other two identity categories, the concept of existential identity brings in the temporal/historical dimension as subjectively experienced, thereby stressing the transituational or transcendent self. It is the individual's biographical self (a term which Hewitt, 1976, uses to express this aspect of self).

The experiences of continuity and uniqueness in existential identity are closely related. To a large extent, our sense of uniqueness is grounded in our sense of personal continuity, that is, in our biographical self. More than our role-identities and character identities, which many others might also possess, our biographical self we typically claim as unique; it is the unique configuration and sequencing of our experiences over time. Like finger-prints, no two are alike.

But existential identity, or the biographical self, does not have the same 'facticity' as fingerprints. Existential identity is a mental construct which keeps changing over the life of the person. These changes are not merely the result of new experiences which the person undergoes in life, but more importantly they are the result of continuing *reconstruction* of the past, as well as the anticipated future, from the perspective of the present. Each new present gives the individual a new perspective on the past and the future (in the form of goals, plans and aspirations). Chandler's concept of 'narrative reconstructions of self' (see Chapter 7) also favours this view of the biographical self. As Chandler *et al.* point out, these autobiographical accounts, or narrative structures, are creative reconstructions of the past in ways which make the present comprehensible.[1]

Not surprisingly, the synthesising function of the self is emphasised here, along with the experiences of uniqueness and continuity (see, for example, Erikson, 1968). This perspective on the existential self has the added virtue of viewing the self as a producer, as well as a product, of one's life course.[2]

The second broad aspect of self-concept we consider is self-evaluation. People evaluate themselves on various criteria, such as competence, morality, worthiness, beauty, etc., and these evaluations have experiential consequences. Cooley (1902) called them self-sentiments, and considered them the most important aspect of self. Their importance lies in the strong positive and negative feelings associated with them and in their motivational significance. Three self-sentiments are particularly important in this regard: self-esteem, self-efficacy and authenticity.

Self-esteem and, to a lesser extent, self-efficacy are well established in the social psychological literature as important self-evaluation outcomes. Self-esteem refers to the positive or negative regard in which one holds oneself. It is experienced and expressed in such feelings as pride and shame. These feelings have strong motivational implications and people typically seek to experience the former and avoid, or at least diminish, the latter. This, in fact, is the basis for the self-esteem motive, i.e. the motivation to view oneself favourably and to act in such a way as to protect or increase a favourable view of oneself. The self-esteem motive is the basis for a number of contemporary theories in social psychology (see Gecas, 1982, for a review).

More recently, self-efficacy has emerged as an important self-evaluation, largely because it has been found to be consequential for a wide range of behaviours and experiences (see Bandura, 1977; Gecas and Schwalbe, 1983; and Gecas, 1982). Self-efficacy refers to the sense of mastery, causality and control in affecting one's environment. Like self-esteem, self-efficacy has a strong motivational component, i.e. people are motivated to experience themselves as agents in their environments, having some control over their circumstances. Much of the support for the self-efficacy motive comes from cognitive and developmental psychology (e.g. de Charms, 1968; Deci, 1975; Brehm, 1966). But it can also be found in Marx's (1844) theory of alienation and in humanistic psychology (Smith, 1968).

The concept of authenticity is much less visible in the literature on self-concept than are self-esteem and self-efficacy. Yet authenticity refers to a very fundamental sense of self, one's sense of reality. Authenticity addresses the question of whether the various identities constituting the self-concept are meaningful and 'real' to the individual. Some identities are obviously more 'real' in this subjective sense than are others: we feel that more of the 'true self' is expressed in these identities. Turner's (1976, 1987) concept of the 'real self' is used in this way when he distinguishes between individuals who locate their sense of authenticity in the performance of institutional roles versus those whose sense of 'real self' is located in the expression of impulse. Turner's treatment of authenticity is highly contextualised (Turner and Billings, 1985), focusing on the identification of contexts within which some feel authentic and others inauthentic. But the concept has also been treated in more transituational terms to characterise an individual's overall or pervasive self-evaluation. It is this latter condition which Frankl (1939) had in mind when he developed logotherapy as a means of helping the patient to see meaning and purpose in his or her life.[3] Etzioni (1968) also considers inauthenticity in this more pervasive sense as a function of social structures which are unresponsive to 'basic human needs'. For Etzioni, inauthenticity and alienation are closely related since both are products of environmental unresponsiveness to human needs.[4] The concept of authenticity also overlaps with Stryker's (1968) concept of identity salience and Rosenberg's (1981) concept of 'Mattering' (i.e. the feeling that we are important to others, that we matter), to the extent that these concepts involve the evaluation of identities on the basis of their significance, centrality and meaningfulness.

A somewhat different vision of 'authenticity' is found in existentialist writings, which generally provide a much more felicitous home for the concept than does social science. Here, inauthenticity refers to a condition of falseness, either to oneself or to others. Olafson, writing on Sartre, describes it this way:

> Authenticity (or entschlossenheit) may indeed be regarded as the
> prime existentialist virtue. It consists in the avoidance of that false
> relation to oneself and to others that is set up when choices are
> represented as something other than what they are – something for
> which the individual is not responsible. Inauthenticity, by contrast, is
> the arch-principle of mystification in the relationship between human
> beings and in the relationship of an individual human being to
> himself. As Sartre's writings make very clear, it is the main obstacle in
> the way of any truly human relationship based on a reciprocal
> recognition of one another as fully responsible moral agents (1971,
> p. 138).

A special case of inauthenticity is self-deception, or what Sartre called *mauvais fois* (sometimes translated as 'bad faith'). Self-deception constitutes an interesting paradox, which Sartre described thus: 'I must know in my capacity as deceiver the truth which is hidden from me in my capacity as the one deceived' (1956, p. 49). He goes on to state that all self-deception has as its point the evasion of responsibility by escaping oneself. Authenticity is central to Sartre and other existentialists because it is the prime criterion of a life well lived as well as the basis for the moral order in society.

The existentialist perspective on authenticity is rich in meaning and scope. It goes well beyond the boundaries of our more limited concern with self-concept in this chapter. What we would retain from the existentialist view of authenticity is the emphasis on what is 'real' and what is 'false', but only as perceived by the individual and then used as a basis for self-evaluation. Furthermore, from our more sociological perspective we see authenticity as a consequence of commitment to systems of meaning in society. Without commitment to role identities or to character identities, there is no sense of authenticity.

All three of these self-evaluations (self-esteem, self-efficacy and authenticity) are important because they each have motivational, as well as evaluative, significance: individuals are motivated to maintain or enhance their self-esteem; to view themselves as efficacious; and to feel authentic (Gecas, 1986).

Processes of self-concept formation

The development and maintenance of the several categories of identity and self-evaluation discussed above depend on a wide range of socialisation processes, involving role-learning, reinforcement, internalisation of values and beliefs, identification and various situational encounters where identities are forged in the negotiations of social reality. Certainly, role-relationships are important to the development of role-identities, such as entrance into and exit from specific roles (e.g. marriage, parenthood, retirement), commitment to particular roles (see Turner, 1978, on conditions of person–role merger) and involvement in various role-sets. Similarly, the development of character and existential identity is affected by the broad range of socialisation processes involved in role-relationships. In short, the process of socialisation in its broad and generic sense is thoroughly involved in the development of self-concept.

The self-concept, though affected by these general socialisation processes, is particularly dependent on three more delimited processes: reflected appraisals, social comparisons and self-attributions (for more extensive discussions of these processes, see Rosenberg, 1979, 1981, and Gecas, 1982). The most visible of these in the sociological literature is reflected appraisals. Based on Cooley's (1902) influential concept of the 'looking-glass self' and Mead's theory (1934) of role-taking as a product of symbolic interaction, the concept of reflected appraisals emphasises the essentially social character of the self-concept, e.g. that our self-conceptions reflect the appraisals and perceptions of others, especially significant others, in our environments. It should be noted, however, that research on this proposition has consistently found that our self-concepts are much more strongly related to our *perceptions* of others' evaluations than to others' actual evaluations of us (Shrauger and Schoeneman, 1979). Reflected appraisals are particularly important in the development of self-esteem.

Also important to self-concept are social comparisons. Social comparison is the process in which individuals assess their own abilities and virtues by comparing them with those of others. Local reference groups or persons are most likely to be used as frames of reference for these comparisons, especially under conditions of competition, such as athletic contests, classroom performance, etc. (Covington and Beery, 1976; Rosenberg, 1975). Here as well, individuals frequently structure the situation or select reference groups which enable more favourable comparisons of self.

Self-attributions refer to the tendency to make inferences about ourselves from direct observation of our behaviour. Bem's (1972) 'self-perception theory' proposes that individuals determine what they are feeling and thinking by making inferences based on observing their own overt behaviour. Self-perception theory can be subsumed under the more general attribution theory in psychology, which deals with how individuals make causal inferences about their own and others' behaviour. This process is particularly relevant to the development of self-efficacy (Bandura, 1977).

Even though the literature on reflected appraisals, social comparisons and self-attributions has focused on their importance for self-evaluations (primarily, self-esteem and self-efficacy), these processes are also important in the development of identities. To a large extent, we come to know who and what we are from the responses of others, from the inferences we make from observing our own behaviour and from the reference groups we use in our social comparisons.

Stability and change in the self-concept

The mechanisms for change and for stability reside both within the self-concept itself and within its environment. Let us consider change first. For many self theorists, change is the natural state of the self-concept (Goffman, 1959; Gergen, 1977). Since the self-concept is built on the human capacity for reflexivity, we have within the self a mechanism for constant change, a mechanism that involves continual self-examination and alteration. Furthermore, since the self is also an *active* agent in the environment, whose actions reflect to some extent the unpredictable 'I', there is usually an element of surprise in human action.

Change in the self-concept may also be due to changes in the environment affecting the processes of self-concept formation. Changes in interpersonal relations and social structural circumstances may, for example, alter one's self-esteem and self-efficacy through less favourable reflected appraisals, social comparisons and self-attributions. Changes in the contexts of social interactions (such as getting a new job) may be associated with the addition or loss of role-identities, having consequences for the organisation of the self-system.

Even if change is considered to be the natural state of self-conceptions, we still can speak of *relative* stability and change. In general, change in the self-concept increases under conditions of conflict, confrontation or discrepancy. The theme of conflict is pervasive in the literature on self-concept change. It is prominent in Mead's (1934) pragmatic social psychology within which the emergence of mind and self depend on confrontation with, and resistance from, the environment. Erikson (1968) also emphasises the importance of conflict for human development: 'I shall present human growth from the point of view of the conflicts, inner and outer, which the vital personality weathers' (p. 92). For that matter, Erikson's epigenetic theory of individual growth has at its centre the idea of a particular conflict or dilemma characteristic of each 'stage' of the life course. Similarly, in Piaget's (1954) developmental theory, the development of the person's cognitive complexity and competence depend on the existence of a challenging environment.

The emphasis on confrontation or conflict as a mechanism for self-concept change is quite evident in contemporary cognitive social psychology as well. For example, Rokeach (1973) found that self-awareness which results in *self-dissatisfaction* leads to change in self-concept. He developed a method of self-confrontation in his studies which demonstrated substantial and persistent changes in self-conception (in terms of central values) as a result of experimentally induced self-dissatisfaction.

As many observers have noted, adolescence is a stage of life in our society particularly characterised by increased and often acute self-consciousness – due to rapid physical changes, peer involvement and the transition from family to adult worlds – which is often associated with self-dissatisfaction as well. This is the stage which Erikson identified as involving the crisis of identity, in which the main psychological task for the individual is the crystallisation of self-concept and its expansion in new directions. The mechanisms for change in the self-concept are indeed pervasive and the conditions for change are conspicuously favourable during this segment of the life course, from adolescence to adulthood.

But there are also mechanisms for self-concept stability, both external and internal to the individual. External stability depends on the constancy or stability of the social environment within which the self-concept exists, specifically the stability of the reference groups, significant others and contexts of interaction within which selves engage in reflected appraisals, social comparisons and self-attributions.

Perhaps a firmer ground for self-concept stability, in our rapidly changing society, is found in mechanisms operating *within* the self-concept itself. There is a general tendency toward the persistence and continuity of attitudes and beliefs. Some of this is due to inertia, but most of it is due to motivations of the individual to *maintain* self-concept stability. One such motivation is based on a functional argument: stable self-conceptions enable more effective action in the world, since without a clear conception of who and what one is, action becomes confused, uncertain or even paralysed. Lecky (1955) viewed the maintenance of a unified self-theory as the overriding need of the individual. Markus (1977), who views the self-concept as an organisation of self-schemata (cognitive generalisations), considers these self-schemata to be increasingly resistant to change once they are established. Greenwald (1980) identifies this motivational element in the self-concept as 'cognitive conservatism', which he describes as 'the disposition to preserve existing knowledge structures, such as precepts, schemata, and memories' (p. 606). In short, the perceived stability of the self-concept is functional for the individual.

Beyond functionality, the individual is motivated to maintain those elements of the self-concept which contribute to a positive view of self. This is commonly referred to as the 'self-esteem motive'. It underscores the point that the self is an object of value which the individual protects and defends. The ego defence mechanisms of psychoanalytic theory could be considered as operating in the service of protecting a favourable view of self (Hildegard, 1949). Rosenberg (1979) discusses the importance of selectivity (for example, in perception of self-relevant information) in the maintenance of self-esteem. The self-esteem motive, therefore, can contribute to the sense of self-concept stability through selectivity and reconstruction of one's social reality. Conversely, negative aspects of the self-concept which give rise to self-dissatisfaction are more likely to be an impetus for change rather than stability in the self-concept.

Lastly, stability is an important feature of that aspect of the self-concept called existential identity. It will be recalled that existential identity refers to the individual's sense of selfsameness, uniqueness and temporal continuity. It contributes to a perception of stability in the self-concept, even if the stability has no basis in fact.

At this general level of discourse, then, we can argue for both stability and change in the self-concept. What we must now consider is which aspects of the self-concept discussed above are more or less likely to change (and through which processes of self-concept formation) during the transition from adolescence to adulthood.

From adolescence to adulthood in the life course

It could be argued that the transition from adolescence to adulthood is the most significant segment in the life course. It marks the person's entry into adult status in society. The changes associated with this period are sometimes stressful and disturbing, both to adolescents and to those who are close to them. Several role changes during this segment of the life course are particularly important for the self-concept: the shift from family and peer group to love relationship or intimate other, and typically to parenthood, as the most significant contexts of interpersonal, expressive interaction; and the shift from school to work as the major institutional context.[5]

Both of these transitions can be expected to have important consequences for self-conceptions. At the level of role-identities, several new identities are added (spouse, worker, provider, and perhaps parent), and some are lost or recede in importance (student, boy/girlfriend, son/daughter). The structure of the self-concept in terms of its role-identities becomes significantly altered, and existential identity, to the extent that it encompasses various role-identities to which the individual is committed, is substantially expanded. For Erikson (1968) the crystallisation of identity (largely in terms of the kind of person one is) is the central task of adolescence. He considers satisfactory resolution of this identity task a precondition for the successful engagement in the next developmental problem, which he (appropriately enough) identifies as 'intimacy vs. isolation'. Involvement in an intimate love relationship may further affect the process of self-concept development. At least, it may increase self-esteem and perhaps shift the locus of self-authenticity from family and peers to activities with the intimate other.

The transition from school to work is the major institutional change during this age segment. Along with the identity implications that this transition involves, it is particularly consequential for the efficacy dimension of self-evaluation. To be sure, school does provide a context for the development of competencies and the experience of self-efficacy, but these are largely under imposed (involuntary) conditions. Furthermore, school is primarily concerned with the acquisition of skills; work is more likely to involve the application of skills. This application has an effect not only on self-efficacy, but on the content of our self-conceptions as well. The consequences of our productive activity in the form of objects, creations, services performed, constitute a basis for self-definition; they become a 'looking-glass' for the self. This, of course, is more likely to be the case in occupations which allow greater autonomy, self-direction, creativity and involvement of problem-solving skills than in occupations which are dull, highly routinised, closely supervised and unchallenging. The latter occupations are more likely to result in low self-efficacy, alienation and feelings of inauthenticity at work (conditions and consequences which Marx discussed as alienated labour). These occupational conditions are largely class related, such that middle- and upper-class occupations and work situations are more likely to involve the set of favourable conditions for self-concept, whereas lower-class occupations involve the conditions unfavourable to self-definition and evaluation (Kohn and Schooler, 1983). In general, the transition from school to work has less favourable consequences for self-esteem, self-efficacy and authenticity for lower-class youth than it does for middle- and upper-class youth.

We might also ask if this transition from school to work, as well as the transition from family/peers to love and marriage, is different for men and women. Historically, work has been a more important context of role-identities and self-definitions for men in American (and Western) society than have marital and parental roles. The reverse has been true for women. But this gender difference in sources of self-definition is rapidly decreasing, as the proportion of women in the labour force continues to rise, as family size continues to decline and as the ideology of sexual equality makes family and work roles more equally shared by men and women.[6]

Research on stability and change in self-concept from adolescence to adulthood

Research on self-concept change during the transition from adolescence to adulthood is sparse. Although it is often stated that adolescence is a time of major change in self-conceptions, neither these changes nor the processes through which they occur have been well documented in the empirical literature. Few studies have spanned the period of adolescence and followed their subjects into adulthood: the Berkeley and Oakland studies (Elder, 1974; Eichorn *et al.*, 1981), the Fels study (Moss and Kagan, 1972), the Terman study of the gifted (Oden, 1968) and the Grant study of Harvard men (Vaillant, 1977). Other research focuses on more limited time periods, such as the years in college (King, 1973; Feldman and Newcomb, 1969; Astin, 1978), or those spanning the teens to the twenties (Offer and Offer, 1975; Symonds, 1961; Golden *et al.*, 1962).

Generally, these studies have not focused on the self-concept. Instead, they examine broad personality dispositions and abilities (which do have some relevance for self-evaluation and character). For example, ability, as defined by grades in school or by performance on intelligence and achievement tests, has been found to be exceedingly stable (Kagan and Moss, 1962; Bloom, 1964; Oden, 1968; Cunningham and Owens, 1983). Investigators have also noted continuity in motivation, as defined by task involvement and perseverance, and in behaviour, as indicated by dependency, spontaneity and aggressiveness (Kagan and Moss, 1962; Oden, 1968; Block and Haan, 1971; Vaillant, 1974). Indicators of adjustment and mental health have also been found to be quite stable through this period (Mortimer and Lorence, 1981).

But if personality and adjustment are generally so stable over time,[7] why does the literature on adolescence emphasise this as a major period of self-concept change? It is evident that most prior studies focus on the underlying personality structure (including dimensions of character, temperament and ability) that are quite enduring even over the relatively turbulent period of adolescence. Because, for the most part, they have been undertaken by psychologists, they do not focus on particular (and differential) social contexts and their distinct consequences for the self-image (see Dannefer, 1984, for a critique of psychological perspectives on the life course). Certain aspects of personality and adjustment may be highly stable, but we contend that the particular contents of identity, as well as dimensions of self-evaluation and character, are highly responsive to the role changes that are experienced during this phase of life.

Evidence from two longitudinal studies

The remainder of this chapter will review some findings obtained from two data sets. The first is the 1966–74 Youth in Transition Study, obtained from a national panel which began with 2,213 tenth-grade boys under the direction of Jerald Bachman at the University of Michigan's Institute for Social Research (see Bachman *et al.*, 1978, for a description of the sampling frame). Data were collected during each of three years in high school, each year after graduation and five years after graduation.[8]

The second data set is the Michigan Panel Study, a longitudinal study of over 500 highly educated men, covering the period from college entry in 1962 and 1963 to a decade beyond graduation.[9] This panel is highly advantaged with respect to both its social origins and its destinations (for further information about the panel, see Mortimer and Lorence, 1981). Unfortunately, since both of these studies are of men, the exploration of gender differences in self-concept formation must rely on other research. We use the findings drawn from these studies to examine the effects of family, school and work on the development of self-concept as persons move from adolescence to adulthood.

Data from the Michigan Panel Study enable assessment of the development of self-esteem, as indicated by a sense of well-being, the perception of self as happy (vs. unhappy), relaxed (vs. tense) and confident (vs. anxious), over the period of transition to adulthood (Mortimer and Lorence, 1981). Our analysis clearly showed that social support is important in sustaining a perception of self as happy, relaxed and confident, but the source of this support changes as individuals shift their allegiances from the family of origin to the intimate other. At the time of entry into college, the quality of relationships with parents appeared to play a major part in enhancing or detracting from psychological well-being. The impact of support from the parents steadily weakened over time (though it was still significant in the senior year). It was supplanted, in early adulthood, by support from the spouse. It is noteworthy that these changing interpersonal influences were far more important for well-being than achievements in college (indicated by grades) or thereafter (measured by socioeconomic attainments), which had no significant effects on well-being during the period of investigation.

The relatively high level of correlational stability of well-being, both during college (.63) and over the decade following (.58), coupled with these patterns of causation, illustrates a more general point. Whereas a substantial portion of the variance is predictable over time, as a result of underlying personality dynamics as well as consistent external influences, we find evidence that the sources of well-being change from adolescence to adulthood. Thus, moderate to high levels of stability manifest in measures of the self-concept do not preclude the existence of changing social determinants of self over periods of life-stage transition.

Like well-being for the Michigan Panel, the self-esteem of the Youth in Transition respondents exhibits substantial correlational stability through the adolescent and early adult years. This demonstrates the preservation of interindividual differences. For example, our analyses (Mortimer and Finch, 1983) showed that self-esteem stability was .62 from the tenth to the eleventh grade, and .72 from the eleventh to the twelfth. Bachman *et al.* (1978, p. 98), using a more comprehensive self-esteem measure, report even higher correlations.

It should be recognised that the level of correlational stability tells us nothing about the mean pattern of change. This interindividual stability in self-esteem occurs within a context of a general rise in mean level throughout adolescence and early adulthood. In the Michigan Panel Study, the average level of well-being declined significantly during college, and then increased during the succeeding decade.

This trend is consistent with the presumption that adolescence is a difficult, stressful period, while problems diminish with successful adaptation to adult roles. Further indication of the stressful character of this transition derives from a trend in a construct we called 'self-doubt' (Mortimer and Lorence, 1981), encompassing elements of inauthenticity. The Michigan respondents were most likely to report concerns about being a 'normal person', about 'always acting, never being true to myself or being myself' and 'social sensitivity – a feeling that I get hurt too easily' at college entry. These concerns declined continuously over the three periods of observation.

With the same data, we examined patterns of change in efficacy and a dimension of character, that of sociability, during the college period and over the decade beyond graduation. The patterns are highly consistent with the changing cultural context for the formation of identity in these phases of life. That is, our culture places great emphasis in adolescence on friendship, popularity and the peer group; whereas in early adulthood, predominant values stress the importance of instrumental achievement, the establishment of a career and attaining financial independence and security. Accordingly, we find a decline in sociability over the fourteen-year period of the Michigan Panel Study, and an increase in competence after college.

The Youth in Transition data demonstrate that adolescent self-efficacy is influenced by instrumental achievements centred on school activities. In adolescence, the sense of individual self-competence is defined largely by the ability to perform well in school. The overall pattern suggests that the sense of efficacy is more responsive to processes of self-attribution, to observation of actual achievements and demonstrations of competence than to processes of interpersonal influence (Maruyama *et al.*, 1985).

One of the most important structural features of interaction contexts affecting both self-efficacy and self-esteem is the degree of autonomy which the context allows the individual. In adolescence, we find a clear relation between indicators of internal motivation and control with respect to school work and self-esteem. Autonomy in both family and school were found to have a significant positive effect on self-esteem of high school students in the Youth in Transition study. Work autonomy had a positive impact on self-esteem five years after graduation (Mortimer and Finch, 1986). The Michigan Panel Study also points to the importance of work autonomy as a source of efficacy in early adulthood. It was found that work experiences offering challenge, the opportunity for innovative thought and independent decision-making increase the individual's sense of personal efficacy and competence (Mortimer and Lorence, 1979b, p. 320).

We observe here a dynamic reciprocal process of influence of person and environment. Those men who felt more competent as college seniors had stronger intrinsic values, which led to the more autonomous occupational positions ten years later. For self-evaluations of efficacy we may find the clearest patterns of spiralling success and failure. Initial conceptions of self-efficacy, from whatever source, may tend to become self-fulfilling prophecies, encouraging the taking of risks and giving confidence in the undertaking of new and challenging tasks. Subsequent success in these endeavours fosters an increasing sense of personal efficacy over time. Similarly, in early adulthood, a sense of competence fosters high occupational attainment (including intrinsic and extrinsic rewards) which, in turn, stimulates greater personal efficacy. In fact, efficacy may be an important intervening variable in studies relating indicators of achievement – such as social class, upward mobility and autonomy – to self-esteem (Rosenberg and Pearlin, 1978; Staples *et al.*, 1984).

The interrelations characteristic of the self-evaluation components (e.g. self-esteem and self-efficacy) are also evident with regard to identities, especially the connection between character and role-identities. Aspects of the adolescent's character are of major importance for choices of adult roles (as well as social environments and personal associates), which, in turn, may have major consequences for the further development of the self.[10]

We illustrate this process by describing the interrelations of adolescent occupational values, here conceptualised as components of character, and work experiences in early adulthood. Prior studies (Rosenberg, 1957; Davis, 1965) have reported significant associations between values and occupational choices prior to the individual's entry into the work-force. The Michigan Panel data enabled assessment of the effects of prior values on features of subsequent adult work roles. Following a question about their career decisions, the college seniors were asked, 'How important would you say the following things are in your decision about whether to go into this kind of work?' The list of items that followed was reduced to three value factors, corresponding to extrinsic (prestige, advancement and high income), intrinsic (involving the use of abilities, expression of interests and opportunity to be creative) and people-oriented (involving the chance to be helpful to others and to work with people rather than things) rewards of jobs. It is noteworthy that these values, like self-esteem or the sense of well-being, were quite responsive to the influence of parents, particularly fathers (Mortimer, 1975; Mortimer and Kumka, 1982), during adolescence. But from our present standpoint what is most important is the power of these values, as dimensions of character, to predict features of occupational roles – and, presumably, corresponding role identities – ten years later (Mortimer and Lorence, 1979a). Those seniors who placed a high value on people-oriented rewards were more likely to have work with high social content a decade later, as they occupied work roles involving welfare, teaching and service functions. Similarly, intrinsic values predicted autonomous work activity (involving innovative thinking, high decision-making latitude and challenge), such as college teaching. High extrinsic reward values in college predicted income attainment and careers in business management. Thus, we find that earlier components of character are clearly linked to subsequent role acquisition.

Moreover, our analyses demonstrate the dynamic, reciprocal interrelations of character and social environment (Mortimer and Lorence, 1979a). Initial values, constituting the basis of occupational selection, were reinforced by the very same work experiences. For example, earlier intrinsic values predicted work autonomy, and work autonomy significantly strengthened intrinsic orientations over time. This pattern has been confirmed by findings from a national panel (Lindsay and Knox, 1984). Through this process, occurring over long periods of time, the level of congruence of self and role may be heightened. One might expect that such reciprocal processes would foster a continually increasing compatibility of personal values and needs, on the one hand, and social demands and rewards, on the other, accompanied by feelings of increasing satisfaction, adjustment and, perhaps, self-esteem. Thus, adolescent character may not only affect the choice of adult roles, but the continuing interrelations of character and role can influence the level of perceived 'success' in roles at subsequent points in time. As in the case of self-efficacy, these processes may generate a spiralling reinforcement of earlier character traits.

Conclusion

In the course of addressing the issue of stability and change in the self-concept from adolescence to adulthood, we have distinguished between several dimensions of the self-concept, considered several processes involved in their development and utilised empirical evidence, primarily from two longitudinal studies, to examine how time and the contexts of interaction characteristic of this segment of the life course affect these components of the self-concept. In the process, we have formed several general observations. First, in spite of the important role transitions characteristic of this segment of the life course, there is considerable stability in the self-concept during this ostensibly turbulent period. This stability is reflected mainly in the 'character' dimension of identity and in two self-evaluation dimensions: self-esteem and self-efficacy. Even though we were unable to assess the course of existential identity in these longitudinal data sets, we will venture the hypothesis that the observed stability in key aspects of the self-concept contributes to the individual's sense of continuity and uniqueness (a speculation also offered by Costa *et al.*, 1983, when they assessed the implications of their own longitudinal findings). Second, there is considerable reciprocity between several of the self-concept components considered: self-esteem and self-efficacy are clearly interdependent; as are role-identities and character identities. And, although again we have no empirical evidence, we expect sense of authenticity to be strongly dependent on commitment to role-identities, values and other character identities, and on favourable assessments of one's competence and worth. And finally, we reaffirm an increasingly common observation: that the self-concept and its social environment are reciprocally determined. The self is not a passive recipient of external influences, but an active selector and constructor of its worlds. In particular, the person strives to establish and maintain situations which foster valued identities. This reciprocity is most clearly evident in cases of spiralling development, such as our observation that sense of self-efficacy tends to lead to situations (i.e. challenges, stimulating environments) which further enhance the sense of self-efficacy. The basis for positive or negative spirals of development is located within the reciprocity between self and environment, and is evident in the transition from adolescence to adulthood.

Acknowledgments

Work on this paper was supported in part by Project 0364, Department of Rural Sociology, Agricultural Research Center, Washington State University. Research reported herein from the Youth in Transition Study was supported by the National Institute on Aging (AGO 03325). The Michigan Panel Study was supported by grants from the Center for Studies of Work and Mental Health, National Institute of Mental Health (MH 26421) and the National Science Foundation (NSF SOC 75–21098). Both studies were also supported by the Computer Center of the University of Minnesota. The authors would like to thank Michael Finch for performing several analyses in the preparation of this paper.

Notes

1 See Erica Haimes's account (Chapter 22) of what happens when the biographical self is perceived to be 'incomplete', as in the case of adoptees in search of their roots.

2 Our identity typology overlaps to a considerable extent with the one proposed by Sheila Rossan in Chapter 19: 'role-identities' correspond to her concept of 'subidentities', 'character identities' are similar to her 'generalised traits', and there is some similarity between our 'existential identity' and her 'core identity'.

3 Meaning, for Frankl, has a strong motivational significance as well, which he calls a 'will to meaning': 'The striving to find a meaning in one's life is the primary motivational force in man' (1939, p. 153).

4 We would more sharply distinguish between 'alienation' and 'inauthenticity', retaining the concept of alienation to refer to the experiential consequence of powerlessness and environmental unresponsiveness (associated with feelings of inefficacy), and reserving the concepts 'authenticity/inauthenticity' for the domain of meaning and sense of reality.

5 It should be noted, however, that these are not inevitable changes and not the only alternatives for individuals moving from adolescence to young adulthood. There are a number of other directions that may be taken: love involvements may be postponed, formal education may be continued into college or professional schools, graduation from high school may be followed by entrance into the armed forces, the Peace Corps or unemployment. But for most people, in industrial societies, these alternative directions merely postpone and prolong the period of transition to the two most central role contexts associated with adult states: marriage and family of procreation, and work or occupation.

6 Nevertheless, we must be wary of generalising from studies based on male samples (such as the Michigan longitudinal studies discussed below) to female populations. There may be an androcentric bias in much of our developmental theorising, as Gilligan (1982) persuasively argues.

7 However, the conceptualisation and measurement of personality change are variable and sometimes ambiguous (see Mortimer *et al.*, 1982). Even as high a correlation as .7 between adolescent and adult psychological measures (usually the associations are lower) is subject to diverse interpretations, depending on the predilections of the investigator. Those who emphasise personality stability will be impressed by the magnitude of this relationship, but those focusing on the potential for change will note that half the variance is unexplained. It is beyond the scope of this paper to attempt to resolve this dilemma. We wish to point

out, however, that even high stabilities of personality measures over time (such as those reported by Bachman *et al.*, 1978, p. 98; and Mortimer and Lorence, 1981) leave much room for external influence.

8 Although sample attrition is a major problem in all longitudinal studies, 73.5 per cent of the original study participants were included in the final wave.

9 Upon entry to the University of Michigan in 1962 and 1963, the men joined an extensive research project, initiated by Theodore Newcomb and Gerald Gurin, on the impacts of college life. This study extended through their college careers. In 1976, 75 per cent of the seniors were located and persuaded to return a mailed questionnaire.

10 It is, of course, recognised that these processes are especially pronounced in those circumstances in which there is a voluntary choice of roles. For example, graduating college students generally have a wide range of occupational opportunities from which to choose, especially when the economy is favourable. This is less likely to be the case for those at lower socioeconomic levels at the time of entry to adulthood, such as high school dropouts.

References

Alexander, N. C. and Knight, G. W. (1971), 'Situated identities and social psychological experimentation', *Sociometry*, 34, pp. 65–82.

Astin, A. W. (1978), *Four Critical Years. Effects of College on Beliefs, Attitudes and Knowledge*, Jossey-Bass: San Francisco.

Bachman, J. G., O'Malley, P. M. and Johnston, J. (1978), Adolescence to Adulthood – Change and Stability in the Lives of Young Men, in *Youth in Transition*, vol. VI, Survey Research Center, Institute for Social Research, Ann Arbor, Mich.

Backman, C. W. (in press), 'Identity, self-presentation and the resolution of moral dilemmas: Toward a social psychological theory of moral behavior', in B. R. Schlenker (ed.), *The Self and Social Life*, McGraw-Hill: New York.

Backman, C. W. and Secord, P. F. (1968), 'The self and role selection', in C. Gordon and K. J. Gergen (eds), *The Self in Social Interaction*, vol. 1, Wiley: New York.

Bandura, A. (1977), 'Self-efficacy: Toward a unifying theory of behavioral change', *Psychological Review*, 84(2), pp. 191–215.

Bem, D. J. (1972), 'Self-perception theory', in L. Berkowitz (ed.), Advances in Experimental Social Psychology, vol. 6, Academic Press: New York.

Block, J. and Haan, N. (1971), *Lives Through Time*, Bancroft: Berkeley, Calif.

Bloom, B. S. (1964), *Stability and Change in Human Characteristics*, Wiley: New York.

Brehm, J. W. (1966), *A Theory of Psychological Reactance*, Academic Press: New York.

Burke, P. J. (1980), 'The self: Measurement requirements from an interactionist perspective', *Social Psychology Quarterly*, 43(1), pp. 18–29.

Cooley, C. H. (1902), *Human Nature and the Social Order*, Scribner: New York.

Costa, P. T., Jr., McCrae, R. R. and Arenberg, D. (1983), 'Recent longitudinal research on personality and aging', in K. W. Schaie (ed.), *Longitudinal Studies of Adult Psychological Development*, Guilford Press: New York, pp. 222–65.

Covington, M. V. and Beery, R. G. (1976), *Self-Worth and School Learning*, Holt, Rinehart & Winston: New York.

Cunningham, W. R. and Owens, W. A., Jr. (1983), 'The Iowa State study of the adult development of intellectual abilities', in K. W. Schaie (ed.), *Longitudinal Studies of Adult Psychological Development*, Guilford Press: New York, pp. 20–39.

Dannefer, D. (1984), 'Adult development and social theory', *American Sociological Review*, 49(Feb.), pp. 100–16.

Davis, J. A. (1965), *Undergraduate Career Decisions: Correlates of Occupational Choice*, Aldine: Chicago.

de Charms, R. (1968), *Personal Causation: The Internal Affective Determinants of Behavior*, Academic Press: New York.

Deci, E. L. (1975), *Intrinsic Motivation*, Plenum Press: New York.

Eichorn, D. H., Clausen, J. A., Haan, N., Honzik, M. P. and Mussen, P. H. (1981), *Present and Past in Middle Life*, Academic Press: New York.

Elder, G. H., Jr. (1974), *Children of the Great Depression*, University of Chicago Press: Chicago.

Erikson, E. H. (1959), 'The problem of ego identity', *Psychological Issues*, 1, pp. 101–64.

Erikson, E. H. (1968), *Identity: Youth and Crises*, Norton: New York.

Etzioni, A. (1968), 'Basic human needs, alienation and inauthenticity', *American Sociological Review*, 33(6), pp. 870–85.

Feldman, K. A. and Newcomb, T. M. (1969), *The Impact of College on Students, vol. 1, An Analysis of Four Decades of Research*, Jossey-Bass: San Francisco.

Frankl, V. E. (1963), *Man's Search for Meaning*, Simon and Schuster: New York (originally published in 1939).

Gecas, V. (1982), 'The self-concept', *Annual Review of Sociology*, 8, pp. 1–33.

Gecas, V. (1986), 'The motivational significance of self-concept for socialization theory', in E. J. Lawler (ed.), *Advances in Group Processes: Theory and Research*, vol. 3, JAI Press: Greenwich, Conn.

Gecas, V. and Schwalbe, M. L. (1983), 'Beyond the looking-glass self: Social structure and efficacy-based self-esteem', *Social Psychology Quarterly*, 46(2), pp. 77–88.

Gergen, K. J. (1977), 'The social construction of self-knowledge', in T.

Mischel (ed.), *The Self: Psychological and Philosophical Issues*, Blackwell: Oxford.

Gilligan, C. (1982), *In a Different Voice*, Harvard University Press: Cambridge, Mass.

Goffman, E. (1959), *The Presentation of Self in Everyday Life*, Anchor Books: New York.

Goffman, E. (1963), *Stigma*, Prentice-Hall: Englewood Cliffs, N.J.

Golden, J., Mandel, N., Glueck, B. C., Jr. and Feder, Z. F. (1962), 'A summary description of fifty "normal" white males', *American Journal of Psychiatry*, 119(July), pp. 48–56.

Greenwald, A. G. (1980), 'The totalitarian ego: Fabrication and revision of personal history', *American Psychologist*, 35(July), pp. 603–18.

Hewitt, J. P. (1976), *Self and Society: A Symbolic Interactionist Social Psychology*, Allyn and Bacon: Boston.

Hewitt, J. P. and Stokes, R. (1975), 'Disclaimers', *American Sociological Review*, 40, pp. 1–11.

Hildegard, E. R. (1949), 'Human motives and the concept of the self', *American Psychologist*, 4, pp. 374–82.

Kagan, J. and Moss, H. A. (1962), *Birth to Maturity*, Wiley: New York.

King, S. H. (1973), *Five Lives at Harvard: Personality Change During College*, Harvard University Press: Cambridge, Mass.

Kohn, M. L. and Schooler, C. (with the collaboration of Miller, J., Miller, K. A., Schoenbach, C. and Schoenberg, R) (1983), *Work and Personality: An Inquiry into the Impact of Social Stratification*, Ablex: Norwood, N.J.

Lecky, P. (1955), *Self-Consistency: A Theory of Personality*, Island Press: New York.

Lindsay, P. and Knox, W. E. (1984), 'Continuity and change in work values among young adults: A longitudinal study', *American Journal of Sociology*, 89(Jan.), pp. 918–31.

Markus, H. (1977), 'Self-schemata and processing information about the self', *Journal of Personality and Social Psychology*, 35(2), pp. 63–78.

Maruyama, G., Finch, M. D. and Mortimer, J. T. (1985), 'Processes of achievement in the transition to adulthood', in Z. S. Blau (ed.), *Current Perspectives on Aging and the Life Cycle*, JAI Press: Greenwich, Conn, pp. 61–87.

Marx, K. (1963), *Early Writings* [1844], T.B. Bottomore (ed. and trans.), McGraw-Hill: New York.

McCall, G. J. and Simmons, J. L. (1966), *Identities and Interactions*, The Free Press: New York.

Mead, G. H. (1934), *Mind, Self and Society*, University of Chicago Press: Chicago.

Mills, C. W. (1940), 'Situated actions and vocabularies of motive', *American Sociological Review*, 5, pp. 905–29.

Mortimer, J. T. (1975), 'Occupational value socialization in business and professional families', *Sociology of Work and Occupations*, vol. 2, pp. 29–53.

Mortimer, J. T. and Finch, M. D. (1983), 'Autonomy as a source of self-esteem in adolescence', Paper presented at the American Sociological Association meetings.

Mortimer, J. T. and Finch, M. D. (1986), 'The development of self-esteem in the early work career', *Work and Occupations*, 13, pp. 217–39.

Mortimer, J. T., Finch, M. D. and Kumka, D. (1982), 'Persistence and change in development: The multidimensional self-concept', in P. D. Baltes and O. G. Grim, Jr. (eds), *Life-Span Development and Behavior*, vol. 4, Academic Press: New York, pp. 263–313.

Mortimer, J. T. and Kumka, D. (1982), 'A further examination of the "occupational linkage hypothesis" ', *Sociological Quarterly*, 23(Winter), pp. 3–16.

Mortimer, J. T. and Lorence, J. (1979a), 'Work experience and occupational value socialization: A longitudinal study', *American Journal of Sociology*, 84(May), pp. 1361–85.

Mortimer, J. T. and Lorence, J. (1979b), 'Occupational experience and the self-concept: A longitudinal study', *Social Psychology Quarterly*, 42(Dec.), pp. 307–23.

Mortimer, J. T. and Lorence, J. (1981), 'Self-concept stability and change from late adolescence to early adulthood', in R. G. Simmons (ed.), *Research in Community and Mental Health*, vol. 2, JAI Press: Greenwich, Conn., pp. 5–42.

Mortimer, J. T., Lorence, J. and Kumka, D. (1986), *Work, Family, and Personality: Transition to Adulthood*, Ablex: Norwood, N.J.

Moss, H. A. and Kagan, J. (1972), 'Report on personality consistency and change from the Fels longitudinal study', in D. R. Heise (ed.), *Personality and Socialization*, Rand McNally: Chicago, pp. 21–8.

Oden, M. H. (1968), 'The fulfillment of promise: 40 year follow-up of the Terman gifted group', *Genetic Psychology Monographs*, 77(Feb.), pp. 3–93.

Offer, D. and Offer, J. B. (1975), *From Teenage to Young Manhood*, Basic Books: New York.

Olafson, F. A. (1971), 'Authenticity and obligation', in M. Warnock (ed.), *Sartre: A Collection of Critical Essays*, Anchor Books: Garden City, N.Y.

Piaget, J. (1954), *The Construction of Reality in the Child*, Basic Books: New York.

Rokeach, M. (1973), *The Nature of Human Values*, Free Press: New York.

Rose, A. M. (1962), 'A systematic summary of symbolic interaction theory', in A. M. Rose (ed.), *Human Behavior and Social Processes: An Interactionist Approach*, Houghton Mifflin: Boston.

Rosenberg, M. (1957), *Occupations and Values*, Free Press: Glencoe, Ill.

Rosenberg, M. (1975), 'The dissonant context and the adolescent self-concept', in S. Dragastin and G. H. Elder (eds), *Adolescence in the Life Cycle: Psychological Change and Social Context*, Hemisphere Publications: Washington, D.C., pp. 97–116.

Rosenberg, M. (1979), *Conceiving the Self*, Basic Books: New York.

Rosenberg, M. (1981), 'The sociology of the self-concept', in M. Rosenberg and R. Turner (eds), *Social Psychology: Sociological Perspectives*, Basic Books: New York.

Rosenberg, M. and Pearlin, L. I. (1978), 'Social class and self-esteem among children and adults', *American Journal of Sociology*, 84(July), pp. 53–77.

Sartre, J.-P. (1956), *Being and Nothingness*, trans. by H. E. Barnes, Philosophical Library: New York.

Scott, M. B. and Lyman, S. W. (1968), 'Accounts', *American Sociological Review*, 33, pp. 46–62.

Shrauger, J. S. and Schoeneman, T. J. (1979), 'Symbolic interactionist view of self-concept: Through the looking glass darkly', *Psychological Bulletin*, 86(3), pp. 549–73.

Smith, M. B. (1968), 'Competence and socialization', in J. A. Clausen (ed.), *Socialization and Society*, Little, Brown: Boston, pp. 270–320.

Staples, C. L., Schwalbe, M. L. and Gecas, V. (1984), 'Social class, occupational conditions, and efficacy-based self-esteem', *Sociological Perspectives*, 27(Jan.), pp. 85–109.

Stryker, S. (1968), 'Identity salience and role performance', *Journal of Marriage and the Family*, 30, pp. 558–64.

Stryker, S. (1980), *Symbolic Interactionism: A Social Structural Version*, Benjamin/Cummings: Menlo Park, Calif.

Symonds, P. M. (1961), *From Adolescent to Adult*, Columbia University Press: New York.

Turner, R. H. (1976), 'The real self: From institution to impulse', *American Journal of Sociology*, 84(5), pp. 989–1016.

Turner, R. H. (1978), 'The role and the person', *American Journal of Sociology*, 84(July), pp. 1–23.

Turner, R. (1987), 'Articulating self and social structure', in K. Yardley and T. Honess (eds), *Self and Identity: Psychosocial Processes*, Wiley: Chichester.

Turner, R. and Billings, V. (1985), 'The social contexts of self-feeling', Paper presented at the American Sociological Association meetings, Washington, D.C.

Vaillant, G. E. (1974), 'Natural history of male psychological health. II. Some antecedents of healthy adult adjustment', *Archives of General Psychiatry*, 31(July), pp. 15–22.

Vaillant, G. E. (1977), *Adaptation to Life*, Little, Brown: Boston.

Weigert, A. J. (1983), 'Identity: Its emergence within sociological psychology', *Symbolic Interaction*, 6(Fall), pp. 183–206.

18 Identity changes as outcomes of work-role transitions

Michael West, Nigel Nicholson and John Arnold

Introduction

If careers are seen as journeys from entry to retirement, then researchers have devoted much time and effort to the study of starting points, destinations and the major routes. Far less attention has been paid to the connections that determine direction for each part of the journey. The events which together form the pattern of careers – work-role transitions – have received only limited attention. In particular, the effects on personality and identity of work-role transitions have been obscured in many cases as a consequence of the macroscopic view of the relationship between careers and identity.

Indeed it is only recently that social scientists have started to study systematically the influence of work roles upon people over time. Most industrial psychologists have been concerned with matching people and jobs – selecting candidates who are most qualified to perform a particular job or training employees to cope with job demands. A more recent emphasis has been on job design and how work requirements can be shaped to match employee needs and skills (Wall, 1982).

However, these matching approaches are being critically augmented by developmental views, studying how jobs affect people's personality and cognitions cumulatively over time (Kohn and Schooler, 1983; Gecas and Mortimer, Chapter 17). This approach is consistent with identity theory in social psychology, which would predict that the work roles we perform affect our perceptions of ourselves and our relation to others in the social world in fundamental ways (Stryker, 1981, 1987). Identity theory also proposes that commitment (how extensive and intensive are the social relations surrounding a role) impacts identity salience, which in turn impacts role performance (Stryker, 1981, 1987). Clearly, for most people this kind of commitment is found in their work roles, compelling relations with co-workers, supervisors, subordinates, customers, clients, etc. Identity salience is the hierarchical ordering of subidentities within the self according to how likely they are to be invoked in different situations. Role performance in Stryker's theory (Stryker, 1987) is the time spent in those activities. Thus 'identities motivate interactional performances whose function is to reaffirm, in interaction, that one is the kind of person defined by the identities'. Given the generally high degree of commitment entailed in work roles we can predict from the theory that the salience of one's work-role identity will be high and will therefore be powerfully influential upon identity and behaviour.

Until recently there was little empirical research to support the predictions of identity theory in relation to work roles. Research in the 1960s had shown correlations between aspects of personality and the characteristics of the jobs that people perform (Kornhauser, 1965; Kohn and Schooler, 1969). However, there was no way of sifting out cause from effect in this research. Did people move into jobs on the basis of their stable orientations, values and personalities, or were they socialised to grow and develop until they fitted the job requirements? Since that time a number of investigations have been conducted, confirming that both selection and socialisation processes are moulding the relationship between identity and work. Mortimer and Lorence (1979), using a sample of 435 male college students from shortly before graduation to ten years on, demonstrated a congruence of work values and the differing characteristics of job rewards and experiences. Specifically, they found that work autonomy (decision latitude, innovative thinking required by the job and job challenge) has positive effects on people-oriented values (desire to be helpful to society and to work with people rather than things) and on intrinsic occupational values (desire to exercise one's skills and abilities, to express one's personal interests and to be creative). Mortimer and Lorence concluded that their analysis provides convincing evidence that occupational autonomy has significant socialising effects on the self-concept during the early work career. Brousseau (1978) found that engineers, scientists and managers in a petroleum products company over a six-year period experienced increased levels of optimism, enthusiasm for taking on new projects, willingness to take risks and greater feelings of energy, vitality and general well-being to the extent that their jobs involved high task identity (performing 'whole' tasks from beginning to end) and high task significance (performing work perceived to have important consequences for others). Later analysis (Brousseau and Prince, 1981) showed that these job characteristics were positively associated with changes in general activity level, restraint, social ascendency and friendliness. Karasek (1979) also found that decision latitude affects well-being in a ten-year longitudinal study of the Swedish labour force, with increasing levels of emotional depression the longer people are in low decision-latitude jobs. But the most ambitious longitudinal research on this theme to date has been conducted at the National Institute of Mental Health, in Maryland. In a major programme of large-scale cross-sectional and ten-year longitudinal studies, plus a number of cross-cultural studies, using complex and rigorous modelling techniques, the research has demonstrated consistent and reciprocal causal relationships between identity and work (Kohn and Schooler, 1983). Jobs which involve complex work with people, data and things increase employees' intellectual flexibility and self-directedness (i.e. beliefs and values opposing fatalism, authoritarianism, conformity and self-deprecation, and favouring truthfulness and high standards of personal responsibility). They also found that high levels of intellectual flexibility predict future movement into more complex jobs and high self-directedness leads people towards jobs with greater freedom. The researchers also were able to demonstrate how ideational flexibility both positively affects and is positively affected by self-directedness, and how self-directedness negatively affects and is negatively affected by distress. These findings show how work experiences not only have effects on specific aspects of personality but can have broader effects on the structure of personality.

These longitudinal studies have taken us towards a more sophisticated understanding of the reciprocal relationship between people and jobs – and between identity and social structure (Stryker, 1981). But it could be argued that focusing on the long-term relationships between job characteristics and individual differences does not reveal the underlying dynamics of social process, and that these are most tellingly revealed at points of discontinuity and change (Nicholson, 1984).

Hall and Schneider's (1973) investigation of the career progression of priests and Becker *et al.*'s (1961) study of the socialisation of medical students demonstrated how powerfully transition can affect identity changes. A classic example of this transformation of identity is Lieberman's (1956) study of how attitudes change as a function of transition between the shop steward and foreman roles. Although early research on job change demonstrated that attitudes change as people switch roles, other writers have taken a longer and broader view, proposing that changing jobs is a first step towards new 'career subidentities' (Hall, 1971) or that they can shift the 'anchorage' of career values that predominate in people's choices and values (Schein, 1978). Research described earlier (Mortimer and Lorence, 1979; Kohn and Schooler, 1983; Brousseau, 1984) confirms the potential of work experiences to engender such identity change. Brett (1984) sees the stresses of transitions as potentially counteracting and inhibiting their developmental potential for the individual, particularly when they involve relocations that require major family adjustments. Approaches to the understanding of work-role transitions and their outcomes in terms of identity change are thus diverse, but it is only recently that comprehensive attempts to explain and predict the outcomes of work-role transitions have been offered (e.g. Brett, 1984; Schein, 1971; Nicholson, 1984).

Nicholson (1984), arguing from the basic premise that work-role transitions involve both personal change and (following Schein, 1971) role innovation, proposes that the outcomes of work-role transitions can be successfully predicted. Four extremes of outcomes of work-role transitions are conceived. An outcome in which there is a change in both the individual (personal change) and in the new role (role innovation) is labelled 'Exploration'; one in which change is primarily along the individual dimension is termed 'Absorption'; where only the role is markedly changed, the outcome is called 'Determination'; and 'Replication' is the term for the outcome in which neither person nor role is much changed following the work-role transition. Nicholson proposes that these outcome modes can be predicted from a knowledge of individual personality characteristics, prior occupational socialisation, present work-role characteristics and organisational culture. It is proposed that role requirements will influence the outcome of work-role transitions in the following ways: (i) high novelty of job demands (in the sense that the individual has to acquire new skills to meet them) is more likely to lead to absorption or exploration as outcomes; (ii) low novelty will favour replication or determination as outcome styles; (iii) discretion or freedom to alter the characteristics of the role will be more likely to lead to determination or exploration; (iv) low discretion or very little latitude to alter role characteristics will be more likely to produce replication or absorption patterns of outcome types. Integrating these predictions, the theory proposes four configurations of role characteristics and four associated outcomes (Figure 18.1).

Personality is incorporated into the theory as an important influence on the outcomes of work-role transitions. Nicholson argues that there are two contrasting clusters of personality characteristics which influence the outcomes of personal and role development. These are desire for feedback from and desire for control over the external environment (both social and non-social). It is argued that low need for feedback will influence outcomes in the direction of replication or determination. Low need for control would predispose towards outcomes of the replication or absorption types (Figure 18.1). Thus, low need for control and low need for feedback are linked with an outcome involving replication. Low need for control and high need for feedback are associated with absorption. Determination is a likely consequence of a high need for control and a low need for feedback, and finally exploration is the most likely outcome for the person who has a high need for both feedback and control (all other things being equal).

Research findings

The research we are conducting at the Social and Applied Psychology Unit at the University of Sheffield provides an opportunity to test a number of

Low discretion + low novelty → Low personal change + low role innovation

Low desire for control + low desire for feedback → Replication

Low discretion + high novelty → High personal change + low role innovation

Low desire for control + high desire for feedback → Absorption

High discretion + low novelty → Low personal change + high role innovation

High desire for control + low desire for feedback → Determination

High discretion + high novelty → High personal change + high role innovation

High desire for control + high desire for feedback → Exploration

FIGURE 18.1   *Job discretion and job novelty as determinants of adjustment modes*

predictions of the theory and, in particular, we are able to examine the relationship between role requirements, self-concept, motivational orientation and mode of adjustment. The study which provides most of the data described below was a questionnaire survey examining career development and work-role transitions. Initially, 4,000 questionnaires were distributed by mail from the University of Sheffield, accompanied by an explanatory letter and pre-paid return envelope, to a random sample of the 55,000-strong membership of the British Institute of Management. Because of the small proportion of women in the sample, a further mailing to all of the 775 females on the membership of the British Institute of Management was carried out. There were 1,882 respondents, of whom 412 were female. A further 422 female managers completed the questionnaires as a result of mailshots through other professional women's groups and contact with a businesswomen's magazine, providing a total sample of 2,304. The survey sought to gather biographical details of respondents, educational qualifications, occupational details, information about work preferences, life preferences, self-concepts (measured using bipolar adjective scales), career history and detailed information about respondents' last job change. Present work characteristics were also elicited from respondents, and details of performance appraisal and organisational career policies were gathered. (For further details see Alban-Metcalfe and Nicholson, 1984; Nicholson *et al.*, 1985; Nicholson and West, 1987; West *et al.*, 1987.)

Two further complementary longitudinal studies were undertaken as part of our research programme on work-role transitions and career development. These were undertaken to examine the magnitude, timing and types of personal change occurring in the year prior to graduation from university and in the immediately subsequent years. Measures of self-perceived abilities, emotional well-being and self-concept were used. The first of these studies was based on interviews with 173 1983 graduates and 144 1984 graduates. The interviews were conducted on three occasions: Winter 1982/83; Summer 1983; Winter 1983/84. The second study examined personal change amongst graduates in the first five years after graduation. Subjects were 146 graduates working in a multinational corporation who entered the organisation in the years 1978 to 1982. Interviews were conducted in Autumn 1982, Summer 1983 and Autumn 1983.

Job changes were defined in the major questionnaire survey as any move between jobs or any major alteration in the content of work duties or activities. The moves reported by respondents were classified as changes in function and/or changes in status and/or changes in employer. In relation to their last work-role transition respondents were asked to indicate whether adjusting to their new jobs had changed them in any way. They were asked to indicate change on each of four dimensions: values ('what is important to me in life'), attitudes ('the things I like and dislike'), career goals ('my plans about my future') and personality ('what sort of person I am').

The extent and pattern of personal change following transition were related to the type of transition involved. Changes in function did not appear to produce significant change in either the person or the way the role was performed. However, changes in employer were associated with self-reported changes in values, attitudes and career goals, though not in personality (Table 18.1). In contrast, changes in status were associated only with self-reported changes in personality and not with changes in attitudes, values and career goals (Table 18.1). One interpretation of this is that the individual who changes employers is more likely to perceive change in private aspects of the self (likes, dislikes, values and goals), whereas those who change their status perceive a more public transformation in identity as a consequence. Thus it might be argued that, whilst private aspects of the self-concept change in conjunction with changes in employer, transformations in social identity are the more likely consequence of status changes.

When people change employers their roles clearly change dramatically, since place of work, type of work and outside life are all likely to alter. If we use Heiss's (1981) definitions of roles: 'a set of expectations attached to a particular combination of actor–other identities ... and all the roles associated with one of the actor's identities is that identity's role set' (p. 95), it is clear that the employer-changer's role set is likely to alter

TABLE 18.1 *Reported personal and role changes following changes in employer and changes in status*

	Change in employer			Change in status		
	X^2	df	*p*	X^2	df	*p*
Values	14.4	4	<0.01	4.7	8	NS
Attitudes	10.3	4	<0.05	7.1	8	NS
Career goals	15.3	4	<0.01	11.4	8	NS
Personality	6.9	4	NS	31.4	8	<0.001
Innovation	4.2	2	NS	3.7	4	NS
Number	1,354			1,367		

NS = not significant

dramatically. The person will be surrounded by an entirely new set of working colleagues or, to use Turner's (1978) term, 'social circle'. Thus, whatever personal change takes place as a result of the role change is likely to be observed only by the individual herself or himself. However, when status changes but not employer changes constitute the work-role transition, the likelihood is that many role partners will remain the same – the social circle will be less dramatically altered. To a much greater extent, therefore, personal change will be subject to public observation. Personal change in this circumstance must also be influenced by the change in relationship between the role partners (in Heiss's sense) and the individual, occasioned by the latter's change in status. We would argue therefore that self-reported personality change following a status change is a consequence of a change in 'those aspects of the self located in the social ecology – the public or social self' (Allen and van de Vliert, 1984), or identity. On the other hand, attitudes, values and goals which are arguably private cognitions represent the global changes in self-concept which occur following a change in employer.

The distinction between public and private components of the self-concept system is not a new one. Turner (1984), following Gergen (1971), refers to social and personal identities. The former refers to self-descriptions consequent upon formal and informal group memberships like sex, nationality, occupation, race, etc. (status would therefore clearly represent a social identity rather than a personal identity). Personal identity refers to specific attributes of the individual such as feelings of competence, bodily characteristics, intellectual concerns, personal tastes and interests. The distinction is not seen by Turner as a hard and fast one and certainly the social determinants of personal identity are not denied. Turner argues that the main merit of the distinction 'is to recognise the simple fact that sometimes we seem to perceive ourselves primarily or solely in terms of our relevant group memberships rather than as differentiated unique persons:

social identity is sometimes able to function to the relative exclusion of personal identity' (p. 527). Turner suggests that the function of social identity is to produce group behaviour and attitudes and represents an example of the situational specificity of self-images (Gergen, 1971). This distinction also echoes the work of Mead (1934), who envisioned two aspects of self: the 'me', or the organised attitudes/expectations of others incorporated into the self; and the 'I', or the responses of the person to the organised attitudes of others.

An alternative explanation for the findings we report is that those who change employers are different in terms of self-concepts from those who change status, and that the differences reported above are related to these base-line differences. Analyses of variance revealed significant relationships between type of most recent move and reports of self-concept and work preferences. Those whose most recent move involved a change in employer tended to describe themselves as dominant, intellectual and sociable and reported lower work preferences for material rewards in the form of opportunities for high earnings and fringe benefits, higher preferences for congenial work colleagues and a desire for work to be in a suitable location and to fit in well with life outside work. Those whose most recent move involved a status change, on the other hand, described themselves as well adjusted and dominant and expressed strong needs to have opportunities for growth, development and achievement at work. They were less concerned than other respondents with their work being in a suitable location or with work fitting in well with their lives outside. However, when the effects of self-concepts and reported work preferences were controlled, the relationship between type of work-role transition and perceived personal change was sustained. Analyses of variance controlling for self-concepts and work preferences confirmed the pattern of self-reported change in values, attitudes and career goals following employer changes and self-reported personality change following status moves (Table 18.2). They also showed that reported personality change was associated with employer changes, and to a greater degree with status change (Table 18.2). When the relationship between the number of upward-status moves over the last five job changes and reported change in personality as a consequence of the most recent transition was examined, a similar pattern was found ($F = 3.61$; $p = <.01$). More upward-status shifts were associated with self-reports of personality change but not with self-reports of shifts in attitudes, values or career goals following the most recent work-role transition.

The two longitudinal studies of graduates confirmed the impact of role transitions indicated in the management survey. The first study revealed that the transition period of graduation was associated with a cessation of the steady increases in self-perceived abilities (such as thinking, dynamism and communication skills) which were characteristic of the pre-graduation

TABLE 18.2 *Analysis of covariance of personal change and type of work-role transition with self-concepts and work preferences as covariates*

Variable	Main effects and interactions	F	Significance of F
Change in attitudes	Employer	15.88	<0.001
	Status	5.34	0.005
	Function	0.04	NS
	Employer × status	8.07	<0.001
	Employer × function	5.45	<0.05
Change in values	Employer	20.61	<0.001
	Status	2.42	NS
	Function	0.74	NS
	Employer × status	3.50	<0.05
Change in career goals	Employer	14.52	<0.001
	Status	7.88	<0.001
	Function	4.84	<0.05
	Employer × status	8.79	<0.001
Change in personality	Employer	10.79	0.001
	Status	19.28	<0.001
	Function	0.79	NS
	Employer × status	0.02	<0.05
All personal change	Employer	23.48	<0.001
	Status	10.33	<0.001
	Function	1.76	NS
	Employer × status	7.19	0.001
	Employer × function	5.39	<0.05
	Status × function	0.91	NS

NS = not significant

period. The second study revealed significant decreases on measures of emotional well-being among graduates recruited in 1982 to the multinational corporation, while those who had been employed in 1978 and 1979 showed increases in emotional well-being over the period of study (1982 to 1983). The overall pattern suggested that the impact of the encounter with new roles and the development of new identities was associated with an initial decline and, following a period of accommodation, a recovery in emotional well-being between two and three years later.

We were also able to test the possibility that retrospective reports of personal change might not correspond to measured change over time in the studies of university graduates, using similar measures to those used in the study of British managers. Retrospective reports of change in personality were correlated with measured change over time in emotional well-being ($r = 0.19$) and self-perceived abilities ($r = 0.24$). Retrospective reports of change in attitudes and career goals were positively correlated with measured change in emotional well-being (0.19; 0.22) and work interests (0.18; 0.20).

To what extent are personal change and role innovation mediated by individual characteristics and role requirements? Those who reported high personal change indicated a high degree of anxiety before starting their new job. They also reported a high level of need for opportunities for growth and development at work and stressed a need for jobs to fit in well with life outside work (Tables 18.3 and 18.4). Those who perceived their new jobs as very different were more likely to report personal change as a consequence of the transition. They also perceived more freedom or discretion in their new jobs in comparison with their previous jobs, and described their working environments as less predictable than did those who reported low personal change (Figure 18.2). High personal change was also predicted when the transition involved an upward-status move. Finally, a belief that career opportunities in their organisations were influenced by organisational policies, luck, prejudice and impersonal decisions within the corporation (which might be interpreted as an external locus of career control) was associated with reports of personal change. Thus, the picture painted by these results is that novelty of job demands and discretion are together associated with higher levels of self-rated personal change, as predicted in Nicholson's theory.

The theory also predicted that role innovation would be most likely to occur where task novelty was low and discretion high. Respondents in the survey were asked to report the extent to which they did their present jobs differently from the person who did the job before them. They were asked to indicate degree of innovation in relation to four areas: setting work targets or objectives, deciding the methods to achieve objectives, deciding the order in which different parts of the job were to be done and choosing whom to deal with in order to carry out work duties. The results showed that role innovators were somewhat older and scored above average on dominance (self-concept) and need for growth and development (work preferences) and low on need for job predictability (work preferences) (Table 18.4 and Figure 18.2). Anxiety before the most recent transition was a negative predictor of role innovation. They were more likely to perceive career opportunities within their organisation as being influenced by external factors (e.g. luck, prejudice) and less likely to see career opportunities as influenced by individual performance. The perceived situational variables which predicted role innovation were high job discretion (but not job novelty) and a change in employer during the most recent transition (Figure 18.2).

In the longitudinal studies of university graduates we were able to show that self-reported dominance (on measures identical to those in the management survey) was a significant predictor of reports of role innovation one year later. This research also confirmed the relationship between perceived discretion and role innovation revealed in the management survey and thus provided some support in two important respects for

TABLE 18.3 *Individual and situational characteristics as predictors of attitude, value, career goal and personality change (statistics based on stepwise multiple regression analysis)*

Variable	Attitudes		Value		Career goal		Personality	
	Beta	Significance	Beta	Significance	Beta	Significance	Beta	Significance
Job discretion	NS		0.072	$p = 0.017$	NS		0.111	$p = 0.0003$
Job novelty	0.109	$p = 0.0003$	0.133	$p < 0.0001$	0.148	$p < 0.0001$	0.123	$p < 0.0001$
Job stress	0.084	$p = 0.005$	NS		NS		0.102	$p = 0.0008$
Job predictability	−0.117	$p = 0.0001$	−0.096	$p = 0.0016$	−0.104	$p = 0.0005$	−0.104	$p = 0.0006$
Upward status shift	NS		NS		NS		0.086	$p = 0.006$
External career influences	NS		NS		0.062	$p = 0.04$	0.072	$p = 0.015$
Adjustment (self-concept)	NS		NS		NS		−0.085	$p = 0.005$
Pre-transition anxiety	0.160	$p < 0.0001$	0.185	$p < 0.0001$	0.167	$p < 0.0001$	0.173	$p < 0.0001$
n Growth and development	0.094	$p = 0.0018$	0.072	$p = 0.015$	0.107	$p = 0.0003$	0.088	$p = 0.003$
n Environment	0.094	$p = 0.0017$	0.099	$p = 0.0009$	NS		0.100	$p = 0.0005$
r^2	0.093		0.095		0.123		0.168	
F	18.02		18.38		24.44		21.10	
Significance of F	<0.0001		<0.0001		<0.0001		<0.0001	

n = 1,452; NS = not significant

TABLE 18.4 *Individual and situational characteristics as predictors of personal change and role innovation (statistics based on stepwise multiple regression analysis)*

Variable	Personal change		Role innovation	
	Beta	Significance	Beta	Significance
Job discretion	0.090	$p < 0.01$	0.216	$p < 0.0001$
Job novelty	0.159	$p < 0.001$	NS	
Job predictability	−0.147	$p < 0.001$	NS	
Employer change	NS		0.081	$p < 0.01$
External career influences	0.069	$p < 0.05$	0.090	$p < 0.01$
Internal career influences	NS		−0.098	$p < 0.001$
Age	NS		0.100	$p < 0.001$
Dominance (self-concept)	NS		0.155	$p < 0.001$
Pre-transition anxiety	0.224	$p < 0.001$	−0.072	$p < 0.05$
n Predictability (work preferences)	NS		−0.090	$p < 0.01$
n Growth and development (work preferences)	0.106	$p = 0.001$	0.187	$p < 0.001$
n Environment (work preferences)	0.093	$p = 0.001$	NS	
r^2	0.167		0.153	
F	26.12		21.04	
Significance of F	$p < 0.001$		$p < 0.001$	

the management survey findings. Firstly, the studies confirm the relationship in a different sample of people of a somewhat different age group; and secondly they show that the relationship between self-reported dominance and innovation holds over time and is not limited to cross-sectional data.

Nicholson's theory receives some support from our findings in so far as patterns of personal change and role innovation following work-role transitions do appear to be systematically related to role requirements and personality. Figure 18.3 shows that both low job discretion and low job novelty in last transition are associated with low perceived personal change and low role innovation – the outcome labelled in the theory as Replication. Low discretion and high novelty are associated with higher personal change (Absorption). High discretion and low job novelty are associated with low personal change and high innovation (Determination). Finally, high novelty and discretion together are associated with the highest levels of personal and role change (Exploration). Thus the major predictions of the theory, as shown in Figure 18.2, are supported by these data.

Turning to the theory's predictions concerning motivational orientation and mode of adjustment, role innovators in the present study described themselves as forceful, confident, ambitious and controlling and expressed lower preferences than others for predictable working environments. Thus a high propensity to control and a relatively low desire for feedback were, as

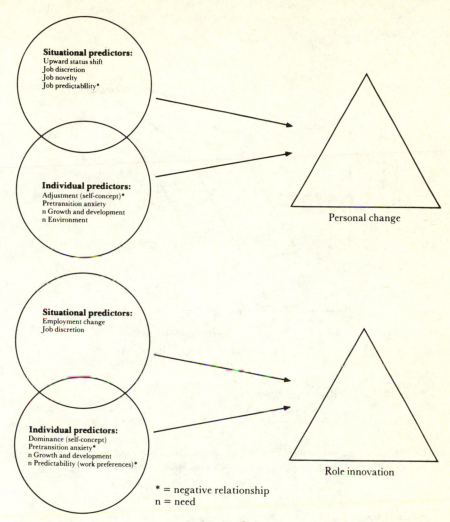

Situational predictors:
Upward status shift
Job discretion
Job novelty
Job predictability*

Individual predictors:
Adjustment (self-concept)*
Pretransition anxiety
n Growth and development
n Environment

Personal change

Situational predictors:
Employment change
Job discretion

Individual predictors:
Dominance (self-concept)
Pretransition anxiety*
n Growth and development
n Predictability (work preferences)*

Role innovation

* = negative relationship
n = need

FIGURE 18.2   *Situational and individual predictors of personal change and role innovation following work-role transitions*

the theory predicts, associated with innovation. The theory is less successful in its prediction of personality and motivational patterns amongst those reporting high personal change following work-role transitions. It may be argued, however, that the higher pre-transition anxiety reported by those perceiving personal change following transition is an indicator of desire for feedback. It is also interesting to note that those reporting personal change tended to describe their working environments as unpredictable, which may reflect as much an underlying motivational orientation of a high desire for feedback as a reflection of their work situation.

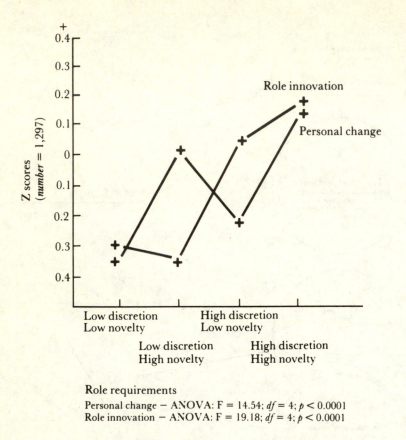

FIGURE 18.3   *The relationship between reported role requirements and degree of personal change and role innovation following work-role transition (standardised group means)*

Conclusions

One major criticism of the study reported here is that the results rely entirely on respondents' perceptions of work environments, job novelty, job discretion, role change and personal change. It might be, therefore, that the relationships we describe are a product of individual differences rather than interactions between objective role requirements, motivational orientations and other individual differences. Further research is therefore needed employing longitudinal designs and methodologies which utilise alternative methods of measuring the variables which are pivotal elements of the theory. The stability of the patterns of results across subgroups of age and sex does give grounds for optimism about the validity of the general conclusions.

As we achieve a more sophisticated understanding of the relationship between social structures, roles and the self, it becomes clearer that there is no simple causal directionality. The people who make particular types of work-role transitions describe themselves differently from those who make other kinds of job moves. They experience different patterns of change in their self-concepts consequent upon the transition. But undoubtedly, too, these people affect the social structures that influence their self-concepts, and they also affect their patterns of change differentially through role innovation (West, 1987). Mead (1934) argued that as society shapes the self, so does the self shape society through the I–Me dialectic. This theme is echoed, with more acknowledgment of the place of social structure, in Stryker's (1981) theorising on identity development: 'The person is shaped by interaction, but social structure shapes the interactions. Conversely, when persons creatively alter patterns of inter-action, ultimately social structures can change' (p. 23). Mortimer *et al.* (1982), on the basis of their results, assert that the relationship between self-concept and objective circumstances is dynamic. They argue that an individual's outlooks can become self-fulfilling prophecies of reciprocal relationships between personality and events through the life course. 'The individual actively creates the environmental context, both objective and subjective, which in turn feeds back on the personality, contributing to the subsequent development of the self image' (p. 304). This theme has been discussed at length by Gergen (1977), who argues for the unpredictability and indeterminacy of human development. He sees the individual's interpretation of life experience as critically formative: 'a given environ-mental condition has the capacity to stimulate virtually any symbolisa-tion. . . . And such symbolisation could dramatically influence the impacts of life experiences on the further course of development' (p. 151).

The findings discussed here provide support for Nicholson's theory as a framework within which to test the reciprocal relationship between the self and social structures by observing the personal change and role innovation consequent upon work-role transitions. The theory focuses on the points of discontinuity and change in the individual's development and advances both a set of predictions and, implicitly, a paradigm for testing the effects of transitions on people's lives and on organisational structures. A focus on work-role transitions also has important applications in everyday life, and this is now more widely acknowledged (cf. Allen and van de Vliert, 1984).

A greater understanding of the processes and outcomes of work-role transition promises useful contributions to understanding adult adjustment and development, organisational change and family adjustment. To return to the analogy of the journey, the choices we make at particular junctions can have lasting effects upon future directions, our attitudes to the journey and to the ways in which we are viewed both by ourselves and by our fellow travellers. The present research suggests that understanding of self and identity in adulthood can be considerably deepened by the study of the junctions which form the course and direction of the career journey.

References

Alban-Metcalfe, B. and Nicholson, N. (1984), *The Career Development of Male and Female British Managers*, British Institute of Management: London.

Allen, V. L. and van de Vliert, E. (1984), *Role Transitions, Explorations and Explanations*, Plenum Press: London.

Becker, H., Gear, B., Hughes, E. and Strauss, A. (1961), *Boys in White*, University of Chicago Press: Chicago.

Brett, J. M. (1984), 'Job transitions and personal and role development', in K. M. Rowland and G. R. Ferris (eds), *Research in Personnel and Human Resources Management, vol. 2*, JAI Press: London.

Brousseau, K. R. (1978), 'Personality and job experience', *Organizational Behavior and Human Performance*, 22, pp. 235–52.

Brousseau, K. R. (1984), 'Job–person dynamics and career development', in K. M. Rowland and G. R. Ferris (eds), *Research in Personnel and Human Resources Management, 2*, JAI Press: London.

Brousseau, K. R. and Prince, J. B. (1981), 'Job–person dynamics: An extension of longitudinal research', *Journal of Applied Psychology*, 66, pp. 59–62.

Gergen, K. J. (1971), *The Concept of Self*, Holt, Rinehart & Winston: New York.

Gergen, K. J. (1977), 'Stability, change, and chance in understanding human development', in N. Datan and H. W. Reese (eds), *Life-Span Developmental Psychology: Dialectical Perspectives on Experimental Research*, Academic Press: New York.

Hall, D. T. (1971), 'A theoretical model of career subidentity development in organizational settings', *Organizational Behavior and Human Performance*, 6, pp. 50–76.

Hall, D. T. and Schneider, B. (1973), *Organizational Climates and Careers: The Work Lives of Priests*, Seminar Press: New York.

Heiss, J. (1981), 'Social roles', in M. Rosenberg and R. H. Turner, *Social Psychology: Sociological Perspectives*, Basic Books: New York.

Karasek, R. A. (1979), 'Job demands, job decision latitude, and mental strain: Implications for job redesign', *Administrative Science Quarterly*, 24, pp. 285–306.

Kohn, M. L. and Schooler, C. (1969), 'Class, occupation, and orientation', *American Sociological Review*, 34, pp. 659–78.

Kohn, M. L. and Schooler, C. (1983), *Work and Personality*, Ablex: Norwood, N.J.

Kornhauser, A. (1965), *Mental Health of the Industrial Worker*, Wiley: New York.

Lieberman, S. G. (1956), 'The effects of changes in roles on the attitudes of role occupants', *Human Relations*, 9, pp. 467–86.

Mead, G. H. (1934), *Mind, Self and Society*, University of Chicago Press: Chicago.

Mortimer, J. T., Finch, M. D. and Kumka, D. (1982), 'Persistence and change in development: The multidimensional self-concept', in P. B. Baltes and O. G. Brim (eds), *Life-Span Development and Behavior*, vol. 4, Academic Press: London.

Mortimer, J. T. and Lorence, J. (1979), 'Work experience and occupational value socialization: A longitudinal study', *American Journal of Sociology*, 84, pp. 1361–85.

Nicholson, N. (1984), 'A theory of work role transitions', *Administrative Science Quarterly*, 29, pp. 172–91.

Nicholson, N. and West, M. A. (1987). *Managerial Job Change: Men and Women in Transition*, Cambridge University Press: Cambridge.

Nicholson, N., West, M. A. and Cawsey, T. F. (1986), 'Future uncertain: Expected vs. attained job mobility among managers', *Journal of Occupational Psychology*, 58, pp. 313–320.

Schein, E. H. (1971), 'Occupational socialization in the professions: The case of the role innovator', *Journal of Psychiatric Research*, 8, pp. 521–30.

Schein, E. H. (1978), *Career Dynamics*, Addison-Wesley: Reading, Mass.

Stryker, S. (1981), 'Symbolic interactionism: Themes and variations', in M. Rosenberg and R. H. Turner (eds), *Social Psychology: Sociological Perspectives*, Basic Books: New York.

Stryker, S. (1987), 'Identity theory: Developments and extensions', in K. Yardley and T. Honess (eds), *Self and Identity: Psychosocial Processes*, Wiley: Chichester.

Turner, J. C. (1984), 'Social identification and psychological group formation', in H. Tajfel (ed.), *The Social Dimension*, vol. 2, Cambridge University Press: Cambridge.

Turner, R. H. (1978), 'The role and the person', *American Journal of Sociology*, 84, pp. 1–23.

Wall, T. D. (1982), 'Perspectives on job redesign', in J. W. Kelly and C. W. Clegg (eds), *Autonomy and Control at the Workplace: Contexts for Job Redesign*, Croom Helm: London.

West, M. A. (1987), 'Innovation in the world of work', *British Journal of Social Psychology*, in press.

West, M. A., Nicholson, N. and Rees, A. (1987), 'Transitions into newly created jobs', *Journal of Occupational Psychology*, in press.

19 Identity and its development in adulthood

Sheila Rossan
In memory of Anne Murry

The theoretical framework

Much of the research purporting to investigate identity is on self-esteem (see, for example, Webster and Sobieszek, 1974; Wylie, 1979), although self-esteem appears to be a minor component of the spontaneous self-concept (McGuire and Padawer-Singer, 1976). Perhaps it is investigated so frequently because it is relatively easy to assess, compared with assessing changes in the content of identity, particularly changes of a complex nature. Why are multifaceted, complicated changes in identity rarely investigated? It may be that there is no generally accepted theory about its structure. This chapter addresses itself to just this issue: What is identity? How can it be envisaged in a way that is meaningful to researchers? Although the research reported here is concerned with changes for women during pregnancy and early motherhood, the period chosen is less crucial than the development of the theory itself. Why this particular time-span was chosen is clarified later in the chapter.

Identity, as used herein, is defined as the set of complex, more-or-less integrated attitudes which the individual has concerning him/herself. It is hypothesised that it has three principal components: subidentities, generalised traits and a core.

The first of these, subidentities, arise as a result of role enactments and are tied to positions held in the social structure (Miller, 1963; Stryker, 1968). An illustration of this is 'I am a wife' or 'I am a loving wife'. Hypothesising the existence of a number of different subidentities allows for changes to occur in different contexts and at different times of life, without negating the sense of continuity which arises from other components, to be discussed below. Subidentities are particularly meaningful to the individual when the position has specified role partners (McCall and Simmons, 1966). 'Father' is usually a more salient construct than 'member of the middle class', since 'father' requires 'son' or 'daughter' for interactions, whereas 'member of the middle class' does not imply intimate interaction with a

304

designated partner. The most important role partners, as described by the women in our research, are included in Figure 19.1. For these women, at least, the number of 'significant others' is relatively small: the marital partner, friends, own child, parents and parents-in-law, other kin and regular contacts at work.

The second component, generalised traits, are characteristics the individual attributes to him/herself because they are common to many role enactments, or are related to a particularly salient subidentity. 'I am intelligent', 'I am usually a happy person' and 'I am good with my hands' are illustrations.

The third set, the core, includes the most generalised, salient attributes: it is the fundamental sense of self. It probably begins early in life, long before the individual can manipulate symbols in a conscious, controlled fashion. It may include attributes that are only partly in awareness. 'I am a woman' or 'I am Catholic' are core attributes. With the passage to adulthood, women who adopt the pervasive, long-lasting roles of wife and mother, it is argued, add many elements from these roles, including the labels, to their core sense of self.

Each of these three categories may include: (1) identificatory tags, such as names ('Robert', 'Honeybun', 'Titch'), which serve to accentuate the uniqueness of the individual or of a particular relationship; (2) qualities, traits and competencies ('helpful', 'proud', 'articulate'); (3) bodily images ('I am too fat', 'I am tired all the time', 'I don't have enough milk to breastfeed'). Note that many of these terms include an evaluative component which, when all of these are summed, provides an overall self-evaluation, or index of self-esteem. Using this model, however, permits not only global evaluations to be made, but also evaluations based on generalised qualities, on traits associated with specific subidentities and on the subidentities themselves. Note also that the model allows for contradictory attributes in the generalised identity. In Figure 19.1, for example, the woman sees herself as warm as a wife and mother, but cool as a daughter-in-law. As a typist, the trait does not appear at all.

Subidentities and the characteristics associated with them are likely to change most frequently, generalised attributes less so, and core elements least of all. The core itself does change, however, as new elements are added to it, which necessitate its reorganisation. It is unlikely that elements are ever eliminated from the core. It is probably elements of the core, and to some extent generalised traits, that contribute heavily to a person's sense of self-continuity.

In the theory presented here, it is suggested that many forces affect identity, and that major changes occur as a result of experiences in adulthood as well as in childhood. Although their work derives from a different tradition, the conclusions of Kreitler and Kreitler (Chapter 21) support this contention. Most theories of influences on identity are limiting

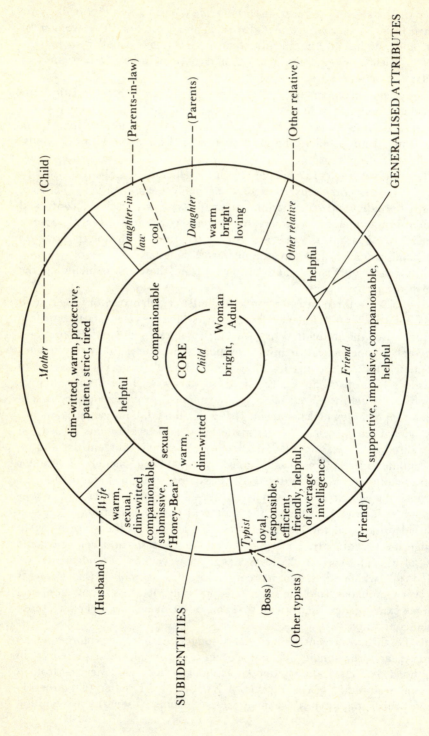

FIGURE 19.1   *The structure of identity*

and, in any case, seem most relevant to development during childhood (Gecas, 1982). Seven sources of adult identity discussed in this chapter are: reflected appraisals, the outcome of role negotiations, social comparison, the setting of and reacting to personal standards, interpretations of bodily changes, cognitive complexity and, naturally, the current identity. Some of these arise directly from intimate social interaction; others do not require such interaction, although they may take place in social contexts.

Most theorists of identity, beginning with Cooley (1964) and Mead (1934) have discussed reflected appraisals as an important source of information about oneself. In interaction, a participant behaves in ways that communicate his or her attitudes about the other to him or her. The other, it is assumed, internalises these communicated attitudes and responds to self as others have responded in the past. A young child, for example, labels himself a 'good boy' when he does something for which significant others have rewarded him in the past. Theorists assume that meanings are shared to the extent that such meanings are identical. This may not be so. It may be that some meanings shared by participants are identical, and others are not. It may also be true that meanings are only partly shared. It is rare to find investigators (see, for example, Felson, 1981a, 1981b) who distinguish empirically between the message intended by the actor, the 'objective' communication, if you like, and the message received by the partner, the 'subjective' communication (Miller, 1963). Observers of social interaction agree that much social behaviour is ambiguous, and the meaning attached to it depends not only on the intentions of the actor as expressed in the action, but also on the context in which the action occurs, the past history of the participants with each other, the past experiences in general of the receiver and his or her current emotional and motivational states. Lopata (1980) adds another reason. She states that a communication may be received differently from its intended meaning, or even ignored, because the meaning is not compatible with the receiver's current sense of self. Not only is the interpretation important, so are the feelings associated with it.

A husband, for example, may tell his wife that he likes the way she looks, now that she is eight months pregnant, because she looks so feminine. His wife may feel pleased that her spouse likes her current shape. Or she may be pleased that he is pleased, but not certain that she wants to look feminine. Or she may wonder why he likes her fat, rather than slender. Or she may be unhappy that he prefers her temporary body shape to her permanent one. Or she may be angry that he likes her manifesting an aspect of woman's traditional role, rather than her more usual competent role in a masculine milieu. Or she may not care what he thinks of her temporary shape, so long as he likes her permanent one as well. Or she may ignore the communication, because she does not care what he thinks. She may even incorporate some elements from more than one of these interpretations into her self-image. It is evident that the interpretations of what, at first glance, would appear to be objectively complimentary to his wife (whatever were his own intentions) are varied, depending on factors other than, or in addition to, what her husband meant to communicate. Each of these interpretations is likely to affect identity differently. If we are to understand the impact of reflected appraisals on the development of identity, we must recognise not only the receiver's interpretations of the communication, which may not be identical with the sender's intentions in the communication, but also the feelings associated with it. In our own research, we asked how other people important to the respondent acted – what they did and said – and also how these made her feel, and how she reacted to these actions of significant others.

A second variable influencing identity is an important one, not much discussed or investigated, which takes as its model an active, potent, controlling human being. A person has expectations, which she or he tries to enforce, about how both self and role partner are to think, act and feel. The partner has expectations about own and the other's behaviour as well. The partners must negotiate together the appropriate overt and covert behaviours for both of them. As these patterns are legitimised and habitualised, the person comes to view him/herself in terms of the qualities and evaluations inferred from these actions. 'Thus, the actor chooses the personage he or she will become at each choice-point in an activity sequence' (Alexander and Wiley, 1981, p. 288). It is possible for different individuals to infer different qualities and evaluations from the same set of habitualised behaviours, and also for the same qualities and attributes to be inferred from radically different conduct. We need to investigate these processes of selective inferences, if we are to understand in what directions, and how, change occurs in images of self. Additionally, because the negotiations differ depending on the context, expectations and partner, different attributes may be relevant for different subidentities. Being sexual, for example, is inappropriate in an employer–employee relationship and is not likely to be part of the occupational subidentity. The traits of 'companionable' and 'helpful' may be part of many subidentities and hence be part of the generalised sense of self (see Figure 19.1). Being sexual, however, is a generalised quality because of its salience in the marital subidentity (and probably also because of its relevance in earlier heterosexual relationships), not because of its prevalence in many current subidentities.

Subidentities may change. Strauss (1977, p. 37) states that 'involvements are evolvements', suggesting that some aspects of intimate relations may be negotiated and renegotiated, leading to changes in subidentities as role enactments change. Our own data reveal the striking extent to which marital, filial, occupational and friend subidentities change as a result of the birth of the first child.

The remaining categories of influences: social comparison, setting standards, bodily changes, cognitive complexity and current identity are not so closely tied to intensive interaction as those already described. They may take place in social contexts or even be influenced by interaction, but the latter is not part and parcel of their influence.

The first of these is the influence of comparing one's own conduct with that of others (Festinger, 1954; Gergen, 1971, 1977; Rosenberg and Kaplan, 1982). Gecas and Mortimer (Chapter 17) refer to the importance of comparing oneself with others in order to evaluate oneself. The processes of social comparison have greater impact than on self-esteem alone. One sees others more or less like oneself doing things, expressing values and feelings which can be compared with one's own styles and reactions. On the basis of many such observations, one learns about the typicality of one's own behaviours, sees new actions to try, watches the reactions of others to these as-yet-untested actions, evaluates a variety of ways of doing, perceiving, feeling which are not yet, but which have the potential to become, a part of one's own repertory of competencies and expressions. These comparisons allow one to evaluate one's own (and one's partners') current states, but they also suggest the possibility of change and the directions these changes could take, any of which could reinforce or alter identity. Psychological research on the use of models ought to be pertinent to an understanding of this variable. As Rosenberg (1973) points out, however, questions such as how one decides which aspects of another's behaviour to select have yet to be addressed.

Another set of influences is subsumed under the heading of meeting one's own standards and includes the recognition of success and failure, meeting moral standards and acquiring skills and abilities (Coopersmith, 1968; Gecas and Mortimer, Chapter 17; Mortimer *et al.*, 1982). All of them entail the individual setting standards, then comparing the outcome with the original goals. Issues of competence and autonomy, as well as feelings of success, failure, pride and guilt, result from the establishment of these standards and the assessment of performance based upon them. Although other people may be important in the establishment of standards and the evaluation of performance, they are not essential. Whatever one's friends say, one still knows whether or not one's own goals have been met. Other people may be important in helping one to set standards and to learn appropriate behaviours, particularly when one adopts new roles. Most of the women in our sample, who had little direct experience of caring for children, sought out ways of learning maternal behaviours and maternal standards. Not only did they speak with women they knew who had children, such as mothers, sisters and friends, but they also read books on child care, attended mothercraft classes or watched relevant television programmes. They were also absorbed in watching strangers with children. One woman said, 'I tend to think about it [being a mother] more when I see other people who are pregnant or who have babies. I wonder how I will compare with them'.

Yet another important influence on identity is one's interpretations of the physical and physiological changes occurring at various points in life. Theorists (*i.a.* Erikson, 1968) recognise the tremendous impact that changes in bodily shape and physiological functioning have on adolescent identity. There are anatomical and physiological developments during adulthood as well (Rossi, 1980): changes in shape, weight, texture of skin and hair, amount of bodily hair, athletic and sexual abilities, and length and types of illnesses. Premenstrual tension and male and female menopause are recognised syndromes, yet there is little discussion of changes in image of the body as they relate to changes in image of self generally. Pregnancy, childbirth and parenting affect the body and its functioning, thereby changing images of the body, which can affect identity specifically and generally, specifically by affecting the contents of one or more subidentities, and generally by bringing about changes in generalised attributes, global self-esteem and the 'core'.

An important intrapersonal factor affecting identity is the cognitive complexity or cognitive style of the person. People may think about themselves in different ways. They may be able to tolerate more or less ambiguity in their identities. They may be happy to recognise contradictory traits in themselves, or they may strive towards cognitive consistency. They may have many or few elements in their self-vocabularies. They may be able to describe themselves using words that shade into subtle nuances or only be able to describe themselves in black and white. They may have given long and considered thought to their self-images, or they may rarely think about themselves. In listening to the women of our sample, it was clear that their linguistic styles differed, and that because of this we gained different impressions of them.

One's current identity affects one's future identity. Current identity may help to determine the roles to which one aspires (Backman and Secord, 1968), the kinds of negotiations about roles into which one enters, as well as the outcome of such negotiations, may influence the interpretations of the appraisals of others and one's feelings about these appraisals, may determine the objects of comparison chosen as an interested bystander as well as the elements chosen, may function as one source of standards (Mortimer *et al.*, 1982) and probably affects the salience and meaning of changes in bodily status and functioning.

Major changes in identity, then, may result from changes in significant others, in roles, in social settings that permit different bystander observations, in experiences of success and failure as a result of setting standards and in the body and its functioning. It is clear that all of these conditions obtain for women who become pregnant for the first time. It thus seemed an appropriate period to study, when many of the factors affecting identity are in flux.

The research design

The sample consists of forty Caucasian women, pregnant for the first time, drawn from two teaching and three non-teaching hospitals in the London area. Approximately half of the women come from the middle class; half from the working class. The aims of the major study are to describe the changes in the women and their babies, to characterise their developing relationships and to assess their babies' achievements. To this end, the women were interviewed, the mothers and babies were videotaped, the babies were tested, and data were collected from hospital records and from nurses who cared for the newborn babies. The data presented in this chapter come from the interviews with the mothers. They were interviewed six times during a span of eighteen months: once each during the second and third trimesters of pregnancy, shortly after the birth of the baby, usually on the fourth day postnatally, and then again when the baby was 3, 6 and 12 months of age. The women were asked questions about their pregnancy, how they spent their time, their most important relationships, their work and, following labour, their baby. Each question was phrased generally, but was followed by a series of probe questions, should the women not volunteer the required information. Each interview consisted of between twenty-two and twenty-six principal questions. The same questions, when appropriate, were asked at each interview. In addition, at each interview the women were asked how they and their lives had changed since the last time they had been seen. Change in the women's identities could be assessed in two ways: by comparing their answers from one interview to the next, and by using their own responses to the questions concerning change. Only one investigator collected all of the data from any one family, so that adequate rapport was established and maintained throughout the period of the study. Each interview lasted, on average, two to three hours. By the end of the project, we had collected transcripts of the women talking for twelve to fifteen hours about themselves and their lives.

An illustrative case

Before proceeding to a discussion of our general findings, we present, by way of illustration, a summary of our interviews with 'Margaret'. Given the space limitations, we focus here on her final interview. (More detailed case reports are available from the author.)

At the final interview, when Chris, her son, is 12 months old, Tony, her husband, has just returned from being hospitalised for three weeks for an injury. Margaret feels well physically but is putting on weight (part of her perennial struggle) because of the worries stemming from Tony's hospitalisation. She says she is exhausted by dinner time. This was also a feature of the previous interview, feeling 'drained' at the end of the day. She has taken up knitting to help her to relax. She is less 'weepy' than she was six months ago, except for the last three weeks since Tony's accident.

As a wife, she feels much more affiliative towards Tony. They are interdependent, and share activities, feelings and decisions. She feels closer to him now than previously: 'We have Chris in common'. She also feels that Tony is more responsible than previously, so she is less demanding of him.

She identifies strongly with her son, Chris. She noticed that he was particularly naughty when Tony was in hospital, so she became more permissive and affectionate with him during this time. She still plays with him and tries to keep him amused and takes him outside most afternoons. She loves playing with and bathing him, as earlier. She takes great delight in his antics. She anticipated eagerly his learning to walk, and now that he does, 'he's much more interesting and much more fun'. She characterises him as being very active and very sociable: he loves attention and prefers to play with people rather than toys.

Margaret also describes Chris as 'a handful', 'cheeky', 'crafty'. 'I feel ready to crack sometimes, so I leave Chris for five minutes, but he looks so forlorn that I melt and give him a cuddle.' She also empathises with him when he cries. The battles she now has with Chris make her impatient and angry – she does not like being defied. She is still particularly focused on his food and is strict in this area. If he does not like the foods she prepares, he is given nothing else.

She loves being a mother but finds it hard work, harder than she had originally anticipated. She still lacks some confidence, wondering whether she is 'doing the right thing'. But she is more confident than in earlier interviews. Her worries now centre less on her own abilities and more on Chris's (long-distant) future – whether he will be clever, have 'nice ways', whether he will marry and what kind of job he will have. She does not want to return to work in the foreseeable future: she feels a strong obligation to stay at home to care for Chris (and future children). 'It is important for the mother to be at home for the first five years.'

As a daughter, she has drawn closer to her mother. She now sees her daily. Her mother continues to be a source of support for her, providing practical and emotional assistance: 'She calms me down'. She feels able to accept her dependency on her mother in a 'mature' way. She discusses Chris and her problems with her mother-in-law as well, but feels closer to her own mother.

Her sociability, although invested to a greater extent in her mother than previously, has lessened towards friends, particularly if going out with them as a couple, rather than as a family. She and Tony now go out only fortnightly. She says she is too tired to dress up and put on make-up. 'I've become a fuddy-duddy.' Generally, she describes her life as more tiring, more chaotic. Yet she describes both herself and Tony as being more organised, less free and impulsive, more responsible and mature and more homebound.

From her own words, we can also see that, compared with eighteen months ago, her figure is less youthful, she suffers from chronic fatigue and she is frequently tense. As a wife, she is highly affiliative and shares most things with her spouse, including, quite importantly, their first child. Their social activities have altered radically: they go out as a couple much less frequently; they engage in more single-sexed social activities; they spend more time in family activities, both with their son and also with their own parents.

Her fantasies concerning what it would be like to have a baby are quite different from the reality she ultimately meets. Instead of a quiet, non-crying, self-sufficient baby, she finds an active, attention-seeking, rebellious, 'crafty' child. He offers her many maternal gratifications, however. As a mother, she is exceptionally warm, attention-giving, sociable, nurturant, empathic, although strict in specialised areas. Her lack of confidence in her abilities at the beginning of motherhood have lessened, but she is not nearly so assured of her maternal skills as are some other mothers. Her determination, expressed in the first interview, that a child would not dominate her life, that she would not devote her whole life to her child, has vanished in the presence of that child. What she has done, quite successfully it seems, is to integrate the child into her life as much as she could, while at the same time having to forgo, quite regretfully, many satisfying activities.

As a daughter, she has drawn closer to a mother to whom she was already highly affiliative. By the final interview, she is able to draw on her mother's skills and assistance in a way that she herself said she could not do earlier.

General findings

The analysis of all the interviews is still in its early stages, so that the following discussion is only the beginnings of elaboration of the issues. It is presented in order to show how the model can be used to explore changes and constancies in identity.

Some of the most profound changes for women in this sample are related to the introduction of a new temporary subidentity of 'pregnant woman' and that of 'future mother', which transforms later into 'mother'. All of the women recognise that being pregnant and, later, being a mother has had major consequences for them. Some of these changes can be seen as indications of increased maturity, as Handel (see Chapter 20) found among the respondents in his sample. All of the women, for example, talk about how the 'responsibility hits you' once the child is born. Some even talk of the 'looming responsibility' during pregnancy. They discuss the immediacy of their babies' needs, and how they themselves have become more patient, more interested in other children, more organised and may feel more 'adult'. Many other changes are not seen to be so advantageous. The women describe how they feel more tied to the home than previously, and many are more lonely than when they were childless. Like the women in LaRossa and LaRossa's sample (1981), these women have less free time than they did previously. They mention that, compared with pre-pregnant days, they are always tired, 'scruffier', occasionally with a more matronly (and less sexy) figure, suffering from more aches and pains and less able to play sports. Their sexual activities, and frequently interest, have declined, although a few report sensuous feelings arising from breastfeeding or touching their babies' skins and, rarely, from the physical intimacy of husband, self and baby as a trio, for example, when the baby is brought into the marital bed for an early-morning, three-way playtime.

The adoption of the maternal role has an impact on other relationships and, consequently, subidentities. All of the mothers discuss how their marriages have changed. As Osofsky and Osofsky note (1984, p. 384), 'they experience important shifts in themselves and their relationship with one another; few, if any, individuals are the same afterward as they were before'. Following the birth of the baby, activities which were formerly pursued as a couple are now pursued singly or as a triad. They spend less time with their husbands than they did as a couple, not only because of the babies' demands on the mothers' time, but also because one partner babysits while the other shops, meets other familial responsibilities or socialises. Hence, activities once shared by husband and wife outside the home are now performed singly. Other formerly dyadic activities become triadic. Meeting relatives and friends, particularly when it occurs indoors, some shopping trips and taking holidays are the kinds of activities in which the family, rather than the couple, engage.

There is also a shift in the focus of the marriage. Many of the mothers comment that their discussions with their husbands are almost exclusively concerning the baby, particularly during the first six months of new parenthood, and that they spend little time alone with their partners. The latter complaint is evident throughout the entire year following the birth. Many of these changes begin some time during the pregnancy when, because of illness or fatigue, the women begin to decrease the number of out-of-home activities, to shift tasks to their partners and to decrease sexual activity. Perhaps it is because of changes such as these that many investigators (for example, Belsky *et al.*, 1985; Entwisle and Doering, 1981; Miller and Sollie, 1980) find a significant decline in reported quality of the marital relationship among new parents.

Relations with friends change as well. Women tend to seek out as friends other women with small babies, and sometimes see childless friends less frequently than they used to do. The process seems to begin during pregnancy, when friends who have not been pregnant are thought to be sated quickly by comments on pregnancy, childbirth and their attendant issues. Once the babies are born, they are quickly integrated into the women's circles of friends (principally those who also have children): the babies are taken to friends' houses in baskets or carry-cots; friends with children bring them to play with or see the newborn; friends' children ask questions about the progress or state of the babies; friends provide advice, used clothing and toys and are called upon in emergencies as babysitters. Discussions with friends focus on children, and the new mothers state how they used to be uninterested in such issues, and how unsympathetic they were to the problems of friends with children. The subidentity of 'friend' includes fewer references to 'out for a good time' and 'with them for a laugh' and more to 'helpful', 'supportive' and 'caring'. Many of these women meet other mothers whilst they are in hospital, at 'well baby' clinics or just as they push their prams in the neighbourhood. Such friendships rarely extend beyond daytime meetings, so that the husbands are frequently excluded from sharing in these new friendships, although the wives may discuss these new-found friends with their spouses. As a consequence, adopting the role of mother affects the role of friend, which has repercussions for the role of wife.

For many women, being a daughter is different following pregnancy and motherhood (Ballou, 1978). The most extreme comment noted so far in the interviews is 'Now we have something to talk about'. It does seem that the common experiences of pregnancy, childbirth and caring for a child increases the range of sharing that it possible between generations. 'Now I understand her [my own mother]' is a frequent realisation of these women. The filial subidentity seems to undergo changes in the direction of feeling more adult and equal in the company of parents, being more empathic to the conditions experienced by one's own mother and changes in the feelings of autonomy. The changes in autonomy are quite complex. In some ways, some of the women feel more independent of their parents, now that they have families of their own. In other ways, some feel more dependent on their parents or parents-in-law, particularly for advice, financial assistance, help with babysitting and child care. For some of the women, this increased dependence seems to affect adversely their own sense of autonomy, confidence and self-esteem. For other women in the sample, their sense of independence, competence and confidence increases: they view the help proffered differently than they did earlier in their lives, and feel their parents offer it to them in a way that allows the women themselves to control what is received and what is ignored or rejected.

A major change also occurred in the women in our sample, in that all of them stopped working, and almost all of them intend to stay out of the labour market until the last-born child starts school, a span of perhaps ten years for some of them. Many of them, even those in the professions, found, rather unexpectedly, that their occupational subidentities were no longer important to them. Few of them maintained friendships with colleagues from work, and even fewer visited their former places of work more than once. Only three had returned to part-time work during the study. One, a hairdresser, began to accept a small number of clients willing to come to her home. She dressed hair whilst her baby slept, but rarely worked more than eight hours a week. The second, a typist, began to work part time at home when her baby was 12 months old but only worked a few hours a week. The third, a scientist, returned to work at three months postnatally but had quit five months later. Her decision was made only after considerable thought and extended discussions with others. It was her involvement with her baby and the intensity of domestic life that decided her to leave. By the twelve-month interview, she was quite firm that she would not return to work in the foreseeable future. Most women echoed the comment: 'Being a Mum is much more fulfilling than working'. A surprising number of women – more than one-third – also reported feelings of guilt, ambivalence or unhappiness at any time taken away from nurturing their babies. We tentatively conclude from these reports that they experience mothering as occupying twenty-four hours a day.

The decision to remove themselves from full-time and part-time employment was surprising to us, given the reports that women do not enjoy being housewives (Gavron, 1975; Oakley, 1974) and given the current concerns within society for equal employment opportunities for women. In a study of women doctors, Mandelbaum (1981) reports that women in full-time work must sometimes place a higher priority on their occupational activities than on the needs of their children. From their comments, the women of our sample would have difficulty doing so. A review of studies conducted in Great Britain and the United States (Warr and Parry, 1982) finds a positive association between women working and their psychological health, except for one category of women, for whom the association does not obtain. For women like those in our sample, wives with children, there is no significant correlation between whether or not the women are in paid employment and their psychological well-being or satisfaction with life.

In an attempt to assess standards and values, women were asked at each interview for their views of the ideal mother and, once they were mothers themselves, how well they measured up to their ideals. Many changes took place between the time of the first and final interviews, a period of eighteen months. In the first interview, women relate their ideal image to their own mothers, occasionally mothers-in-law or older sisters, wanting to be either like them or different from them. As their mothers' role partners, they have themselves in mind, as adolescents or young adults, and the qualities they discuss are those suited to mothers of grown-up daughters: tolerance, encouragement of independent thought and getting on well with her children. By the final interview, the new mothers have quite different ideal images, implicitly seeing their partner as a baby. Two common comments are 'I don't reckon they [ideal mothers] exist' and 'the patience of a saint'. Hence, with the introduction of a child into the household, the women's frame of reference alters drastically. Most of the women believe they are managing fairly well, and the number of positive comments they make about themselves increases with time. The data show clearly that the first three months is the most difficult time to see oneself as a 'good mother'. The women incorporate 'progress reports' into their standards, by which they judge their current behaviour on the basis of how well they have done before. The behaviours of their babies have a profound impact on how they judge themselves. Those who have 'easy' babies, who sleep and eat well and who are responsive to their mothers' ministrations, see themselves in a more positive fashion than do those mothers who have 'difficult' babies, who have problems in establishing routines and who are not so responsive to what their mothers do for them.

Even with such a sketchy description of the data, it can be seen that major changes in identity result from changes in these women's lives. The new mother is faced with a baby for whom she has principal responsibility (LaRossa and LaRossa, 1981). In many ways the role negotiations of this relationship are quite different from all others: the partner, a newborn baby, cannot negotiate in the way that adults do, nor does a mother usually impute sophisticated beliefs, intentions and self-control to her new role partner. Yet, she does regularise her actions with the baby, and by so doing takes on new actions, attitudes and feelings, which she will incorporate into her new subidentity.

In summary, the pregnant woman, and subsequently the new mother, can be seen to compare herself with others, and may change her actions and self-attributions as a result. Her body and its functioning change, and she cannot and does not ignore these in her picture of herself. In addition, her standards can be seen to change, as do the form of her relations with many significant others. Finally, the typical woman, in our sample, loses, not too regretfully, her occupational subidentity. Such profound changes make the period an especially interesting one for exploring the different facets of the identity theory introduced here.

References

Alexander, C. and Wiley, M. (1981), 'Situated activity and identity formation', in M. Rosenberg and R. Turner (eds), *Social Psychology: Sociological Perspectives*, Basic Books: New York.

Backman, C. and Secord, P. (1968), 'The self and role selection', in C.

Gordon and K. Gergen (eds), *The Self in Social Interaction*, vol. 1, Wiley: London.

Ballou, J. (1978), *The Psychology of Pregnancy*, Lexington Books: London.

Belsky, J., Lang, M. and Rovine, M. (1985), 'Stability and change in marriage across the transition to parenthood: A second study', *Journal of Marriage and the Family*, 47, pp. 855–65.

Cooley, C. (1964), *Human Nature and the Social Order*, Shocken Books: New York.

Coopersmith, S. (1968), 'Studies in self-esteem', *Scientific American*, 218, pp. 96–106.

Entwisle, E. and Doering, S. (1981), *The First Birth*, Johns Hopkins University Press: Baltimore.

Erikson, E. (1968), *Identity: Youth and Crisis*, Norton: New York.

Felson, R. (1981a), 'Ambiguity and bias in the self-concept', *Social Psychology Quarterly*, 44, pp. 64–69.

Felson, R. (1981b), 'Self- and reflected appraisal among football players: A test of the Meadian hypothesis', *Social Psychology Quarterly*, 44, pp. 116–126.

Festinger, L. (1954), 'A theory of social comparison processes', *Human Relations*, 7, pp. 117–40.

Gavron, H. (1975), *The Captive Wife*, Penguin: Harmondsworth.

Gecas, V. (1982), 'The self-concept', *Annual Review of Sociology*, 8, pp. 1–23.

Gergen, K. (1971), *The Concept of Self*, Holt: London.

Gergen, K. (1977), 'The social construction of self-knowledge', in T. Mischel (ed.), *The Self: Psychological and Philosophical Issues*, Blackwell: Oxford.

LaRossa, R. and LaRossa, M. (1981), *Transition to Parenthood*, Sage Publications: London.

Lopata, H. (1980), 'The self concept: Characteristics and areas of competence', Paper given at American Sociological Association.

Mandelbaum, D. (1981), *Work, Marriage, and Motherhood*, Praeger: London.

McCall, G. and Simmons, J. (1966), *Identities and Interactions*, Macmillan: London.

McGuire, W. and Padawer-Singer, A. (1976), 'Trait salience in the spontaneous self-concept', *Journal of Personality and Social Psychology*, 33, pp. 743–54.

Mead, G. (1934), *Mind, Self and Society*, University of Chicago Press: Chicago.

Miller, B. and Sollie, D. (1980), 'Normal stresses during the transition to parenthood', *Family Relations*, 29, pp. 459–65.

Miller, D. (1963), 'The study of social relationships', in S. Koch (ed.), *Psychology: Study of a Science*, vol. 5, McGraw-Hill: New York.

Mortimer, J., Finch, M. and Kumka, D. (1982), 'Persistence and change in development of the multidimensional self-concept', in P. Baltes and O. Brim (eds), *Life-Span Development and Behavior*, vol. 4, Academic Press: London.

Oakley, A. (1974), *The Sociology of Housework*, Martin Robertson: London.

Osofsky, J. and Osofsky, H. (1984), 'Psychological and developmental perspectives on expectant and new parenthood', in R. Parke (ed.), *Review of Child Development Research*, vol. 7, University of Chicago Press: London.

Rosenberg, M. (1973), 'Which significant others?' *American Behavioral Scientist*, 16, pp. 829–60.

Rosenberg, M. and Kaplan, H. (eds) (1982), *Social Psychology of the Self-Concept*, Harlan Davidson: Arlington Heights, Ill.

Rossi, A. (1980), 'Life-span theories and women's lives', *Signs*, 6, pp. 4–32.

Strauss, A. (1977), *Mirrors and Masks: The Search for Identity*, Martin Robertson: London.

Stryker, S. (1968), 'Identity salience and role performance: The relevance of symbolic interaction theory for family research', *Journal of Marriage and the Family*, 30, pp. 558–64.

Warr, P. and Parry, G. (1982), 'Paid employment and women's psychological well-being', *Psychological Bulletin*, 91, pp. 498–516.

Webster, M. and Sobieszek, B. (1974), *Sources of Self-Evaluation*, Wiley: London.

Wylie, R. (1979), *The Self Concept* (rev. ed.), vol. 2, University of Nebraska Press: Lincoln.

20 Perceived change of self among adults: A conspectus

Amos Handel

Have I changed or not compared with what I was like at some point in the past? Am I likely to change or remain unchanged in the near or distant future? These questions presumably absorb the attention of many individuals from adolescence onward; yet they have rarely been focused upon in empirical studies about developmental changes in the self-concept of adults and of both younger and older individuals.

In view of the recently growing interest in the phenomenology of identity crises and transformations among adults (cf. Berger, 1963; Berger *et al.*, 1974; Erikson, 1959, 1968; Levinson, 1979; Lifton, 1976; Musgrove, 1977; Sheehy, 1976), it is rather surprising that the topic of self-perceived change and sameness has been rarely explored in the relatively large number of nomothetic studies recently published on the development of various dimensions of the self-concept (Wylie, 1974, 1979). The participants in these studies were rarely requested to compare their present and their retrospective (or prospective) view of themselves and to report their own resulting conclusions about the similarity of the two self-conceptions. Yet, such individual comparisons seem to be called for, and are indeed imperative, if the researcher is interested in securing information about the individuals' subjective sense of continuity and change, i.e. their own personal view of whether: (a) they have changed or remained the same in comparison to what they were – in retrospect – at some specific point in their past; (b) they anticipate that they are going to change at some point in their future, e.g. five or ten years from now, or in the wake of a future, expected life event. Rather than eliciting the individual's own self-appraisals of change and sameness of his or her self, some researchers relied on their own inferences in appraising the subjective sense of continuity underlying, in their view, the responses which they solicited from various groups of subjects. In their inferences about this distinctly intraindividual phenomenon, these researchers drew their implications from one of the following parameters, each of which seems to be rather irrelevant for appraising that particular phenomenon:

320

1. the magnitude of the difference between the means of various age groups on self-report scales administered to them in the context of cross-sectional studies which originally have been designed to assess the gradient of the age-bound progression of a particular dimension of the self-concept (Kokenes, 1974; Monge, 1973);
2. the magnitude of correlation coefficients of temporal stability obtained for repeated measurements of a self-report measure administered to a group of individuals in the context of a longitudinal study (Costa and McRae, 1980; Mischel, 1969, 1971; Moss and Sussman, 1980);
3. the magnitude of increase or decrease in self-evaluations of groups of subjects who were individually exposed to a brief experimental manipulation which was especially designed to determine whether the level of their self-esteem would change as the result of a brief, pre-planned encounter with another person acting as a confederate of the experimenter (Gergen, 1982; Gergen and Wishnow, 1965; Morse and Gergen, 1970).

On the other hand, the very notion of the individual's sense of continuity has been of special interest to clinicians, and to theorists in developmental psychology, in personology and social psychology. Most of these publications, which have been markedly influenced by Erikson's (1959, 1968) conceptualisations of ego-identity and by his elaboration of the sense of continuity as one of the major components of self-identity, have been limited, however, to analyses of one of the following, rather specific, phenomena or topics: (a) the relatively rare experience of a drastic disruption in the sense of continuity of one's personal identity as it occurs in states of grave psychopathology (Bender, 1950; Cattell, 1966; Erikson, 1968; Hilgard, 1949; Jacobson, 1959; Reed, 1972); this uncommon experience had already caught the attention of James (1890), who described in detail the extreme, drastic manifestations of depersonalisation as they are reflected in what he called 'abnormal alterations of self', the worst of which 'induce the patient to think that the present *me* is an altogether new personage' (p. 375), totally unrelated to the past self; (b) radical transformations in the core of one's identity in the wake of 'extreme situations' (Tyrikian, 1968), such as conversion (James, 1961; McDowell, 1978), coercive persuasion (Lifton, 1961; Schein, 1961), and similar, mostly unexpected, rather uncommon experiences of drastic losses (Marris, 1975; Parkes, 1972a, 1972b) which are deemed to affect the inner regions of one's life space; (c) global, holistic impressions and implications drawn by researchers from detailed, unstructured life-history interviews which they have conducted with relatively small, rather selected samples of adults who agreed to participate in such studies (cf. Cottle and Klineberg, 1974; Krantz, 1978; Levinson, 1979, 1981; McDowell, 1978; Musgrove, 1977; Osherson, 1980; Rubin, 1976, 1979; Sheehy, 1976, 1981). The design of these studies suggests that they were mostly centred on some broadly phrased issues of personality development in adulthood, e.g. the evolution of the individuals' life structure, the nature of their developmental crises, their strategies in coping with these crises. Although published versions of these studies contain some clues about the broad areas of self which are liable to change in adulthood, they unfortunately contain only few, casual references indicating: (1) the specific nature of the sense of continuity or the amount of change perceived by the interviewees; (2) the self-perceived changes in specific attributes, attitudes, interests, role expectations, etc., which may have been explicitly related by the interviewees in reconstructing the course of their development.

This chapter is focused upon the retrospective dimension of perceived change of self ('self-in-awareness') as a segment of the phenomenological reality that is reflected in self-narratives of 'typical', 'ordinary' adults about the course of their own development. Previously studied among adolescents (Handel, 1980), middle-aged kibbutzniks (Handel *et al.*, 1983) and among adults who have changed their name (Zadik, 1979), the concept of perceived change of self delineates a field of study designated to accommodate investigations of: (a) self-appraisals of change and sameness made by the individual in the context of comparing present and retrospective (or prospective) views of self; (b) self-perceptions evoked by this process of individual comparisons, e.g. evaluations made by the individual about the relative importance, psychological centrality (Rosenberg, 1979) or positive/negative quality of such self-perceived changes.

The notion of perceived change of self rests on the following assumptions: (a) self-appraisals of change refer to those 'changes in the Me recognised by the I' (James, 1890, p. 373); these changes evidently can only be recognised and discerned against the background of those aspects of the self-as-an-object (Me) which at that given point in time are perceived by the individual as having remained the same and unchanged; (b) self-appraisals of change and sameness are the outcome of comparisons made by the individual himself or herself between the present and the retrospective or prospective views of oneself; (c) self-appraisals of change and sameness, like any other class of self-perceptions, are available to the researcher only in the form of self-presentations which the individual is able and willing to communicate in the form of verbal, first-person, self-referent statements; (d) self-appraisals of change and sameness may pertain to more or less inclusive components of the self-as-an-object; the range of the components includes: (1) specific self-perceptions, e.g. a particular trait or role conception; (2) a somewhat broader facet of the self, e.g. one's feelings about one's body, one's view of life; (3) the self-as-a-whole, as a global entity.

The distinct nature of perceived change of self becomes further clarified when contrasted with four other relevant notions of change and continuity of self. Two of them, estimated change of self and observed change of self (Handel, 1980), involve systematic comparisons of the individuals' present and retrospective (or prospective) self-images; yet these particular comparisons are made not by the individuals themselves but by the researchers, who employ their own frame of reference as they compare the self-report data they have obtained from these individuals and draw from these comparisons their own conclusions about the extent to which each of them has indeed changed.

In the case of estimated change of self, the researcher compares two sets of self-descriptions which were separately elicited from the person on the same occasion: (1) the person's present self-image; (2) the retrospective or prospective self-image reported by the person, using the same set of self-descriptions (e.g. a Q-sort, a self-report inventory). The magnitude of the discrepancy between these two self-images represents the amount of estimated change in the retrospective or prospective dimension (cf. Bell, 1976; Hauser and Shapiro, 1973; Lewis, 1971). The proposed distinction between perceived and estimated change of self seems to be also justified on empirical grounds in view of the relatively small amount of common variance shared by such measures in the studies of Zadik (1979; 23 per cent) and Handel (1980; 18 per cent), as well as in the present study (sample A: 24 per cent; sample B: 3 to 19 per cent, for four different measures of perceived change which were solicited only from the group of nurses).

The notion of observed change of self is based on a comparison made by the researcher between repeated measurements (time 1 and time 2) for any self-report measure (e.g. self-esteem) which has been solicited from a group of subjects within the context of a longitudinal study. Here the significance of the difference between the two means or the magnitude of the correlation coefficient between the two measurements represents the amount of observed change (cf. Mischel, 1969, 1971; Moss and Sussman, 1980).

A markedly different approach to the study of continuity is evident in studies which were designed to elicit the wide range of explanatory statements and reasons employed by children and adolescents in order to account for: (a) the sense of their *own* personal continuity and their certainty in its actual existence, as reflected in their responses to the following critical question: 'If you change from year to year, how do you know you are always you?' (Hart *et al.*, Chapter 8); (b) their personal continuity as reflected in their responses to questions in which they were requested to consider the continuity (or lack of continuity) of *other people*, that is, fictional story characters who were described by the researchers as having come through periods of radical change (Chandler *et al.*, Chapter 7).

The barometric self (Rosenberg, in press) represents yet another notion of change of self. In this particular notion, the emphasis is on the level of self-reported volatility of the self-concept, i.e. on our own self-appraisal about whether we experience rapid shifts and fluctuations of self-attitudes from moment to moment or whether our feelings and thoughts about self are, in our own eyes, just the opposite, namely, high stable, fixed and constant over time.

Method

This chapter presents a summary of selected findings from hitherto unpublished studies about perceived change of self in four different groups of adults. The participants in these studies were asked to compare themselves with what they were like: (a) ten years ago (206 women; age range, 30 to 40: sample A); (b) before starting their professional training (68 and 55 trainees in nursing and teaching, respectively; age range, 19 to 30: sample B); (c) about three years ago when they were still illiterate (60 women who were trained to become literate in Hebrew; age range, 38 to 65: sample C); (d) before having joined the army (59 ex-servicemen, recently discharged after three years of service in the army; age range, 22 to 26: sample D). In addition to these major sources of data, I shall avail myself of some unstructured data about perceived change of self. These data have been obtained by means of open-ended interviews with a group of students from overseas who came to Israel for a one-year programme of studies ($N=14$) and with a small group of middle-aged professionals ($N=9$).

The principal measure of perceived change of self solicited in the four samples was the Retrospective Change Inventory (RCI). The RCI contained a list of specific, dimensional self-attributes which were represented in the RCI by a variety of traits, dispositions, values, attitudes, interests, habits, etc. Below are some examples of RCI items: 'I am optimistic', 'I am energetic', 'I go my own way regardless of the opinions of others', 'I support the orientation of "let us eat and drink, for tomorrow we shall die" ', 'I believe that the major source of satisfaction in life is the attainment of a great achievement', 'I like to read thrillers', 'I am in my element when I am with a group of people who know how to enjoy life' (a fuller listing is available in Handel *et al.*, 1983). The RCI version administered to each group contained a list with different items, ranging in number from 35 to 70. These self-attributes were selected for their particular relevance to the presumably salient and/or mutable aspects of self in each of the four groups.

In responding to each RCI item, all the participants in the four samples were requested to follow through the three parts of the RCI. In part 1, which was designed to solicit their present view of self, each individual was requested to indicate to what extent the particular self-attribute 'characterises me now', using a 5-point scale from 'very much' to 'not at all'.

Part 2 of the RCI was intended to obtain the individuals' self-appraisals about the amount and direction of retrospective change of self as it applies to each attribute. Here, the respondents were requested to compare themselves with what they were like in the past, e.g. ten years ago (sample A), and to specify whether they were now 'optimistic', 'energetic', etc., 'much more than in the past' (score 5), 'slightly more than in the past' (score 4), 'the same as in the past' (score 3), 'slightly less than in the past' (score 2) or 'much less than in the past' (score 1). Sample C underwent a simplified format and simplified scoring system. The original scores of directional change were also transformed into a 3-point scale of absolute change: values of 2, 1 and 0, representing the categories of 'much change', 'slight change' and 'no change', were assigned to responses which obtained the original, directional-change scores of 1 and 5, 2 and 4, and 3, respectively. Based on this transformation, a summary score was computed for each subject. This summary score (SRC) was the sum of scores for the absolute amount of change assigned to all RCI items.

In part 3 of the RCI, the respondents were asked to: (a) evaluate the positive/negative quality of the self-perceived changes reported by them in part 2 (samples A and D); (b) indicate their own attributions of each of these changes to either the factor of schooling, to 'other factors', or to a combination of both schooling and 'other factors' (samples B and C).

Further information on the composition of each of the four samples and on the other questionnaires administered to them is available from the author.

Results

The findings selected for presentation in this chapter represent a summary of salient, recurrent themes which seem to characterise the self-appraisals of change and sameness of our respondents.

1. Self-appraisals about the amount of retrospective change one perceives in oneself with respect to various self-attributes tend to be closely interrelated. Composite scores of the self-appraisals for all the RCI items show a high degree of internal consistency (alpha coefficients of 0.90 and above in samples A, B and D). The pattern of intercorrelations between the different measures of the absolute amount of retrospective change further supports the notion that what underlies most judgments of self-perceived change and sameness is a phenomenologically consistent, rather pervading self-schema of having either changed much, or little, or not at all. That self-schema enters into, and possibly determines, the

appraisals of change made by the individual with respect to a specific self-attribute, or a facet of self, or the self-as-a-whole.

2. Most of the respondents in each of the four groups perceive only slight changes in themselves or none at all when they compare themselves to what they were like in the past. The mean proportion of endorsement of each of the three response alternatives of absolute change for all the RCI items was as follows:

   a) 'no change': 40 per cent, 53 per cent, 40 per cent, in samples A, B, D, respectively;

   b) 'slight change': 38 per cent, 31 per cent, 38 per cent, in samples A, B, D, respectively;

   c) 'much change': 22 per cent, 16 per cent, 22 per cent, in samples A, B, D, respectively;

   In sample C, the predominance of self-appraisals of sameness was even more pronounced; here the 'no change' response was endorsed on average by 83 per cent of the women and only 17 per cent indicated the existence of 'change' in themselves on the RCI self-attributes.

3. Given the opportunity to present their own evaluation of the nature of each self-perceived change, a large majority of the respondents viewed such changes as being a gain rather than a loss (samples A and D).

4. There is a substantial correlation between the *amount* of perceived change and the relative *importance* assigned to each particular change. Nevertheless, the self-reports of our respondents suggest that they tend to distinguish between amount and importance of self-perceived change (sample B).

5. Even respondents with minimal education (sample C) are able to make distinctions between self-perceived changes which have occurred, in their own view, due to the impact of a critical experience, i.e. transition to literacy, and those changes which they attribute to the impact of other factors.

6. When the individuals in each of the samples compare themselves with what they were like in the past, we find a striking similarity in the connotation of the self-attributes which have changed the most. These changes occur with great regularity: a subjective sense of having reached a higher level of self-knowledge, of having become more self-confident, of having gained more control over one's impulses, etc. It is as if our respondents availed themselves of a commonly held, implicit theory about the developmental meaning of 'maturity'. Factor analyses of the RCI data (samples A and D) support this notion inasmuch as those attributes that have changed the most do have significant loadings on a factor of 'increased self-perceived efficacy'.

7. The life history of those who perceive themselves as having minimally changed, as compared with those who report many changes, indicates

that they have been exposed to fewer critical life events and experiences (sample A).

8. Individuals who perceive themselves as having minimally changed exhibit a relatively low level of cognitive complexity in construing both themselves and their significant others (samples A and B). Furthermore, they manifest a slightly higher level of well-being and satisfaction (samples A and B) and show a slightly higher need of approval than those who view themselves as having considerably changed (sample A).

9. The test–retest reliabilities obtained for self-appraisals of change and sameness for the RCI self-attributes were substantial. They were in the same order of magnitude as those found for self-descriptions of one's present view of self.

Discussion

The predominant theme of the 'collective' self-narrative of our respondents seems to be that of stability. In most cases, this theme is attended by what appears to be a clearly positive, 'progressive' self-narrative (Gergen and Gergen, 1983) reflecting the sense of improvement and gains accruing to one's self from the past.

Before considering some qualifications and implications which are called for by these findings, two matters deserve brief attention. First, these and other forms of self-narratives evidently are in 'no way to be construed as objective reflections of one's personal life' (Gergen and Gergen, 1983, p. 260). In principle, such self-narratives may have indeed little in common with the actuality of one's personal history. However, our findings do indicate a significant and meaningful relationship between the two accounts (sample A). Secondly, the stability and progressive aspects of the self-narrative are not mutually inconsistent and may actually coexist in the context of one's narrative. The data from our interviews suggest that frequently the two aspects blend in one's ontology, which can be summarised by the following epitome: 'By and large I have remained the same as I was in the past and have hardly changed; the relatively few changes I find in myself have been mostly gains rather than losses and on the whole I now seem to be better off than I was in the past.'

The predominance of self-appraisals of sameness and of little change which characterises the judgments made by the majority of our subjects is in accord with the pattern of self-appraisals found among adolescents (Handel, 1980) and middle-aged adults (Handel *et al.*, 1983) on a comparable set of specific self-attributes. All in all, our findings do not support the general notion of radical change in adult identity. Thus, our findings do not support the idea that the nature of the identity of modern people is characterised by an awareness of and a pride in the capacity for marked transformations of identity, as suggested by the protean self-process of Lifton (1971, 1976), the fluid self-identity of Kilpatrick (1975) or the conversion-prone notion of Berger *et al.* (1974).

Several points need to be kept in mind with regard to this general finding. First, we should note that our studies have been focused upon self-in-awareness and deal only with those self-appraisals of change and sameness which the individual is aware of and willing to report to the researcher in a first-person format. Other operational definitions of these concepts have produced different results. Thus, Fiske (1980) reports radical changes in the self-concept of adults as she probes into their self-reported values and self-perceptions by means of a 'semiprojective approach' (p. 245) and makes inferences about what she takes to be the 'truth' (p. 245) with respect to their value structure and the hierarchy of their commitments. She is thus adopting the formulation of Epstein (1983) that the researcher analyse the actor's self-theory at not only the conscious, but also the preconscious and unconscious level of awareness.

Secondly, we find that the amount of perceived change is contingent upon the degree of specificity of the self-descriptions called for from the subject. The more specific the description, as in the RCI, the less change reported. The more general or global the aspect of self being described, the more change. We can document this generalisation only in samples B and C, and additional data would be necessary to confirm this tendency.

Thirdly, the findings of our studies support the notion that self-appraisals of the amount of perceived change should not be considered apart from other aspects of such self-perceptions, such as their positive/negative quality and the relative importance of each self-perceived change. Also, there is some evidence that the emotional intensity and the degree of personal involvement of the individual need to be considered in perceived change of self. Taylor (1983), in interviews with women with breast cancer, found emphatic statements reflecting a marked discontinuity as they compared their present selves and their retrospective, pre-morbid selves. On the other hand, two of our middle-aged interviewees, both survivors of the Holocaust, testified vigorously that notwithstanding their experiences during that period they still believed that they have remained basically the same, unchanged and untouched by the pain and misery of the Holocaust.

The conclusion that individuals report a sense of having changed, if at all, for the better, i.e. the presentation of 'progressive' self-narratives, manifests itself in our studies in various ways: (a) in evaluating their self-perceived changes on the RCI, a large majority of the respondents view these changes as being gains rather than losses (samples A and D); (b) a large majority of the critical events which have occurred in the course of one's life history are regarded in retrospect as having had a positive rather than a negative impact on one's self (sample A); (c) the overall quality of the changes that have occurred in the self-as-a-whole is similarly regarded as positive rather than negative (sample B). The hopeful nature of that 'progressive' self-narrative is further evident in predictions made about one's personal future. The typical chart obtained for self-evaluations made by each subject with respect to the level of her self-esteem from early childhood onward shows that the level of the self-esteem in the present is higher than in the past, ten years ago. Moreover, the forecast for the future indicates an expectation for further improvement and for an additional increase in the level of self-esteem (sample A). Along with this general trend, there is also a strong relationship between self-ratings of the favourability of retrospective and prospective change; those who view themselves as having by and large changed for the better expect to change in the same direction in the future, and vice versa (sample B).

The belief that one has changed in a positive way, i.e. that one has become more competent, mature, self-confident, etc., than in the past, seems to provide the individual with a personally meaningful and a subjectively 'realistic' indication of what might be achieved in the same areas in the future. Thus, individual comparisons with a retrospective self and the resulting self-appraisals about the direction and the amount of change of self do not merely serve as a 'historical' record of what has been accomplished so far, but function as a point from which to extrapolate to the future. Viewed in this perspective, the favourability of retrospective, self-perceived changes is obviously related to and affected by the general tendency to protect and enhance one's self-esteem. Guided by this tendency, we may affect the outcome of our individual comparisons and boost our belief that we have made a definite progress by selecting for such comparisons either a particularly deficient self from our past or a specific, previously undeveloped aspect of any of our previous selves.

While the 'progressive' self-narrative seems to be predominant in most evaluations of one's self-perceived changes, the full range and variety of the evaluations obtained from the respondents calls for some additional remarks. First, individuals differ widely in evaluating the positive/negative quality of self-perceived changes. The 'regressive' self-narrative is relatively rare among our respondents, yet we find self-reports with numerous changes listed as losses and a small percentage of records in which the sum of RCI changes evaluated as losses actually exceeds the total number of self-perceived changes regarded as gains (9 per cent and 5 per cent in samples A and D, respectively). Interestingly enough, our findings further indicate that the greater the negative evaluation of the retrospective changes, the lower the level of both the present and the prospective self-esteem.

Secondly, the data obtained from the interviews suggest that our understanding of such evaluations about the favourability of one's self-perceived changes may be significantly enriched if supplemented by information about the relative importance and psychological centrality (Rosenberg, 1979) of gains and losses in these changes. Thus, for some of our interviewees, the middle-aged professionals, what was psychologically central was the idea of self-sameness. For them, the tendency to enhance one's self-esteem called for a self-narrative of pronounced stability, rather than for a notion of having changed even for the better, in some desired, specific direction.

Finally, it should be noted that the process of individual comparisons and the resultant judgments that one has changed, improved or remained the same are not fanciful products of one's imagination. There is a definite relationship between self-perceived changes and the course of one's life. Individuals who perceive themselves as having radically changed report a significantly higher number of critical experiences that have occurred in their past than individuals who view themselves as having minimally changed (sample A). This relationship between the amount of self-perceived change and the number of critical experiences in the past applies to events for which there is an 'objective', public record, e.g. change in marital status, employment, etc. (L-data; Cattell, 1965) and also to experiences that are more 'subjective' such as self-perceived changes in one's interpersonal relationships, intrapsychic functioning, etc.

Thus, it is both the factual nature of one's life history as well as its subjective interpretation and reconstruction by the actor which are significantly related to the amount of self-perceived changes reported by the individual. The findings of our studies further suggest that a pronounced sense of continuity, a self-schema of having minimally changed, seems to be related to three additional characteristics: (a) a sense of well-being and satisfaction (samples A and B), and a positive adjustment as expressed in self-ratings (Handel, 1980) or peer ratings (Handel *et al.*, 1983); (b) a rather simple-minded, unsophisticated approach to the psychological analysis of oneself and of others (samples A and B); (c) a tendency to seek approval of others by adhering to socially desirable norms (sample A).

In the present study, the process of individual comparisons of the respondents' present and retrospective self was initiated and more or less guided by the researcher. The quality of individual responses to both the structured questionnaires and the open-ended interviews, however, clearly suggests that our respondents are definitely familiar with that process and have engaged in it more than once spontaneously, on their own initiative, and did so perhaps in the same manner as lay people presumably proceed when they 'spontaneously engage in attributional activities' (Wong and Weiner, 1981, p. 650).

While the specific properties and determinants of the process of individual comparisons are yet unknown and remain to be explored, the mainly qualitative findings of our study call for some further remarks on the following aspects of that process.

First, it seems that in our individual comparisons we do not limit ourselves to the assortment of retrospective selves which are part of our recent past. On the contrary, the interview data of our middle-aged professionals and the comments volunteered to the researcher by some of the hitherto illiterate women (sample C) suggest that in their 'spontaneous', individual comparisons, middle-aged individuals are oftentimes inclined to select a temporally distant self from their childhood or adolescence, dated even several decades ago. Such a definitely extended temporal perspective is also clearly evident in individual comparisons made by middle-aged (and older) autobiographers as they describe the course of their development and choose to elaborate upon similarities and differences between what they are now and what they were like (in retrospect) as much as four, five and more decades ago (cf. Handel, 1986 and in press, for specific, autobiographical examples of such an attitude). The time perspective of adults, as it is revealed in these sources, exceeds by far the time span designated for individual comparisons which researchers have solicited from participants in nomothetic studies, i.e. no more than three, five or ten years in studies of adults and middle-aged individuals, and fifteen years at most in the case of elderly persons (Blau, 1956).

Secondly, our interview data suggest that individual comparisons involve (explicitly or implicitly) not only one's present and retrospective self but at least one, and more often two, additional selves, e.g.: (a) a desired self (Rosenberg, 1979) of myself as I would like to be, or the opposite picture of one's negative identity (Erikson, 1968), the image of myself as I might become if the worst possible things were to happen to me; (b) a prospective, anticipated view of myself, after I become a mother (or father) for the first time in my life, after my retirement, etc. Sometimes the additional element in such comparisons is a significant other, e.g. my close friend, my spouse, a rival who threatens the position I now hold at my work, a person who in my eyes is a model of aging in a graceful or ungraceful manner, etc. Thus, social and individual comparisons converge and shape together the resulting self-appraisals of change and sameness. Moreover, the image of another person is sometimes introduced into these comparisons in order to assist us in reviving a dimly recollected self from our past. Such a strategy was adopted by some individuals in the group of U.S. students who came to Israel for a one-year programme of studies. In elaborating upon their difficulties in concluding whether they had changed (or not) during the sojourning experience, these students expressed the feeling that on seeing their friends again back home in the U.S.A. they might be reminded of what each of them was like a year ago, and thus be able better to relate to their retrospective self. The anticipated reunion with their close friends was regarded by them as important for yet another reason; in the face-to-face, intimate interaction with their friends they expected to receive some personally meaningful feedback about how they appeared in the eyes of their friends and thus to obtain an important piece of evidence for corroborating their own subjective impression about any changes that might have occurred in them. The notion of friends providing confirmation of change in oneself, which was shared by half the individuals in that sample, suggests: (a) the close connection between cognitive processes of social and individual comparison on the one hand and the expected impact of social interactions with one's significant others on the other hand; (b) that Berger's (1963) plausible but questioned thesis about the critical, prevailing role of social interactions in sustaining and transforming the identity of adults in general (Musgrove, 1977) may actually apply to a specific age group, namely, adolescents and young adults. In their attempts to consolidate their self-identity, adolescents may well seek and eventually find ample opportunities for both projecting their self-image on their peers and seeing themselves reflected, clarified and eventually confirmed in their interactions with them. Thus, some aspects of individual comparisons and the pattern of social interaction which is associated with that process may well be age-specific and change during the life course.

Thirdly, there is the question of what it is that induces us to initiate the process of individual comparisons. Is it indeed the experience of personal failure which activates that process, as is implied by the theory of objective self-awareness (cf. Wicklund, 1975)? Or is it just the encounter with any of the personally unexpected events, losses as well as gains, which upsets our inborn tendency to 'assimilate if you can; accommodate if you must' (Block, 1982, p. 286) and leads us to ruminate on why it is that today we didn't handle a situation of this kind as easily as we did in the past? The notion about the evolutionary, built-in priority of the assimilative over the accommodative mode (Block, 1982; Piaget, 1970) suggests that we are likely to initiate the process of individual comparisons when we have failed to assimilate a new experience and have perceived that it does not fit our conception about the essence of our continuous self. An essentially similar position is adopted by Swann (1983), and by Strauss (1969) who further maintains that the recognition of change in ourselves is determined by the relative importance we attach to our new experiences and by our ability to assign to them a personally meaningful interpretation within the system of our terminology (or the 'construction system', in the parlance of Kelly, 1955, p. 57). The new experience has to be both of importance to me and lie outside the range of convenience of my constructs (Kelly, 1955) if it is to induce me to engage in the process of individual comparisons. The responses of our interviewees suggest yet another noteworthy factor which might influence our willingness to initiate that process: the need to justify in retrospect the wisdom of a previously made, important decision which deeply affects our present, everyday life. This need becomes urgent as we start questioning the good sense of such a decision and set in motion the distressful combination of remorse, guilt and self-abasement. At this juncture, individual comparisons may serve a defensive function and fend off that distress, if only the preconceived, summary conclusion of these comparisons leads me to believe in the end that: all in all, I am now better off than I was in the past, e.g. before I emigrated to Israel, before I decided to quit my job, inasmuch as I am now calmer, more satisfied, less bogged down in the trivialities of life than I was in the past, etc. In these instances, such decisions can be justified in retrospect by my sense of improvement, which in this case rests on the results of individual comparisons I myself have activated in order to reach just that particular conclusion.

Fourthly, it is clear that generalisations about the sense of sameness, continuity or change of self of any group of individuals are bound to be meaningless unless we specify the conceptual and operational definition of each of these terms and delineate our usage of them. Moreover, any such generalisation about the durability, permanence, resistance to change of self, of self-as-a-subject, of self-identity, of personal identity, or about the fluid, protean, chameleonic nature of these unfortunately ambiguous constructs may be misleading if we have failed to specify their stipulative definition. On the other hand, a systematic comparison of the manifestations of these separate constructs, as they are actually reflected in various groups of individuals, may enrich our understanding of the variety of developmental changes which occur in the self-concept of a particular group. For example, an intriguing analogy is that between subjective manifestations of a disruption in the sense of continuity of one's self-identity (see Erikson, 1968) and the pattern of a below-par level of well-being and adjustment reported in our research. The latter characterises individuals who perceive themselves as having considerably changed, particularly when self-evaluation relates to losses rather than gains (sample A). Further connections between the particular notion of Erikson (1968) and the self-schema of perceived change are suggested by data obtained from some of our interviewees. These data suggest the special significance of changes which in one's own view pertain to the core of one's self and are of major importance in presenting the differences between one's present and retrospective self. A multitude of such changes, which at the same time are perceived as personal losses, seems to characterise individuals whose self-presentation suggests that they are at present in a state resembling the phenomenology of an identity crisis as described by Erikson (1968).

These are some of the topics and issues which need to be further explored in order to gain a better understanding of the concept of perceived change of self. Thus far, however, our findings suggest the potential viability of this construct and the usefulness of its measures for at least the following purposes: (a) to assess one's overall sense of sameness and change at various stages of the life course; (b) to assess the differential amount of change which applies to various dimensions of perceived change of self, e.g. the amount of change which applies to the core or the periphery of self, to important or trivial changes, to gains or losses, etc.; (c) to explore one's implicit theory about the course of development of self as it is reflected in the direction and amount of change in various self-attributes and in some broader facets of self; (d) to compare the magnitude, quality and importance of the self-perceived impact of broad developmental processes (e.g. maturation, aging) and of specific critical life events and experiences, designated also as psychological transitions, milestones or turning points, e.g. conversion, bereavement, professional training, immigration, transition from illiteracy to literacy; (e) to study the connections between perceived change of self and the process of individual comparisons and other related concepts, e.g. life review, mid-life crisis, self-image disparity.

References

Bell, B. D. (1976), 'Role set orientations and life satisfaction: A new look at an old theory', in J. F. Gubrium (ed.), *Time, Roles, and Self in Old Age*, Human Science Press: New York.

Bender, L. (1950), 'Anxiety in disturbed children', in P. H. Hoch and J. Zubin (eds), *Anxiety*, Grune & Stratton: New York.

Berger, P. L. (1963), *Invitation to Sociology: A Humanistic Perspective*, Anchor Books: New York.

Berger, P., Berger, B. and Kellner, H. (1974), *The Homeless Mind: Modernization and Consciousness*, Penguin Books: Harmondsworth.

Blau, Z. S. (1956), 'Changes in status and age identification', *American Sociological Review*, 21, pp. 198–203.

Block, J. (1982), 'Assimilation, accommodation, and the dynamics of personality development', *Child Development*, 53, pp. 281–95.

Cattell, J. P. (1966), 'Depersonalization phenomena', in S. Arieti (ed.), *American Handbook of Psychiatry*, vol. 3, Basic Books: New York.

Cattell, R. B. (1965), *The Scientific Analysis of Personality*, Penguin: Baltimore.

Costa, P. T. and McRae, R. R. (1980), 'Still stable after all these years: Personality as a key to some crises in adulthood and aging', in O. G. Brim and J. Kagan (eds), *Constancy and Change in Human Development*, Harvard University Press: Cambridge, Mass.

Cottle, T. J. and Klineberg, S. L. (1974), *The Present of Things Future: Explorations of Time in Human Experience*, Free Press: New York.

Epstein, S. (1983), 'The unconscious, the preconscious, and the self-concept', in J. Suls and A. G. Greenwald (eds), *Psychological Perspectives on the Self*, vol. 2, Erlbaum: Hillsdale, N.J.

Erikson, E. H. (1959), *Identity and The Life Cycle*, International University Press: New York.

Erikson, E. H. (1968), *Identity: Youth and Crisis*, Norton: New York.

Fiske, M. (1980), 'Changing hierarchies of commitment in adulthood', in

N. J. Smelser and E. H. Erikson (eds), *Themes of Work and Love in Adulthood*, Harvard University Press: Cambridge, Mass.

Gergen, K. J. (1982), 'From self to science: What is there to know?' in J. Suls (ed.), *Psychological Perspectives on the Self*, vol. 1, Erlbaum: Hillsdale, N.J.

Gergen, K. J. and Gergen, M. M. (1983), 'Narratives of the self', in T. R. Sarbin and K. E. Scheibe (eds), *Studies in Social Identity*, Praeger: New York.

Gergen, K. J. and Wishnow, B. (1965), 'Others' self-evaluations and interaction anticipation as determinants of self-presentation', *Journal of Personality and Social Psychology*, 2, pp. 348–58.

Handel, A. (1980), 'Perceived change of self among adolescents', *Journal of Youth and Adolescence*, 9, pp. 507–19.

Handel, A. (in press) 'Personal theories about the life-span development of one's self in autobiographical self-presentations of adults', *Human Development*.

Handel, A. (1986) 'Sense of estrangement from one's previous self in the autobiographies of Arthur Koestler and Edwin Muir', *Biography*, 9, pp. 306–23.

Handel, A., Kimhi, S. and Leviatan, U. (1983), 'Perceived retrospective change of self among the middle-aged in the kibbutz', *International Journal of Behavioral Development*, 6, pp. 241–60.

Hauser, S. T. and Shapiro, R. L. (1973), 'Differentiation of adolescent self-images', *Archives of General Psychiatry*, 29, pp. 63–8.

Hilgard, E. R. (1949), 'Human motives and the concept of the self', *American Psychologist*, 4, pp. 374–82.

Jacobson, E. (1959), 'Depersonalization', *Journal of the American Psychoanalytic Association*, 7, pp. 581–610.

James, W. (1890), *The Principles of Psychology*, Holt: New York.

James, W. (1961), *The Varieties of Religious Experience*, Macmillan: New York.

Kelly, G. A. (1955), *A Theory of Personality: The Psychology of Personal Constructs*, Norton: New York.

Kilpatrick, W. (1975), *Identity and Intimacy*, Dell: New York.

Kokenes, B. (1974), 'Grade level differences in factors of self-esteem', *Developmental Psychology*, 10, pp. 954–8.

Krantz, D. L. (1978), *Radical Career Change: Life Beyond Work*, Free Press: New York.

Levinson, D. J. (1979), *The Seasons of a Man's Life*, Ballantine Books: New York.

Levinson, D. J. (1981), 'Exploration in biography: Evolution of the individual life structure in adulthood', in A. I. Rabin, J. Aronoff, A. M. Barclay and R. A. Zucker (eds), *Further Explorations in Personality*, Wiley: New York.

Lewis, C. N. (1971), 'Reminiscing and self-concept in old age', *Journal of*

Gerontology, 26, pp. 240–3.

Lifton, R. J. (1961), *Thought Reform and the Psychology of Totalism: A Study of 'Brainwashing' in China*, Norton: New York.

Lifton, R. J. (1971), 'Protean man', in B. B. Wolman (ed.), *The Psychoanalytic Interpretation of History*, Basic Books: New York.

Lifton, R. J. (1976), *The Life of the Self: Toward a New Psychology*, Simon & Schuster: New York.

Marris, P. (1975), *Loss and Change*, Doubleday: New York.

McDowell, V. H. (1978), *Re-creating: The Emergence of Life-change and Religion*, Beacon Press: Boston.

Mischel, W. (1969), 'Continuity and change in personality', *American Psychologist*, 24, pp. 1012–18.

Mischel, W. (1971), *Introduction to Personality*, Holt, Rinehart & Winston: New York.

Monge, R. H. (1973), 'Developmental trends of factors of adolescent self-concept', *Developmental Psychology*, 8, pp. 382–93.

Morse, J. and Gergen, K. J. (1970), 'Social comparison, self-consistency, and the concept of self', *Journal of Personality and Social Psychology*, 16, pp. 148–56.

Moss, H. A. and Sussman, E. J. (1980), 'Longitudinal study of personality development', in O. G. Brim and J. Kagan (eds), *Constancy and Change in Human Development*, Harvard University Press: Cambridge, Mass.

Musgrove, F. (1977), *Margins of the Mind*, Methuen: London.

Osherson, S. D. (1980), *Holding on or Letting Go: Men and Career Change at Midlife*, Free Press: New York.

Parkes, C. M. (1972a), *Bereavement: Studies of Grief in Adult Life*, Penguin Books: London.

Parkes, C. M. (1972b), 'Components of the reaction to loss of a limb, spouse or home', *Journal of Psychosomatic Research*, 16, pp. 343–9.

Piaget, J. (1970), 'Piaget's theory', in P. H. Mussen (ed.), *Carmichael's Manual of Child Psychology*, vol. 1, 3rd ed., Wiley: New York.

Reed, G. (1972), *The Psychology of Anomalous Experience: A Cognitive Approach*, Hutchinson University Library: London.

Rosenberg, M. (1979), *Conceiving the Self*, Basic Books: New York.

Rosenberg, M. (in press), 'Self-concept development from middle childhood through adolescence', in J. Suls and A. G. Greenwald (eds), *Psychological Perspectives on the Self*, vol. 3, Erlbaum: Hillsdale, N.J.

Rubin, L. B. (1976), *Worlds of Pain: Life in the Working Class Family*, Basic Books: New York.

Rubin, L. B. (1979), *Women of a Certain Age: The Midlife Search for Self*, Harper: New York.

Schein, E. H. (1961), *Coercive Persuasion: A Socio-psychological Analysis of Brainwashing of American Civilian Prisoners by Chinese Communists*, Norton: New York.

Sheehy, G. (1976), *Passages: Predictable Crises of Adult Life*, Dutton: New York.

Sheehy, G. (1981), *Pathfinders*, W. Morrow: New York.

Strauss, A. L. (1969), *Mirrors and Masks: The Search for Identity*, The Sociology Press: San Francisco.

Swann, W. B. (1983), 'Self-verification: Bringing social reality into harmony with the self', in J. Suls and A. G. Greenwald (eds), *Psychological Perspectives on the Self*, vol. 2, Erlbaum: Hillsdale, N.J.

Taylor, S. E. (1983), 'Adjustment to threatening events: A theory of cognitive adaptation', *American Psychologist*, 38, pp. 1161–73.

Tyrikian, E. A. (1968), 'The existential self and the person', in C. Gordon and K. J. Gergen (eds), *The Self in Social Interaction*, vol. 1, Wiley: New York.

Wicklund, E. A. (1975), 'Objective self-awareness', in L. Berkowitz (ed.), *Advances in Experimental Social Psychology*, vol. 8, Academic Press: New York.

Wong, P. T. P. and Weiner, B. (1981), 'When people ask "why" questions and the heuristics of attributional research', *Journal of Personality and Social Psychology*, 40, pp. 650–63.

Wylie, R. (1974), *The Self Concept: A Review of Methodological Operations and Measuring Instruments*, vol. 1 (rev. ed.), University of Nebraska Press: Lincoln.

Wylie, R. (1979), *The Self Concept: Theory and Research on Selected Topics*, vol. 2 (rev. ed.), University of Nebraska Press: Lincoln.

Zadik, Y. (1979), 'Perceived retrospective change of self-concept in the wake of changing one's name', Unpublished master's thesis, University of Haifa, Israel.

21 The psychosemantic aspects of the self

Shulamith Kreitler and Hans Kreitler

Shared assumptions

The recent resurgence of interest in the concept of the self has been marked by consensus in regard to at least three basic assumptions. The first is that the self is a cognitive construct, as may become evident in its conceptual nature, its contents or its functions. Accordingly, the self is often described as 'cognitive generalizations about the self' guiding the processing of self-related information (Markus, 1977, p. 64), a set of beliefs (Cantor *et al.*, 1982) or attitudes about the self (Rosenberg, 1965), general information about oneself (Fiske and Taylor, 1984) or a theory for assimilating knowledge (Epstein, 1983).

A second widely shared assumption is that the self is a complex construct, which has different dimensions (McGuire and McGuire, 1981), categories (Lewis and Brooks-Gunn, 1981), domains (Harter, 1985) and manifestations, e.g. the 'real', 'ideal' and 'social' selves (Glick and Zigler, 1985).

A third common assumption is that the self is deeply enmeshed in the social sphere, as may become evident in its origins (Harré, 1983; Lewis and Brooks-Gunn, 1981), its contents (Shane and Shane, 1980) and its function, e.g. to provide a frame of reference for evaluating others (Markus and Smith, 1981).

Remarkably all three assumptions were strongly supported by major investigators in previous generations too: the first and second assumptions by William James (1890) and Kelly (1955), the third by Freud (1964) and Mead (1934) among others.

Controversial issues

Despite the sharing of such basic assumptions the investigation of self is characterised by more disagreements than consensus, and by more problems than resolved issues. Paradoxically, the major controversial issues are all related to the three aforementioned assumptions.

One problem, intimately bound up with the cognitive assumption, concerns the dualistic nature of the self as both 'the knower' and 'the known', the 'subject' and the 'object', of psychological functions (Wylie, 1961). The fact that most investigators acknowledge the duality but deal with self in only one of the two senses (Wylie, 1974) indicates that no conceptual bridge has yet been found between the view of the self as an active agent (e.g. Bandura, 1982) and as an epistemic construct (e.g. Bromley, 1977).

A second problem, related to the complexity assumption, hinges on the issue of unity versus multiplicity of selves. Despite the common experience of the self as a unity and its importance for mental health (Rosenberg, Chapter 13), psychologists have been sufficiently impressed by the diversity of the aspects (Spitzer *et al.*, 1971), presentations (Jones and Pittman, 1982) and changes of the self (Jordan and Merrifield, 1981) to suggest a series of different 'selves' (Anderson, 1981; Epstein, 1973). The problem then is: How can the unity of the self be upheld experientially and conceptually despite the multiplicity of its manifestations and changes?

A third problem, bound intimately to the social assumption, derives from the fact that despite the close theoretical bond between the conceptions of self and others, these two fields of research have hardly been bridged up to now, so that the search for the relations between the self-concept and information-processing in social psychology (Rosenberg, 1977), or for the rules binding the microcosmos with the macrocosmos (Smith, 1980), has hardly begun (Kuiper and Derry, 1981; Markus and Smith, 1981). The problem then is: How can the self resemble others and yet differ from them? (Hart *et al.*, Chapter 8).

A fourth major problem, related to all three shared assumptions, concerns the contents of the 'self-space' (McGuire and McGuire, 1982). About 95 per cent of the research into the self has dealt with only one aspect of the contents – self-esteem. This approach violates the complexity assumption and is inadequate because self-evaluative responses constitute fewer than 10 per cent of the free descriptions of the self (Kreitler and Kreitler, 1967; McGuire *et al.*, 1979). The minority who broke away from the restrictive tradition (Bugental, 1964; McPartland, 1965; McGuire and McGuire, 1981) were bound to devise categories for describing the contents of the self. Thus, Bromley (1977) suggested 'a comprehensive and exclusive system' of thirty-three categories (e.g. possessions, life history), of which only twelve correspond to any of the thirty categories in Gordon's (1968) system, only seven correspond to any of the eleven categories set up by Kreitler and Kreitler (1967) and only two correspond to the categories on which the McGuires (Chapter 9) focused, yet all used similar stimulus questions for the subjects.

A categorisation system is, nevertheless, of the utmost importance since it determines to a large extent the research results and the answers they may provide. To our mind, an optimal system should have the following properties: (a) it should be anchored in a theoretical framework that renders it independent of the data given by particular respondents and experimenters' biases; (b) it should be sufficiently broad and diversified to enable the responses of individuals in different populations to be coded, doing justice to the assumption about the self's complexity; (c) it should be able to include categories devised by other investigators of the self since their similarity to each other indicates that they probably tap important and common aspects of the self; (d) it should allow comparisons of self-descriptions provided by different respondents and by the same respondent in different contexts or stages; (e) it should have a specifiable level of abstractness and the possibility of modifying it systematically so as to meet the needs of different research goals; (f) it should have a high level of reliability, particularly intercoder reliability; (g) it should be applicable also to the description of others, doing justice to the assumption about the social involvement of the self-concept.

It may be expected that a system of categorisation with these properties could help in promoting the process of solving some of the controversial issues that have hampered progress in the study of the self.

Purpose of the chapter: Questions and hypotheses

In this chapter we shall describe a system of categorisation of self-descriptions that has the properties mentioned above as optimal. In later sections we will illustrate its use by applying it to self-descriptions yielded by individuals of widely different age groups. The application has the aim of answering four general questions. First, is there a cluster of particular aspects or features characterising the self-concept of the individual as she or he describes himself or herself spontaneously? and how does this change with different ages and genders? We focused on adulthood and old age (16 to 90) because very few studies have been devoted to the self-concept in this period (L'Ecuyer, 1981; Rossan, Chapter 19; Suls and Mullen, 1982) in contrast to the many that deal with the self-concept in childhood and adolescence.

The second general question is: How does the spontaneous, context-free description of the self relate to descriptions of the self from various selective viewpoints, i.e. the self in the present, the self in the past, the self in the future, the self as described by the individual to a friend and the self as the individual assumes a good friend would describe him or her? Specifically, we wanted to find out to what extent the same aspects and features would be used in the general and the selective descriptions. The higher the number of shared aspects or features the more support there would be for the view that the self is inherently a unitary entity rather than a multiplicity of context-bound selves.

The third question is: How does the spontaneous self-concept relate to beliefs and attitudes the individual holds in regard to matters of import for the self, i.e. what would constitute self-betrayal, what would constitute change in oneself, what makes the self lovable, what makes the self worthy of rejection, what are the distinguishing features of the self, under what conditions would one feel well/content/happy, and under what conditions would one feel frustrated/discontented/unhappy? The purpose of these explorations was to investigate to what extent individuals used the same aspects and features in describing themselves spontaneously and in forming beliefs in matters that concern the self directly, yet constitute a distinct domain of self-related contents.

The fourth question is: How does the spontaneous self-concept relate to descriptions of other persons? Specifically, we wanted to find out to what extent individuals use the same aspects and features in describing themselves spontaneously and in describing other people. In view of previous findings about differences of liked and disliked persons (Leahy, 1976; Livesley and Bromley, 1973), we distinguished between persons the individual loves/respects/accepts and those he or she hates/does not respect/rejects. Notably, previous research has centred on studying either descriptions of the self or of other persons (Hamilton, 1981; Livesley and Bromley, 1973) but rarely the relations between these tantalisingly close kinds of descriptions (e.g. Markus and Sentis, 1982). This part of the study was designed to fill this gap to some extent. We expected to be able to show that our system of categorisation, which is adequate for coding self-descriptions, applies also to descriptions of others. This would lend support to the assumption that essentially a person treats himself or herself as (s)he does the figures of other people (Wegner and Vallacher, 1977, Chapter 6).

In addition to the four questions, we had two hypotheses which referred to developmental trends across the studied age span. The first was that between the ages of 16 and 90 years the self-concept would gradually become broader and richer, i.e. would include a greater number of aspects and features. Our rationale was that increase in the differentiation of cognitive abilities and in the extent of exposure to life experiences would promote continued development after the age of 16. The second hypothesis was that the extent of similarity between the features used in self-descriptions, on the one hand, and those used in selective descriptions of the self, self-related beliefs and descriptions of others, on the other hand, would decrease with time because age may bring about an enhanced awareness of the distinctiveness of the self.

The system of meaning

The set of categories we suggest for coding descriptions of the self and others is anchored in the system of meaning (Kreitler and Kreitler, 1976, 1986b, 1987) which was developed in order to enable the coding of verbal and non-verbal meanings for purposes of assessment, comparison and manipulation. A brief description of this system is necessary for understanding the method and findings of the study.

The most basic cognitive process in our system is initial input identification. It involves predication, which, to paraphrase Sapir (1949, p. 119), could be defined as 'saying or thinking something about something'. In our terms, an input to the cognitive system, namely, some external or internal phenomenon, is identified by assigning to it one or more units of cognitive contents called 'meaning values'. Since the meaning values mostly refer only to particular aspects of the attended input, we call the aspects to which they refer 'referent', thereby distinguishing between the input as such, defined in physical, physiological or even social terms, and the referent which is the focus of the assigned meaning values. For example, the input may be a given phrase or a presented picture while the referent would be a word included in the phrase or some figure in the picture. The meaning value is a minimal unit of cognitive contents, verbal or non-verbal, assigned to the referent as its meaning, or, in simpler terms, as an answer to a particular implicit question about the referent. If the referent is, say, 'a rose', the meaning values could be 'It is red', 'I don't like it', 'It has petals', and so on. Accordingly, *meaning is defined as a referent-centred pattern of meaning values.*

In the framework of the meaning system the meaning values are coded in terms of variables which were derived empirically on the basis of data collected from thousands of subjects (differing in age, gender, education, occupation, SES, cultural background and nationality) in a standard experimental situation in which the individual is requested to communicate to a hypothetical other the meaning of a standard set of stimuli. There are four sets of meaning variables: (a) *meaning dimensions*, which characterise the contents of the meaning values, e.g. actions, material (set I, Table 21.1); (b) *types of relation*, which characterise the quality of the relation of the meaning values to the referent, e.g. attributive, comparative (set II, Table 21.1); (c) *forms of relation*, which characterise the logical–formal relation of the meaning values to the referent, e.g. assertive, conjunctive (set III, Table 21.1); and (d) *referent shift* variables, which characterise the changes in the referent that often occur in the course of meaning assignment, e.g. fragmentation, association (set IV, Table 21.1).

In coding materials in terms of meaning we use meaning variables of all four kinds for each unit of response, one from each set. Both verbal and

TABLE 21.1 *Major variables of the meaning system*

I. Dimensions of meaning

1. Contextual allocation
2. Range of inclusion
3. Function, purpose or role
4. Action(s) and potentialities for action
5. Manner of occurrence or operation
6. Antecedents and causes
7. Consequences and results
8. Domain of application
9. Material
10. Structure
11. State and possible changes in it
12. Weight and mass
13. Dimensionality and size
14. Quantity and number
15. Locational qualities
16. Temporal qualities
17. Possessions and belongingness
18. Development
19. Sensory qualities
20. Feelings and emotions
21. Judgements and evaluations
22. Cognitive qualities

II. Types of relation

1. Attributive
   a. Substance–quality
   b. Agent–action
2. Comparative
   a. Similarity, including identity
   b. Dissimilarity, including contrast
   c. Complementariness
   d. Relationality
3. Exemplifying–Illustrative
   a. Exemplifying instance
   b. Exemplifying situation
   c. Exemplifying scene

4. Metaphoric–Symbolic
   a. Interpretation
   b. Metaphor
   c. Symbol

Modes of meaning

Lexical (interpersonally shared) meaning
(1 & 2 under Types of relation)

Symbolic (personal–subjective) meaning
(3 and 4 under Types of relation)

III. Forms of relation

1. Assertion (positive)
2. Denial (negative)
3. Restricted positive (sometimes)
4. Conjunctive

5. Disjunctive
6. Mixed positive and negative (not this but this)
7. Double negation
8. Obligatory

IV. Referent shift variables

As compared with previous or presented referent, referent is:

1. Identical
2. Opposite
3. Partial
4. Previous meaning value
5. Modified

6. Higher level
7. Association
8. Grammatical variation
9. Linguistic label
10. Unrelated

non-verbal materials can be coded. The veridicality of the responses is not considered. The intercoder reliability was uniformly found to be over .95 across a set of responses. Summing the individual's coded responses across stimuli produces the individual's profile of meaning, i.e. a specification of the frequencies with which she or he has used the meaning variables in a standard situation. By summing across individuals one may obtain in a similar way meaning profiles of stimuli, situations, etc.

It will be noted that the meaning variables include as special cases the definitions of meaning used in the assessment of meaning by other investigators. For example, the dimension of function was emphasised by Goldstein and Scheerer (1941), contextual allocation and sensory qualities by Werner and Kaplan (1963), consequences by Peirce (1958), judgments and evaluations, state and actions by Osgood *et al.* (1958), interpersonally shared and personal–subjective modes of meaning by Ogden and Richards (1949), Piaget (1948), and so on.

The meaning variables play an important role in cognition. Studies showed that particular meaning variables correlate highly with performance on particular cognitive tasks, e.g. the meaning dimension 'locational qualities' correlates positively with performance on tests of mazes and of spatial orientation (Kreitler and Kreitler, 1986a), the meaning dimension 'manner of occurrence and operation' correlates positively with planning (Kreitler and Kreitler, 1987). Further, types of relation play an important role in creative thinking, forms of relation in logical tasks and rule learning, and referent shift variables in problem-solving, particularly when decentring, contextualisation and integration are called for. Owing to the complexity of most cognitive tasks, the performance on a cognitive task is almost always correlated not only with one dominant meaning variable but with a whole set of meaning variables, e.g. in addition to the meaning dimension 'locational qualities' high performance on a mazes test is correlated also with the meaning dimensions of structure, size and sensory qualities (form) and the comparative type of relation of similarity. More importantly, the study of the relations between meaning variables and cognitive performance shows that the meaning variables are involved sometimes as processes and sometimes as contents. Thus, a person who scores high in the meaning profile on the meaning dimension 'antecedents and causes' performs better on tasks that require causal thinking (e.g. inferences) than a person who scores low on this dimension. But, in addition, the high scorer would also perform better those tasks in which causes appear as contents; for example, he or she would categorise or remember better items that refer to causes (Kreitler and Kreitler, 1986a). Moreover, it was shown that modifying particular meaning variables by means of systematic training raises the level of performance in predictable domains, for example, in retarded children (Kreitler and Kreitler, 1986a) or normal adolescents (Arnon and Kreitler, 1984). Because of the systematic and predictable involvement of the meaning variables in the most diverse forms of cognitive functioning, spanning the field from perception (Kreitler and Kreitler, 1983) to problem-solving (Arnon and Kreitler, 1984), we regard the meaning variables not as hypothetical constructs but as active tendencies of meaning assignment that enable and regulate cognitive action, either as processes or as contents, depending on the context or the point of observation. Further, the meaning assignment tendencies may combine with one another and thus allow for delineating or focusing on highly specific domains of contents. When the meaning dimension of 'consequences and results' is combined in turn with the dimensions of 'feelings and emotions' or 'actions' we obtain more specific categories of results, i.e. emotional results and behavioural results, respectively. These combinations of meaning variables allow for adjustments in the level of abstractness or for devising finer-grained categories, in line with the needs of research or diagnosis. The latter remarks lay the groundwork for a new emerging psychosemantic theory of cognition that defines cognition as the meaning-processing system: a system that assigns, elaborates, transforms, analyses, combines, integrates, produces, applies and stores meanings.

Subjects and procedure of the study

There were 160 subjects of four age groups: 16 to 18 years, 20 to 30 years, 30 to 60 years and 60 to 90 years. In each group there were twenty men and twenty women matched in occupations and cultural background. In each group half were of Middle Eastern or North African background, and half of European or North American background. All subjects were of medium SES. The questionnaires were administered individually, in an oral form, in two separate sessions, the one devoted to self-descriptions, the other to descriptions of others. In half the cases, randomly determined, interviews about the self were given first, in the other half interviews about others were first. All the material was coded, by individuals who did not participate as experimenters, in terms of the four groups of meaning variables (intercoder reliability was .89).

The system of meaning was chosen for coding because it has all the properties of the optimal system. Let us now illustrate the use of the system for coding self-descriptions. For the response 'I am a woman' we get: meaning dimension: contextual allocation; type of relation: attributive; form of relation: positive; referent shift: referent identical to input. For the response 'My eyes are smaller than my sister's' we get: meaning dimension: size; type of relation: comparative; form of relation: positive; referent shift: referent is part of input. For the response 'Mother does not buy me a bicycle' we get: meaning dimension: actions (passive); type of relation: exemplifying instance; form of relation: negative; referent shift: referent identical to input.

Findings and conclusions

The results showed that in describing themselves in general subjects used a large number of different meaning variables (12 to 24). Since the means are higher than for other referents we have studied, the self appears to be the focus for a particularly rich matrix of meanings. This wealth of meanings highlights the limitations of the research on the self that has traditionally focused on evaluative aspects only. The means rise linearly from the youngest to the oldest age group (Table 21.2), which indicates that even beyond adolescence there is – as expected in line with our first hypothesis – a steady extension in the self-concept. The extension is so far-reaching that, whereas adolescents use 37.5 per cent of the meaning variables in the meaning system in communicating about the self, subjects beyond 60 use 74 per cent. One could almost say that beyond 60 there is a tendency for the self and the world to converge. In the two younger age groups (16 to 18 and 20 to 30) there is a difference between women and men in the number of meaning variables used for describing the self: women use more. The difference disappears in the older age groups.

When the raw scores of meaning variables of each kind are converted into percentages of the total number of meaning variables used in the group, the comparison across groups indicates that there is a tendency for a decrease in the use of different meaning dimensions and the referent shift

TABLE 21.2   *Means of meaning variables used in self-descriptions by subjects in four age groups*

	Age groups			
Groups of meaning variables	16 to 18 Years	20 to 30 Years	30 to 60 Years	60 to 90 Years
Meaning dimensions	6.2	7.9	8.3	11.4
Types of relation	2.1	2.8	3.5	4.6
Forms of relation	1.3	1.2	2.2	3.9
Referent shifts	2.4	3.1	3.0	3.8
Total	12.0	15.0	17.0	23.7
Gender: Men	10.0	13.2	16.2	22.6
Women	14.0*	16.8*	17.8	24.8
Percentage of all meaning variables[a]	37.5	46.9	53.1	74.1

* The difference is significant at the level of $p < .05$.

[a] For the sake of this computation the total number of meaning variables in the system of meaning was considered as 32 (i.e. 22 meaning dimensions; 4 types of relation, i.e. II.1., II.2., II.3. and II.4. in Table 21.1; 3 forms of relation, as defined in note *a* in Table 21.3; and 3 referent shifts, as defined in note *b* in Table 21.3).

variables (the percentages are, for dimensions, 51.7, 52.7, 48.8 and 48.1 per cent and, for referent shifts, 20.0, 20.7, 17.6 and 16.0 per cent in the four groups, respectively) and a tendency for increase in the use of different types of relation and forms of relation. These tendencies are not a function of the distribution of the kinds of variables in the meaning system (since the distribution in each age group differs significantly from the distribution in the whole system) but rather they indicate a growing differentiation in the interrelations and structural elements used for communicating the self-concept.

More revealing about the contents of the self-concept are the differences between the age groups in the frequencies of particular meaning variables. The most salient dimensions in the youngest age group (16 to 18 years) are actions the self does, emotions, size, weight and physical characteristics; in the medium age groups (20 to 30 and 30 to 60 years) they are actions the self does and actions done to or with the self, manner of operation (which indicates among other things concern with style), emotions, possessions and domain of application (which indicates concern with interpersonal relations); and in the oldest age groups they are actions done to or with the person, state (e.g. health), contextual allocation (e.g. to which groups the individual belongs), development, and judgments and evaluations.

These findings suggest that in terms of contents the self-concept becomes embedded in an ever-widening context. In adolescence the predominant orientation is focused on action and physical characteristics, in the middle-range groups the orientation is amplified by further emphases on passive actions, style, emotions, interpersonal relations and possessions, and in old age it is amplified by the characteristic consideration of judgments and evaluations, state (which includes health, strength and friendships) and a developmental perspective. Thus, in contrast to preadolescent developments in the self-concept that seem largely to fit the schematic progression from the actional and external poles to the psychological and internal poles (Keller *et al.*, 1978; Montemayor and Eisen, 1977), the postadolescent extensions in the self-concept cannot be adequately characterised in global terms, such as movement from the actional to the emotional pole or an increased differentiation of the psychological orientation. The extensions appear to be more complex, diverse and multidirectional.

In addition, there is with age an extension in the use of other meaning variables (Tables 21.2 and 21.3). Concerning types of relation, already in adolescence there is an enhanced use of the attributive type of relation which reflects lexical interpersonally shared meaning and of the exemplifying type of relation that reflects personal–subjective meaning. With age there is a bolstering of these two tendencies. First, in the ages 20 to 60 years there is an extension of lexical meaning through an increased use of the comparative type of relation, indicating an enhanced tendency to compare the self with others; second, above age 60 there is an extension of personal

TABLE 21.3   *Percentages of subjects in the four age groups who used each meaning variable in their self-descriptions*

Meaning variables	Age groups			
	16 to 18 Years	20 to 30 Years	30 to 60 Years	60 to 90 Years
Meaning dimensions				
Contextual allocation		18	10	41
Range of inclusion	12			8
Function	6	22	31	15
Actions (active)	94	89	78	41
Actions (passive)	20	35	49	87
Manner of occurrence	7	58	55	12
Causes and antecedents	5			6
Consequences and results	17		10	14
Domain of application (subject)		65	72	20
Domain of application (object)	20	46	34	29
Structure	10			21
State	14	29	40	85
Weight	29			10
Size and dimensions	48	12	15	6
Locational qualities				10
Temporal qualities				18
Possessions and belongingness		52	56	10
Development		12	8	37
Sensory qualities (of referent)	66	21	11	7
Sensory qualities (experienced)	50			18
Feelings and emotions (evoked)	42	27	30	18
Feelings and emotions (experienced)	69	65	69	29
Judgments and evaluations		20	22	96
Cognitive qualities	16			20
Types of relation				
Attributive	96	98	99	96
Comparative	10	49	69	23
Exemplifying–illustrative	45	23	30	54
Metaphoric–symbolic	2	5	14	43
Forms of relation[a]				
Positive	100	100	100	100
Negative	20	45	36	14
Complex	11	14	26	67
Referent shift variables[b]				
Near shifts	95	100	100	75
Medium shifts	20	51	70	68
Far shifts		7	18	99

meaning through an increased use of the metaphoric–symbolic type of relation, indicating an enhanced depth in considering the self, perhaps along the lines of individuation suggested by Jung (1956). As might be expected, there is also evidence for an increased structurisation of the self-concept. In adolescence assertion is the main form of relating contents to the self (i.e. 'I am x, y'), after adolescence there is an increased use of negation (i.e. the self is also described through what it is *not*, such as 'I am not a fascist', 'I do not drink'), and in old age there is an increased use of complex forms of relation (e.g. conjunction – 'I take care of my health and also try to get pleasure out of living' – or disjunction – 'Either I feel a sympathy with a person or I completely reject him'). Of particular interest is the evidence concerning the growing tendency to use referent shift variables that are increasingly distant from the self. This tendency starts in subjects 20 to 30 years old and reaches its climax in the subjects of the oldest age group, who in describing themselves use referents apparently far removed from the self more than they use the self itself as a referent. This finding indicates that with age there occurs an extension in the referents considered when describing the self. When people grow older, more themes, i.e. other people, objects, acts, events and concepts, become relevant for expounding the meaning of the self. This finding complements the above-noted extension that occurs in the use of meaning variables. Together the two findings illustrate most clearly the mentioned extension of context in describing the self that is particularly prominent in the oldest age group.

A different domain of findings concerns the correspondence between the meaning variables used for describing the self and those used in other domains: selective descriptions of the self, beliefs in matters of import to the self and descriptions of others. Table 21.4 shows that the majority of meaning variables used for selective descriptions of the self ($\bar{X}=72.1$ per cent) and for beliefs in matters of import for the self ($\bar{X}=71.8$ per cent) are identical to those used in describing the self-concept. Notably, the correspondence tends to be higher in the case of positive than negative aspects of the self, e.g. it is 94 per cent in regard to features that make the self lovable and only 69 per cent in regard to those that make the self deserving of rejection. But, on the whole, the correspondence is sufficiently high to suggest that the self-concept is in fact a broad, surprisingly stable matrix of meaning variables, out of which specific subsets may be sampled – and even further differentiated in terms of different meaning values for the

---

The percentages are rounded to the closest unity. Percentages below 5 per cent are not mentioned in the table.

[a] 'Positive' forms include III.1 and III.3–8; 'Negative' include III.2, III.6 and III.7; 'Complex' include III.4 to 7 (see Table 21.1).

[b] 'Near shifts' include IV.1, IV.3, IV.8; 'Medium shifts' include IV.2 and IV.4–6; 'Far shifts' include IV.7, IV.9, IV.10 (see Table 21.1).

TABLE 21.4   *Correspondence between meaning variables used for the self-concept and for related domains*

Domains and themes	Age groups			
	16 to 18 Years	20 to 30 Years	30 to 60 Years	60 to 90 Years
Selective descriptions of the self				
Self in the present	91	90	90	93
Self in the past	62	45	71	84
Self in the future	80	68	66	87
Self described to a friend	75	59	54	93
Self described by another	54	51	56	74
Mean percentage of correspondence	72.4	62.6	67.4	86.2
Mean interprofile correlation	.29	.35	.48	.77
Matters of import for the self				
Self-betrayal	78	70	76	97
Change in oneself	40	41	44	90
That which makes oneself lovable	100	90	88	100
That which makes oneself deserving of rejection	64	60	63	88
Distinguishing features	100	85	87	100
Good times for oneself	56	51	54	76
Bad times for oneself	47	50	52	62
Mean percentage of correspondence	69.3	63.9	66.3	87.6
Mean interprofile correlation	.31	.30	.41	.80
Descriptions of others				
Positive figures	67	65	64	66
Negative figures	49	51	53	63
Mean percentage of correspondence	58	58	58.5	64.5
Mean interprofile correlation	.37	.42	.59	.75

same meaning variables – in line with the requirements of particular situations.

In so far as different situations may demand emphasis on different aspects of the self or even different self-presentations, the subsets sampled from the self-concept matrix should not be expected to be highly similar if flexibility is to be upheld. Indeed, the means of the interprofile correlations between selective self-descriptions ($\bar{X}=.36$) and self-related beliefs ($\bar{X}=.33$) are not high in the age range 16 to 60 years. Thus, there must be context-guided selectivity of descriptions from a larger set in order for it to be possible to preserve the constancy of the self-concept and coherence in the broad domain of self-related responses, without giving up flexibility and adaptability. This principle may underlie the observation that with age the correspondence between the self and selective descriptions of the self, as well as self-related beliefs, does not decrease (as expected in line with our second hypothesis) but remains fairly constant up to the age of 60 years and then even increases.

The findings for the oldest age group require special mention. Beyond 60 there is a change in the data: both the correspondence of the subsets to the basic self-concept increases from the means of 66.5 to 67.5 per cent to the means of 86.2 to 87.6 per cent *and* the mean interprofile correlations increase from .33 to .36 to .77 to .80. It seems that beyond 60 the self preserves its full identity to a greater extent in different relations and situations while the changes in self-presentation in different contexts become more limited, so that flexibility decreases.

Both of these phenomena are probably functions of the increased number of meaning variables used by older people for describing the self. We do not know to what extent physiological or emotional changes play a role in broadening the self-concept in older ages but it seems likely that cognitive development does, both because there is evidence about the extension in the use of meaning variables from 2 to 18 years, and because training of meaning based on directed intensive multimodal experiences was shown to lead to an enduring extension of meaning variables in retarded children (Kreitler and Kreitler, 1986a). Since the training differs from exposure to life experiences mainly in being more systematic, condensed and time-limited, we assume that it is the cognitive assimilation, i.e. elaboration in terms of available meaning variables of an increasing number of life experiences, that underlies the gradually enriched view of oneself reflected in what is often called the 'wisdom' of old age. Thus, cognitive level may be a determinant of the self-concept not only in younger age groups (Bromley, 1977; Leahy, 1985; Rosenberg, 1977) but along the whole developmental span.

However, our findings about the increased number of meaning variables and the decreased flexibility in old age are intriguing. Although psychologists often claim that a differentiated and extended self-concept is an indicator of mental health and adaptability (Epstein, 1973; Gergen, 1971; Kelly, 1955; Scott, 1974), we observed that the increase in differentiation (as assessed by the increase in the number of meaning variables used) is coupled with a decrease in flexibility (as assessed by increase in the mean of interprofile correlations). One possible reason is that the expected positive correlation between the two variables is restricted to a certain range. That is, differentiation only up to a certain degree would make for an increase in flexibility, while differentiation beyond that degree would lead to a decrease in flexibility, perhaps by threatening one's sense of coherence and integration, thereby producing anxiety (see also Wegner and Vallacher, 1977). Hence one would expect both low and high differentiation to be related to low degrees of flexibility, though possibly for different reasons.

There is a further domain in which the self-concept is manifested: descriptions of others. Our findings (Table 21.4) show that the majority of meaning variables used for describing others are identical with those used for the self-concept. The range of correspondence for the different kinds of figures and age groups is 51 to 67 per cent and the mean is 57.5 per cent. This mean is significantly lower than the means for selective descriptions of the self (72.1 per cent) or for self-related beliefs (71.2 per cent). This is to be expected because, though others may be close to oneself, they do not constitute integral parts of the self in the same sense as, say, the image of oneself in the past or the future. Again, as in the cases of selective self-descriptions and self-related beliefs, the correspondence does not decrease with age (as expected in line with our second hypothesis) but remains constant for the ages 16 to 60 and then even increases. Yet, on the whole, the correspondence is sufficiently high to indicate that the individual uses for describing oneself and others cognitive tools (processes and contents) sampled from the same sphere of meaning variables. The correspondence is higher in the case of positively evaluated persons ($\bar{X}=65.5$ per cent) than negatively evaluated persons ($\bar{X}=54$ per cent). The reason may be that sympathy enhances the judgment of similarity or vice versa (Byrne, 1971). Another difference in the description of positively and negatively evaluated persons is that in regard to the former the correspondence percentages remain the same for the four age groups, but in regard to the latter there is an increase in correspondence in the oldest age group. Here again one may be tempted to remark that in older people the self-concept becomes so broad that it is sufficiently stable to allow for describing in the same terms not only friends and loved ones but even one's enemies. Moreover, the higher interprofile correlation in this group (.75) indicates that, with age, people tend increasingly to describe both loved and rejected people in terms of the same meaning variables. Thus there is a decreased differentiation in the sphere of interpersonal concepts.

Attempts at some answers

Analysis of the data in terms of the meaning system has provided findings that can be used for answering some of the questions raised. First, the specific questions of this study (see 'Purpose of the chapter: Questions and hypotheses'). The study showed basic characteristics of the contents and structure of the self-concept across the age span 16 to 90, which were the concern of the first question. These characteristics consist of specific categories of contents and modes of interrelating these contents which form part of the meaning system. Further, it was shown that the meaning of the self is communicated by means of an increasing number of meaning variables. Thus, the self is a matrix of cognitive processes and contents subject to extensions after 16 years of age in contents, in reflection of interpersonally shared and personal–subjective meanings, in references to other referents and in increased complexity of patterning – all of which make for a developmentally significant increase in breadth, stability and adaptability. The self-concept of people after 60 was found to be very broad but less flexible than that of people younger than 60.

Concerning the second question, since a high degree of similarity ($\bar{X} \approx 72$ per cent of correspondence) was found in the cognitive means used for describing the self in general and from various specific viewpoints, it is justified to conclude that there is a unitary self, partial manifestations of which are based on particular samples selected from the comprehensive pool.

Concerning the third question, since a high degree of similarity ($\bar{X} \approx 72$ per cent of correspondence) was found in the cognitive means used for describing the self and beliefs about matters of import to the self, the self-concept may be considered as a comprehensive matrix shaping cognitive activity in the broad sphere of self-relevant matters and information.

Concerning the fourth question, it was shown that individuals use to some degree ($\bar{X} \approx 60$ per cent of correspondence) the same cognitive means for describing themselves and others so that it seems justified to consider the self-concept matrix of meaning variables as shaping to some extent interpersonal perception in general.

Let us turn now to the more general questions involved in the study of the self (see 'Controversial issues'). Concerning the dichotomy between the self as 'the knower' and as 'the known', it seems that a bridge can be formed when we consider, first, that the meaning variables may be manifest both as processes basic for general information processing (thus underlying the active facet of the self as 'the knower') and as contents (reflected in the conceptual facet of the self as 'the known'). Second, there is a high similarity between the meaning variables used in self-related beliefs which enter as active elements into the shaping of behaviour (Kreitler and Kreitler, 1976) (and hence manifest the self as 'the knower') and those used for describing the self (which manifest the self as 'the known').

Concerning the issue of unity versus multiplicity of manifestations and stability versus variability through changes, a possible solution can be outlined by considering, first, that the self may function as a basic matrix from which different samples may be drawn in line with specific contextual requirements and, second, that a meaning variable may remain unchanged whereas the meaning values subsumed under it may change. Thus, the self can be assumed to be a unitary entity, though its particular manifestations may differ in different situations or roles, and as a stable entity, though it may undergo developmental change.

Concerning the issue of self versus others, a possible solution for upholding both the similarity and the difference between self and others may be envisaged by considering, first, that similarity may refer to identical meaning variables used for describing self and others, while difference may refer to the different meaning values used in the actual descriptions, and, second, that only about 60 per cent of the meaning variables used for describing others are identical to those used for self-description.

Finally, concerning the issue of the contents of the self, our suggestion is to define the contents in terms of the meaning system that provides a set of categories which has all the properties of an optimal system: it is rooted in cognitive theory; it is stable, independent of context, free of experimenter bias, sufficiently broad and highly reliable; it includes other sets of categories in this field; it is applicable for coding contents in other spheres; and, above all, it is adequate for analysing descriptions of self and others. Since its application to the study of self has led to some insights concerning basic controversial issues in the conceptions of self and others, it is likely that meaning variables and meaning values are basic constituents of human reality, which is defined mainly by 'self' and 'others' and the network of their multiple interrelations.

References

Anderson, L. W. (1981), 'An examination of the nature of change in academic self-concept', in M. D. Lynch, A. A. Norem-Hebeisen and K. Gergen (eds), *Self Concept: Advances in Theory and Research*, Ballinger: Cambridge, Mass., pp. 273–82.

Arnon, R. and Kreitler, S. (1984), 'Effects of meaning training on overcoming functional fixedness', *Current Psychological Research and Reviews*, 3, pp. 11–24.

Bandura, A. (1982), 'The self and mechanisms of agency', in J. Suls (ed.), *Psychological Perspectives on the Self*, vol. 1, Erlbaum: Hillsdale, N.J., pp. 3–39.

Bromley, D. B. (1977), 'Natural language and the development of the self', in H. E. Howe, Jr. and C. B. Keasey (eds), *Nebraska Symposium on Motivation 1977*, University of Nebraska Press: Lincoln, pp. 117–67.

Bugental, J. F. T. (1964), 'Investigations into the self-concept: III. Instructions for the W-A-Y method', *Psychological Reports*, 15, pp. 643–50.

Byrne, D. (1971), *The Attraction Paradigm*, Academic Press: New York.

Cantor, N., Mischel, W. and Schwartz, J. C. (1982), 'A prototype analysis of psychological situations', *Cognitive Psychology*, 14, pp. 45–77.

Coopersmith, S. (1967), *The Antecedents of Self-Esteem*, Freeman: San Francisco.

L'Ecuyer, R. (1981), 'The development of the self-concept through the life span', in M. D. Lynch, A. A. Norem-Hebeisen and K. Gergen (eds), *Self Concept: Advances in Theory and Research*, Ballinger: Cambridge, Mass., pp. 203–18.

Epstein, S. (1973), 'The self-concept revisited: Or a theory of a theory', *American Psychologist*, 28, pp. 404–16.

Epstein, S. (1983), 'A research paradigm for the study of personality and emotions', in R. A. Dienstbier and M. M. Page (eds), *Nebraska Symposium on Motivation 1982: Personality – Current Theory and Research*, University of Nebraska Press: Lincoln, pp. 91–154.

Fiske, S. T. and Taylor, S. E. (1984), *Social Cognition*, Addison-Wesley: Reading, Mass.

Freud, S. (1964), 'New introductory lectures on psycho-analysis', in *Standard Edition of the Complete Psychological Works of Sigmund Freud*, Hogarth Press and the Institute of Psycho-Analysis: London, pp. 3–182.

Gergen, K. J. (1971), *The Concept of Self*, Holt, Rinehart & Winston: New York.

Glick, M. and Zigler, E. (1985), 'Self-image: A cognitive-developmental approach', in R. Leahy (ed.), *The Development of the Self*, Academic Press: New York, pp. 1–53.

Goldstein, K. and Scheerer, M. (1941), 'Abstract and concrete behavior: An experimental study with special tests', *Psychological Monographs*, 52, no. 2.

Gordon, C. (1968), 'Self conceptions: Configurations of content', in C. Gordon and K. J. Gergen (eds), *The Self in Social Interaction, vol. 1., Classic and Contemporary Perspectives*, Wiley: New York, pp. 115–36.

Hamilton, D. L. (1981), 'Cognitive representations of persons', in E. T. Higgins, C. P. Herman and M. P. Zanna (eds), *Social Cognition: The Ontario Symposium*, vol. 1, Erlbaum: Hillsdale, N.J., pp. 135–59.

Harré, R. (1983), *Personal Being*, Blackwell: Oxford.

Harter, S. (1985), 'Competence as a dimension of self-evaluation: Toward a comprehensive model of self-worth', in R. Leahy (ed.), *The Development of the Self*, Academic Press: New York, pp. 55–121.

James, W. (1890), *Principles of Psychology*, 2 vols, Holt: New York.

Jones, E. E. and Pittman, T. S. (1982), 'Toward a general theory of strategic self-presentation', in J. Suls (ed.), *Psychological Perspectives on the Self*, vol. 1, Erlbaum: Hillsdale, N.J., pp. 231–82.

Jordan, T. J. and Merrifield, P. R. (1981), 'Self-concepting: Another aspect of aptitude', in M. D. Lynch, A. A. Norem-Hebeisen and K. Gergen (eds), *Self Concept: Advances in Theory and Research*, Ballinger: Cambridge, Mass., pp. 87–95.

Jung, C. G. (1956), *Symbols of Transformation*, Routledge & Kegan Paul: London.

Keller, A., Ford, L. and Meacham, J. (1978), 'Dimensions of self-concept in preschool children', *Developmental Psychology*, 14, pp. 483–4.

Kelly, G. A. (1955), *The Psychology of Personal Constructs*, Norton: New York.

Kreitler, H. and Kreitler, S. (1967), *Die Kognitive Orientierung des Kindes*, Ernst Reinhardt: Munich and Basel.

Kreitler, H. and Kreitler, S. (1976), *Cognitive Orientation and Behavior*, Springer Publishing: New York.

Kreitler, S. and Kreitler, H. (1983), 'Meaning assignment in perception', in W. D. Froehlich, G. J. W. Smith, J. G. Draguns and U. Hentschel (eds), *Psychological Processes in Cognition and Personality*, Hemisphere: New York, pp. 173–91.

Kreitler, S. and Kreitler, H. (1986a), 'The cognitive rehabilitation of the retarded', Unpublished manuscript, Tel Aviv University.

Kreitler, S. and Kreitler, H. (1986b), 'Traits: The cognitive perspective', Unpublished manuscript, Tel Aviv University.

Kreitler, S. and Kreitler, H. (1987), 'Plans and planning: Their motivational and cognitive antecedents', in S. L. Friedman, E. K. Scholnick and R. R. Cocking (eds), *Blueprints for Thinking: The Role of Planning in Cognitive Development*, Cambridge University Press: New York, pp. 110–178.

Kuiper, N. A. and Derry, P. A. (1981), 'The self as a cognitive prototype: An application to person perception and depression', in N. Cantor and J. F. Kihlstrom (eds), *Personality, Cognition and Social Interaction*, Erlbaum: Hillsdale, N.J., pp. 215–32.

Leahy, R. L. (1976), 'Developmental trends in qualified inferences and descriptions of self and others', *Developmental Psychology*, 12, pp. 546–7.

Leahy, R. L. (1985), 'The development of the self: Conclusions', in R. L. Leahy (ed.), *The Development of the Self*, Academic Press: New York, pp. 295–304.

Lewis, M. and Brooks-Gunn, J. (1981), 'The self as social knowledge', in M. D. Lynch, A. A. Norem-Hebeisen and K. Gergen (eds), *Self Concept: Advances in Theory and Research*, Ballinger: Cambridge, Mass., pp. 101–18.

Livesley, W. J. and Bromley, D. B. (1973), *Person Perception in Childhood and Adolescence*, Wiley: New York.

Markus, H. (1977), 'Self-schemata and processing information about the self', *Journal of Personality and Social Psychology*, 35, pp. 63–78.

Markus, H. and Sentis, K. (1982), 'The self in social information processing', in J. Suls (ed.), *Psychological Perspectives on the Self*, vol. 1, Erlbaum: Hillsdale, N.J., pp. 41–70.

Markus, H. and Smith, J. (1981), 'The influence of self-schemata on the perception of others', in N. Cantor and J. F. Kihlstrom (eds), *Personality, Cognition and Social Interaction*, Erlbaum: Hillsdale, N.J., pp. 233–62.

McGuire, W. J. and McGuire, C. V. (1981), 'The spontaneous self-concept as affected by personal distinctiveness', in M. D. Lynch, A. A. Norem-Hebeisen and K. Gergen (eds), *Self Concept: Advances in Theory and Research*, Ballinger: Cambridge, Mass., pp. 147–71.

McGuire, W. J. and McGuire, C. V. (1982), 'Significant others in the self-space: Sex differences and developmental trends in the social self', in J. Suls (ed.), *Psychological Perspectives on the Self*, vol. 1, Erlbaum: Hillsdale, N.J., pp. 71–96.

McGuire, W. J., McGuire, C. V. and Winton, W. (1979), 'Effects of household sex composition on the salience of one's gender in the spontaneous self-concept', *Journal of Experimental Social Psychology*, 15, pp. 77–90.

McPartland, T. S. (1965), *Manual for the Twenty-Statements Problem* (rev. ed.), Greater Kansas City Mental Health Foundation: Kansas City.

Mead, G. H. (1934), *Mind, Self and Society*, University of Chicago Press: Chicago.

Montemayor, R. and Eisen, M. (1977), 'The development of self-conceptions from childhood to adolescence', *Developmental Psychology*, 13, pp. 314–19.

Ogden, R. M. and Richards, I. A. (1949), *The Meaning of Meaning*, Routledge & Kegan Paul: London.

Osgood, C. E., Suci, G. J. and Tannenbaum, P. H. (1958), *The Measurement of Meaning*, Illinois University Press: Urbana.

Peirce, C. S. (1958), *The Collected Papers of C. S. Peirce*, Harvard University Press: Cambridge, Mass.

Piaget, J. (1948), *Language and Thought of the Child*, Routledge & Kegan Paul: London.

Rosenberg, M. (1965), *Society and the Adolescent Self-Image*, Princeton University Press: Princeton.

Rosenberg, S. (1977), 'New approaches to the analysis of personal constructs in person perception', in J. K. Cole and A. W. Landfield (eds), *Nebraska Symposium on Motivation 1976*, University of Nebraska Press: Lincoln, pp. 179–242.

Sapir, E. (1949), *Language: An Introduction to the Study of Speech*, Harcourt Brace Jovanovich: New York.

Scott, W. A. (1974), 'Varieties of cognitive integration', *Journal of Personality and Social Psychology*, 30, pp. 563–78.

Shane, M. and Shane, E. (1980), 'Psychoanalytic developmental theories of the self: An integration', in A. Goldberg (ed.), *Advances in Self Psychology*, International Universities Press: New York, pp. 23–46.

Smith, M. B. (1980), 'Attitudes, values and selfhood', in H. E. Howe, Jr. and M. M. Page (eds), *Nebraska Symposium on Motivation 1979*, University of Nebraska Press: Lincoln, pp. 305–50.

Spitzer, S., Couch, C. and Stratton, J. (1971), *The Assessment of Self*, Sernoll: Iowa City.

Suls, J. and Mullen, B. (1982), 'From the cradle to the grave: Comparison and self-evaluation across the life-span', in J. Suls (ed.), *Psychological Perspectives on the Self*, vol. 1, Erlbaum: Hillsdale, N.J., pp. 97–125.

Wegner, D. M. and Vallacher, R. R. (1977), *Implicit Psychology*, Oxford

University Press: New York.

Werner, H. and Kaplan, B. (1963), *Symbol Formation*, Wiley: New York.

Wylie, R. (1961), *The Self Concept*, University of Nebraska Press: Lincoln.

Wylie, R. C. (1974), *The Self-Concept*, vol. 1, University of Nebraska Press: Lincoln.

22 'Now I know who I really am.' Identity change and redefinitions of the self in adoption

Erica Haimes

Introduction

This chapter examines the concepts of self and identity in relation to adoption. It is based on a study of the law which gives adopted adults in Britain access to their original birth records (Section 26, Children Act, 1975). This legislation is used by adoptees to obtain a copy of their original birth certificates: from the information contained therein, they may trace their natural parents, if they wish. The information they gain leads them to question their 'true' identity and hence to reformulate their self-knowledge.

Although the chapter is based on an empirical piece of research, I shall attempt to fuse those empirical findings with certain theoretical perspectives on self and identity. More specifically, I shall attempt to relate the idea of personal or ego-identity to the concept of 'social identity'. In doing so I shall be drawing particularly from the work of sociologists such as Anselm Strauss and Erving Goffman as well as from the work of the social philosopher, Alastair MacIntyre. I share Strauss' view when he argues,

> Identity as a concept is fully as elusive as is everyone's sense of his
> own personal identity. But whatever else it may be, identity is
> connected with the fateful appraisals made of oneself – by oneself and
> by others. Everyone presents himself to others and to himself and sees
> himself in the mirrors of their judgements (Strauss, 1977, p. xxx).

I shall begin by presenting some of the experiences of a group of adult adoptees in making enquiries about their background, and some of the well-established explanations for this behaviour. This should demonstrate the particular uses made of concepts such as 'self' and 'identity' in this context. I shall then, by relating the individual adoptee's experience to the wider social aspects of adoption, argue that the individual adoptee's sense of identity, and how that is viewed by others, is inextricably tied up with the identity of adoption itself as a socially constructed institution.

Adoption and the theory of the 'identity crisis'

Discovery of his or her adopted status frequently leads the adopted person to question his or her 'true identity'. Such profound questions about the self as 'Who am I really?' reveal the impact such knowledge can have. For many this is compounded by the change in name undergone as part of the adoption process. Adoptees now experience a sense of disjuncture from what they had hitherto assumed to be their 'real identity'. Consequently, they talk, for example, of having two identities or even of having no fixed identity. This can lead to a desire to know the 'real story' of their lives, and they seek to do this by finding out further information about their background and/or by tracing their natural parents.

Such a quest is usually explained as a 'search for identity' by social work practitioners, psychiatrists and child psychologists, all of whom can be implicated in particular instances of adopted children, adolescents and adults making enquiries about their past.

Generally, however, this search is seen by researchers and practitioners alike as a reflection on the individual's adoptive experience: the poorer the adoptive experience, it is argued, the stronger the desire to trace. (See, for example, Triseliotis, 1973.) Those adoptees who were so interested in their past as to wish actually to meet their natural parents were, it has been argued, suffering in some way from a flawed, if not failed, adoption. Their wish was not the product of a natural curiosity, but a 'deep psychological need' (Triseliotis, 1973). Tracing and meeting natural parents was seen as some sort of self-therapy. Certainly aspects of adoption have been stressed in a language that can only serve to emphasise the psycho-pathological aspects of that experience. Earlier writers have written of the necessity for adoptees to undergo periods of grief and mourning for their loss of the past: Shawyer (1979) has even written of the adoptee's 'death by adoption'.

Curiosity about the past is taken, then, as a sign of psychological stress. The adoptee is pictured as confused and lost, and terms such as 'identity crisis' and 'genealogical bewilderment' (Sants, undated) have become accepted explanatory concepts. Adoption as an institution survives, however, because, it is also argued, the number of adopted people who want to trace their natural parents is actually very small, and most adoptees do not suffer such stress or anxiety about their sense of identity.

However, the findings of our research[1] suggested the need for an alternative explanation of why adopted people seek information about their past. This research was primarily intended to be a policy study of the implementation and use of the provision of access to birth records by adopted adults. As part of the project, the author conducted a series of semi-structured interviews with forty-five adoptees, each lasting at least an hour, some much longer. From these detailed discussions it was apparent that, although aware of their public image, these adoptees resisted the labels suggesting current stress or compensation for past experiences. Certainly to the researchers they displayed little evidence of psychological damage: our assessment of them was of normal, well-adjusted adults. Therefore, although initially not a study of the issues of identity in adoption, it became obvious that such issues would have to be addressed if we were to understand, first, why adopted people applied for birth record access under this law and, second, the use to which they put this information once they had acquired their birth certificates.

Quite how these points could be considered emerged quite clearly from our data. Again, given our prime concern with the study of legislation, we felt we wanted to resist the temptation to allow our interviewees simply to tell us their life histories; we wanted to focus the interview on their opinions of the legislation. However, after only a couple of interviews we realised that it was exactly these life histories that, to the adoptees, explained their actions in terms of the legislation. This point is best illustrated by an example.

Mrs A discovered she had been adopted when she was tracing the man she thought was her 'real' father. Her parents had divorced and she had had no contact with him for thirty years. Her interest in regaining contact was stimulated through a family tree project her son had been given at school. Mrs A felt that her adoptive mother's death freed her to start making enquiries.

> I found my father very easily . . . and it just came out in conversation
> that I was an adopted daughter, I just hadn't any idea. I was
> absolutely stunned. . . . I wasn't upset, but I was shocked . . . but it
> answered a few questions.

Mrs A had for a long time felt that in appearance she was totally different from her family and that her consuming interests in life had 'never stemmed from my environment at all'.

Her first action was to 'phone her relations,

> and they all knew . . . and never told me . . . one or two thought I
> knew and all my aunts kept saying, 'Oh, but you were a lovely baby'.
> That's not the point. 'What do you know, what can you tell me?'

The official start of Mrs A's search came when she applied under Section 26 and saw a social worker, to receive the counselling which is a compulsory part of the application procedure. Her original birth certificate revealed her mother's maiden name: 'I just saw this name in print and I said to my son, "Look, that's my mother." It meant so much to me . . . this was my blood mother . . . it was an emotional thing.' She was then able, through her adoptive father, to trace the family her natural mother had worked for when she became pregnant. She heard that her mother 'was on her own, just a young girl on her own, no family I found out since, so she could not keep me'. She also traced a half-brother and through him, eventually, her natural mother. The first contact with her mother, using an aunt as an intermediary, brought forth a denial that her mother had any knowledge of a child with Mrs A's Christian names. Mrs A then wrote to her mother.

> I said, 'I don't want in any way to interfere with your life, cause you
> any embarrassment or upset' . . . how I'd had a happy childhood with
> no trouble there; I didn't want anything from her, I said, 'but you,
> your son and daughter, besides my own children are my only blood
> relatives, and I just want to meet you once, if only once . . .'

Mrs A's mother regretted her earlier denial and invited her to visit. 'So we went the next day and she was lovely and it was just the likeness. . . . I am so like her. . . . I've met my half-brother and he was struck by the resemblance between my mother and me.'

Mrs A supported the legislation for at least two reasons: first, it had given her her mother's name, 'I had this name . . . and I thought that is my mother – real mother, and before . . . you know all sorts of things go through your mind, whether she was somebody grand or somebody poor'; and second, 'it's essential that you have access to your own identity.'[2]

For Mrs A, then, the legislation was only one small, albeit important, step in discovering something about her past. Mrs A's story is not untypical of the other adoptees interviewed for this project, particularly in the portrayal of the search as arising not from stress but from curiosity. She displays a feature of talk which is very common and which we have labelled 'just-talk', since adoptees use the word 'just' to minimise the potential threat of their actions, as in, 'It was just curiosity', 'I just wanted to find out who my mother and father were', 'I just wanted to find out who I was basically'. They are aware of, and to a certain extent share, the image held of adoptees; as one person who was tracing his parents said, 'I used to wonder, naturally you do, but I never had a sort of obsession that I know some people have when they know that they're adopted, to find out their parents.'

The use of 'just-talk' is an attempt to overcome the public image of obsession and to present in its place a rational explanation. As Goffman (1963) argued, 'The painfulness then of sudden stigmatization can come not from the individual's confusion about his identity but from his knowing too well what he has become.'

We would agree that a rational explanation is available and is one which, unlike the psycho-pathological model of ego-crisis, takes into account that social image of adoption and adopted people. We argue specifically for an interactional perspective on adoption, which removes the image of adoptees as 'psychological vagrants' in search of a new set of family relationships and replaces it with a model of adoptees seeking to place themselves socially, in order to remove the unease they and others feel about their adoptive status. We have described this as a psycho-social model of identity.

The key to this explanation lies in what adopted adults themselves say about their reasons for tracing. As one person said, 'I'd like to see her [her natural mother] to finish the story. . . . I'd like to know beginning, middle and end, in general order.' The concept of the story is very common in the explanations adoptees give and this is critical in understanding their experience. Having been placed at birth with adoptive parents they have in a sense been 'dis-placed' from their origins – from their original name, their original parents and their original place of birth. They are unsure how important those unknown features of their lives are and they cannot know this until they know the original facts. The 'search for identity' then can be understood as the search for their life-story, as an attempt to compile a complete consistent biography. The discovery of their adoptive status leads to a reformulation of their life histories and the need to know the full facts.

The importance of having a biography cannot be overstated since this provides the necessary account of one's life that everyone needs, not just adopted people. As MacIntyre (1981) says,

> To be the subject of a narrative that runs from one's birth to one's
> death is . . . to be accountable for the actions and experiences which
> compose a narratable life. It is . . . to be open to being asked to give a
> certain kind of account of what one did or what happened to one or
> what one witnessed at any earlier point in one's life. . . . The other
> aspect of narrative selfhood is correlative: I am not only accountable,
> I am one who can always ask others for an account, who can put
> others to question. I am part of their story as they are part of mine.
> The narrative of any one life is part of an interlocking set of
> narratives. Moreover this asking for and giving accounts itself plays
> an important part in constituting narratives. Asking what you did and
> why, saying what I did and why, pondering the differences between
> your account of what I did and my account of what I did, and vice
> versa, these are essential constituents of all but the very simplest and
> barest of narratives (pp. 202–3).

It is just such a 'narratable life' that adoptees lack until they have the full facts of their life-story. Barbara Hardy (1968) points out how important a narrative sense of self is:

> We dream in narrative, daydream in narrative, remember, anticipate,

hope, despair, believe, doubt, plan, revise, criticise, construct, gossip, learn, hate and love by narrative. In order really to live we make up stories about ourselves and others, about the personal as well as the social past and future . . .

The difficulty for adoptees is that there is very little certain knowledge available about their origins. A second difficulty particular to adoptees is that, as well as having such gaps in their knowledge as we all do, their attempts to fill these gaps are met with censure, some of it self-imposed. The swapping of accounts which MacIntyre considers essential to have all but 'the very simplest and barest of narratives' is the most difficult to achieve for the adopted person, given the barriers of guilt and secrecy she or he has to overcome. However, as one adopted adult argued, unaware of course that he was echoing MacIntyre's words:

> I've thought about it [tracing my natural parents] as the only method of finding out. I mean it's a very difficult decision to make, but I suppose as I get older I realise more and more life is such an extraordinary thing in what happens to one, it's terrible not having part of one's story, it's very hard to account for the way one is.

Those adopted people who overcome the barriers to discover some or all of the facts about their background talk of a feeling of knowing, of completion and of certainty. As one woman said,

> It just confirms – it gives you a little bit more of an identity. It's very hard to explain. I'm not the sort of person that really *cares* what was before. What's in the past is in the past, but at the same time it was something that I wanted to know about, and I did know most of it. I just wanted it confirmed. I like things nice and tidy – I don't like loose ends hanging around.

However, discovering such facts about the self obviously leads to a reformulation of one's personal identity. Two distinct groups emerged from the adopted adults we spoke to: the members of the first group see their individual life histories as comprising the one single-strand narrative, about which they now have more details with which to fill the gaps. There are five stages to their life history in terms of their identity:

Group 1
(i) Period of stable identity → (ii) Discovery of adopted status →
(iii) Discovery of facts about pre-adoption self → (iv) Reappraisal of self →
(v) Original (embellished) identity

In sharp contrast to this are the members of the second group, who view their life history in terms of a true identity which has been hidden from them until now. Looking back on their lives they can identify six distinct periods:

Group 2
(i) Original identity (at birth) → (ii) False identity (as a result of adoption) → (iii) Discovery of adoptive status → (iv) Discovery of facts about pre-adoption self → (v) Reappraisal of self → (vi) Return to their real (i.e. original) identity

For this second group, their life history has two strands of identity running through it, one real but until now hidden, the other false. If we accept Rossan's notions (explained earlier, in Chapter 19) of 'identity' consisting of the core, subidentities and generalised traits, we can see that in this second group of adoptees, it is the *core* of their identities which they consider they have discovered. Since it is argued that it is this aspect of identity that changes least we can only begin to guess the strength of the emotions experienced by members of this group.[3] Examples of the way members of the two groups differ can be seen in their reactions to discovering their original names. As one person who falls into the first, single-identity group said, she expected her original name to make a great impact on her. 'It's who you are, yes, that's it. "Who am I?" And when I did find out my name it didn't make a damn bit of difference.' In contrast to this, a member of the second group said, 'I wanted an identity, you know. Oh, once I got my name I was thrilled to bits. In fact I was all for changing it there and then.' Although this person did not formally change her name, she used her original Christian name in her new job and said, 'I'm getting called by my *proper* name now.'

Whichever of the two groups adoptees fall into they each individually had to work to incorporate their newly acquired knowledge into their lives.[4] As one adopted person mentioned, it felt very odd to discover he had been born in a place he thought he had never even visited before. Similarly, another felt strange on hearing her natural father had been Polish, 'because I had always considered myself wholly British before'. New knowledge such as this involves an immediate rearranging of the facts of the individual's life and a 're-placing' of him/herself in a new biography. Although there are at least these two different ways of reacting to information about themselves, the adoptees share a newly acquired ability to recount their life histories, whether this be done in terms of one single or two interwoven threads. Their social identity, that is, their ability to place themselves in their own and in the life histories of others, becomes clearer as can be seen by Mrs A. Gone, or less frequent, are those embarrassing situations when she and other adoptees lacked social accountability: such as, when pregnant, being unable to furnish details of their own mothers' medical history, or as job applicants being unable to produce full birth certificates when necessary; or as parents being unable to provide their children with a family tree. It is through these apparently 'trivial' social negotiations that any individual demonstrates his/her social competence. Barham (1984), in adapting MacIntyre's ideas, explains it this way:

> Problems of personal identity are thus properly understood as problems in the narrative ordering of human lives, as difficulties that arise for the agent in his efforts to make his life intelligible either to himself or to others.

Identity then can be seen in interactional terms as an ability: the ability to give an intelligible account and hence to be seen to be accountable. The development of this ability is vital for *any individual* to be seen as a full member of society:

> In the development of *the capacity to assimilate 'stories' and to tell them* . . . the child also learns what it is to be that creature which, in Nietzsche's phrase, is capable of making promises, of 'remembering forward' as well as backward, and of linking his end to his beginning in such a way as to attest to an 'integrity' which every individual must be supposed to possess if he is to become a 'subject' of (any) system of law morality or propriety (emphasis added; White, 1984, pp. 13–14).

The social identity of adoption

If one accepts that the issues of identity in adoption have more to do with constructing a narratable self than with crisis, it becomes necessary to seek the origins of the theory that imputes pathological identity problems to these adoptees seeking what is in fact a normal, rational aim. From the evidence of our research we would argue that the psycho-pathological view is an expression of social uncertainty about adoptees, which arises not from their dispositions as individuals but from a basic uncertainty about adoption itself. Barham (1984) argues that we cannot adequately understand the individual's actions without placing them not only within his/her own narrative history but also within the narrative history of the particular social context. Thus, the individual adoptee's sense of personal identity is bound up with his/her social identity and that is inseparable from the social identity of adoption. And the social identity of adoption is bound historically to the twin stigmata of infertility and illegitimacy. Consequently, it has also been associated with secrecy, which has served to preserve certain social standards of morality and normality, as well as, within certain constraints, the reputations of individuals. In the case of illegitimacy, social standards were preserved by separating, symbolically and physically, the child from his/her past. Donzelot (1980) describes how this was accomplished in eighteenth-century France, by use of a special turret enabling unmarried mothers to abandon their children anonymously.

> In this way the donor would not have been seen by any of the house staff. And this was the objective: to break, cleanly and without scandal, the original link identifying these individuals as the off-spring of objectionable alliances, to cleanse social relations of progeny not in conformity with the law of the family, with its ambitions and its reputations (p. 26).

In twentieth-century Britain the techniques are more subtle. The break occurs through the renaming of the child, thereby immediately transforming what little social identity a baby has at that age and producing, through that same action, a fictionalised past biography. Adoption has been a conscious attempt to change the individual's identity. Strauss (1977) argues,

> The changing of names marks a rite of passage. It means such things as that the person wants to have the kind of name he thinks represents him as a person, does not want any longer to be the kind of person that his previous name signified. . . . The phenomenon of 'passing' is often marked by name-changing: you disguise who you were or are in order to appear what you wish to be . . . secrecy sometimes gets mingled with personality transition (pp. 16–17).

Adoption, then, was arranged through different modes of institutionalised secrecy to disguise the fact of illegitimacy. As a consequence the fact of any infertility was also hidden. With the prescription to 'treat the child as if it were your own', adoptive parents were initially encouraged to keep the matter a secret within the family too. Their own feelings of failure and uncertainty arising from infertility provided encouragement to follow this advice.

Such were the circumstances under which many of our respondents were adopted in the 1940s and 1950s. Even when in the 1950s it was recognised that it was better to tell children they were adopted, on the basis that secrets within the family were not healthy and the knowledge that children tended to discover them anyway, the institutional secrecy remained in the form of changed names and secret registers. Adoptive parents were being given a double message: on the one hand they were told to be open with their children; on the other, they could witness that official secrecy persisted, and in some instances was increased. Adoptive parents were also, then as now, very dependent on the agencies for information about the natural parents. As there was a tendency in some cases to edit that information, including of course withholding the natural mother's name, adoptive parents did not always have the chance to be open with their children. Gaps in their knowledge resulted in gaps in the adoptee's knowledge. Historically, therefore, adoptees *and* adopters, through the linking of adoption with illegitimacy and infertility, were associated with stigma. Adopted children could as a result suffer on two levels: be labelled 'illegitimate' and thus suffer their natural parents' social marginality; be labelled 'adopted' and suffer from their adopters' marginality. Any failing on the adoptive parents' behalf to be open with their children can be partly attributed to their awareness of their own and their child's potentially damaging social identity, and partly because of the double message they could witness institutionally.

It might be argued that since the 1960s the social identity of adoption was such that the individual's identity need not suffer, since the stigma attached to illegitimacy and to infertility has diminished. However, the image of adoption remains uncertain, as new worries replace old. Increasingly concerns are expressed as to what is actually being done through the practice of adoption, and the separation of child from parent. Rautenan (1976), an adoption social worker, says of adoption, 'We have to face the fact that we establish relationships that are artificial . . . giving individuals new names and identities. We may really act as kinds of Gods' (p. 27).

The concern about identity does not just rest with the individual; it is not simply a case of 'Who am I?', but also 'Who are they?'. The uneasiness about adoption *per se* attaches itself to the adoptees also, because of the fear that they might be damaged by the experience and also because they too are not easily placed in any one category. Since they are not rooted in natural relationships it is thought that there is no certainty as to where they might align themselves: to natural or adoptive families or perhaps to no one at all. The notion of a psychological vagrant, with no particular ties to anyone, is apt. The only feature by which they might be identified, and hence categorised, is their adoptive status – an adopted child – so, Sorosky *et al.* (1978) argue, they remain within that category. 'One of the common complaints of adoptive adults is that they continued to be treated by society as "children"; they are never allowed to grow up.'

This spreads into all areas of the adoptee's life. Their calculations as to who their parents might be, or attempts to place themselves, come to be seen as fantasies; other attempts to discover information are regarded as potentially dangerous or even vindictive. Even when Section 26 empowered them to gain at least some information, they were still not regarded as sufficiently responsible and/or capable to cope with that sort of information, so special procedures involving age limits and compulsory counselling were established. The process of being adopted and of growing up adopted becomes then a process of being separated as a consequence of that status. Adoption is an experience of being different by virtue of membership of a statistically defined minority group; it is also experience of being made marginal by a set of social processes embodied in the structural arrangements for adoption.

Adoption, then, presents problems for practitioners and for society as a whole. Consequently adoptees also present a problem: we cannot place it or them easily. The uneasiness that is felt about the process is attributable to the individual and extends to questioning their stability. In viewing adoptees potentially at least as damaged and in need of help, the psycho-pathological model attributes the uncertainty about adoption to the adopted people themselves. Conversely, the social identity model attributes the uncertainty to the relationship between the adopted and the non-adopted, as Goffman (1963) explains,

> The attitudes we normals have towards a person with a stigma and
> the actions we take in regard to him, are well known, since these
> responses are what benevolent social action is designed to soften and
> ameliorate . . . we construct a stigma theory, an ideology to . . .
> account for the danger he represents.

The ideology constructed for adoption is that of the individual pathology of the identity crisis, but as we have pointed out, and as Barham (1984) makes explicit,

> Once we have identified the role of narrative in the constitution and
> understanding of individual and social life we can be brought to see
> why the concept of personal identity is inexplicable in the sort of
> account that the empiricist tradition provides which restricts itself to
> the description of psychological states and events (p. 98).

Conclusion

Adopted people experience social marginality both on a general level as a socially differentiated minority and on the individual level through their lack of accountability. We would suggest that enquiries that adoptees make about their past, including those under Section 26, signify an acknowledgment of their difference and, further, represent an attempt to account for it. In this way adopted people, though they cannot change their status of being different and in many cases would not want to, can at least repair any lacunae in their social identity arising from their failure to account for themselves. The 'search for identity' results in the ability to provide a narrative history that is intelligible to the self and others and which interconnects with the narratives lived out by others (Barham, 1984, p. 89).

Notes

1. This research was undertaken by the author and Professor Noel Timms, whose contribution both to the original research and to the ideas contained here I should like to fully acknowledge. Full details of the methodology and analysis of the original research may be found in Haimes and Timms (1983).
2. This example reflects Honess and Edwards's (1984) analysis of the case study which divides into narrative and themes. The narrative addresses the question 'What happened?' and the theme addresses 'Why?' Our answer to 'Why?' is explicated in the text, but, like Honess and Edwards, our explanation is 'data-driven'. (See also Honess and Edwards, Chapter 16.)
3. Rossan also argues that identity can be said to change as much in adulthood as in childhood. Her analysis of pregnancy, together with our analysis of adoption, substantiates that claim.
4. It would be interesting to pursue Handel's analysis (Chapter 20) of 'perceived life change' by re-interviewing these adoptees in the future to see how the impact of tracing natural parents compares with the magnitude of the impact of other critical life events.

References

Barham, P. (1984), *Schizophrenia and Human Value*, Blackwell: Oxford.

Donzelot, J. (1980), *The Policing of Families: Welfare Versus the State*, Hutchinson: London.

Goffman, E. (1963), *Stigma: Notes on the Management of Spoiled Identity*, Prentice-Hall: Englewood Cliffs, N.J.

Haimes, E. and Timms, N. (1983), *Access to Birth Records and Counselling of Adopted Persons under Section 26 of the Children Act, 1975*, Final report to the Department of Health and Social Security, London, May 1983.

Hardy, B. (1968), 'Towards a poetic of fiction: An approach through narrative', *Novel*, 2, pp. 5–14.

Honess, T. and Edwards, A. (1984), 'A case study approach to the examination of the development of identity in adolescents', Paper presented to the British Psychological Society Development Section Conference, Lancaster, England.

MacIntyre, A. (1981), *After Virtue: A Study in Moral Theory*, Duckworth: London.

Rautenan, E. (1976), 'Work with adopted adolescents and adults', in *The Search for Identity*, Association of British Adoption and Fostering Agencies.

Sants, H. J. (undated), 'Genealogical bewilderment in children with substitute parents', in *Child Adoption*, Association of British Adoption and Fostering Agencies.

Shawyer, J. (1979), *Death by Adoption*, Cicada Press: Auckland.

Sorosky, A., Baran, A. and Pannor, R. (1978), *The Adoption Triangle*, Anchor Press: New York.

Strauss, A. (1977), *Mirrors and Masks: The Search for Identity*, Martin Robertson: London.

Triseliotis, J. (1973), *In Search of Origins*, Routledge & Kegan Paul: London.

White, H. (1984), 'The question of narrative in contemporary historical theory', *History and Theory*, vol. xxx, pp. 1–33.

Subject Index

Author Index